The purpose of the author is to explain the psychological nature and function of religion, especially Christianity, in the development of wholesome personality.

How does religion originate in the individual? Under what conditions are its potentialities realized? What is its contribution to human welfare? How does religion control personality? How is religion related to mental health? What specious religious beliefs and practices are mentally debilitating? How can thwarted and defeated individuals be led to freedom and victory? What is a religiously mature personality? What implications for religion are discovered in the various modern schools of psychology? These are some of the questions which this book answers with an approach at once scientific, evangelical, and practical.

This volume is not only a contribution to the psychology of religion and to mental hygiene, but also background material for religious education.

THE PSYCHOLOGY OF
RELIGIOUS LIVING

THE PSYCHOLOGY OF RELIGIOUS LIVING

By

KARL R. STOLZ

DEAN, HARTFORD SCHOOL OF RELIGIOUS EDUCATION

COKESBURY PRESS
NASHVILLE

SET UP, ELECTROTYPED, PRINTED, AND BOUND
BY THE PARTHENON PRESS AT NASHVILLE
TENNESSEE, UNITED STATES OF AMERICA

C

TO MY BROTHER

FREDERICK

A Faithful Minister of the Gospel

PREFACE

THIS book contains the substance of lectures delivered in several theological seminaries, universities, and summer schools conducted for ministers and laymen. The reduction to manuscript form of material orally presented produced a number of baffling problems. In the first place, it was necessary to decide which topics should be discussed in a volume of moderate size. It was imperative to formulate a principle of inclusion. On the whole it seemed wisest to select those aspects of religious living which are of special importance to lay and ministerial workers. That some of the subject matter discussed contributes to the attainment of this objective indirectly rather than directly is perhaps unavoidable. In the second place, the development of the chosen topics entailed the sifting of the available stores of theories and findings. It was necessary to perform the delicate task of choosing from the vast amount of material accumulated over a period of almost a quarter of a century that which would best further the ends in view, adequately represent current thought, and embrace dependable knowledge. It has been as difficult to determine what to discard as what to incorporate.

Several of my professional responsibilities have constantly stimulated me to explore the psychological fundamentals of religious personality. For example, my clinical work in mental hygiene and therapy, practical experience with undeveloped or disorganized individuals, made the formulation of a theory of human nature and of a religious philosophy urgent. One purpose of the present volume is to provide a background for the concrete activities of the personal worker. The chapter on prayer, which offers an interpretation of the psychological principles undergirding prayer rather than an extended exposition of the various techniques of prayer, is an instance in point. A knowledge of the dynamics, functions, and dimensions of religious personality is a precondition of the effective

7

application of psychological methods to the mastery of life-situations.

The psychological position of the following pages may on the whole be interpreted as a combination of functionalism and voluntarism. The insights of other schools of psychology are by no means ignored as the attentive reader will observe, but the union of dynamic principles with integrative values has been accorded the pre-eminence. An eclecticism which is simply a complication of incompatible elements is repugnant to every educated man. The current varieties of psychology embrace so many seeming and real contradictions that a writer in the domain of the psychology of religion may be pardoned if he hesitates to commit his enterprise entirely to any single and rather restricted school. The predominance of a dynamic outlook coupled with functional insight should obviate the charge of adhering to a narrow perspective or of bringing together conflicting psychological theories.

Theologically, the initiative, the aggressiveness, of God in the world of humanity is upheld. Religion is man's response to the direct action of God upon human life. The various religious ideas, customs, and obligations which one encounters among different peoples are regarded as mankind's diverse reactions to a cosmic Purposiveness. So far from being interpreted as static and disinterested, the central Power is believed to be active, responsive, alert, and questing. Without divine aid man could not have discovered God; rather man could not have been found by God if God had not first sought man. The theological attitude maintained inclines toward the doctrine of the transcendence of God rather than toward the doctrine of the divine immanence. The origin of the teaching that God is objectively and consciously within every man is Greek rather than Christian. The distinction between fellowship with God and metaphysical identification with him suggests the theological trend of the volume.

In developing many of the selected topics considerable Bible material has been laid under tribute. The purpose has been manifold. Since the governing interest is the psychology of Christian personality the Bible naturally furnishes pertinent references and illustrations. The origins and growth of certain beliefs and practices among the Hebrews, Jews, and Christians are recorded in the Bible. Its value for the history of religion is recognized in the following pages. It will be evident that modern psychology teaches much that the Bible in its own idiom reveals. Furthermore, Christian experience should be evaluated in the light of the cardinal principles of the New Testament. Its most significant passages constitute a norm for Christian character. The Christian faith has a literature to transmit, an experience to mediate to successive generations, principles of conduct to inculcate, and theological beliefs to disseminate. The Bible, especially the New Testament, is for the Christian a point of reference which gives personality continuity and consistency of experience.

As a reader in the psychology of religion and allied fields for many years, it is impossible in the majority of instances to make specific acknowledgments of indebtedness to other workers. On the other hand, many direct references to sources upon which I have drawn have been made throughout the volume. No doubt my own thinking has been influenced by a multitude of writers whose contributions are not recognized in footnotes. The appended bibliography indicates a wider circle of authors to whom I owe stimulation and guidance. The trenchant responses of hearers to my classroom and platform presentations have done more than I can record not only to clarify but to determine and develop my positions.

To several of my colleagues, especially to Professors Farmer, Hart, Hodous, and Shaw, and to Professor H. L. Pritchett of Southern Methodist University, I am under heavy obligations for critical readings of those portions of the manuscript to which they are respectively and especially competent to react. Not one of them is, however, personally responsible for any conclusions I have stated. The fellowship and inspiration which have accrued from my associations with these and other scholars make life an amazingly fascinating adventure in the field of personality relationships.   K. R. S.

CONTENTS

11

PART ONE

BACKGROUNDS OF THE RELIGIOUS QUEST

CHAPTER I

ORIENTATION

THERE are four major approaches to this interesting world in which our lot is cast—the scientific, the philosophical, the aesthetic, and the religious. By means of each, man seeks to catch the spirit of the universe. Each has its characteristic method and particular goal. Many individuals in their quests for the fullness of life combine two or more of these four fundamental relations.

The scientific approach is centered in the exploration of the reportable events of what we call the natural or phenomenal order. Its instruments are observation, experimentation, and inference. Ideally, pure science as contrasted with applied science proceeds without regard to the practical ends which its findings may serve. The goal of pure science is the disinterested acquisition of knowledge of facts of perception. Manifestly, science so understood abstracts, investigates, describes, and correlates sensory aspects of the universe, and therefore relies on a procedure which is avowedly, if not actually, objective, impersonal, and candid. Pure science and applied science in practice if not in principle interlock, the one frequently leads to or stimulates the other; the distinction between the two forms must not be pressed too hard. Men whose dominant interests are rooted in the world of nature, its structure, its laws, and its utilities, derive satisfaction from the study of science. Evidences of regularity and dependability in nature suggest an orderly, universal underlying principle to many such persons.

The philosophical approach to the world is intellectual and comprehensive. Philosophy endeavors to submit a conception of the world which will enable us to grasp its significance as a whole. It strives to construct a self-consistent and coherent ideology or body of thought which will evaluate and correlate the contributions of science and the spheres of experience which

17

science is unable to penetrate and bring under subjection to itself. Its chief instrument is logic, its incentive is love for speculation, its end is intellectual harmony and satisfaction. That the universe is amenable to this approach, despite the profusion of divergent thought systems which have been advanced, will be affirmed by men of philosophical temper.

Art is a normative approach to the universe when it is concerned not with mere data of sensory experience but with beauty as a cherished value. The aesthetic impulse at its best is more than an emotion to be released or a spark of genius to be expressed in an appropriate form; it is intrinsically an aspiration for an experience of reality. Art in its higher forms is a type of idealism and a quest for finality. It is the recognition of something in the vast ranges of the cosmos which is other and greater than man. The pursuit of beauty is ideally a member of a triad of interpenetrating enterprises. It is significant that the creation and appreciation of beauty have been linked in a dynamic relation with the search for truth and the cultivation of goodness. The noblest of the fine arts which are allies of goodness and truth, is music. In their most inspired hours such composers as Bach, Beethoven, and Brahms have served as mediums through which the ultimate order seems to have been manifested.

Art furthers man's adjustment to the world by fostering a sensitiveness to beauty which is a category of worth. A peculiar quality of sympathetic imagination is the central characteristic of the aesthetic attitude. Aesthetic experience comprehensively considered includes a feeling of kinship with nature in its various manifestations, with the humblest sentient creatures beneath our feet as well as with the awesome heavenly bodies. The truly cultured man sees in every bush a flaming world of loveliness and inspiration. The art relation embraces not only evaluations of human productions but also the emotional penetration of the works of nature.

The Religious Quest

The goal of the religious approach to the universe is the satisfaction of man's deepest yearnings for inward peace and unity, for security and self-realization, for deliverance from moral evil and condemnation through co-operation with a suprasensible cosmic finality. Religion and applied science are practical, philosophy is intellectual, art is disinterestedly appreciative. The generously endowed and harmoniously developed personality employs the four main approaches to the world and its resources for abundant living. The universe is so complex that only by the employment of various mediums can it be apprehended and appreciated, but in man's response to the demands of life religion can play a unique part. When science has exhausted its ways and means and is silent, when philosophy is incoherent and confused, when art is depressed by ugliness in the world, prophetic religion still has a forward-looking message of hope, reproof, assurance, and certainty.

There are eleven great religious systems, all of them originating in Asia and each divided into sects, through which men of our own generation are seeking adjustment to the universe.[1] In this array of religions both unity and diversity are discoverable—unity of fundamental purpose which is to make the universe friendly, and diversity of concepts of the nature and requirements of final Reality. It is estimated that the adherents of these eleven forms of religion number approximately 1,465 millions of persons. The combined following of the eleven amounts to almost three-fourths of the globe's total population of two billions.[2] Zoroastrianism has the smallest constituency, claiming only 100,000 followers; Christianity has the largest, embracing as it does 557 millions, or more than twice as many as any other religion can muster.[3] Some of these living religions, including Christianity and Mohammedanism, are growing statistically; others, especially Zoroastrianism and Shintoism, are losing adherents; the nu-

---

[1] Hinduism, Judaism, Shintoism, Zoroastrianism, Taoism, Jainism, Buddhism, Confucianism, Christianity, Mohammedanism, and Sikhism.

[2] Each day about 100,000 persons die and 150,000 are born.

[3] No method has been devised by which those who are Christians in reality can be statistically separated from the merely nominal followers of Jesus Christ. No doubt the enumeration given above includes many who are more pagan than Christian. Of course an analogous statement may be made of any other type of religion.

merical strength of still others, like Judaism and Taoism, remains comparatively stationary.   Impressive numbers do not, of course, validate the actual or alleged superiority of a specific religion, but they do attest the wide recognition it has won. The following of the leading religions, considered as a whole, is maintaining itself, which indicates that millions still treasure the values which the religious approach to the universe discloses and makes available.   Unless human nature changes in unpredictable ways, religion will indefinitely continue to be a dominant cultural asset.

The Psychological Standpoint

The religious enterprise is so old, so diversified, and so significant that it may be studied from various angles.[4]   The scientist has made it the object of inquiry.   The religious approach to the universe may be examined through the medium of psychology to the advantage of both religion and science. The psychologist cultivates a limited area of religious knowledge and discovery.   He makes a systematic study of religious relations, in so far as these are amenable to his techniques. He occupies himself with both the behavior and the subjective events which possess religious significance.[5]   Our special project is the exploration of religiously meaningful attitudes, ideas,

[4] For example, the history of religion, comparative religion, the philosophy of religion, and systematic theology.

[5] H. L. Hollingworth, in his *Psychology, Its Facts and Principles* (New York: D. Appleton & Co., 1928), defines mental behavior as activities which can be reinstated by a reduction in the original stimulus.   A sick child may react violently to the disagreeable taste of the prescribed medicine and thereafter exhibit the characteristic responses of disgust and repulsion at the mere sound of the approach of the nurse or physician.   Some one part of the original complicated situation is sufficient to induce the observable original reaction or behavior.   Psychological activities do not obey the law of mechanics, which is that only when all causal factors are present can an effect be reproduced.   I accept this description of behavior.   Hollingsworth makes discrepancy of report the criterion of subjectivity.   When several persons disagree in their accounts of a common experience, psychic problems emerge. That concerning which there is general agreement may be regarded as objective.   A number of persons may examine a portrait and be in accord as to its size and location, but there may be differences of opinion as to whether the artist has expressed the dominant characteristics of the sitter.   The conflicting elements constitute the subjective events and as such are proper objects of psychological investigation.   Hollingsworth's distinction between objectivity and subjectivity is suggestive and worth pondering and testing.

and responses in their direct bearing on the organization and
control of personality.

The psychologist assumes that religion exists as a fact not
created by him but available as an object of investigation.
Strictly speaking he is under no obligation to raise or answer
questions concerning the validity of the ultimate claims of
religion. For example, he should not be called upon in his
capacity of a scientist to determine whether God is objectively
real, for this is a metaphysical issue and as such not under the
control of the instrumentalities of science; but he should be
able to tell us why men put their trust in God, how they have
arrived at the belief that God exists, how faith in God affects
conduct, what tensions confidence in God relieves, what emotions it arouses, what needs it satisfies, what ends it serves,
and how it controls personality as a whole. It is within his
province to raise and at least in part answer the question, To
what extent and in what terms does psychology describe religious personality? On the other hand there is no valid reason
why as a religious inquirer he should not address himself to
such a problem as the nature and reality of God.

The utterly impersonal interpretation of the psychological
data of religion is, of course, an unrealized if not unrealizable
ideal of scientific perfection. Any world-view seriously held
colors more or less the explication of facts of perception. The
psychologist, the philosopher, and the theologian are often
united in the same individual. A competent psychologist may
be a poor or a good philosopher, but in either case it is humanly
impossible to eliminate from scientific description every vestige
of personal conviction of the structure and relationships of
ultimate reality. Only an intellectual automaton could make
a completely successful attempt to keep his personal attitude
toward religion considered as a God-centered enterprise from
affecting his scientific decisions.

To be sure, there are psychologists who hold it permissible
to develop the philosophical or theological implications of their
scientific conclusions. They would make contributions to what
is presumably a scientifically based theory of reality. Others
go even farther. They put no restraints upon their philosoph-

ical predilections and consequently most of their more inclusive psychological pronouncements are dictated by a governing world-view. As one would anticipate, psychologists who uphold divergent philosophies draw dissimilar inferences from the same reportable aspects of religious experience. In fact, adherents of the same school of psychology may be in accord in their scientific descriptions but disagree in their final evaluation of religion.

Although science and philosophy occupy separate spheres of responsibility the fact remains that certain findings of psychology possess philosophical involvements which the student of religious living should not ignore. The psychological and theological standpoints of this study of religious personality may be suggested at the outset. An indication of what they are should serve as a guide to the reader. In general a dynamic viewpoint will characterize both the psychological and theological positions held. The implications of religiously integrated personality will be developed. The function of religion as the rallying center of personality will be discussed in its various bearings. The contributions of psychology to a better understanding of the governing passion of religious personality will be introduced. Furthermore, the concept of the divine initiative will be espoused as the core of the theological background. Religion in its essence will be interpreted theologically as a relationship arising from man's response to the promptings of a conscious, creative, and final form of reality. So long as the elements of religious personality are accurately described and related to the larger context of psychological principles to which they belong, surely no valid scientific objections can be raised against such a world-view.

Limitations of the Scientific Approach

Invaluable as the scientific study of religion is, it is by no means an infallible, accurate, and inclusive procedure. The specialized forms of investigation have severally and in the aggregate expanded our knowledge of the nature and function of religion. That these methods will be progressively refined and made correspondingly more productive and that others will be devised may be safely predicted. Whether all the limitations which at the present characterize the scientific approach in its various forms will be dispersed by future technical improvements time alone can tell, but it is probable that at least some of them inhere in the nature of science itself and are therefore ineradicable.

The psychological analysis and explication of religious data should not deprive us of the insights and fruits of appreciation. Faith is still justified by its consequences. To say the least, science is only one of the several approaches to the world and its manifold resources. An excess of zeal for objective measurement is likely to father the assumption that whatever is not caught in the net which the scientist spreads is either illusory or of secondary importance. A more dispassionate comprehension of the relations of mankind includes an order of meanings, values, and goals to which the religious personality tenaciously clings and which may be described by psychology but the validity of which can be neither affirmed nor negated by science. The scientist may become entangled in and be religiously and aesthetically strangled by his own techniques. A religion based on science alone would be void of appreciations and creations which are distinctive of religion and would therefore not be a religion at all. Science gives us a partial knowledge of the total universe.

Again, attention should be called to the insufficiency of scientific analysis apart from creative synthesis. The exercise of critical intelligence in the psychological study of religious personality is a primary necessity, but it should be observed that in the analysis of religious experience the quintessence of religion escapes. When a medical student has dissected a dog there is no longer a dog on the dissecting table but only the physiological remains of a dog. That which developed the several organs and made them function as a co-ordinated whole, that which responded to the call of his master, chased a cat up a tree, and protected a child has not been laid bare by the scalpel of the budding medical practitioner. A consequence of the dissection of the dog is a deeper understanding of anatomy and physiology, but a live dog is an organic union of parts animated by a form of vitality which as such is not subject to analysis. A dog is more and other than the sum of the parts exposed to view by the process of dissection.

Totality possesses a uniqueness which is necessarily sacrificed in the analytic project. A religious experience involves the personality as a whole and is prompted and supported by values which the analyst, however competent he may be, cannot capture. It is possible to abstract from conversion as a religiously motivated and directed reintegration of personality, psychological functions, to dissect them, relate them to like phenomena, and draw an inference in the nature of a law, but that which unifies the experience and makes it significant in its entirety eludes scientific analysis. Conversion transcends the aggregation of factors subject to the technique of science. Analysis is a scientific indispensability, but its inadequacy, even its destructiveness, should be recognized, and overcome by a creative synthesis which includes all the constituents and values. Fire, as Horace Bushnell once remarked, is a great analyst, but its product is a handful of ashes; nevertheless, one is inclined to add that fire may be harnessed to constructive purposes.

Furthermore, the psychologist tells us less than we suppose. In many cases factual knowledge which is the common property of intelligent lay observers is disguised in technical terminology. Old facts are described in new words and thus invested with a dignity and impressiveness they have not hitherto possessed. Frequently one wonders why the psychologist employs a plethora of scientific jargon when the language understood by the laity would serve the purpose of conveying his thought equally as well if not better. The reader of a ponderous treatise may conclude that he is engaged in a language study rather than in the acquisition of new scientific information. A new vocabulary does not necessarily contribute to a knowledge of religious personality.

On the other hand, the psychologist may tell us less than we suppose for an entirely different reason. The more truly scientific he is, the more abstract his deductions are and the less meaning his reports entail. The ideal conclusion of the scientist is the one which can be stated in mathematical symbols. In the realization of the mathematical ideal the physicist has the advantage over the psychologist. Nevertheless, the application of the scientific method to the study of certain psychological phenomena yields quantitative findings or measurements which can be indicated by mathematics. How much do such abstractions tell us? If the psychologist translates his formula into the language of common social intercourse, he is likely to convey more than his mathematical calculations warrant. If he utilizes a technical vocabulary, he is in a similar predicament. If he submits a mathematical formula, the content of his report is too indefinite and abstract to impart much meaning. Eddington says that a mathematical reading is related to the fact to which it applies as a telephone number is related to a subscriber.[6]

The existence of a variety of competing psychologies imposes an additional limitation upon the scientific study of religious personality.[7] As a comparatively new science, psychology is a house divided against itself. Psychologists of divergent schools disagree as to many points of special concern to the religious personality, such as the nature of the self and the existence of the subconscious. The multiplicity of discrepancies is, negatively, the outcome of the immaturity of the science of psychology and, positively, an evidence of the subtlety and illusiveness of psychological problems. As the body of substantial and verifiable knowledge of human personality increases there will in all probability be more and more uniformity of psychological inference. In the course of time, decay and extinction will overtake the schools of psychology whose basic principles are contradicted by scientific progress.[8]

[6] Eddington, Arthur Stanley, *The Domain of Physical Science* (New York: The Macmillan Company, 1929).

[7] The fundamental theories of the leading schools of psychology and their implications will be considered in Chapter X.

[8] Bertrand Russell in his readable volume, *The Scientific Outlook*, pp. 74 ff. (New York: W. W. Norton & Co., 1931), describes several limitations of the scientific method which I have not included in my survey, such as doubt of the trustworthiness of induction and the difficulty of drawing valid inferences from the known to the unknown. The quantum theory which has to do with individual atoms and electrons, Russell reminds us, throws doubt

The inference should not be drawn that the psychological interpretation of religious personality, since it is exposed to the limitations of science, should be abandoned. The undertaking is by no means futile. Precaution, not discontinuance, is the wiser course. The recognition of the probability of error should lead to an improvement in method, a closer scrutiny of results, a testing of generalizations, and the cultivation of the spirit of open-minded inquiry.

Benefits to Be Derived

Why should one engage in the study of religious personality? Apart from the gratifying of curiosity, do any benefits accrue to the learner? He who undertakes an attentive and systematic inquiry, particularly if he is sustained by the Christian philosophy of life, may be assured that he will be enriched by a number of definite contributions. Cognizance and anticipation of the benefits which may be reaped will motivate and direct study of the psychology of religion.

In the first place, the scientific understanding of religion entails a cultural asset which no educated man can forego without loss. For ages religion has been a chief concern of mankind. No one can lay claim to a comprehensive knowledge of civilization, past or present, who has not made the structure, function, and evaluation of religion an object of diligent study. One ventures to say that he who deliberately fosters a progressively sympathetic appreciation of humanity in its manifold relations is a cultured man. Nothing that deeply affects humanity is alien to his interests. The person of culture has a desire to know and understand and think, and presupposes

upon the universality of causality. Perhaps atoms have a certain degree of freedom; if so, the doctrine of physical determinism is undermined. In the atom there are various states which are separated by tiny gaps. The gaps may be over-leaped so that the states in the atom are rearranged. At present no laws are known which determine which of the possible transitions shall occur under a given condition. If upon further investigation it should be established that in this respect the atom is not subject to law, something in nature analogous to free will in man might be posited. Eddington in his book, *The Nature of the Physical World,* has applied this possibility to the problem of human freedom of choice. The quantum theory is, however, undergoing rapid development and seems at present to be far from its final form.

that these employments in the field of religion are in themselves
worthy ends.

Closely allied to the cultural value is the release from bondage to one's own religious beliefs and practices. The individual is predisposed to assume that his own religious outlook,
necessities, and activities are the proper measure of those of
others, especially of the persons for whose guidance in the
things of the spirit he is responsible. The leader who is conversant with the results of the scientific investigation of religion learns that no two persons who profess the same religious
culture have identical convictions, desires, purposes, and outlets.

Each personality is unique, although individuals possessing
outstanding characteristics in common may be grouped and
given a general distinguishing label. The wise guide's attitude
toward religious responses which differ from his own is not
that of captious criticism, or superior toleration, or bare suf-
ferance, but that of understanding and respect. He may be
amazed to discover that what he has considered of no consequence or deleterious or been entirely unaware of has actually
fructified the lives of others. Through the recognition and
appraisal of the values which others cherish, the religious
worker may be delivered from subserviency to his own experience. The preacher, for example, who has been ministering
to a minor fraction of his audience because his message has
been circumscribed by his own outlook, may be led by the
psychological study of the range of personality problems so
to broaden the scope of his service that those of his constituency whose dispositions and needs vary from his will be
nourished.

In the third place, the psychological exploration of religion
should result in the clarification and reconstruction of the individual's ideal of the good life. To learn what are the essentials of religious idealism may revive a spiritual life for a long
time dormant or in a state of decline because religion has been
adjudged illusory or outmoded. Knowledge of the conditions
under which religion is effective in personal experience may
unlock resources hitherto neglected, if not willfully disowned.
The practice of prayer rejected as a magical and superstitious

performance beneath the dignity of an intelligent person may be reinstated, its place in the scientifically described universe ascertained, and its techniques appropriated. Other areas of religious significance may be creatively re-evaluated. Concepts which are defective may be revised or replaced, and unwholesome attitudes discontinued or transformed. The formulation of a religious philosophy of life which commands the respect of reason and furthers adjustment to an active order of higher sanctions is a normal and desired outcome of constructive psychological inquiry.

Finally, the psychology of religious personality provides a background for other disciplines and thus adds to the usefulness of the pastor, social worker, teacher, or parent. There is no part of the entire formal preparation for Christian leadership which cannot be quickened and enriched by the psychology of religion. It is one of the several cultural developments which conspired to launch religious education as a modern movement. It places at the disposal of the religious educator its methods and findings and supplies pedagogical hints. It furnishes the pastor with suggestions for the use of religion in the solution of the personality problems of his constituency. It contributes to the conduct of worship for the various age or social groups within the local church. It offers guidance to the preacher in the art of sermon composition and delivery. It is instrumental in the interpretation of Bible characters and narratives. Christian nurture, work with maladjusted individuals, homiletics, Biblical exegesis, and other forms of religious service can lay under tribute the technique and results of the psychological study of religious living.

CHAPTER II

THE NATURE OF RELIGION

THE psychology of religion occupies itself with three main problems—the structure of religion, the beginnings and evolution of religion, and the function of religion. It raises and seeks to answer the questions, What constitutes religion? How did it originate? and, How does religion affect the individual and social institutions? The present inquiry has to do chiefly with the answer to the first question. In determining the nature of religion one may employ the method of analysis and comparison. The investigator may reduce representative religions to their constituent common principles and weave these into a generalization or definition. That which gives any one religion its peculiar quality is not specified in a statement broad enough to comprehend the essentials of the variety of religions. The basic structure of a given type of religion, the framework alone, is incorporated in a descriptive summation of all religions.

Definitions of Religion

Let us quote representative definitions of religion from the works of scholars whose conclusions, while not necessarily final and absolute, are worthy of favorable consideration. All fourteen descriptions which will be introduced stress a form of relationship subsisting between an invisible order and human beings. They are in accord with the historic understanding of the nature of religion. A comparison of these concise statements will reveal points of agreement which exist among specialized forms of religion. A reduction of different religions to their common factors provides the materials for a general definition of religion.

Religion is "the belief in Spiritual Beings." [1]

[1] Tylor, E. B., *Primitive Culture*, p. 424 (New York: Henry Holt & Co., 1874).

⊣ Religion is "a propitiation or conciliation of powers superior to man which are believed to direct and control the course of nature and human life." [2]

"Religion is the worship of higher powers from a sense of need." [3]

⊢ "Religion shall mean for us the feelings, acts, and experiences of individual men in their solitude, so far as they apprehend themselves to stand in relation to whatever they may consider the divine." [4]

"Religion is the serious and social attitudes of individuals or communities toward the power or powers which they conceive as having ultimate control over their interests and destinies." [5]

Religion, considered subjectively, "is the recognition of all our duties as divine commands." [6]

"Religion is that part of human experience in which man feels himself in relation with powers of psychic nature, usually personal powers, and makes use of them." [7]

Religion is "the persistence of value." [8]

"Religion is the endeavor to secure the conservation of socially recognized values through specific actions that are believed to evoke some agency different from the ordinary ego of the individual, or from other merely human beings, and that imply a feeling of dependence upon the agency." [9]

[2] Frazer, James George, *The Golden Bough,* Vol. I, pp. 222, 223 (London: The Macmillan Company, 1911).

[3] Menzies, Allan, *History of Religion,* p. 11 (New York: Charles Scribner's Sons, 1906).

[4] James, William, *The Varieties of Religious Experience,* p. 41 (New York: Longmans, Green & Co., 1911).

[5] Pratt, James Bissett, *The Religious Consciousness,* p. 2 (New York: The Macmillan Company, 1930).

[6] Kant, Immanuel, *Kritik der praktischen Vernunft,* p. 155 (Riga: Johann F. Hartknoch, 1788).

[7] Leuba, James Henry, *A Psychological Study of Religion,* p. 52 (New York: The Macmillan Company, 1912). Leuba cites forty-eight definitions of religion, dividing them into three classes, the intellectualistic, the affectivistic and the voluntaristic. *Ibid.,* pp. 339-360.

[8] Höffding, Harald, *The Philosophy of Religion,* p. 95 (New York: The Macmillan Company, 1914).

[9] Wright, W. K., *American Journal of Theology,* Vol. XVI, p. 393.

Religion is "man's consciousness of relation to his larger environment: (a) his feeling of relation to God and to humanity; (b) his thought about these relations; (c) the action resulting from this feeling and belief." [10]

"What doth Jehovah require of thee, but to do justly, and to love kindness, and to walk humbly with thy God?" [11]

"Thou shalt love the Lord thy God with all thy heart, and with all thy soul, and with all thy strength, and with all thy mind;[12] and thy neighbor as thyself." [13]

"Pure religion and undefiled before our God and Father is this, to visit the fatherless and widows in their affliction, and to keep oneself unspotted from the world." [14]

The various definitions of religion quoted imply at least five elements—a sense of human need, a conception of an existence that satisfies man's deepest desires, an attitude of dependence on the superhuman, moral and social implications, and the involvement of all one's personality relationships. The genius of religion as an intimate and integrating experience is perhaps most characteristically expressed in these five attributes and principles. Increasing numbers of people mean by religion not a book, nor a church, nor a theological system, but response to reality, reaction which issues in moral control, inward peace, and devotion to ideals. Specific religions differ in the range of human need they undertake to satisfy, the character of the superhuman being relied on, and the conditions of intercourse between man and his deity. In addition, most of the great living religions have evolved a cult, a sacred literature, and a creed. Although these three products are not the core of religion itself, they do throw light upon the nature of religion and possess significance for the conservation and propagation of religion.

[10] The author of this suggestive definition is unknown to me.
[11] Micah 6: 8.
[12] Deuteronomy 6: 5.
[13] Leviticus 19: 18; Luke 10: 27.
[14] James 1: 27.

Human Need

The definitions of religion submitted presuppose a felt human need, a craving for a form of good, physical, moral, or spiritual. This desire, however crude it may be among primitive peoples, is one of the sources of religion. Without it religion cannot exist. The intensity of it gives to religion vitality, urgency, and direction. It motivates the human quest for reality and redemption. Early man sought the aid of his deities when he planted his crops or went into battle with his enemies. The votaries of an ethical religion seek release from attitudes considered contrary to the will of the deity, and crave fellowship with the object of worship, inward peace, and a sense of security.

The Objective Reference

A basic factor in religion is a belief in a type of ultimate reality with which man may cultivate correspondences. The great historic religions are centered in this belief and its application. The above definitions of religion affirm the existence of a potent cosmic agency. One writer refers to "spiritual Beings," another to "powers superior to man," still another to "the Divine," Pratt to "a Determiner of Destiny," Micah to "Jehovah," St. James to "God the Father," Mohammed to "Allah." Under many names and titles the nature of the object of religious devotion is indicated.

Can religion exist without an objective existence other than mechanistic or human? If we give to religion its historic value, the answer is negative. To relieve religion of its reliance on a power not ourselves nor nature is to rob it of its most distinctive quality. The term loses the connotation which imparts to it its peculiar identity and character. That which is conceived apart from a personal attitude toward a cosmic Presence is not religion but something else. The implications of such a practical philosophy of life which we call humanism will be stated and evaluated in another chapter.

Is ultimate reality personal? The fundamental datum of religion cannot be comprehended in human concepts, nevertheless personality is the most complex form of being in structure and function which we know.   It is reasonable to suppose that we catch glimpses of the nature of ultimate reality through the highest processes we ourselves are capable of, such as the pursuit of truth, the appreciation of the beautiful, and selfless living.   To philosophy and theology rather than to psychology falls the task of describing the structure of ultimate Being. Nevertheless, psychology must take into account the indisputable fact that historically religion is identified with a type of reality that is extra-human and psychic.   Furthermore, psychology must include in its survey of religious phenomena the outcome of the belief in a cosmic agency which affects the welfare and destiny of man.   It cannot ignore the results of the response to what is regarded as a divine prompting, such as the transformation and invigoration of personality, the sanction of conduct, the impartation of comfort in an hour of sorrow, the generation of hope, and the empowerment for service to mankind.

Faith

The religious personality travels the path of faith to certainty and power.   The object of worship is recognized as the possessor and dispenser of the good sought.   The worshiper holds that the highest values are the outcome of a venture of confidence in the existence, potency, and reliability of his deity. He feels dependent on a cosmic entity or existence which controls his destiny.   He responds to what he interprets as a divine challenge of expectation.   An attitude which is by turns self-committal and receptivity, is the source of vitality and peace in daily life.

The method whereby religion seeks deliverance from evil and the possession of the good differs radically from that employed by science in the conquest of natural forces.   The approach of religion is synthetic, that of science is analytic. The attitude of the one is subjective, that of the other is objective.   The one is appreciative, the other is skeptical.   Religion affirms the validity of inward certainties; science questions them.   The resources of religion are released by confidence in the surmise of the heart and not alone by the control of the laws of the physical world.

Faith as simple trust in the presence and good will of God is central in the religion of Jesus. The Father is easily accessible to those who turn to him in the simplicity of childlike assurance. Jesus lived in the intuitive atmosphere of the poet rather than in the cognitive climate of the scientist. He advanced no arguments for the existence of God, but assumed that he who has experienced a saving sense of loving Reality will require no other proof. As compared with the precision and clarity of an objective demonstration of a law of nature, the practice of redemptive faith may seem vague, elusive, and inconclusive. Nevertheless, the results of faith as Jesus exercised it are as real as the products of applied science.

Ethical Requirements

The higher forms of religion impose moral and social obligations. Religion and morality are not identical, they are not one and the same. Religion is more than "morality touched by emotion." It transcends the guidance of man by the principles of honesty, justice, and sympathy. Religion postulates a power other than our own which makes for righteousness. In Kant's phraseology religious personality interprets moral obligations as divine obligations.

The ethical element as we practice it was in primitive religions in all probability negligible. The divine commands as understood and obeyed by early man were for the most part ritualistic. Although ceremonies were originally quite void of what we would call morality they were of tremendous value. The elaborate religious exercises which were conducted in a crisis possessed a personal and tribal significance which it would be folly to ignore. The funeral rites, for example, which seem to us weird and meaningless were a solace and a stabilizing force. They helped the surviving mourners to make the difficult adjustment to loss by death. Other ritualistic performances contributed to tribal solidarity, or ministered to the private concerns of the individual.

The scope of moral obligation among the ancient Hebrews

was restricted to the welfare of the members of the tribe or of the citizens of the nation and the protection of their interests. The transient, the temporary resident, the refugee who sought a brief asylum in the land of Israel was generally not a client of Jehovah and was, therefore, not to be treated as a fellow-Hebrew. Interest on loans could be exacted from him and the carcass of an unbled animal could be sold to him. Only with the growth of the concept of the universality of the domain of Jehovah could Gentiles be considered on a parity with Jews, an implication which was, in fact, never fully developed by the Jews as a whole.

Religious and moral practices interpenetrate in Christianity; in fact, they constitute a whole. They are comprehended in a synthesis of insight and power. It is impossible to dissociate the one from the other in religious living although they are not identical. Morality apart from the sanction and support of a relationship with a suprasensible being is humanistic but not religious. The God-centered life has moral consequences.

Religion in Life

Religion is not an entity having its existence apart from human affairs. It is not detachable in actual practice. It is the leaven in the lump. True religion is a mode of life, a spirit which transfuses all the manifold relationships of man, but is never an isolated quality. Religion loses its existence when it seeks independence. Only by arousing and regulating a profusion of ideas, attitudes, and practices does religion expand and truly live.

An outstanding fact of the great ethnic religions is the fact that they permeated and animated all aspects of the cultures of their votaries. Hunting, planting, reaping, making war, marrying, giving birth, burying the dead were all engaged in according to the religious statutes. Human relationships were not divided into holy and profane areas. All were religious. Our modern world distinguishes between the Church and the state, religious education and general education, things sacred and things secular. The result has been the impoverishment or the evaporation of religion from large areas of our culture.

Furthermore, it is a fundamental principle of Christianity that the functions of personality constitute an organic system. Christianity in its best estate is a certain synthesis of God, the individual, and his fellow men.   Jesus, quoting with approval, affirms, "Thou shalt love the Lord thy God with all thy heart, and with all thy soul, and with all thy mind, and with all thy strength. . . . Thou shalt love thy neighbor as thyself." [15]   When the importance of any one of these three terms in the equation of Christianity is eliminated this form of religion is fatally stricken.   When God is dismissed as superfluous and only the well-being of man retained, when the self-sufficiency of man is assumed, when the individual relies solely upon his own resources, when all reference to cosmic reality is abandoned, the religious attitude is dissipated.   On the other hand, when man as an individual is degraded to a worm in the dust, when he practices undue mortification of the body or cultivates a morally sterile sentimentalism, the dignity of personality as recognized by Jesus is violated and religion as he taught and lived it loses a distinguishing characteristic.   Self-respect is a cardinal virtue.   Furthermore, when the social implications of Jesus' teaching are ignored and an extreme individualism is fostered, true religion languishes.   Christianity is not a solitary religion.   Private solicitude may become selfishness incarnate.   Social injustice, rivalry, and strife, to all of which Christianity is unalterably opposed, are in some instances the melancholy consequences of the religious mind turned upon itself.

True and undefiled religion holds in proper proportions divine reality, man himself, and social obligations.   To love God, to love oneself, to love one's fellow man—to embrace not one of these but all of them—is to catch the spirit of Jesus. A balance of the cosmic reference, the personal reference, and the social reference marks the mature religion which Jesus sanctioned and exemplified.

[15] Mark 12: 30, 31.

Cults

Religion manifests itself in worship, rites, and ceremonies. Such crises as birth, death, puberty, and marriage have been variously recognized in religious practices. Seedtime, harvest, and war have been occasions of appropriate religious celebrations. Dances, processions, sacrifices, and liturgies have invested the pivotal experiences of the individual and group with religious meaning.

The genius of Hebrew religion developed an elaborate cultus in charge of a priesthood. The Hebrew priest was a mediator between man and God, officiated at the altar, conducted the worship according to prescribed forms, and applied the legal regulations to particular cases. In addition, the priest instructed the people in the law and served as adviser to those who sought his counsel. The priest was a conservator rather than an originator of religious and moral attitudes. He did not possess the ethical perception, the religious penetration, the social vision which so splendidly characterized the glorious succession of the Hebrew prophets. The progressive religious interpretation of life in its manifold relations was foreign to the cultus with its settled convictions, conservatism, and note of finality.

It would be unjust to impute only legalism and ritualism to the priests who promoted the cultus of Israel. The nineteenth chapter of Leviticus, for example, imposes demands which disclose the moral and humanitarian aspects of the cultus. Together with the admonitions not to mar the corners of the beard and not to wear a garment of two kinds of stuff mingled, are the mandates to respect the aged, to protect the helpless, to rise above deceit and dishonesty, and to permit the poor to glean in the grain fields and gather the fallen fruit in the vineyards. In the same chapter lies embedded the commandment, "Thou shalt love thy neighbor as thyself," which was in due course given universal application by Israel's greatest prophets.

Christianity in the course of its historical development expressed itself in a cult. Baptism, the Eucharist, and formal worship characterized the group religious life at an early period. Gradually the cultus, through the absorption and adaptation of foreign religious customs as well as through innovations of its own, became exceedingly elaborate. We shall have occasion to take cognizance of representative features when we survey the types of public worship prevalent in the Christian Church. Ecclesiastic etiquette and devotional proprieties when they aid the thoughtful and reverent approach to God are to be commended, but when they dull the religious perceptions and obscure the obligations of justice and love they are to be condemned. A sensitiveness to the refinements of worship ennobles and purifies. In every prescribed cultus a menace lurks, the menace of divorcing religion and life, the menace of obeying the letter of a commandment while violating the intent of it, the menace of living in the dead past and scorning the urgent present. It is possible for a devotee to be far more perturbed when a ceremonial regulation has been neglected than when a fellow-man has been wronged.

In order that organized religion may be delivered from an endless round of restrictions and technicalities void of moral significance, a liberal infusion of the prophetic spirit with its expanding vision of the purpose of God must occur from time to time. The prophetic voice is energizing. The prophet tends to destroy the rigidity of a cultus controlled by the priestly element. He calls attention to religion as a personal response to God and to the divine obligations of justice and compassion. A religion develops characteristic institutions and forms which crystallize and become ends in themselves unless the prophetic influence serves as the corrective.

Religious Writings

Adherents of a given religion may acknowledge and esteem a body of writings as possessing for them a certain specific authority. Only a highly developed religion can acquire a sacred literature. Several of the great religions other than Christianity possess what might well be termed an authoritative canon. Every "Bible" is a literary outgrowth of religious living. Religion precedes its book or Bible. First of all a considerable number of people accept a religious faith and practice. A religious movement exists. If the movement is strong and spreads, it creates a literature. The writings are eagerly read. Some of the literature is more serviceable than the rest. As time passes, what finds favor is regarded with veneration. At length this is considered sacred and authoritative. The literary output of other religions is regarded as of much lesser value if not repudiated altogether. The traditional illustration of exclusiveness and intolerance is the destruction of the library in Alexandria, Egypt, on the grounds that if the books were in harmony with the Koran they were needless and if they contradicted it they were false and should be burned.

The Bible of Christianity is priceless. It is a library of sixty-six books written by nobody knows how many authors scattered over a period of more than a thousand years. Poets and sages, prophets and priests, kings and shepherds, men and women contributed to its varied lore. It represents every literary device known to the people from which it sprang. The living God is revealed and interpreted in the Bible. It is gratefully admitted that God has spoken to peoples past and present who do not possess our Bible, but Christians believe that it records the experiences of men who have had a more intimate fellowship with God. Our Bible is progressive; it is a record of a quest culminating in the life and work of Christ. The priceless possession of Christianity is Christ, and the New Testament contains accounts of his life and words. Our Bible alone introduces us to Christ and we believe his character and his teaching have vouchsafed a unique disclosure of the love and will of God. The documents of non-Christian religions afford varied concepts of a superhuman order, but the message of Christ sets our Bible apart from and above all other sacred literature.

Creeds

A creed is a condensed statement of religious beliefs. Some ancient peoples like the Babylonians and the Assyrians, although intensely religious, did not formulate and use a creed as we understand the word today. The general prevalence of the worship of local deities differing in demands accounts for the lack of a comprehensive creed in early Egypt. The concise declaration of the fundamentals of Gautama Buddha may be regarded as a creed. It contains the essential elements of Buddhism. Buddha asserted that life is suffering, that suffering is produced by the will to live, that cessation of suffering occurs in the state of nirvana, and that nirvana is achieved by discipline, knowledge, meditation, and insight. Articles of a creed in the modern sense were not formulated by the Jews until later post-Biblical times. The Biblical statement, "Hear, O Israel: Jehovah our God is one Jehovah," [16] which affirms an uncompromising monotheism, is the basis of the creed of Judaism. The literary and religious education of the Jewish child began with the writing and reading of these words. The chief tenet of Islam may be recalled, "There is no God except Allah and Mohammed is his prophet."

Of the various creeds which the Christian Church has produced the Apostles' Creed is an outstanding specimen. This creed has survived in the Western Church, and another but similar summary of doctrine is used in the Greek Orthodox Church. The name, Apostles' Creed, is misleading. It was not compiled or written by the twelve apostles of Jesus. Tradition, to be sure, does assign the authorship to the twelve and goes so far as to credit separate clauses to individual members of the apostolic group. The Apostles' Creed is a growth. Although various articles of it may be supported by the New Testament, it is really the product of post-Biblical men distributed over a period of several hundred years. It seems to have been formulated to meet the practical needs of religious teachers to whom the instruction of those who applied for admission into the Church was entrusted. At the time of baptism it was probably repeated by the candidate as a confession of faith. An original simple statement was expanded in order to give a fuller outline of Christian doctrine.

The Apostles' Creed has undergone subtraction as well as

[16] Deuteronomy 6: 4. See also Deuteronomy 6: 5, 6; 10: 12; Isaiah 45: 5-7; Micah 6: 8; Psalm 15.

addition. A conspicuous example is the omission of the article, "He descended into hell," in the form in which the creed is recited by several leading denominations. These communions, although gratefully acknowledging the boundless concern of God for men, hesitate to affirm that Christ during the period when his body lay in the grave visited either a general abode of the dead or a place of torment. They do not judge this creedal article to be sufficiently historical to warrant its retention. There is nothing in the creed itself which claims perfection and finality. Men wrote the Apostles' Creed, good men, men who served their day, and when fresh insight and experience in our time demand revisions and restatements other men, equally good and capable, are confronted with a duty which they should not shirk.

It is evident that the misuse of the Apostles' Creed may be an obstacle to the religious development of certain persons. When the acceptance of every article of it is made the condition of church membership the doctrinal requirement is far more stringent than that which Christ exacted of his personally chosen disciples. The responsibility of dictating in fine detail what a person must believe in order to be a Christian is one which a thoughtful religious leader will hesitate to assume. Exactly what shall be the principles of inclusion or omission is an issue which to date is difficult to meet. A creed excludes much of importance. The Apostles' Creed skipping from "born of the Virgin Mary" to "suffered under Pontius Pilate" ignores the intervening prophetic ministry of Jesus, the Sermon on the Mount, his prayer life, and his labors for the establishment of the kingdom of God. Religious experience is far more comprehensive than any abbreviated report of it. In fact, life outruns our intellectual formulation of it.

The bitter doctrinal wars which various factions of the Church waged against one another have left their impress on the Apostles' Creed. The historic creeds which have won the enthusiastic assent of men are summaries of doctrinal differences rather than statements of agreements. A formulation of beliefs unified and solidified one party and sharply separated it from antagonistic factions in the Church. In order to combat what were regarded as doctrinal irregularities, references to the incarnation, the passion of Christ and his resurrection were added to the Apostles' Creed. The creed became not only authoritative teaching material but also a weapon to be wielded against the heretic.

Summary

It is evident that religion is compounded of various attitudes, beliefs, and practices. An array of definitions of religion as it is historically conceived discloses a complexity of responses, values, and objectives. Some definitions stress the emotional element, others the intellectual element, and still others the volitional element. A desire for a form of good, a belief in the existence of a psychic Power competent to meet man's deepest needs, a reliance on such a cosmic Being, and the discharge of accepted obligations are factors which the definitions as a whole lift into prominence. A cult, a sacred literature, and a creed may be regarded both as products of religion and as instruments for the propagation of religious principles and practices. The origin and evolution of religion and its varied functions in personality integration now claim our attention.

CHAPTER III

ORIGINS OF RELIGION

THE beginnings of religion are lost in the mists of the prehistoric life of the human race. Where and how religion began we can never know with certainty unless our present sources of information are unexpectedly transcended. The speculations in which we engage rest on an inadequate knowledge of primitive cultures. It is, however, reasonable to suppose that the racial beginnings of religion were interwoven with the primary concerns of early man such as nutrition, reproduction, personal security, and property rights. The differentiation of the religious attitude from the sum total of early man's relations was probably accompanied by an increased complexity of his personal, social, and economic status.[1]

Is Religion Instinctive?

The inference that religious behavior is the response of an instinct to the universe as a whole has been generally discarded. Those who have attempted to identify religion with a single instinct, separate and distinct from all other inborn reaction patterns, have been of divergent opinion in important aspects. If the religious adjustment were the outcome of a definite instinct, one would anticipate more uniformity than actually exists in the conceptions of religious obligations and actual practices. One would expect the religious expressions of different men and peoples to be similarly definitive and predictable. Such is, however, not the case.

A critical resurvey of original human nature discloses a relatively small number of instincts. The short list of man's instincts, if one may group the findings of several outstanding psychologists, is composed of anger, fear, sexuality, self-expression, self-preservation, and gregariousness. The popular

[1] See King, Irving, "The Evolution of Religion from the Psychological Point of View," *American Journal of Sociology,* 1909, Vol. XIV, pp. 433-450.

usage of the word "instinct" includes far too many learned directive reactions. Most of the automatic activities of man are habits and the resultants of social interaction.[2] It appears that with the growth and progressive complexity of man's nervous system, many human instincts have deteriorated or become extinct. Man controlled wholly by instinct could have survived only in a static world. Man has created a psychosocial environment. Of all creatures, only man is responsive to tradition and custom, and conceives abstract ideas and symbols. In these areas of major human achievements, intelligence and creative imagination, rather than instinct, play the stellar parts. Again, not all instinctive behavior is advantageous; fear of a loud sound like thunder does not further the welfare of the infant; a moth driven by instinct persists in flying into a flame. Man's instinctive equipment is both meager and not in every case serviceable in making adjustments to his environment.

Man is born with a capacity to respond to a higher order of existence, not with a religious instinct which functions without previous cultivation or conscious direction and control. The regulation of personality by religion is a deliberately cultivated form of integration, an ability acquired through training and exercise. As man is endowed with a capacity for verbal expression, but in complete isolation would not learn to speak any language, so it is certain that if infants were placed in charge of savages who have no religion, if any such could be discovered, they would grow up without developing the native capacity for religious living.[3] There are in man

[2] See Bernard, L. L., *Instinct, A Study of Social Psychology* (New York: Henry Holt & Co., 1924).

[3] "We read of an ancient king, who, being desirous to know what was the natural language of men, in order to bring the matter to a certain issue, made the following experiment: He ordered two infants, as soon as they were born, to be conveyed to a place prepared for them where they were brought up without instruction at all, and without ever hearing a human voice. And what was the event? Why, that when they were at length brought out of their confinement, they spake no language at all, they uttered only inarticulate sounds, like those of other animals. Were two infants in like manner to be brought up from the womb without being instructed in any religion, there is little room to doubt but (unless the grace of God interposed) the event would be just the same. They would have no religion at all:

leanings toward religion, but they do not in their summation constitute an instinct with a quality and function peculiar to itself.

Religious adjustment centers in the organization of the varied interests and relationships of man around the governing conviction of the existence and aggressiveness of cosmic reality. One may think of personal religion as a drive which is the determinant of a special form of idealism. A drive, although not biologically inherited but acquired, once it is established and has gained momentum, controls the personality. A drive becomes potent to the extent to which it is exercised with a supporting emotional accompaniment. At first, religion is almost altogether an external or social pressure, but gradually, if the process of religious nurture is successful, it becomes an internal motive force, a powerful drive. The pedagogical reference is obvious. The responsibility for the inculcation of the religious purpose and ideal is the obligation of the home, the church, and kindred institutions.

It is evident that the origin of religion cannot be traced to the first appearance in mankind of a certain instinct. Furthermore, to insist that religion had its inception in a religious instinct which has perished in the course of the evolutionary progress of human nature is to make an assertion for which not the slightest direct proof can be adduced. The few instincts which are included in man's biological inheritance are in themselves void of any moral quality. It is the uses to which they are put, the purposes to which they are subordinated, the manner in which they are consciously employed, that are either good or bad in the light of an accepted moral standard.

Is Religion an Outgrowth of Magic?

It has been asserted that religion is a child of magic. Some go so far as to maintain that as religion has largely supplanted

they would have no more knowledge of God than the beasts of the field, than the wild ass's colt. Such is natural religion, abstracted from traditional, and from the influences of God's Spirit." (Wesley, John, *Sermons on Several Occasions,* Vol. I, p. 395, New York: Carleton & Porter, 1825).

magic, science should retire religion.[4]   A deeper understanding
of both magic and religion, however, warrants the inference
that they differ in origin and method.   That the simpler forms
of magical practices antedated religious behavior seems highly
probable.   It is also patent that religion developed some magical
beliefs and rites and adopted others in the course of its evolution.   In many instances religion and magic interpenetrate to
such an extent that it is difficult to distinguish the one from
the other.   Baptism, the Lord's Supper, the sign of the cross,
and formal prayers are in our own time invested with magical
properties by many Christians.

Both religion and magic imply a belief in the potency of
unseen powers.   The ways in which the belief in the existence
of such powers arose are dissimilar.   The sources of magical
practices are legion.   Early man probably in most instances
did not analyze into distinguishable data a problem which
exasperated him.   Desire or anxiety incited in him the mood
to do something which would control a situation.   Like was
believed to produce like.   A rat is skillful in dodging projectiles
hurled at him; hence the man who possesses the skin of a rat
acquires this agility.   Things once in contact with each other
continue to exercise the same power at a distance when the
contact has been severed.   An old woman in South Africa took
a white child into her arms, praised his beauty, rubbed his head
against her own which was gray, in order to communicate to
him her own length of days.[5]   An implement or article employed with success was naturally supposed to possess magical
qualities and was therefore used again.   The hook that had
caught a fish and the arrow that had reached its mark were
supposed to be lucky.   The belief that the cooling of an arrow
keeps a wound from inflaming may have arisen in such a
manner.   Unity of apprehension dominated by emotion, which
is a relatively uncritical process, is perhaps the explanation of

[4] Frazer, James George, *The Golden Bough,* 12 volumes (New York:
The Macmillan Company, 1907-1915).   See also Lang, Andrew, *Magic and
Religion* (New York: Longmans, Green & Co., 1901).

[5] Allier, Raoul, *The Mind of the Savage,* p. 58 (London: G. Bell & Sons,
1929).

such beliefs and practices. Moved by a similar state of mind, the young son of a theological professor insists that his father repeat the use of a golf ball with which a long and straight drive has been made.

It is likely that many magical rites originated in senseless rumors or idle gossip. In Africa a hen is placed on a number of eggs and a certain decision will be determined by the sex proportion of the chicks hatched.[6] One might be told by an irresponsible person that the killing of a snail produces rain, and spread the tale. If such an act is really followed by a shower, a magical belief and practice may be the result. The impulse to aid others finds natural expression in magical activities. It is supposed by some primitive peoples that when the men are engaged in a battle the women at home can give them strength and victory by hacking at fruit with sticks or other crude weapons. The motivating impulse of such performances is not critical but emotional.

In a relatively advanced stage of social evolution an amber necklace is worn to protect children from the pain of teething, coral is believed to preserve one from the evil eye, and gold from bullets in battle. It is said that the prime minister of Syria issued a decree against the yo-yo top introduced into that country. The Moslem leaders complained that the use of these tops had caused a drought which ruined the grazing lands. As a result, cattle starved to death. It was declared that the up-and-down movements of the yo-yo tops counteracted the prayers for rain. According to a newspaper dispatch, the next day after the prime minister had issued his decree against the tops it rained. Often cause and effect are unconsciously inverted. It is said that a missionary in the course of a prolonged drought was requested, by the savages among whom he labored, to wear his raincoat. Inquiry revealed that the people drew the conclusion that rain would be produced by the raincoat which the missionary had worn in a previous downpour.

[6] Allier, Raoul, *The Mind of the Savage*, p. 176 (London: G. Bell & Sons, 1929).

We should bear in mind that magic in its various forms was born of uncritical psychic states. When we refer to imitative or sympathetic magic and the operation of the laws of association we are employing concepts which were foreign to early man. We are imposing upon him processes of reasoning in which he did not engage. The rationalism of nineteenth-century philosophy and the categories of modern psychology should not be imputed to the simplest forms of culture. The probability is that emotions of fear, awe, and wonderment extended in several directions by critical circumstances swayed primitive peoples. The emotional unity of apprehension, rather the processes of reasoning, gave rise to the profusion of magical attitudes, beliefs, and practices which played so prominent a part in the lives of our distant ancestors. In an analysis of the origin and nature of magical rites we should avoid the transference of our patterns of thinking to peoples who lived so largely in a complex of emotions. The conclusions, correct or fallacious, which they drew were for the most part emotional. Our explanations of primitive religion should be in terms of apprehension motivated by emotion rather than in terms of comprehension of relations.[7]

Both religion and magic are employed in enlarging life, but the methods adopted are opposed.[8] The magician may control a potency outside himself or he may himself be the seat of a mysterious agency. In general, it may be said that the magician by the exercise of his unique power compels persons, gods, or unseen impersonal potencies to do his will. The method of magic is essentially a form of coercion. Pressure upon the mysterious entity may be exerted by the proper intonation of the voice of the magician or by other accredited means. Of course the services of specialists in magical practice are not indispensable in all circumstances. The layman or the profession-

---

[7] Representative of this approach are the following: Lévy-Bruhl, Lucien, *How Natives Think* (London: George Allen & Unwin, Ltd., 1926); *The Soul of the Primitive* (New York: The Macmillan Company, 1928); Malinowski, Bronislaw, *Argonauts of the Western Pacific* (London: George Routledge & Sons, Ltd., 1922).

[8] See Leuba, James H., *A Psychological Study of Religion*, pp. 151 ff. (New York: The Macmillan Company, 1912).

al may assume that whatever is done to a tooth will befall its former possessor, and proceed to bring this form of pressure to bear upon an enemy. There is, then, in magical practices the underlying principle of compulsion.

In seeking to accomplish its purposes religion employs not force but supplication and entreaty. The gods are implored to come to the aid of the worshiper. Sacrifices, rites, and prayers are depended upon to persuade, appease, placate, and reconcile the higher agencies. Religion implies dependence on unseen psychic powers; magic implies the direct and arbitrary control of the mysterious potencies. If the right formula is used in the magical performance, the appropriate result must of necessity follow; in religious practice the help for which an appeal is made depends on the will of the deities. In the one case the will of man is supreme; in the other the will of the gods is sovereign.

Religion is progressive, magic is static. The genius of religion at its best includes creativity and adaptability, which principles insure at once growth in theory and accommodation to unusual or novel situations. The inner flexibility of religion gives rise to endless variation and development. In the course of a century the implications of religion may be made explicit. On the other hand, magic is the same from generation to generation. By their very nature magical procedures are fixed and unalterable. The efficacy of magic is supposed to inhere in an undeviating conformity to the established rites and methods. Change in practice is believed to defeat the purpose magic is intended to serve. Once accepted as an effective control of natural or human forces, magic brooks no variability.

Magic is opposed to rigorous methods of experimentation which is the life of science. For example, only when the magical element was abandoned did chemistry as a science arise. Rigidity and finality are of the very essence of magic; adjustability and improvement mark religion. Magic arrests the intelligence of man, but religion is a mental stimulus. The capacity for reflection is developed by ethical religion; a disinclination to scrutinize, analyze, and criticize is fostered by magic.

Superstition and credulity are prominent characteristics of magic. That these attributes have debased various forms of religion, cannot be denied, but religion as a whole rests on a broader and firmer foundation. Superstition is a baseless belief in the existence and power of occult agencies. It is an irrational confidence that through the domination of supernatural powers, of the spirits of the dead, and of the secret forces in nature, desired effects may be produced. Held by the disturbing attractiveness of the mysterious, the individual who is given to the magical is at the mercy of his emotions and fantastic suggestions.

The contention is, then, that magic is not the mother of religion. Religion and magic are dissimilar in origin and method of operation. Both are ancient means by which man sought to further his welfare. Magic is older than religion. Magical beliefs and performances appear in greater or lesser variety in most, if not all, known forms of religious behavior. As a given form of religion becomes progressively refined in theory and practice, it gradually eliminates its magical accretions. The one is arbitrary, stationary, and irrational; the other is reasonable, experimental, and adaptable. In nature, structure, and procedure magic and religion are fundamentally uncongenial. That two such conflicting ways of enlarging human life should subsist in a relation of cause and effect is not likely.

How Did Ideas of Gods Arise?

It is highly probable that certain ideas preceded and prepared the way for early man's belief in the existence and influence of spirits and gods. The notion that all objects in nature are sentient, all substances alive, antedated the oldest conception of psychic beings of superhuman power.[9] It seems likely that according to primitive ideology no one and only power inhabited or manifested itself in all the different material objects. At first, it was supposed that everything was mysteriously

[9] Durkheim, Émile, *The Elementary Forms of the Religious Life,* translated by Joseph Ward Swain (New York: The Macmillan Company, 1912), concludes that primitive religion and primitive society are totemistic. The god of the clan is the clan itself objectified in terms of the visible animal or vegetable that serves as a totem.

animate. Each thing was in its own right a power. Works of nature conspicuous for their contribution to the welfare of men, like trees, or for the injury they may inflict, like falling rocks, or for their tendency to inspire awe, like stars, attracted the special attention of man and were believed to be more powerful than other objects. That man strove to live on good terms with such phenomena is a logical inference.

It is doubtful that early man attributed to inanimate but significant things or even to animals a soul like his own. The idea of a soul could have arisen only after prolonged reflection, and implies a relatively advanced stage in the evolution of religion. More reasonable is the theory that primitive man imagined that natural objects, plants, and animals are simply alive. At least a part of the raw materials of religion consisted of a naïve conception, accompanied by the emotion of fear, awe, or reverence, that each entity is sentient.[10]

Religion itself emerged when man entertained and took seriously the idea that superior powers exist and determine human welfare and destiny. The conception of the existence and potency of gods did not spring from a single fountainhead. The sources of ideas of gods were numerous and various because the relationships and functions of personality are many and diverse. To restrict the beginnings of religion to a sole experience or concern of human nature is to exclude from consideration an almost infinite variety of man's necessities, in-

[10] The theory outlined and propounded is opposed on the one hand to that of E. B. Tylor (*Primitive Culture*, 2 volumes; New York: Henry Holt & Co., 1883), who argues that animism, the belief that objects have human life or spirit, is the origin of religion; and on the other hand to that of R. R. Marett (*The Threshold of Religion;* London: Methuen & Co., 1909), that religion arose in animatism, a sense of awe inspired by the belief in the presence of a diffused vague mysterious power, not personal, pervading all things but manifesting itself in concentrated form in conspicuous objects. The theory of Marett, although simpler and more cogent than that of Tylor, presupposes, in the opinion of the present writer, a less ingenuous primitive mind than seems necessary to attribute to early man. The hypothesis, advanced by E. Washburn Hopkins (*The Origin and Evolution of Religion;* New Haven: Yale University Press, 1923) and used as basis for the processes suggested above, that each thing was believed to be a separate sentient power, implies a more naïve and primitive form of mental life. The ability to generalize, to comprehend all under one head, is more advanced and complicated than the ability to see in each thing a distinct entity. Monism in its incipient stage is more advanced than the crudest forms of nascent pluralism.

terests, and desires. Furthermore, it is reasonable to presume that the origins of religion are inextricably interwoven not only with the satisfaction of his social and intellectual wants and responses, but also with the gratification of such primary needs as food, sex, and safety. The deities of a people were explicitly related to its social and economic life. Personality develops in participation in the life of a group; and religion, as the control of man's entire being, evolved in a social setting.

Professor King shows what may occur when a gap arises between human activity and the end toward which it is being directed.[11]   The gap may be filled with powerful emotions when anxiety and uncertainty exist. When the gap has been created by suspense or delay, the end sought is lifted into mental prominence and invested with additional desirability and value. It can be readily understood that the agency relied on by early man to meet a need or grant a response was invoked and entreated. If relief or aid actually comes, the object, natural force, plant, or animal accredited with the boon is raised above the ordinary powers in the estimation of the beneficiaries. An appropriate attitude is assumed toward it. The agency to which extraordinary ability is ascribed is enmeshed in personal associations. Just as one seeks help or a favor from a fellow man, so one naturally seeks help or a favor from non-human entities to which superior powers have been attributed. Some of these may be placated for the harm or suffering they may impose, others may be worshiped for the good they have done or can do. Does not the individual praise, entreat, and feast the person who surpasses him in the power to hurt or succor? Intimate personal connections with agencies accorded unique significance, once they are established, constitute a source of the idea of gods.

The principal deities of the most primitive people, it seems certain, were animals, trees, stones, and other objects in their immediate environment. The acquisition of an adequate food supply was a fundamental requirement. With the rise of agriculture weather gods arose. The relation of the weather

[11] King, Irving, *The Development of Religion*, pp. 44 ff. (New York: The Macmillan Company, 1910).

to the raising of crops was observed; hence the sun, the rain, and the gentle south wind were propitiated and entreated. From the basic yet humble necessity for food a belief in the presence and power of the gods of the weather, the rain, the wind, and the sunshine developed. It was almost inevitable that beneficent natural forces should be endowed with psychic attributes and transformed into gods. Gratitude for an abundant harvest was indubitably one of the earliest motives for the offering of sacrifices to the generous gods.

Impressive natural phenomena such as thunder, lightning, tempest, and fire were closely associated with the weather deities. The works of nature in action were assigned human functions such as jealousy, hatred, envy, and love. A god for almost every natural force and human activity sprang into being—a sun god, a moon god, a god of water, a god of grass, a god of trees, gods of fertility, and a god of war. An almost endless procession of gods began to invade the primitive group life of man, a profusion quite bewildering to a modern mind accommodated to the monotheistic theory of reality.

Man's emotional and social experiences and intellectual necessities, as well as his physical wants, led to the conclusion that psychic beings of mysterious properties and qualities rule the world of nature and human beings. Among man's personal experiences from which a belief in spirits originated were the dreams in which the sleeper consorted with those long dead or adventured with the living who inhabited places at a distance.[12] The observation of one's image on the polished surface of a stone or on the water, the motion of objects propelled by the mysterious wind, suggested respectively, a "double" in intangible form, and an unseen agency at work. Such abnormal states of mind as insanity or delirium in which the subject

[12] Herbert Spencer maintained that ancestor worship was the first expression of religion. Fear of the dead is the root of religion. Ancestors appearing as ghosts in dreams or reverie aroused fear and an impulse to placate the spirits. Although ancestor worship harks back to ancient times, as the religion of Asiatic peoples testifies, it is too narrow a foundation for the extensive superstructure of religion, for the complication of primitive urges, affairs, and reactions in which religion functioned. Spencer's theory is too far-extended and over-weighted.

seems to be controlled by a foreign power, induced or increased early man's belief in spirits and gods.

The universe in which he lived challenged the intellect of man. The problem of the creation of all things arose in the mind of man, engaged his prolonged attention, and demanded a solution. He speculated, theorized, and philosophized. Whence did the universe issue? What is its significance? What is its ultimate destiny? Some ancients evolved the explanation that all forms of sentient life are the offspring of the union of the gods of the sky and earth. The ancient Babylonians created myths which were taken over by the Jews, relieved of their polytheism and low ethical standards, and projected against a moral monotheism. Several centuries before the Jews told the story of creation in terms of a drama of six acts, the ancient Hebrew reduced to writing a tale that had been orally transmitted for generations. According to this legend God made a figure from the earth, breathed into it the breath of life and thus produced the first human being, placed him in a garden and proceeded to form from the ground, as a child makes figures from clay, birds and beasts, and finally shaped a woman from a rib removed from the side of the man.[13] The world and what it contains necessitated the theory of a maker. The order of nature which man observed raised questions of origins which were answered by the affirmations of creative imagination and thought.

Some of the works of nature are so conspicuously wonderful that they inspired in the beholder a sense of awe and mystery. The contemplation of the starry hosts of heaven, for example, evoked in the heart of man an overwhelming emotion of majesty and glory. It is not strange that the sun and moon were deified and worshiped, stars acclaimed angels, and the heavens searched for changes which presaged events of importance to men.[14]

[13] Genesis 2: 4b-24.

[14] Rudolph Otto (*The Idea of the Holy;* London: Oxford University Press, 1923) postulates a human capacity for experiencing an emotion of great awe. This emotion, he maintains, is non-rational and unique, is aroused in the presence of Reality, and is the source from which the belief in demons

The ancient poet sang, "The heavens declare the glory of God." [15]

As his personal and social relationships multiplied, man felt the pressure of duty. When he failed to rise to the level of group expectations regarded as divine obligations he was seized by a sense of frustration and condemnation. He was bereft of self-esteem and self-approbation. He sought to appease the outraged deity whose commands he had disobeyed. There was present within him an irrepressible urge to meet the demands of the accepted standard of conduct. He craved strength to obey the mandates imposed upon him. Realizing his own insufficiency, he sought resources other than his own. Surely superhuman agencies answer his need.

We can never realize what fear once meant to human beings. Objects of fear were personified by primitive minds. Such personifications so far from relieving men of terror only increased it. Fearsome forces were in many instances reduced to or represented by crude images of stone or wood. The terrible nightmare of pestilence prowled constantly in the homes, and when it struck and slew, fear drove men together for mutual aid. The violence of the plague so far from abating throve in the huddling mass of humanity. No doubt, in some such cases the inference was drawn that an invisible and hostile power was punishing men, or taking vengeance on them, or was capriciously malicious and that therefore it behooved them to placate it. Indubitably fear was one of the earliest active sources of ideas of gods whom it was imperative to conciliate with sacrifice, ritual, and ceremony. When he is the victim of fear, man desperately seeks a refuge of security or a means of extricating himself from the painful situation. Terrifying images were often friendly gods whose fearsome guise was intended to frighten evil spirits away from tormented people.

Other personality necessities originated or intensified and expanded man's belief in responsive divine beings. Sorrow, and gods sprang. Two objections may be raised against this assumption. In the first place, psychology can detect no such peculiar capacity in man. In the second place, to reduce religion to an inarticulate emotion, to a single presupposed human function, seems contrary to the complexities of human personality. [15] Psalm 19: 1.

misunderstanding, and loneliness led to a search for sympathetic comprehension and companionship. Man wanted to be
loved. Was not this desire matched by a love nothing could
quench? He craved an object worthy of his deepest affections
and utmost loyalty. Was there not a Being so perfect in moral
will and constant in love that one was drawn to him in the
mood of reverence and devotion? The desire for fellowship
with a psychic being other than human represents a rather
advanced stage in the development of religion.

Conclusion

Religion, as the worship of gods, arose from man's varied
problems, interests, and experiences. The background of
primitive religion was the belief that every object and force
is sentient. Man's physical needs prompted him to appeal to
the powers of nature which could supply them. Personal associations with inanimate objects; forces of nature, plants, and
animals were established. The endowment of dramatic natural
phenomena, whether hostile or beneficent, with human traits
probably occurred at an early stage of culture. Such experiences and states of mind as dreams and delirium originated or
supported the belief in spirits and gods. Speculation relative
to the production and preservation of the world made the existence of a Creator and Sustainer a reasonable inference.
Threatened with the loss of possessions or life itself, man,
motivated by fear, sought the author of his plight in order to
effect deliverance through appeasement. A desire for aid in
the performance of his recognized duties and a craving for
consolation in tribulation and for fellowship contributed to the
conception of accessible, friendly, understanding, and helpful
superhuman beings. Furthermore, it is not likely that all the
different sources of belief in divine existences were active at
one and the same time. A prolonged period elapsed between
the beginning of the worship of weather gods and the beginning of the worship of gods with whom man could fellowship.

The cosmic activity in the origin of religion should not be
ignored. Man does not inhabit a static universe but one which
is both aggressive and responsive. The religiously regulated

personality feels that a cosmic power impinges upon it, spurring it to progressively refined integrations. Something induces man to seek self-realization by self-surrender to a cosmic overture. Man reaches up because something first reaches down. If the spirit of the universe had not exercised the initiative, man could never have discovered an object of worship which makes religion at its best a stark reality.

The consequence of religion may be considered an emergent. An emergent is the product of a creative combination of conditions or processes. Water is the emergent of two parts of hydrogen and one part of oxygen. It seems almost incredible that such a fluid substance should result from the compounding in proper proportions of two chemical constituents, neither of which resembles water. Such an outcome from the chemical union would not be anticipated by one unfamiliar with the formula for water. Water is more than the sum of the elementary gaseous substances to which chemistry reduces it. Water is the product of interaction, a new and unique creation.

Let this serve as an analogue. Religion was not injected ready-made into man from without, but emerged in the course of his struggle for the enrichment of personality in a dynamic universe. The cosmic impulse acts on man. A human reaction to the stimulus occurs. In divers manners, many of them in our opinion crude and ineffective, man, seeking goods of all sorts, is responsive to the cosmic promptings. Obeying the divine strivings, man becomes a religious being. Religion, thus conceived, is the outcome of the initiative of God in human life. The result is an emergent.

The most familiar verse in the Bible stresses the religious emergent.[16] "For God so loved the world, that he gave his only begotten son"—that is the divine initiative, the theistic action; "that whosoever believeth on him"—that is the human function; "should not perish, but have eternal life"—that is the negative and the positive resultant, salvation from destruction by evil and the derivation from God of a life which is endless and Christlike. The core of the Christian religion is man's acceptance of God's proffered love.

[16] John 3: 16.

CHAPTER IV

THE EVOLUTION OF THE IDEA OF GOD

In order to be adequate a theory of ultimate reality must comply with the ethical, emotional, and intellectual requirements of man. It must include within its scope two worlds, the world of sense perception and the world of imponderability. It must provide a cogent interpretation of the universe, its existence in time and space, its significance and purpose, and its destiny. The theory must, in short, make the universe rational, give its multitudinous aspects underlying unity and cohesion, and supply the whole with creative energy. Some men are incurably philosophical and therefore cannot rest until they find peace in a world-view to which their intelligence gives assent.

In the second place, the core of religion, which is a dynamic appreciation of ultimate determining reality, must satisfy man's deepest cravings for inward harmony. Religious reality must validate, sanction, and organize such cherished values as hope, ethical love, justice, beauty. It must guarantee the idealism of man and supply him with ethical momentum and fervor. The concept of reality characterized by sufficiency answers to genius of the inner world of spirit as well as to the structure of the outer world of nature.

Happily it does not fall within the purview of the psychology of religious personality to sit in judgment upon the objectivity and reliability of the various and often clashing types of religious devotion or the gods to which man has given allegiance throughout the ages. This delicate and sometimes thankless task is a function of philosophy and theology, especially of the philosophy of religion. The psychologist as such has no such mandate. As a scientist in the performance of his duty he has nothing to do with finalities. He is not obligated to determine whether the proffered concepts of the manifold forms of reli-

58

gious worship correspond to actualities. He may, however, express his theological convictions. He is charged with the assignment to trace the personal and social processes which have led man to evolve his ideas of the nature and number of gods, and to tabulate the consequences of such concepts for conduct and for the respective types of personality.

Polytheism

Successive pantheons of gods, many of them, in current opinion, violent and absurd, conquered and ruled men and communities and then passed into oblivion. The record of their palmy days, of the obligations they imposed upon their votaries, of their own idiosyncrasies and rivalries, is preserved in the myths and traditions that have reached us. The worship of several, if not numerous, gods by individuals and communities has not yet perished from the earth. The traveler, if he is so inclined, may have this type of worship under actual observation.

It is not hard to perceive how it came to pass that of several gods a certain one would be singled out for special veneration and devotion. Not all gods, obviously, were of equal importance to the worshiper. The gods that were the guardians of the special interests of communities were of course given preferential consideration. A ranking of the gods would be the natural consequence. From the worship of a number of gods polytheism evolved. Technically, polytheism implies a hierarchy of gods.

Greek polytheism as incorporated in Homer's works is representative. The gods of Homer's writings are superhuman and immortal, and suffer pain and humiliation. Zeus is the father of the gods and men. Hera is his wife. Apollo is the inspirer of prophecy, Artemis his sister is a huntress, Ares is the chief god of war, Aphrodite is the goddess of love, Poseidon is the god of the sea, Athena is a patroness of handcrafts and takes an interest in war, Hermes serves the gods as messenger. The chief virtues enjoined by Homer are reverence for parents, the practice of hospitality, and the keeping of an oath.

It came to pass that in many cases a principal god possessed a city and a priesthood with a prescribed ritual. The leading deity of the city of Haran in Mesopotamia, from which Abraham and his kin migrated to Canaan, was Sin, a moon god. Marduk, a sun god, was the chief deity of Babylon. Aton, also a sun god, was the patron deity of Thebes in Egypt. Pallas Athene was the local goddess of Athens, and Artemis of Ephesus. Images in human or animal form symbolized the gods. Certain animals might be sacred to a deity. Both images and sacred animals were the objects of worship and superstitious veneration. Idolatry or image worship is the inevitable outcome of the tendency to represent gods in the works of human hands.

There is valid reason to suppose that the ancient Hebrews passed through the stage of polytheism in their religious pilgrimage. The Old Testament is a repository of several survivals of polytheistic beliefs and practices of the early Hebrews. Joshua in his last charge to the Israelites, not long before death overtook him, affirmed that the fathers both in Mesopotamia and Egypt served gods other than Jehovah. He exhorted the people to abandon the worship of these gods, which evidently had been imported into Canaan, and to pledge themselves to the exclusive service of Jehovah.[1] Ezekiel, a prophet of the exilic period, pours vials of indignation and condemnation upon the abominations associated with the worship of Egyptian deities, which were practiced both by his forebears and his contemporaries. He is equally caustic in his references to the worship of Babylonian gods by the fathers in Chaldea, the land of their nativity.[2] The transliteration of the Hebrew word translated God is Elohim, which is in the plural number. The designation suggests a polytheistic derivation. The retention of the plural in later usage was perhaps a deliberate enhancement of the prestige of the God of Israel.[3]

[1] Joshua 24: 2, 14.   [2] Ezekiel 23: 1-27.

[3] Reference to demigods, deities of inferior rank, is probably made in the use of the first person plural in the priestly narrative of creation where we read "God said, Let us make man in our image" (Gen. 1: 26), and in the prophetic story of the fall of man where the statement is made, "And Jehovah God said, Behold, the man is become as one of us." (Gen. 3: 22.)

In most instances polytheistic religions have died for lack of sufficient inner vitality and power of progressive adaptation. The ancient religions of Babylonia, Assyria, and Egypt, with an exception to be specified, never advanced beyond a ranking of their many gods. Looking back, polytheism came a long distance, but looking forward it left possible paths untraced. The Hebrews pressed on from polytheism to progressively exalted and refined religious stages.

Henotheism

Among the Hebrews polytheism gave way to henotheism, or allegiance to one god as the patron of the tribe or nation, without abandoning the belief in the existence of the deities of other peoples. The gods of other communities or nations were feared by the Jehovah-serving Hebrews, but they were not worshiped or implored for aid or protection. This advance on polytheism is also called practical monotheism. Moses came before his people in Egypt with the message of deliverance from bondage through the grace and might of Jehovah. Willing and able to succor the enslaved Hebrews, Jehovah merited their unlimited confidence and exclusive devotion. Under Moses, his prophet, Jehovah would become their emancipator, protector, judge, and ruler, if only they, in the hour when they seemed doomed to destruction at the hands of their Egyptian oppressors, would forsake all other gods and pledge him constant single-minded loyalty.

Where and how was Moses introduced to Jehovah? Was Jehovah the god of Jethro, the father-in-law of Moses? As a fugitive from the wrath of Pharaoh, Moses had wandered into the land of Midian and had there found asylum in the tent of Jethro. If Jethro made known to Moses the nature and requirements of Jehovah, where and how did Jethro become a worshiper of Jehovah? Did he separate Jehovah from a collection of gods as the one who merited exclusive veneration and obedience or was the religion of Jehovah transmitted to Jethro by others? The answers to these questions cannot, under the present limitations of our sources of information, be supplied with any degree of assurance. It seems probable that Moses embraced the henotheistic worship of Jehovah while a sojourner in the land of Midian since there is no cogent reason for supposing that he acquired it in Egypt as a member of Pharaoh's court. The call to deliver his brethren in Egypt that resounded through his being one day while herding sheep probably followed prolonged meditation. An inner illumination experienced by a responsive personality prepared by isolation and profound reflection has been the origin of several great religions.

In the desert Israel formally entered into covenant relations with Jehovah. The Hebrews solemnly obligated themselves to render Jehovah passionate loyalty and moral obedience. Other gods might exist, the gods of other peoples, the gods ruling over the lands of non-Israelites, but Jehovah was separated from them all by his superior might and righteousness. He had demonstrated his power by leading the Hebrews under Moses out of the house of Egyptian bondage. The great deliverance marked the birth of a new nation conceived in the acceptance of Jehovah as their god and dedicated to the service of ethical conduct. "Thou shalt have no other gods before me" was his express command. The conviction that Jehovah was without a peer in strength and moral quality was the germ of monotheism, the basis on which all other gods were ultimately retired.

Not that Israel kept absolute faith with Jehovah. It is likely that during the wilderness wanderings the worship of clan and family gods was surreptitiously if not openly performed. When the Hebrews obtained a foothold here and there in Palestine, the temptation to serve the local nature deities, who were popularly credited with the fertility of the soil and flocks, proved to be too strong to be resisted. Jehovah worship was not altogether neglected. It did not suffer the atrophy of complete disuse, but was combined with the worship of the native gods. The resultant syncretism seems not to have elevated the Baal cult, but it did debase the service of Jehovah and violate his commands. Such apostasy constituted a degradation of the Mosaic ideal in the eyes of the early prophets who strove to purge the religion of Jehovah of its pernicious foreign elements.   Elijah opposed the imported Tyrian Baal worship, castigating its priesthood and challenging its presumed superiority and efficacy.   In his attempts to extirpate Baalism he did not shrink from the slaughter of its votaries.   His successor Elisha succeeded by diplomacy in accomplishing what violence had failed to achieve.   It appears that up to the period of the Babylonian exile the religion of Jehovah was adulterated with the recognition of both native and foreign gods; nevertheless it possessed an inner character and potentiality, a persuasive appeal, a moral and intellectual vitality that enabled it to survive and evolve.

Monotheism

Israel's two most precious gifts to the world are the theory of history as a divine determination to realize a lofty purpose, and ethical monotheism.   The belief that only one God in all the universe exists and that he alone is to be acknowledged and obeyed by men everywhere is the culminating stage in the evolution of the concept of ultimate religious reality.   The earliest form of Hebrew monotheism was not final.   It is, for example, a long way from the simple idea of God in the guise of a man, which one encounters in the early narratives of Genesis, to the statement of Jesus, "God is a Spirit: and they that worship him must worship him in spirit and in truth." [4]

Not that monotheism did not appear among peoples other than the Hebrews before it was conceived and accepted by the great prophets of Israel.   A form of monotheism originated in Egypt in the fourteenth century before Christ.   It seems

[4] John 4: 24.   In the oldest Genesis stories Jehovah performs many physical and manual acts.   He forms the first man from the dust, plants a garden in which he places Adam, removes a rib from his side from which he fashions woman.   Jehovah walks in the garden in the cool of the evening, converses with Adam and Eve in human language, and makes clothing for the fallen couple.   In one strand of the flood account Jehovah shuts Noah and his family in the ark, and later smells the sweet savor of the sacrifice offered by the grateful survivors of universal destruction.   Three angels, one of whom is Jehovah himself, visit Abraham and partake of the cakes, butter, milk, and veal set before them by their host.   When we consider these and other anthropomorphisms we should not forget that since we think in terms of experience we are unable to describe a purely spiritual being.   When we impute to God such attributes as love and justice we give them a content derived from human relationships.

to have had its rise in the ambition of Ikhnaton, ruler of Egypt, to conquer the world he knew. He exalted the sun god Aton to sole sovereignty. The service of other gods was forbidden by the decree of Ikhnaton, their priesthoods despite protests were disbanded, and access to their shrines was denied. The worship of one god only was designed to unify Egypt and other lands to be annexed by conquest, and to weld into one vast cohesive whole a new empire. The attempt, premature and despotic, failed to enlist a sufficient number of influential subjects to maintain itself indefinitely. Furthermore, it did not possess enough ethical vitality to survive and expand. After the death of its author and under the reign of his successor the elementary Egyptian monotheism was permitted to recede, and polytheism, with all its complicated paraphernalia, crudities, superstitions, and imperfections, was restored to its former place of power.

Hebrew monotheism grew in the subsoil of minds fertilized by a dignified henotheism. It was rooted in the Mosaic belief that Jehovah possesses power and moral discrimination superior to those exhibited by his rivals. Who the first of Israel's monotheists was is difficult if not impossible to ascertain. The withering scorn which Elijah casts upon the Tyrian Baal and his devotees, his assumption that two such antithetical principles as Baalism and Jehovism cannot long exist side by side, his impassioned exhortation to his countrymen to choose and serve the one or the other, appear to involve an incipient monotheism.[5] The literary prophets of Israel were the teachers of an unequivocal conviction that Jehovah is the sole deity of the whole world. It permeates the message of Amos, who labored about 755 B.C. It is reasonable to infer that reflection on the successive changes through which his nation had passed and on the relations of it to other nations led to a universalized and unified conception of God. The idea of the range of Jehovah's jurisdiction expanded with a broadened and enlarged political outlook. After all, the land of Israel was a bridge which was crossed by nations from the southeast and the north-

[5] 1 Kings 18: 20-40.

west. It was often the battleground of foreign peoples of conflicting political ambitions. Impressions were made upon Israel by surrounding peoples. It dawned upon Amos that the sovereignty of Jehovah extends beyond the confines of Israel and includes all men and all forces of nature. Jehovah's chief function is not to fight the battles of pampered favorites but to establish justice. He disciplines the violator of the principles of justice regardless of his nationality. When the Assyrian falls upon Israel like the wolf upon the fold, the Hebrew is not to infer that foreign gods of war have routed Jehovah, but that he is using the military invasion of the promised land and its consequent devastation as his chosen instrument of punishment. The disruption of Israel is Jehovah's assertion of moral determination.

Isaiah, also an eighth-century prophet, stressed the ethical contrast between Jehovah and the gods of other nations. Since the moral law is supreme in the world, only that God who is ethically upright can have an existence of his own. Jehovah is morally above reproach, the gods of other peoples are not so; hence the God of Israel is the only deity in all the universe.[6] By virtue of his justice and kindliness he must be Lord of all and without rival. Jehovah is thus not a national god, but the international God. The universality of his sovereignty renders all other gods superfluous, makes them nonentities, and practically identifies them with their images. So Isaiah reasoned.

The central teaching of Israel affirms the oneness and unity of the divine Being.[7] The spirit of Israel's great prophets blazes forth in the solemn admonition, "Know therefore this day, and lay it to thy heart, that Jehovah he is God in heaven above and upon the earth beneath; there is none else." [8] The conception and gradual enlargement and enrichment of monotheistic religion is a supreme achievement of the prophets of Israel. It was not until the Hebrews grasped and promulgated it that monotheism became established as a religious belief.

[6] Euripides argued that if gods are base, then they are not gods. Fragment 294.

[7] Deuteronomy 6: 4.

[8] Deuteronomy 4: 39.

The Greeks later evolved a unitary theory of reality. The doctrine which they advanced is called monism. According to Greek monism there is in the universe a single principle or element from which all else is derived. Idealistic monism explains impersonal energy in its various manifestations as a modification of mind. Mechanistic monism resolves mind into a type of physical or chemical phenomenon. A third variety of monism reduces both psychic and physical forces or entities to one underlying agency or substance.

Several of the early Greek monists were candidly and forthrightly materialists. Thales, who flourished in the sixth century B.C., reduced all things to a single primordial substance—i.e., water. Anaximander, who lived in the same century, declared that everything proceeded by processes of separation from an original substance called by him the Indefinite, a limitless something perhaps comparable to the ether which physicists of a later day postulated. Anaximenes, also a sixth-century philosopher, maintained that from air, a breathlike entity, all has been produced by rarefaction and condensation. Heraclitus, a fifth-century thinker, argued that fire was the ultimate originating element.[9]

Not all the great early Greek monists were materialists. Notable exceptions are recorded. Xenophanes, who wandered in Greece in the sixth century, was an idealistic monist, in fact his doctrine might well be called an elementary monotheism. Anthropomorphism, which is the belief that gods are human in form and manifestations, received his contemptuous condemnation. He is reputed to have declared, "If oxen and lions had hands wherewith to portray their gods in art, they would give to them bodies of oxen and lions." He taught that there is but one God, not like man in body or mind, but who sees, hears, and thinks with his whole being. Anaxagoras, of the following century, posited as the ground of all *Nous,* or mind or reason.

[9] Empedocles, who labored in the fifth century, was a pluralist. To the water of Thales, the air of Anaximenes, and the fire of Heraclitus, he added earth. From these four elements in various combinations changes proceed. Love or attraction unites the primordial entities, but hate or repulsion separates them.

Idealist monism, such as that of Xenophanes, may have satisfied the demand of the intellect for an ultimate explanation of the universe. Unlike Hebrew monotheism, Greek monism is cold, dispassionate, and indifferent to human weakness and need. It lacks moral fervor and responsiveness. It may serve as a philosophical principle, but not as an ethical dynamic or emotional stabilizer. The psychological advantage rests with monotheism, glowing as it does with sympathy for the weak and oppressed, burning with indignation for the wrongdoers, and blazing at all times with moral zeal. Monotheism, thought-provoking, heart-warming, conscience-stirring, and packed with social implications, appeals to the whole personality, not merely to this or that human function. For that reason Hebrew monotheism rather than Greek monism has survived as a force in the lives of millions of men. Monotheism achieves its powerful significance in a framework of personal relationships.

Christian Monotheism

The monotheism of contemporary Judaism, Christianity, and Islam has been derived from the doctrines of the Hebrew prophets. Islam as expounded in the Koran and enforced by its founder Mohammed is a form of monotheism which diverges from that of Judaism or Christianity. Allah, the God of Islam, is absolute, despotic, and capricious. It is difficult for the critical reader of the Koran successfully to resist a mounting suspicion that Allah reflects the unstable and autocratic disposition of his prophet Mohammed.

Liberal Judaism stresses the numerical oneness and the unity of the divine Being. It makes the God of the great Old Testament prophets the sole object of worship. Social justice, compassion, and humility are considered the primary requirements of God. Whoever strives to practice these cardinal principles is acceptable in the sight of God. The fundamentals of liberal Judaism possess a simplicity, grandeur, and practical value which carry forward the traditional ethical monotheism.

Christ took over from Judaism the concept of the fatherhood of God, stamped it with his unique personality, and made it central in worship and conduct. He drew sustenance for daily living from the social and religious principles proclaimed by Israel's great prophets. The doctrine of monotheism developed and interpreted in certain prophetic writings of Israel, and taught by some of the later Jewish sages, was given an emphasis by Jesus which makes his message ever new. He made the universal fatherhood of God the dynamic of personal living as well as that of a more equitable social order.

The term Father as a name for God may mean either that God is the creator of human beings in somewhat the same sense in which the bond between an earthly father and son is one of blood, or that God adopts man and that the tie between them is one of mutual responsibility and affection. In the Old Testament the thesis is maintained that God is the Father of Israel in the sense that he is the founder of the nation.[10] He is the creator of men and peoples, but in a special sense Israel is his son. The Christian concept of the fatherhood of God combines the principles of the two postulates. The personal relationship is, however, given the pre-eminence. God is the creator of all men, but the individual becomes his son by adoption.

Monotheism is by no means a rigid and static conception of ultimate reality. The doctrine possessed from its inception sufficient vitality and flexibility to assume various forms and to undergo processes of refinement in the course of time. The main stream of monotheism stresses the transcendence of God. Orthodox Judaism teaches that God is remote from the world of man and nature, dwells in the seventh heaven above the firmament, and has interposed between himself and his people a mass of legal and ceremonial obligations and a host of angels and spirits.

The doctrine known as deism is a type of monotheism which magnifies in characteristic ways the transcendence of God. In one of its cruder forms God is pictured as a venerable patriarchal figure, incomparably good and wise and mighty. At a datable time he created the world and what it contains, and ordained the laws which govern it. He now dwells apart from

[10] See Deuteronomy 32: 6; Isaiah 63: 16; Malachi 2: 10.

the universe, observes its processes and occasionally inter-
rupts the normal course of nature in order to further a special
design of his own or gratify a worshiper who has won his
favor. He is a great artificer and an exalted ruler. A direct
evidence of his existence is an event which contradicts the
natural order. It is evident that with the reduction of the
world to regularity and law, independent episodes are increasingly difficult to discover. God who comes and goes, whose
appearances are sporadic, is likely to vanish altogether from
a law-abiding universe.[11]

The doctrine of the divine immanence is opposed to the
doctrine of the transcendence of God. The word "immanence"
means indwelling, internally resident. The teaching of the
immanence of God implies that God is the soul of the universe,
creating, animating, and sustaining it from within. As the
human mind inhabits and invigorates the body, but is not
identical with the body, God is an all-pervading Presence distinct but not apart from the world. The universe is the continuous and progressive manifestation of the creative energy
of an indwelling divine will. There is no line of demarcation
between nature's work and God's work, for he expands himself
in the progression of natural events. Natural law is divine
energy and purpose organized.[12]

The New Testament in its general drift teaches that God
is transcendent but gracious and accessible. The doctrine of
the immanence of God is Greek rather than Hebrew or Chris-

[11] Another variety of deism holds that the world may be compared with
a huge machine which is so perfectly adjusted in all its interior parts that
having been set in motion it will continue to operate for the appointed time.
The world requires no further care from its maker, the great mechanic, for
it has been originally supplied with forces adequate for all future contingencies and emergencies. God passively regards his masterpiece from afar and
never interferes with its ongoings. He is the great Unknown.

[12] A dualism comprised of impersonal energy and God has been advocated
by some philosophers whose acumen and Christian character command
respect. Dean Inge, influenced by Greek philosophy, for example, holds that
both matter and God are independent existences, and that God manipulates
and utilizes matter or energy. Pluralism is the doctrine that there are several or even many ultimate realities or principles. William James, an outstanding pluralist, declares that monotheism creates the problem of evil, and
only by assuming that evil is an independent actuality is God relieved of all
responsibility for its presence in the world. See his *Pluralistic Universe*.

tian in origin and nature. We read that God arrays the lilies of the field and clothes the grass,[13] that the death of a sparrow is recognized by him, and the hairs of our heads are numbered.[14] Statements of this kind are poetical and pictorial assurances of Jesus that God's watchcare is over all rather than philosophical affirmations of the divine immanence. The Father is in heaven. With a love that knows no bounds he welcomes the penitent sinner. Seeing in Jesus the agent of creation and of salvation, St. Paul could not have taught the immanence of God without flagrant contradiction.[15] Paul's epistles abound in passages in which the transcendence of God is either directly asserted or implied. Only believers, those who by faith are united with the living and glorified Christ, possess the Spirit. The Stoic doctrine that in every man the divine principle is resident is entirely foreign not only to Paul's theology but also to the teaching of the New Testament as a whole.

Christian theology maintains that God so far from being the altogether unknown and unknowable has manifested himself uniquely in the character and mission of Jesus. To declare that we can know all about God is to be guilty of the most deadly sin of presumption; to disclaim any knowledge of God is to be victimized by tragic agnosticism. The direct self-impartation of God according to Christian thinking reaches its culmination in the life of Christ. The mind of Christ is in all probability expressed in the statement, "He that hath seen me hath seen the Father." [16] Jesus' concern for the welfare and reclamation of man invites us to glimpse eternal Love. We

---

[13] Matthew 6: 28-30.

[14] Matthew 10: 29, 30.

[15] It has been repeatedly declared that when St. Paul on Mars' Hill quoted with approval a Greek poet's sentiment that "in him we live, and move, and have our being," he proclaimed an immanent God to the assembled Athenians. Two points should be given due weight. The affirmation of the divine immanence would have contradicted the conception of God which runs throughout Paul's epistles. Again, scholars recognize that the speech on Mars' Hill is recorded in a secondary source of literary information—the Book of Acts—and that at least some of its statements were imputed to the apostle by uncritical reporters.

[16] John 14: 9.

can never discover the God of Jesus through sight and hearing, for he is not a sense datum. God forever prompting the individual to self-realization, can be experienced through the immediate relation of appreciation and faith.

In approaching the concept of God, the peculiar characteristics of scientific knowledge, metaphysical speculation, and religious faith must be distinguished lest confusion abound. Scientific knowledge is obtained by investigation of data determinable by the senses. A deity scientifically discoverable, analyzable, and verifiable would not be the object of religious veneration, the God who transcends our finite experiences. God is not datum of scientific research. Furthermore, speculation as to the nature and functions of God, however cogent, justifiable, and even imperative, does not exactly correspond with the facts.

As soon as we proceed to define God we impose upon him the limitations of our mental processes. After all, God as a religious dynamic is an object of faith and not an inference of speculation or a direct finding of science. Relying on what is beyond the possibility of scientific scrutiny, men by faith appropriate God and embark on adventurous living. Psychology may profitably study the motives, emotions, ideas, and deeds associated with the religious consciousness, but it cannot capture, dissect, and classify God himself.

Who can fully describe how personality is affected by the character of the divine Power acknowledged as the Determiner of destiny? Who can imaginally reconstruct the terror-stricken man who believed implicitly in the existence and dominance of gods whose wrath could be appeased only by the sacrifice of his most cherished possessions, even human blood and gore? Who can analyze the state of mind created by the conviction that divine vengeance would descend upon all who designedly or unintentionally did not scrupulously observe the tangled mass of taboos and obligations imposed by the gods? Who can adequately discuss the tragic condition of the personality haunted by superstition, insecurity, and terror? When fear of capricious and arbitrary gods was cast out by simple trust in a God of love personality was stabilized, the conjunctive attitudes of confidence and security developed, and the individual, released from the burden of torment, was filled with peace.   The relation which exists between the quality of personality and the nature of the deity invoked is positive and determining.

CHAPTER V

HUMANISM

In our time thousands of men and women of intelligence and good will are attempting to make life rich, honorable, fruitful, and satisfying apart from a reliance on God as an objective reality. Without reference to God a way of life is now being advocated by many voices and accepted by multitudes, a way which is generally known as humanism.[1]

Current absolute humanism holds that a passion for the welfare of mankind, together with personal self-fulfillment, should be the dynamic of living and outline the complete range of our responsibilities. Reliance is placed on education, political reorganization, scientific knowledge, and co-operative effort for the elimination of disease, poverty, ignorance, crime, and war, and for the actual realization of personal freedom, self-development, and economic equalization. This is not a new arrangement of life, for throughout centuries persons of culture and humanitarian ideals have disowned the validity and practicability of religion in its historic significance. The one new factor which emerges in the present situation is that this philosophy of life is being proclaimed from the housetops and is winning the allegiance of men and women in increasing numbers.

Is Humanism a Religion?

Humanism as a movement is still in process of development, and further experimentation and clarification will no doubt impose modifications. At present, several varieties are discernible and distinguishable. One representative group of humanists does not formally disavow religion, but declares that

---

[1] This way of life should not be confused with the humanistic movement which during the Renaissance brought into being a revival of the study of the ancient Greek and Roman classics. As a result of this revival attention was directed from the world of nature to the mind and inner needs of man.

the chief end of religion is the earthly welfare of man. The dynamic and sanction of religion are enlisted in a vigorous campaign for the betterment of man's lot here and now. It places special emphasis on the social aspects of religion. A second group consists of those who do not deny the extra-human structure of Reality but maintain that it has nothing to do with man and his affairs. They are practical rather than theoretical atheists. Belief in the existence of God, it is said, may be a philosophical necessity, but all the resources for more abundant living lie within man himself. A third typical group subscribes to the doctrine that humanitarian values are supreme and final. The attitude of humanists of this persuasion toward religion as the integration of life in terms of God-consciousness is negative if not actually hostile. Religion is supposed to be the enemy rather than the ally of mankind in the reconstruction of society and the emancipation of the individual. In fact, it is generally assumed that religion is an opiate which drugs its victims into complacent acquiescence with the *status quo*. It is alleged that religion, stressing celestial prospects and counseling submission to the iniquities of the existing social system, makes a direct, immediate, and urgent solicitude and struggle for the objectives of social idealism, if not actually impossible, at least immeasurably difficult. Religion is evaluated as a phase in the cultural development of the human race, which men of scientific temper, philosophic discrimination, and social vision should dismiss. Although the first group indicated is far from invulnerable, the present discussion takes into account chiefly the second and third groups.

The effects of humanistic propaganda are various and potent. For example, certain sections of the field of religious education have been invaded by the ultra humanists. Attempts attended by more or less success are being made to reduce religious education to character education as such. This program of moral culture ignores the function of religion in the organization of personality. Leaders in religious education who are committed to Christian theism maintain that the present situation should be clarified and that such fundamental questions as the following be answered: How does religious education differ from character education? What is the place of the Bible in Christian education? What is the function of worship? What is the nature of authority in religious culture?

The strict humanist seems to be more interested in the means than the end of human life. Applied science has enabled us to improve the means, but it has not clarified the end. Those for whom philanthropy is everything have no answer to the question, "What shall we do with life?" The question will persist even when everybody is adequately fed, housed, and clothed. The war against hunger and disease must be continued, but man lives not by bread and creature comfort alone. To know, to appreciate, to pursue truth and to integrate personality in terms of cosmic relationships are worthy ends which man cannot forfeit without loss.

Some strict humanists appropriate the terminology of a religion whose real nature and power they reject. One of them claims that "religion is the endeavor of divided and incomplete human personality to attain unity and completion, *usually but not necessarily,* by seeking the help of an ideally complete divine person or persons." [2] Another insists that any activity which is undertaken for an ideal end in the face of obstacles and threats of personal loss is religious in quality. God is simply the unity of the ideal purposes which arouse in us desire and action.[3] To define religion so that it does not indispensably include the deliberate and intelligent response to a Power other than human or physical is to invest the word "religion" with a connotation which is absolutely foreign to it. It would be both clearer and franker to state that strict humanism is not a religion at all but a substitute for or the proposed successor to religion. Such a declaration would clear the air of the confusion which infests it.

The issue should be drawn between religion, a way of life based on God, and ultra-humanism, a way of life based on man. In order to be valid, definitions of both religion and

[2] Potter, Charles Francis, *The Story of Religion,* p. 18 (New York: Simon & Schuster, Inc., 1929). The italics are mine.
[3] Dewey, John, *A Common Faith* (New Haven: Yale University Press, 1934).

humanism should incorporate or imply the differentiation. To insist that religion is the conservation of highest social values does not necessarily include the worship of an extra-human being. A definition broad enough to embrace both theism and strict humanism does not sharply characterize either. Humanism as well as religion is a quest for life, for more and abundant life, for a completely satisfying life, but the religious quest is God-centered, and the ultra-humanistic quest is man-centered. A godless religion is a contradiction of terms.

Roman and Modern Humanism

As has already been intimated, the essence of humanism is an ancient philosophy of life. St. Paul in his day encountered it. We must bear in mind that Paul did not preach the gospel of Christ in a world which had discarded religion and philosophy. The Roman Empire which Paul invaded with the Christian message staged a veritable conflict of philosophies and religions. As a Christian missionary and apologist Paul faced such formidable competing philosophies and religions as Epicureanism, Cynicism, Stoicism, Emperor worship, the mystery cults, and incipient Gnosticism. To these divergent beliefs and practices should be added the Judaistic form of Christianity against which Paul was impelled to set himself.

Epicureanism, still influential in the Roman empire when St. Paul flourished, included elements which are reflected in modern humanism. The adherents of Epicureanism believed that the universe is the outcome of a chance arrangement of atoms, that matter is the sole final reality, that the senses are the only trustworthy guides in the search for truth, that the gods if they do exist care nothing at all for men, that death terminates human personality, and that the chief end of life is satisfaction.[4] It should not be forgotten that Epicurus taught that genuine satisfaction is achieved through virtue. The sturdy loyalty to sense facts, the conduct of life on an exalted level, the mechanistic interpretation of the universe together with the denial of personal immortality, which marked those who were faithful

[4] Glover, T. R., *The Conflict of Religions in the Early Roman Empire,* pp. 218-220 (London: Methuen & Co., 1909).

followers of Epicurus, are all involved in the tenets and programs of certain groups of humanists of the present generation. To be sure, modern humanism transcends these common elements with an intelligent and dominant social passion. Since Epicureanism embodied the freedom, the elegance, and the skepticism of Greece, it is not strange that it was considered the essence of paganism by the early Christians. Containing the seeds of its own corruption, it degenerated in the course of time into license and sensuality. Will that form of current humanism which is akin to Epicureanism suffer a similar moral collapse?

Stoicism was in several important respects different from and superior to Epicureanism. Although the varieties of Stoicism are confusing, they seem to be agreed that there is in man a divine reason which binds him to God, that men are to act for the right without regard to pain or pleasure, and that the prospect of conscious life after death is dim and uncertain. Some of the noblest men in the Roman empire were Stoics, among them being Seneca, Epictetus, and Marcus Aurelius. Stoicism was popularized and carried from the schools to the masses by street teachers. Its influence was widespread and significant. The correspondences between varieties of present humanism and the Stoicism of St. Paul's time are numerous and fundamental.

In a caste-shackled world the humanism of Stoicism, called by the Roman *humanitas,* was an ennobling, liberating, and creative force. It recognized the worth of the individual regardless of his social status. It tried to make the individual self-reliant and to qualify him for effective social participation. Both the Christian and the Stoic considered life a struggle for goodness and truth. To put an end to his faults was the goal of Seneca although he never secured the inner peace which he craved. Of course much of its moral teaching, such as the prohibition of anger, impurity, and self-indulgence, Stoicism did not originate, but is rather the common property of all important systems of morals.

With persuasive eloquence Stoicism preached an ideal of humanity in terms of a spiritual unity. Mankind is a mystic organism permeated and held together by reason, a unity in which all members are related to one another and akin.[5] Among the Stoics there were humanitarians who were sincerely devoted to the relief of the poor, the teaching of the ignorant, the reformation of the degraded, and the improvement of the lot of the outcast. Their plea for the considerate treatment of the slave is typical of their humanitarian angle of vision. Seneca commends his friend Lucilius for his good will to his slaves, and exhorts him so to live with an inferior as he would wish his superior to live with him. "Let some (slaves) dine with you because they are worthy and others so that they may be so," Seneca counsels his friend. The noblest of the Stoics did not challenge the rightfulness of slavery as an institution, but taught that in the final analysis freedom is spiritual rather than moral. Epictetus declares that he whose body is at large while his soul is in fetters is a slave, and, contrariwise, he whose body is in bonds while his soul is at liberty is free. There was, despite the ideal of humanity as a mystic unity, an attitude of condescension and superiority in the intercourse of the typical Stoic with those outside his own social group. True friendship, it was generally believed, can exist only between equals who are wise. Active participation in politics was dictated by human welfare, but many of the Stoics shrank from discharging political obligations because they feared the loss of self-respect through personal contact with the corruption of the times.

In reply to the question, What is God? the Stoic frequently countered with, What is God not? Zeno, the founder of Stoicism, asserts that images, temples, sacrifices, prayers, and worship are of no avail, for the universe is God and may be addressed as God. Divinity may be ascribed to natural manifestations. Seneca insists that all religious observances are futile; prayer may be offered not in order to induce the gods to help us but to remind them of our limiting circumstances, the effect of such a reminder being entirely subjective. In addition, both Seneca and Epictetus strongly recommend as a daily

[5] Angus, Samuel, *The Religious Quest of the Graeco-Roman World*, p. 65 (New York: Charles Scribner's Sons, 1929).

religious practice a review of the events of the day and a self-examination before sleep at night.[6]   Although some of the Stoics exhort men to believe in God, to follow and obey God, and to live as sons of God, their conception of God is nebulously pantheistic. Since men are parts of God, he himself is responsible for human folly and wickedness.

It is not difficult to detect points of contact between modern humanism and the ancient Stoic variety. A high regard for moral integrity, a dependence on the resources of human nature as such in the struggle with hostile forces within and without, an effort to improve the lot of the underprivileged man, the meeting of misfortune with equanimity, the acceptance of what reason and judgment approve, the denial of the personal quality of ultimate Reality, are all common to both the Stoic and some modern types of humanism. To be sure, current humanism in several of its aspects transcends Stoicism. For example, its concern for human welfare is more intense and its social objectives are more daring and radical. Its methods are infinitely more scientific. As contrasted with ancient Stoicism, the humanism of the present functions in an industrial setting.

Humanism and Christianity

Frankly, the strict humanism of today does not derive from Epicureanism or Stoicism but from Christianity; hence its superior social quality. As a movement it exploits the social values of Christianity, but rejects their religious background, their religious incentive and control. Some of our humanists hesitate to employ such terms as "good will," "love," "service," and "sacrifice" which have been appropriated by Christianity and sanctified by its usage. Mr. Lippmann makes disinterestedness the core of his philosophy of life.[7] Whatever the terminology employed, the thing signified which present ultra-humanism exalts is included in but is not co-extensive with Christianity. The values which commend it flow from the

---

[6] Arnold, E. Vernon, *Roman Stoicism*, p. 236 (Cambridge, Eng.: The University Press, 1911).

[7] Lippmann, Walter, *A Preface to Morals* (New York: The Macmillan Company, 1929).

social passion of Judaism and Christianity, and the scientific procedure which it adopts is the product of a civilization in which Christianity has exercised a creative influence.

Could anything be more truly and aggressively social than the religion of the great Old Testament prophets and of Jesus? Amos makes social justice the fundamental requirement of God. Those who have falsified "with balances of deceit," bought "the poor for silver, and the needy for a pair of shoes," sold the "refuse of wheat" are exhorted to "hate the evil, and love the good, and establish judgment," to "let judgment run down as waters, and righteousness as a mighty stream." Isaiah admonishes his erring countrymen to "relieve the oppressed, judge the fatherless, plead for the widow." Running throughout the writings of the prophets is the vision of a new era in which justice, compassion, and the unadulterated worship of God shall reign. Jesus, catching the spirit of the succession of Israel's prophets, becomes the founder of a brotherhood which rejects predatory principles and practices intelligent good will. To be sure, the number of true followers of Christ is still small, for his teaching is so radically opposed to a social system based on self-seeking and warfare that the masses of men have not comprehended and much less applied it. The message of Jesus is freighted with principles which if courageously and intelligently applied would redeem the institutions of society from the giant iniquities which have hampered and thwarted men.

Much the same may be said for the ethical teaching of St. Paul. Although certain precepts which he advocated should be interpreted in the light of his expectation of the cataclysmic return of Christ, he was a consistent champion of the poor, the outcast, the ignorant, and the oppressed. The contention that Christianity even at its best is preoccupied with the intangible and imponderable to such an extent that it ignores, tolerates, and often defends social evils that can be eradicated, does not correspond with the relevant facts. The Christian religion is actually charged with social idealism.

Many humanists have dismissed religion as an escape mechanism. They have declared that religious faith is a narcotic which renders one insensible to the preventable or curable ills of society. It should be conceded that stereotyped concepts of right and wrong, which are promulgated in the name of theism, do often make adjustments to new demands quite impossible. It should be confessed that to cast upon a kindly God tasks which we men should undertake is ethically stultifying. The influence of an indolent belief in God is soporific. On the other hand, one is inclined to inquire whether the humanist's preoccupation with affairs mundane is not a refuge from the passionate demand of the self for adjustment to cosmic forces and eternal values. Humanism may serve as a substitute for religion. It may be an unintended effort to divert the attention from a personal religious crisis. It may be easier to engage one's power in philanthropic enterprises than to face religious uncertainty and perplexity, and to battle one's way to a victorious faith. A religious philosophy that can sustain one in the varying circumstances of life is not a gift imposed from without but the product of inner conflict and conquest. Humanism in its godless form is easily understandable as an attempt in many cases to avoid the anguish of acquiring a redoubtable theism.

The inference that atheism or agnosticism as professed by strict humanists necessarily and inevitably leads to badness is contrary to observable fact. A great company of men and women who do not believe in the existence and potency of God actually undertake to live a good life. One rejoices that many despite their atheism invest themselves in worthful social projects. It would be folly to claim that personal virtues and social sympathy cannot be engendered and cultivated apart from religious idealism. It has been suggested that a moratorium on the worship of God be declared for a generation in order to determine whether we might not make satisfactory moral progress without religious motivation. Such a proposal is the outcome of a distrust of theism as an ethical force, a distrust which should give us pause.

The quality of the personal and social idealism of the theist depends on the quality of the God he worships and the degree of his devotion to the divine will. A god who is solely a superior native impulse, or an abstract principle, or a purposeless form of energy, or social attributes personified, or the *esprit de corps* of a group may not be totally void of moral influence. He—the use of the personal pronoun is permissible by courtesy—is, however, too pallid, vapid, and indefinite to inspire the maximal measure of moral enthusiasm. The God of Christ, passionately served, incites and supports the very attribute that is of paramount importance to the humanist. That God discloses himself in the realm of human experience as an empowering Presence, the socially fruitful careers of men like Savonarola, John Wesley, General Booth, and Henry Ward Beecher testify.

Walter Lippmann describes humanism at its best, and with the utmost candor and clarity reveals the melancholy discontent of men who have no satisfying portion in what remains after the religious attitude has been abandoned. He insists that when men can no longer be theists they must become humanists if they are civilized. He and others of the same opinion seemingly do not appreciate the logical implications of their social idealism. He fails to see that if a man who is civilized follows the ramifications of humanism at its best, he can no longer be a mere humanist but must become a theist. When the strict humanists encourage us to unite as brothers, to understand, inspire, and support one another, to refrain from seeking the competitive individualistic good and to promote the collective welfare, they apparently do not sense that their program involves an organizing ideal and power transcending themselves.

Why should any man adopt the humanitarian idealism which is so persuasively proclaimed? This is a fundamental question and the answer overleaps the bounds of absolute humanism. It is not because our ordinary inborn desires impel us to live the disinterestedly socialized life. Our natural inclinations are opposed to it. Men are by nature selfish. A rebirth, a transformation of our native impulses, motives, and aspirations is involved, a reconstruction of personality which implies a cosmic ground of the imperishable social principle, and an objective ultimate integrating power. Such a recentering of the self occurs in a frame of reference which is cosmic. Only cosmic impressions can move so many men to strive for progressively higher integrations of personal freedom from defects, for the positive moral enrichment of life, and social self-committal. Only when its negations are absorbed in the affirmations of religious values can humanism achieve normal realization.

The contention of the extreme humanist that the God Christ trusted is a grandiose fiction is generally unsupported by either sound argumentation or relevant factual data. He frequently begs the question and thus exposes himself to rebuttal. Sometimes he reasons in a circle. Men of yesterday believed in God as an objective reality, the majority of today conclude that God is merely a projection of the human mind; hence God does not exist in actuality but is a product of the imagination. No thorough and systematic effort is made to establish the chief contention which is that God is non-existent. Even if a statistical study should show that most men in lands where Christianity has been widely proclaimed do not believe in the reality of the God of Jesus, the basic query persists, Is truth determined by a majority opinion? A more liberal infusion of the pale cast of logic would relieve certain humanists of an active tendency to generalize without foundation.

Nothing less than a cosmic order of values can validate and guarantee the idealism which humanism cherishes. For things fundamental there are no adequate substitutes. There are no successors to tested realities. To date, no one has been able to suggest anything that equates theism. If men deify themselves, unchecked selfishness will choke any pre-existing social impulses. If men worship the state, a rampant nationalism will militate against the creation of internationalism and plunge civilization into war. It is not absolutely impossible to worship one's own moral convictions, but since the humanist explains them as by-products of a mechanistic universe, he must experience intellectual difficulty in an effort to deify them. Psychologically, undeviating humanism has nothing to offer which can supplant the theistic tradition. Without cosmic support it falls to the ground and withers.

The Survival of Humanism

In order to survive, humanism must develop its theistic implications. The history of philosophy and religion teaches that when humanism refuses to become positively religious it loses its vitality and its constituency, and perishes. Stoicism, the noblest of the humanistic philosophies contending for the patronage of men in the Roman Empire, centuries ago ceased to be a force. It died from arrested development.

The survival of Buddhism throughout twenty-four centuries is no doubt attributable to its theistic affiliations and developments.[8] Gautama, the founder of Buddhism, taught a variety of humanism the key word of which was renunciation. Salvation is accomplished through self-control and love, apart from rites and ceremonies, priestly intervention, and the help of the gods in whose power men had put their trust. After a career as a mendicant itinerant preacher extending over a period of forty-five years, when Gautama, called Buddha, which in turn means the "Enlightened One," departed this life, his reputed last words were, "Work out your own salvation with diligence."

Buddhism was originally not a religion but a moral discipline. The existence of the gods was not categorically denied, but deities were ignored by Gautama and his faithful disciples in their way of life. Prayer as an appeal to the gods for aid was excluded, for a man ought to summon his own powers in all exigencies. Sacrifices were forbidden because they are a means whereby one seeks to propitiate the gods and thus escape consequences one should accept, and because they entail the shedding of blood. All speculation about the origin and destiny of the world order, the creation of man and other sentient beings is prohibited.

The eight-fold path is the essence of Buddhism as taught and exemplified by Gautama: right view, right aim, right speech, right action, right living, right effort, right mindfulness, right contemplation. Desire is the bane of human experience. De-

---

[8] For a comprehensive account of the origin, rise, and spread of Buddhism and of the sects into which it separated consult Pratt, J. B., *The Pilgrimage of Buddhism* (New York: The Macmillan Company, 1928).

sire for prosperity, pleasure, and for existence itself is empty, misleading, and insatiable. Good will to all men should supplant the evil of self-seeking. Buddha taught that generosity, universal love, and the welfare of others, rather than consideration for self and its temporal condition, should engage the minds of his followers. The caste system is to be abolished. Although humanistic Buddhism lacked social vigor, it did teach a multitude of individuals kindness to all creatures with an insight and patience equaled only by the genius of Christ.

Buddhism failed to maintain itself indefinitely as a humanistic philosophy of life. In the course of time it was supported and modified by many varieties of theism. In India rival sects appropriated from Buddhism what they could use to advantage. It was gradually absorbed by its ruthless competitors. Vestiges of its influences are discoverable in Hinduism. It failed to survive as a separate philosophy of life in the land of its birth.

Buddhism flourishes today in China, Japan, Ceylon, Siam, and Tibet. It is not the humanistic Buddhism of Gautama which has won and held the devotion of millions in these countries, but Buddhism enriched, fructified, and modified by theistic currents. The Mahayana Buddhism of China may serve as a conspicuous and illuminating example. In this form of Buddhism a large and motley collection of gods has developed.[9] The student of Chinese Buddhism encounters a bewildering profusion of systems of gods and trinity groups. The highest class of gods consists of the heavenly Buddhas. The first in rank is the historical Gautama himself. With an irony difficult to match in the annals of religion Gautama, who counseled his disciples to refrain from intercourse with the gods, has himself been deified and is being worshiped by large masses of men. He is portrayed sitting in meditation with half-closed eyes, with legs crossed under him and hands resting on the upturned soles of the feet. His image is a familiar object.

[9] See Reichelt, Karl Ludvig, *Truth and Tradition in Chinese Buddhism*, pp. 171 ff. (Shanghai, China: Commercial Press, Limited, 1927).

Against his own will, as it were, Buddha has joined the cavalcade of the gods.

Mahayana Buddhism includes a remarkable thought-system, and an impressive apparatus of worship. Although much of it is animistic superstition and demon worship, it answers questions of existence, imparts courage for the battle of life, and grants comfort in the hour of sorrow. To the man of culture it offers a broad mystical basis of life and satisfies his craving for a saving sense of reality. The system of Gautama in modified form is thus set in a frame of theistic reference.

Modern humanism possesses implications which make it not the enemy but the ally of the Christian religion. So far from condemning humanism outright, we should apply the logic of its social philosophy and develop its deepest possibilities. Only in a theistic matrix can any type of strict humanism make explicit its potentialities. The history of religion teaches us that men and women will raise fundamental questions about God, the ultimate nature and meaning of the universe, and the destiny of human beings. Man has a thirst for unseen values which ethics alone cannot quench. Science provides the procedures and methods of social rebuilding, but the Spirit of the universe supplies the originating impulse, the stabilizing principles, and an inner tranquillity that survives the shattering of utopian dreams.

CHAPTER VI

ACTION VERSUS REACTION MYSTICISM

RELIGIOUS mysticism centers in the subject's conviction of an immediacy of contact with God. The mystic feels that he is being moved by the divine will without recognizable rational intervention. In the sum total of events which compose the mystical state the impartation of religious insight and power occurs. It is evident that an attempt to formulate a definition of mysticism in rational terms is in the nature of the case beset by insuperable difficulties. Mysticism has its being for the most part in the domain of emotion, intuition, appreciation, and subliminal impressions, which are not directly amenable to the intellectual approach and grasp. The mystical experience is synthetic rather than analytic, an event rather than a critical inquiry; hence, although not necessarily void of ideational components, it is predominantly non-rational.

There are two contrasting forms of mysticism, the action and the reaction.[1] The classification is determined by the instigating source. In action mysticism man by an effort of his own approaches God, in reaction mysticism God approaches man; in the one case the initiative is human, in the other it is divine. When the originating impulse is provided by man himself a practicing mysticism follows, when God as an actual Presence is experienced apart from human striving revelatory mysticism exists.

Action Mysticism

Action mysticism is egocentric, and in practice is a way in which man or his spiritual essence ascends by an effort to God and is united with him in a flood of ecstasy. Primitive re-

[1] See Deissmann, Adolf, *The Religion of Jesus and the Faith of Paul,* translated by William E. Wilson (New York: George H. Doran Company, 1923); also his *Paul* translated by William E. Wilson, pp. 149 ff. (New York: George H. Doran Company, 1926).

ligions are replete with crude and sensuous techniques for the production of mystical states. Music, dancing, fasting, and the use of drugs are among the familiar means by which the devotees of immature forms of religion seek the consciousness of the Divine and knowledge of its purpose. In the more highly developed religions the techniques are refined and combined with a philosophical system. Physical means of mystical practice give way at least in part to a program of spiritual exercises. The tie that binds the many types of action mysticism and their various instrumentalities is man's deliberate attempt to discover the Determiner of human destiny, to secure his co-operation, and to be identified with him.

The framework of action mysticism is non-Christian in origin. The main current of the religion of the Bible is reaction mysticism, but many influential leaders of the Church throughout the centuries of its historical development have been action mystics. It appears that the action philosophies of Greek thinkers like Plato and Plotinus invaded the minds of the Fathers, and largely supplanted the reaction mysticism of the apostolic church.

In his *Symposium* Plato has expounded a form of action philosophy which seems to be the basis of subsequent theories and practices of a large number of mystics of the Church. Plato taught that two opposed worlds exist, the world of forms and the world of sense. Man has affiliations with both, but it is his duty to pass from the world of sense to the world of forms. The world of forms does not consist of forces which of themselves strive with man and seek to dominate him. The driving attribute is resident in man himself. It is called *eros,* and is love with an egocentric quality. Catching an inkling of the existence and beauty of the world of forms, the soul of man is aroused by *eros,* by a desire. Starting with a sense of beauty the soul proceeds to mount a heavenly ladder, climbing upward to progressively higher stages of beauty until at last the pure form of unalloyed Beauty is reached.[2] The Fathers sub-

[2] "When a man proceeding onwards from terrestrial things by the right way of loving, once comes to sight of that Beauty, he is not far from his goal. . . . He should begin by loving earthly things for the sake of the

stituted God for the world of forms, and spiritual exercises for the aesthetic progressions. When the theory of a divine spark inherent in man supersedes the concept of *eros,* as it so frequently has done, the analogy is complete.

Plotinus, who flourished in the third century of our era, directly influenced the mysticism of the Church more than any other non-Christian philosopher. It was he who aroused both the criticism and the emulation of St. Augustine, who in turn became the forerunner of a long line of action mystics. The aim of Plotinus was twofold: the cogent exposition of the philosophy of Plato and the introduction of men to divine Reality. Combining the passion of the missionary and the intellectual pursuits of the philosopher, Plotinus has survived in an active state in the ongoing life of the Church whose traditions he himself rejected. He postulated three stages of ascent to ultimate Reality, stages familiar to students of religion as the codified mystic formula—namely, purification, enlightenment, and ecstatic union with the Highest. The three steps do not in Plotinus constitute a progressive series of independent psychological processes, but rather a unified enterprise with interpenetrating graduated disciplines and results. A brief description of the stages, not necessarily as Plotinus interpreted them, but more specifically as they are understood by many modern mystics, will indicate the importance of the part which the mystical ladder or "way" plays in action mysticism.

The first step is the purgation of the self from errors of thinking, wrong emotional attachments, and moral sloth.[3] The aim is to incline the heart to true wisdom. To the question, By what means is purification accomplished? various answers have been proposed. An historic one is asceticism, or self-discipline having for its ultimate end union with God. Monas-

---

absolute loveliness, ascending to that as it were by degrees or steps, from the first to the second, and thence to all fair forms; and from fair forms to fair conduct, and from fair conduct to fair principles, until from fair principles he finally arrive at the ultimate principle of all and learn what absolute beauty is." (Plato, *Symposium,* translated by Robert Bridges.)

[3] The older practice was negative and consisted largely in an attempt to abstract various states of consciousness; in fact, the process of emptying the mind of its content was carried to such extremes that it fell under the ironic condemnation of men like Luther.

ticism is the community organization of asceticism. Great leaders like St. Benedict and St. Francis attracted large followings and almost inevitably gave the forms of asceticism for which they stood communal expression. The orders which took the names of these men were natural developments. The monastic followers of these mystics assumed the obligations of seclusion, penance, poverty, chastity, and obedience. Life in the monastery was regulated to the minutest detail. Although there was much mortification of the flesh, it is only just to add that some of the outstanding mystics taught that true asceticism is the death of evil desire rather than the torture of the body. That a detachment of the senses and the will from things mundane can be achieved without resort to physical austerities has been maintained. The central principle of the purgative way is the sacrifice of what is regarded as a hindrance to identification with God. Self-control must be practiced until the lower impulses are subdued by the highest functions of personality.

The second stage is the experience of illumination. Here the mind is kindled into burning love by the contemplation of Christ or God. In order to be transformed into the likeness of Christ the action mystic engages in the earnest contemplation of the image of the Master. The worshiper apprehends Reality in concentrated attention; and imagination, sensibility, and emotion are enhanced. Miss Underhill writes that the selfless adoration of God is one of the essentials of the stage of illumination.[4] She attributes to the illuminated way an extensive variety of mystical experiences such as the transitory but true sense of divine companionship achieved in prayer, and the consciousness of standing on the frontier of another world of values, a consciousness which arises when one is stirred by the presence of beauty. She believes that the majority of mystics never advance beyond this experience. Symbols and forms of worship play a significant part in mediating God to

[4] Underhill, Evelyn, *The Essentials of Mysticism*, pp. 17 ff. (New York: E. P. Dutton & Co., 1920). This volume contains a readable chapter on Plotinus in which it is maintained that the infusion of the doctrines of this philosopher into the Church has enriched rather than confused or perverted New Testament mysticism.

the mystic at this stage, but behind the divergent appearances and practices such as the Eucharist of the Catholic Church or the silence of the Society of Friends there is the same consciousness of Reality.

The third stage, intuitive identification with God, is the culmination and true goal of the mystic's quest. Union with the Eternal is generally if not necessarily accompanied by ecstasy, an intense exaltation of personality. The mystic experiences "imageless goodness," "absolute oneness," "the hidden heaven," "the ineffable unveiled world," "a state of song," "the key of the universe." The ecstatic state is so entrancing and engrossing that all other forms of consciousness are suppressed, self-awareness is banished, and individuality is submerged in the Godhead. Deification in some sense seems to be the final desire of the true action mystic. Many refer to a stillness of the senses as an essential of ecstasy. Julie, in *The Fountain,* uses a metaphor to indicate this condition, "The stillness of an axis at the center of a wheel." Narwitz expands the illuminating figure, remarking, "The axis that moves forward with the wheel but never revolves." [5] The mystic way begun with the purification of the self through exercises and disciplines and continued with the focusing of the attention upon religious reality, and the apprehension of it through love, is consummated in an overmastering transport that obliterates all awareness of time and sense and makes the mystic one with cosmic consciousness.

Subjectivism

That the way of the action mystic has often been and is still frequently a means of the avoidance of the arrows of misfortune is plain. The threefold way may be a complex but effective escape mechanism. Mystical absorption is, as has often been said, the refuge of many who have despaired of impinging adverse circumstances but have not lost faith in God. Asceticism expressed in monasticism affords individuals for whom the world is too severe, a haven of retreat and security. The flight

[5] Morgan, Charles, *The Fountain,* p. 311 (New York: The Macmillan Company, 1932).

into the bosom of the Eternal, the egotistical enjoyment of God, may be subconsciously motivated by a desire to elude the world with its duties, its work, and its tormenting conflicts. It may assume the nature of a compensation for social maladjustment, personal disappointment, and even material loss.

If this world and God are mutually exclusive, which is a cardinal tenet of many mystics, the repudiation of things temporal is a solemn obligation; one's citizenship should logically be entirely in heaven, and mundane concerns renounced or at least regarded with indifference. Great mystics, it should be acknowledged, have been aware of these dangers and subversions, have issued solemn warnings against them, and made personal integrity and socialized behavior the criteria of the genuineness of the walk with God. Logically, however, if the submergence of consciousness in a God-experience through an ascending series of religiously meaningful exercises deliberately engaged in is the central purpose of mysticism, excessive individualism cannot be avoided.

Subjectivism is the hallmark of extreme action mysticism. Psychologically, action mysticism is a systematic and progressive endeavor to produce a condition from which everything else is excluded. The action mystic seeks the invulnerability of ecstasy even if it lasts only an instant. While this state of being exists he feels untouchable, timeless, and transcendental. In his striving to apprehend God and to lose himself in him, the action mystic is psychologically akin to the scientist searching for a final order in the data determinable by the senses, to the artist who seeks to identify himself with the spirit of beauty expressing itself in the tangible arts, and to the philosopher devoting his days and nights to the quest for absolute truth. All these alike pursue an end to which they subordinate everything else, and in their most intense moments are detached from themselves and seem to be one with the object of dominant desire.

Action mystics who have been given to self-analysis have confessed that discipline does not complete the state of purification deemed essential. How can the necessary love and humility be engendered by systematic exercises of any sort? Some have maintained that if we will have these virtues they are ours; others have declared that if we realize the existence of our defects we are set free from them by such self-knowledge.[6] Furthermore, the conscious efforts of many mystics to achieve union with God seem at the last to converge upon the condition of expectant receptivity. It is frequently asserted that only when one ceases to strive does union with the Divine ensue. One is inclined to accept the teaching of quietism that if confident relaxation is the one thing needful it should be cultivated from the beginning.

Reaction Mysticism

A study of John Wesley's transition from action mysticism to reaction mysticism, which he describes in theological rather than psychological terminology, is exceeding instructive.[7] He writes that for several years preceding the turning point in his life he kept the commandments to the best of his ability, scrupulously observed the Wednesday and Friday fasts, tasting no food until three o'clock in the afternoon, and did good by his presence or substance to the bodies and souls of others. A man whose name is not mentioned convinced Wesley that works alone are futile and that inward holiness or union with God should be cultivated. The adviser's recommendation that mental prayer and similar exercises be engaged in as effectual means of purifying the self and uniting it with God was adopted. Wesley concludes that his prayers, fasts, acts of charity, and attempted identification with God were in the aggregate nothing more than the essence of self-righteousness. The refined form of reliance on his own works and self-esteem "so zealously inculcated by the mystic writers" failed to give him the sense of peace and release he so diligently sought. He derived no help or comfort from such practices. Finally, stimulated and guided by Peter Böhler, a Moravian brother, Wesley renounced all dependence on his own merits and striving, and

[6] For an extended discussion of these divergent opinions see Hocking, William Ernest, *The Meaning of God in Human Experience*, pp. 380 ff. (New Haven: Yale University Press, 1912).

[7] *Journal*, pp. 466 ff.

began to trust Christ alone for redemption and peace. The attitude of trust in Christ was continued with relapses and periodic dullness, coldness, and indifference until that evening when his heart glowed within him and he was assured that he was a child of God. Persistent and conscientious endeavor to ascend to God at last yielded to acceptance of the divine mercy as a free gift. The egocentric attitude gave way to a theocentric life.

Examples from the Bible

Reaction mysticism is the predominant type of mysticism recorded in the Bible. In its best estate mysticism results in fellowship with God rather than in identification with him, in the moral transformation of personality rather than in loss of individuality, in the conformation of the human will to the divine purpose rather than in the deification of the worshiper, in peace that passeth understanding rather than in aesthetic intoxication. Mysticism as experienced by the great personages of the Bible is a reaction of man to the divine prompting, a reaction which is conscious, ethical, socially beneficial, and personally integrative.

The Old Testament teaches that God moves upon men, vouchsafes a knowledge of his will to those who are qualified to receive it, reproves and comforts individuals, and commissions his chosen to important service. It tells how he called Abraham to desert Haran with its polytheistic taint and to journey to a land where he might establish his posterity and worship God only. It tells how God approached Moses feeding the flocks of his father-in-law in the fields of Midian and from a burning but incandescent bush commanded him to return to Egypt, whence he had fled as a fugitive, and to lead his brethren out of their bondage through the grace and power of Jehovah. It tells how God addressed the boy Samuel in the night, and when the lad responded, "Speak, for thy servant heareth," told him that judgment would descend upon the slack and lax Eli and his wayward sons. It tells how God seized Amos the shepherd with a conviction that would not let him escape and gave him a mandate to proclaim the doom of national destruction to Israel for the sins of social injustice of which its leading citizens were guilty. It tells how God gave Isaiah a vision of divine holiness and glory, a vision that filled the temple and was accompanied by voices hymning the sacred majesty, a vision that prostrated the youth with a sense of his own unworthiness, cleansed him from his sin, and called him to the thankless office of an unheeded prophet. It tells how God through direct self-disclosure with imperious summons induced crises, turning points, in the lives of others who have left their impress on the history of religious progress.

It may be objected that these Old Testament accounts reflect a primitive culture which we may regard with tolerant interest but which we cannot and should not revive. Belief in an anthropomorphic God, a God endowed with human characteristics, a God with a human voice and attributes, is frankly disclaimed. Furthermore, historical criticism, one hears, has rendered doubtful if it has not actually disposed of such stories as those of Abraham and of the Mosaic theophany associated with a bush. Nevertheless, modern theology and the scientific study of the Bible aside, these narratives have preserved religious convictions which undergird both the Old and the New Testament. When we think our way to the significance of the accounts of the crucial religious experiences of Abraham and Moses and Samuel and Amos and Isaiah and others we uncover two priceless fundamentals: the divine initiative in man's life and the beneficent results of the human response.

The New Testament continues and brings to fruition the reaction mysticism disclosed by the Old. The teaching of Jesus is resplendent with it. Some of his parables stress the prevenient redemptive love of God for defeated humanity. The good shepherd plunges into the wilderness in search of the straying sheep; the woman, lighting a lamp, sweeps the house to recover a lost coin; the father, casting dignity aside, runs to meet and embrace the returned profligate, and later entreats the elder son to welcome his brother. In the parable of the spurned overtures of God, of the vineyard and the husbandmen, the dominant element is the persistent and sacrificial effort of God.[8]   The householder in this parable, who is God, plants a vineyard, which is Israel, sets a hedge about it and supplies it with a winepress and a watchtower.   He requires at the hands of the husbandmen, who are the responsible leaders of Israel, the fruits of the vineyard; but they refuse to give him the yield.   With unwearied forbearance the householder sends them servant after servant, during which period of forbearance he stays the merited penalty.   Finally he sends them his own son, but him they kill.   Jesus ingeniously weaves into the parable the impressive conviction that he has a mandate from God himself.   The trend of the teaching and religion of Jesus is determined by his assurance that God is not an impotent prisoner in his world but an originating Being.

The life and message of St. Paul derive their significance from reaction mysticism.   St. Paul was persuaded beyond all cavil that God in Christ had invaded his personality with redemption and a summons to preach the gospel of grace.   "I was not disobedient unto the heavenly vision," [9] is a statement of his which epitomizes his religious career.   Submission to the impact of God rather than an endeavor to bend God to his will, marks the religion which St. Paul lived and adorned.   Time and again he reacts positively to what he interprets as a divine instigation.   He responds to a dream vision, which implores him to carry the gospel to Macedonia.[10]   In Corinth, St. Paul surrounded by hostile forces is comforted and emboldened by a nocturnal visitant.[11]   Psychology may reduce the form in which these impressions were made upon the apostle to such subjective functions and predispositions as imagination, emotion, preoccupation with certain religious concerns, subconscious elaboration of pertinent data and their exterioration in visual and auditory imagery, but superseding all else is a life enriched and made astonishingly fruitful by a succession of responses to a series of events explicated as divine impulses.

St. Paul's doctrine is in accord with his experience.   He believed that the death of Christ is related to man's salvation

8 Mark 12: 1-12.   9 Acts 26: 19.
10 Acts 16: 9, 10.   11 Acts 18: 9.

from sin, although he does not explain the *modus operandi*.
He repeatedly asserts that God, taking the initiative, offered
Christ as a sacrifice for man's sin. As Nygren remarks, St.
Paul's conception of availing sacrifice differs sharply from
that of other religious leaders.[12]   Primitive man offered a portion of his possessions on the altar, a lamb, a kid, a bullock, and
in desperate straits even a child, and by such means sought to
find God and to win his favor. Reaching a higher stage in the
evolution of religion, man tried to secure the approval of God
by sacrificing something of himself, as it were. The sacrifices
of obedience to his commandments, of justice and mercy were
presented to his God. The penitent psalmist proclaims that the
sacrifices of God are a broken and a contrite heart.[13]   Sacrifice is now personal and ethical. St. Paul moves on a still
loftier plane of religious insight and power. The central and
indispensable article of his faith is that on the cross it is God
and not man who is making a sacrifice which in some way is of
inestimable benefit to humanity.[14]   The sacrifice of Christ is
not man's attempt to gain access to God, but it is God's act
whereby he seeks to reclaim man. In other religions man
offers sacrifices which the gods demand and receive as their
due; but the only true God, as St. Paul understands him,
makes the supreme sacrifice when he gives Christ to an unworthy world of sinful men. Christianity is centered in reaction mysticism.

Our fathers engaged in protracted and acrimonious controversies over rival theories of the incarnation and atonement.
Our interest in such historic doctrines may be too slight and our
distaste for polemical disputes too great to divide us into opposing camps, but when we discard them altogether as outgrown
and outmoded theological formulations we do not appreciate
that they bear witness to the Church's conviction that in Christ
God has approached man with love and grace. Such declara-

[12] Nygren, Anders, *Agape and Eros,* translated by A. G. Herbert, pp. 88 ff.
(London: Society for Promoting Christian Knowledge, 1932).
[13] Psalm 51: 17.
[14] Isaiah 53 suggests this conception which may have contributed to St.
Paul's doctrine of the sacrifice of Christ by God.

tions of St. Paul as "God was in Christ reconciling the world unto himself," [15] and "God commendeth his own love toward us, in that, while we were yet sinners, Christ died for us" [16] should have for the Christian a substratum of incalculable and abiding value. Statements of the same or similar import by other leaders in the apostolic church, such as "For God so loved the world, that he gave his only begotten Son, that whosoever believeth on him should not perish, but have eternal life," [17] and "Herein is love, not that we loved God, but that he loved us," [18] indicate the prevalence of reaction mysticism among the earliest Christians.

Love as a Response

Reaction mysticism does not culminate in intoxicated enjoyment of God and unrestrained behavior. It does not produce ethical sluggards or offenders. The love of a man for others is, in the New Testament sense, moral enthusiasm. It is, however, not original and spontaneous but derived. It is a response to the divine stimulus. It is a reaction. "We love, because he first loved us." [19] Love is a derivative. Jesus exhorts men to ask that it may be given to them, to seek that they may find, to knock that it may be opened unto them; [20] but is not their asking, their seeking, and their knocking and their persistent praying after all a result of God's own prompting? We seek him because he has been searching for us.

Christian love as contrasted with egocentric love, so far from being the will to have and to hold, a desire for the good of the self or a noble form of self-assertion, gives and spends itself freely, pours itself out upon good and bad men without partiality, and creates new values in its recipient. St. Francis of Assisi, a most lovable man, who was kind to birds and animals, gentle with erring humanity, courteous, selfless, sympathetic, and generous to the poor, was a mystic who identified himself not only with God but also with all sentient creatures that

[15] 2 Corinthians 5: 19.
[17] John 3: 16.
[19] 1 John 4: 19.
[16] Romans 5: 8.
[18] 1 John 4: 10.
[20] Luke 11: 9.

crossed his path.   Reference has been made to his asceticism,
to his action mysticism.   Because of his fidelity to a high ideal
of service the mysticism of St. Francis, including the stigmata
which appeared on his person, did not expend itself wholly in
an excess of subjectivism.   St. Paul says, "I press on, if so be
that I may lay hold on that for which also I was laid hold on
by Christ Jesus." [21]   Reaction love reverses the cherished ends
of what might be called refined self-regard to such an extent
that only by losing itself can it live.   The gracious invitation,
"Behold, I stand at the door and knock: if any man hear my
voice and open the door, I will come in to him, and will sup
with him, and he with me," [22] graphically stresses the divine
action, the desired human reaction, and a designed interaction.

The Mystical Presence and Illumination

The core of the mystical occurrence is the consciousness of
a Presence interpreted as God.   This awareness transcends
belief in the existence or objective reality of God; it is the assurance of fellowship with God which is independent of sense
perception and is direct and immediate.   It is more than the
perception of consistency and order in the physical universe or
of the adaptations of a unicellular organism to its environment, as evidences of God; it is an unquestioned awareness
that God is revealing himself in person, so to speak.   Ordinary
processes by which knowledge is acquired, the usual media of
sensation and reasoning, are for the time suspended.   The
quality and intensity of the prevailing emotional tone of the
mystical state varies.   The sense of the divine Presence may
simply cast a glow or warmth upon all the relationships of the
individual, or it may induce a conviction of unworthiness as
in the case of Isaiah in the temple or Saul before the gates of
Damascus, or culminate in fellowship with the Divine.   The
more vivid experiences of the Presence are most likely to
occur at life's turning points, such as times of sorrow or joy
or grave responsibility.

Dr. Raven in the following beautifully lucid passage quoted

[21] Philippians 3: 12.
[22] Revelation 3: 20.

from his autobiography describes the sense of Presence which he experienced as a young man: "Hitherto my glimpses of the Eternal had been associated only with nature, sunsets and moonlight, flowers and birds. Now of an evening I took long solitary walks; for at Cambridge I had played cricket and fives regularly, and exercise was necessary after a day at a desk. And on my walks in the mean streets God, as I had learned to call Him, met me, in splendor. Always the sense of His presence was unexpected, even startling in the suddenness of its manifestation; always it had the same effect of exhilaration and enlargement; but now the meaning and poignancy of it was more plain, and the 'little people,' as at such times I called mankind, were transfigured by it and made infinitely dear. Not only was the earth full of the glory of the Lord, but humanity, the crowded folk of the city, were His family, each and all in His keeping." [23]

What is the ultimate nature of the mystical Presence? The answering of the question does not fall within the purview of the psychologist as a scientist. It is a responsibility of the philosopher and theologian. It is the task of the psychologist to describe the mystical state as an experience or a possession, to trace its effects on personality, and to discover uniform underlying processes, or laws. The explanation of the Presence eludes the scope and method of the scientist although the psychologist may provide the philosopher with suggestive data.

The results of psychological experimentation in the realm of religious mysticism are suggestive but not final. Leuba, for example, records an experiment in which a sense of presence was imaginatively induced.[24] Seven subjects, all graduate students, were blindfolded and in succession seated in a dimly lighted room with backs toward assistants stationed at a distance of twenty-five feet. Each subject was told that someone might enter the room and approach the back of the chair. He was requested to indicate the awareness of a presence by rais-

---

[23] Raven, Charles E., *A Wanderer's Way*, p. 109 (New York: Henry Holt & Co., 1929). Note that the experience is reaction mysticism.

[24] Leuba, James H., *The Psychology of Religious Mysticism*, pp. 283 ff. (London: Kegan Paul, Trench, Trübner & Co., Ltd., 1925).

ing the hand and to study the accompanying mental processes. At irregular intervals someone walking on thick rugs would approach the subject and after standing behind him for a number of seconds would silently retire. In about half the cases the approach was unperceived. In the instances in which the approach was heard, the perception was not reported as a sense of presence. At least half of the seven subjects reported an experience of the awareness of presence. In another series of the same experiments the sense of presence was induced in two of the five subjects.

The experiment demonstrates that a vivid sense of presence not datum for the senses yet possessing validity for the subject can be reduced to an illusion compounded of such processes as expectation and imagination. Leuba identifies all cases of divine presence with the subjective elements which in their totality constitute an illusion. Leuba appears substantially to agree with Vaughan that "mysticism is that form of error which mistakes for a divine manifestation the operations of a merely human faculty." [25]   Although Leuba does not categorically reject the reality of the Unseen, he does dogmatically assert that the consciousness of the presence of God is completely explicable in terms of an illusion. Such an inference is bad science and worse metaphysics. How does Leuba know, how can he know, that the sense of the direct manifestation of God to man has been, is, and probably always will be nothing more than an objectification of human mental states? If the psychologist learns how experimentally to induce an awareness of an objectively unseen and unheard presence, does it follow that all experiences of presence are identical? To make a universal philosophical deduction from a certain number of instances psychologically studied is a procedure which does justice to neither science nor philosophy. [26]

[25] Quoted by Inge, William R., *Christian Mysticism*, p. 347 (New York: Charles Scribner's Sons, 1899). In the appendix of this volume Dean Inge quotes twenty-six specimen definitions of mysticism, some of which he analyzes with his customary acumen.

[26] For the critique of Leuba's contention that the mystic's love for God is an ideal expression of a thwarted human love and is a disguised form of organic satisfaction, see Hocking, William Ernest, *The Meaning of God in Human Experience*, pp. 574 ff. (New Haven: Yale University Press, 1912).

The Human Equation

Not that a divine communication received by the individual is by him given an interpretation which is entirely free from human admixture. One's appreciation and understanding of the meaning of the divine Presence is necessarily affected by two important mental processes—the self-activity of the human mind and the apperceptive accumulation. These two interlock, and they modify all impressions to which one responds. In the first place, then, the mind is reactive. It does not passively register external stimuli, but seizes them and utilizes them in the construction of an intellectual life. It does not reflect as in a mirror the objective order. Indeed, it is quite certain that it does not inertly receive the impact of the Presence. By virtue of dynamic principles inherent in its own nature, the mind of man assimilates and transmutes into characteristic thought forms the divine impulses to which it reacts.

In the second place, past experience and personality characteristics color the present and transmute it. Previous experience, the cultural forces which have been playing upon the personality, habits of thought and subconsciously active increments influence the comprehension of a new or novel occurrence. The union of the new and the old constitutes a fresh whole which acquires a unique significance. The spontaneous synthetic activity of the mind combines related events into a system. The experience of the Presence is appreciated in terms of one's mental furnishings and therefore assumes validity and meaning. It is not entirely absorbed by the content of personality, but a formation occurs in which a new insight or state of being emerges. The individual learns and registers progress. God may prompt man, but much that is imperfect is involved in the reception and interpretation of the divine impression.

Despite its limitations and fallibility the human personality may serve as a vehicle for divine revelations. In fact, if God exists, how is it psychologically possible for him to disclose himself directly to man apart from the synthetic activity of minds entangled in their own processes? An inerrant understanding of a divine impression by any of us is hard to con-

cede, but an appreciation of the Presence sufficient to purify
and integrate the constituents of personality is psychologically
credible. "We have this treasure in earthen vessels, that the
exceeding greatness of the power may be of God, and not from
ourselves." [27]

It should be admitted that since all things are subject to
human interpretation there is no absolute criterion of truth in
any realm. The world is full of deceptive appearances, and
fiction, illusions and errors pervade and distort the human
understanding. Man exhibits a tendency to regard the satisfac-
tions which an unsubstantiated belief affords as sufficient proof
of its truth. To be sure, anything which occurs, including an
hallucination, is real in the sense that it exists; but the issue
at stake is the correspondence of belief to what it professes to
represent. Although the senses often betray us, although they
are by no means invariably and entirely reliable, we do daily
put our trust in them and consequently they yield serviceable
data. Our reliance on their reports is not always misplaced.

Religious convictions cannot be scientifically demonstrated.
Truth is not established by speculation however cogent, but by
the realities of experience. Although there is no single objective standard which may be mechanically applied in determining the validity of an interior experience, the inner quality of
a mystical impulse is made manifest in its actual personality
effects. That many who have professed to have been motivated
by a divine mandate have, as judged by their consequent behavior, been either deliberate frauds or the victims of self-
deception, no one with even a modicum of knowledge of life
will be disposed to deny. The pathway of the history of religion is strewn with alleged revelations from heaven, the resulting moral ruin and social havoc of which refute the claims
of divine origin.

On the other hand, there are almost numberless instances in
which the pragmatic test has supplied the ground of justified
religious certainty. A sense of the divine fellowship has remade many a man, sustained him in the hour of sorrow, for-

[27] 2 Corinthians 4: 7.

tified him in the day of temptation, sensitized conscience, inspired him to deeds of valor, given him joy in the face of persecution for the sake of life-giving convictions, empowered him to endure disappointment without bitterness, and created within him a zone of peace which the fret of ordinary existence and the flame of fear and ambition could not invade. Jesus' contention, "By their fruits ye shall know them," [28] is still applicable to all who profess that they are led by the Spirit of God. And it is reasonable to suppose that God desires to make himself directly known to men, and can and does.

[28] Matthew 7: 16.

CHAPTER VII

RELIGIOUS PERSONALITIES AND SCIENCE

It should be generally conceded that religious personality, if it would function most effectively in the modern world, must recognize and in so far as it is possible utilize the findings and the most cogent theories of science. Indeed, one of the present major tasks of theology is to evaluate science and to disclose and appropriate what is of significance for the religious culture of man. On the other hand, in an appreciation of what science has contributed to our understanding of the world in which we live and to human welfare generally, we are prone to overlook what science owes to religious idealism. Absorbed by the fascinations of scientific theories, procedures, and results, we have taken insufficient cognizance of the religious environment in which the scientific spirit originated and the specialized sciences developed. An historical sketch of scientific backgrounds should make us sensible of forgotten or ignored obligations of science to religion. The relation of the Church to science is misunderstood by many and should be clarified in the interests of both causes.

Gifts of Science to Religion

The contributions of science which support and enrich religious faith have been so frequently listed and described that educated men are intelligently familiar with them. A few of them may be recalled. Science, especially astronomy, has disclosed a universe of force and activity which is of incomprehensible dimensions. By arousing one's sense of the majesty, orderliness, and immensity of the universe, astronomy intensifies religious values already cherished. The scientific reduction of natural activity to those constant modes of behavior called laws suggests a consistent and dependable universe. Furthermore, the doctrine of evolution implies a cosmic urge for progression and improvement. Religion senses in a dynamic and creative concept like emergent evolution a type of reality which moves forward with grand strategy to the ultimate realization of a purpose.[1] The course of evolution, organic and social, as we know it, has achieved its consummation in human personality. Outstripping all other forms of sentient life by virtue of such functions and competencies as self-conscious reflection, articulate speech, tool-making, a high order of aesthetic appreciation, moral sense, and the capacity to worship an unseen supreme Being, man is the highest form of life which science knows. Disciplined personality may be a major goal toward which creation moves. Many scientists are inclined to recognize the existence of personality in the interpretation of ultimate reality. The inference has been drawn by many thinkers that the energy expressed in every pulsation of the universe is not mere elasticity or motion or growth or instinct, but essentially consciousness. Science, if not faith-creating, is at least faith-supporting.

Intelligent religion appreciates what science has accomplished in terms of human welfare. Mechanical science has decreased human drudgery by inventing machinery which is more economical than the brawn of the unskilled laborer and permits man to concentrate on the intellectual factor in production. Modern applied science has made it possible to produce all the food, clothing, and other creature comforts which the human race needs. The historical and social sciences tell the story of the rise and fall of nations, of the origin and development of political structures, of our economic relations and our group customs and traditions, and in so doing give us an understanding of the institutional world in which we have a stake. Medical science has eradicated some epidemics and lessened the hazards of others, decreased the virulence of disease, and taught us how to maintain a stronger and healthier physical existence. Psychology teaches us how to develop balanced and wholesome personalities. Educational psychology and mental hygiene have outlined a constructive process of per-

[1] Morgan, C. Lloyd, *Emergent Evolution* (New York: Henry Holt & Co., 1927).

sonality development. Since nothing that adds to the sum of human well-being is foreign to religion, all who value religious progress should be truly thankful for these and other scientific blessings.

Sciences Originating in Ancient World Views

Has religion made any significant contributions to science? Historically religion has been the matrix within which most of our cultural values have originated and been nurtured. The historic body of religion has been so charged with creative vitality that from it have issued ceremony, music, dancing, custom, group regulation, art, science, and morality. There is but little of our culture and civilization which was not at one time within the scope of religion. Science, art, and morality as such were differentiated from religion and organized separately only at relatively modern stages of culture. To be sure, after science was differentiated from religion many special sciences arose or were refined within major departments of science as we now identify them. It is a distinctive function of religion to refine and correlate the manifold institutions, arts, and disciplines to which it has given birth.

The contention that science is the offspring of magic is founded on a misconception of the essential nature of magic. As we have had occasion to observe elsewhere, magic is a spurious system of rules and regulations, the application of which is supposed to determine the sequence of desired events or to forestall imminent danger. It is a fact that both science and magic assume that a succession of occurrences are conditioned by immutable laws, the operation of which can be foreseen and precisely calculated. Both take for granted that caprice and accident are banished from the course of nature. Both present seemingly endless possibilities to him who knows how to set in motion the prodigious and intricate mechanism of the natural order.

But at this point the resemblances end. The fatal flaw in magic is a total misapprehension of the constitution of the natural world. Magic, for example, places reliance on the principles of similarity and contiguity. It presupposes that effects are like their respective causes and can, therefore, be obtained by imitation or reinstatement, and that things in contact with each other are causally connected and will continue in this active relation even after they have been physically separated. Science, on the other hand, critical of such naïve identifications and presuppositions, seeks to acquire a body of interpretations of natural forces, based on objective experimentation and verifiable wherever the contributing conditions are met. Early science, it should be conceded, is a patchwork of true and false ideas; but taken as a whole, the spirit, procedures, and products of science differ so radically from those of magic that the theory that science is rooted in magic lacks cogency.[2]   On the contrary, one is warranted in giving favorable consideration to the probability that many magical practices originated in the inadequacy of primitive man's knowledge of nature, of his science, in the face of crises.

In the nature of the case, it is not quite so easy to tabulate the gifts of religion to science. Since science explores the order of sense data, it is as such relatively impersonal, objective, analytic, and communicable; since religion as a personal experience is interior, synthetic, and tinged with emotion, it is much less tangible and articulate. Nevertheless, a survey of the part which religion has played in the rise and growth of science will disclose certain definite contributions which the mind can seize and estimate. Generally speaking, many special sciences had their inception in ancient and rather crude religious faiths and practices, were adopted and advanced by the ancient Greeks and later by the Arabs, and received their greatest experimental refinement and practical application by men identified with, or at least under the influence of, the Christian Church.

In ancient times there dwelt in Egypt and Babylonia peoples whose religious genius fostered scientific beginnings. The hour

[2] The traditional explanation of the origin of chemistry is alchemy, the effort to invent a formula by means of which base metals could be transmuted into gold, or an elixir which would indefinitely prolong human life. It appears, however, that chemistry originated in the extraction of juices from plants for medicinal purposes. It was medieval rather than ancient alchemy that made the transformation of metals into gold a major objective.

of sixty minutes and the week of seven days are probably of Babylonian origin. The four monthly phases through which the moon successively passes seem to have excited the ancient Babylonian's religious interest. The seven-day week was associated with the heavenly bodies which from ancient times were personified and worshiped. It was generally believed that a person's fortunes could be predicted by a knowledge of the position and aspect of the heavenly bodies at the time of the individual's birth. The interest in astrology no doubt stimulated the priests to make careful observations and records of astronomical phenomena. They believed that when the heavenly bodies were created and arranged in order they were given laws of behavior which they will never transgress. As early as 2300 B.C. the Babylonians made use of multiplication tables in their astronomical calculations.

The Babylonian records of medical practices preserve curious prescriptions mingled with weird incantations. Efforts were made by the priests, who were the first physicians, to exorcise the evil spirits, the possession of which by the patient was believed to account for disease.[3] In many instances gods were implored to heal the sick. The priestly study of the condition of the internal organs of sacrificial animals in order to ascertain the will of the deity or the trend of events to come resulted in an elementary knowledge of anatomy. Humble, indeed, as well as religiously motivated are the origins of medicine which today boasts amazing triumphs of preventive and curative procedures.

The people of remote civilization in Egypt as well as Babylonia felt that it was necessary to promote harmony with the

---

[3] Neolithic man appears to have assumed that frequently malevolent spirits take up their abode in the human body. Delirium, lunacy, headaches, epilepsy, and probably other ailments were evidently diagnosed as the presence of demons within the skull, for perforated skulls have been found in the burial mounds in France, Peru, Mexico, and elsewhere. The skull of the primitive sufferer was scraped, cut, or bored with a piece of flint by the priest or medicine man in order that an avenue of escape might be provided for the offending evil spirit. That the first operation did not always afford relief and the ailment frequently recurred is indicated by evidence that patients submitted to repeated surgical treatment of this kind. Many skulls containing several healed openings testify to the sufferer's survival of several operations and to a persistent belief in spirit possession.

heavenly bodies they worshiped; hence astrology and magical practices arose and flourished. In Egypt as in Babylonia the temples were astronomical observatories closely allied with the religious and other needs of the people. The early priests were elementary astronomers, scanning as they did the heavens for portents of the future. They called the planets, which shift their position in relation to other heavenly bodies, messengers or angels. Meteors, comets, and eclipses were believed to be omens of pestilence, the death of kings or national disaster. The Egyptians carefully observed and recorded the time when certain stars and constellations became visible at dawn. Sirius, whose rising in conjunction with the sun marked the coming of the Nile inundation, was an object of worship.

Progress in mechanics and mathematics was made in Egypt. Geometry originated in the Nile valley. It had its beginnings not only in the measuring of the land for the purpose of restoring the boundaries swept away by the Nile floods but also in the building of temples and pyramids. Triangles were marked out by means of ropes divided into three parts. Religion provided the motive power for the Egyptian advances in architecture. The irrigation projects, the erection of pyramids, obelisks, and the supporting columns of the temples developed engineering skill among the Egyptians, which has excited the admiration of architects and construction engineers of later generations.

The Egyptian dead, the royal dead especially, were regarded with a solemn expectation that was registered in several sciences. The belief that the spirit that had left the body at death might at some future time return to reanimate the corpse led to a process of mummification so successful, after much experimentation, that it arouses present-day curiosity and wonderment. The preservative properties of such things as wine, common salt, cassia, and myrrh and of atmospheric dryness were known and utilized. The earliest embalmers as well as the first physicians were priests. A knowledge of the rudiments of anatomy and physiology was part of the vocational equipment of the priestly embalmer. With amazing skill he removed the brain and viscera of the corpse.

Among the Persians agriculture as the breeding and care of useful animals and plants was believed to be an effective means of undermining the kingdom of impurity. It was a sacred duty, the performance of which was co-operation with the deity. Diversified farming which replenishes the soil was a religious obligation.[4] In lending Ahura Mazda (God) practical aid and comfort in his conquest of Ahriman (the devil) the Persians improved their methods of agriculture. Cattle and dogs are cherished gifts of Ahura Mazda; snakes, scorpions, toads, and lizards, being disposed to inflict injury, are the noxious creations of Ahriman.[5]

These ancient civilizations should be credited with the origin and earliest development of such specialized sciences as astronomy, medicine, anatomy, emblaming, mathematics, mechanics, and agriculture. The majority of them were born and cradled in religion.

Intellectual Greeks at an early date imported Babylonian astronomy and Egyptian geometry and raised these sciences to higher levels of development. The deductive genius of the Greeks was at home in mathematics and speculation. Their generalizations in science and philosophy have been profoundly influential in the growth of European culture. It is obviously not easy to determine the correlation between the religious idealism of the Greek philosophers and their scientific contributions. Many of the most productive thinkers either rejected the then current gods as fabrications of the imagination or refused to take them seriously, but at the same time repudiated a materialistic explanation of the universe. They were philosophical idealists.

Plato was a mathematician and astronomer as well as a teacher of ideal values. He laid insistence upon the study of

[4] See Dawson, Miles Menander, *The Ethical Religion of Zoroaster*, pp. 164 ff. (New York: The Macmillan Company, 1931).

[5] The theory is inherently probable that animals were tamed because they were worshiped in the Nile valley and elsewhere and the practical utilization of them came later—that is, after the priests had completely domesticated them.

geometry, not because this science is useful in daily life, but because he believed that it develops powers of abstract thinking. Only when the mastery of the principles of geometry withdraws the mind from the material and the particular and engages the intellect in a rigorous examination of the immaterial and universal does the pursuit of this branch of mathematics fulfill its mission. Visible things, Plato taught, are imperfect copies of ideal types which, in turn, are not comprehended by the senses but only by the mind. Since there is inherent in the human mind a notion of the ideal types, man knows that objects fall short of perfection. The mind of man is native to the realm of higher values. All perfect types are the product and reflection of the Good. The Idea of the Good corresponds to Absolute Being. Plato's scientific activities were inspired and controlled by his doctrine of ideal concepts.

Aristotle, whose teaching was destined to affect the theology of the Christian Church to an amazing degree, believed the struggle for perfection everywhere present in nature is the response to a non-material principle resident in the universe, a principle called by him the "Efficient Cause." He combined acute observation and classification of natural phenomena with philosophical speculation. His studies enriched astronomy, physical geography, geology, chemistry, botany, anatomy, embryology, and zoology. Such disciplines as logic, ethics, aesthetics, psychology, and political science were remade and enlarged by this stupendous intellect. He not only interpreted and systematized the multitudinous facts which he himself observed, but also critically evaluated the information and opinions then current in learned circles. He was an ardent evolutionist. As a biologist he dissected specimens of no less than fifty species of animals. More than five hundred forms of life are discussed in his extant works. He drew the inference that there is a gradual progression of organisms and that the older and elementary forms have given rise to the younger and more advanced. He formulated a theory of a natural process or agency whereby the continuous succession of evolutionary changes could occur. He sensed in the vast comprehensive dynamic order of nature a reaction to the "Efficient Cause."

The Transmission and Preservation of Science

The earlier body of nature lore has been a valuable asset to the later scientists. From it they have derived background, atmosphere, suggestions, and starting-points for their own investigations. If the primitive sciences had never existed or if they had been altogether lost, later scientists would have been compelled to begin *de novo,* in which case it is doubtful whether modern science could have reached its present stage of development. What remote religions had to pass on to more developed civilizations became the basis of later scientific attainments. Every science has its own pedigree.

Mohammedanism cannot be omitted in our estimate of what religion has done for science. The Moorish schools preserved from destruction much of the learning of the Greeks. The Moslem society called the Brothers of Sincerity produced scientific treatises of merit and stimulated scientific inquiry. The curriculum of the Moorish colleges included arithmetic, geometry, trigonometry, physics, astronomy, and medicine. New discoveries and inventions issued from the scientific studies and experiments of the Moorish scholars.

The experimentation of the Arabs in chemistry are of interest if not of lasting importance. They tried to concoct the elixir of life, to find the philosopher's stone, and to transmute base metals into gold. These ambitious projects were viewed by many with disfavor and alarm. Lacking the power of intense abstract thinking, the Arabs, unlike the Greeks, reveled in detached facts rather than general underlying principles. Nevertheless, the tradition of culture was preserved and transmitted throughout the Dark Ages chiefly by the Arabs. The greater part of the scientific knowledge of the later Middle Ages was in their possession.

In the eleventh century the darkness of medieval barbarism began to recede. The Roman Church resumed its intercourse with the Greek Empire in which the lamp of learning had been kept burning. Contacts with the Arabs in Spain, among whom the sciences were cherished, were established.   The Arabs, stimulated by Greek learning imparted by Christians in Syria, founded celebrated schools in Bagdad and Damascus.   Astronomy, mathematics, and chemistry were devotedly cultivated by Arabian Mohammedans.   Contact with the scientific acquisitions of the Arabs and the revival of the study of Greek philosophy infused new spirit into the schools of the Western Church.

The medieval scholasticism was an attempt by the application of reason to theology to organize and prove the existing traditional beliefs of the Church.   The authority of the Church had been respected throughout the patristic age, but now a supreme effort was made to submit an intellectual justification of what the heart had experienced and what had been accepted on ecclesiastical authority.   The instrument whereby it was hoped that this result might be obtained was the syllogism. The schoolmen reposed unlimited confidence in dialectics.   Marvelous feats of mental gymnastics were performed by such outstanding schoolmen as Anselm, Abelard, Bernard, Alexander of Hales, Albert of Bollstadt, styled "doctor universalis," and Thomas Aquinas.   Alexander of Hales, for example, wrote commentaries on Aristotle which were widely used, and achieved such distinction in his knowledge of the Fathers of the Church and of religion that he was supposed to have exhausted the powers of the human understanding.   This gigantic intellect was steeped not only in ethics and theology but also in physics and psychology.

In these almost superhuman attempts to present consistent intellectual formulations of the traditional doctrines of the Church and religious experience one glimpses that brave spirit of inquiry which in the course of time was bound to be directed toward the world of nature.   From ecclesiastical authority and tradition as such, and via the scholastic efforts to give the Church and religion solid rational foundations, men eventually moved toward objective observation and experimentation which constitute the basis of scientific procedure.   The schoolmen proper, as a class, did not themselves enter the promised land of experimental science but now and then one of their number did catch hazy glimpses of it. Heroic endeavors to reduce religion and doctrine to a logical system seem to have anticipated the attempt of scientists of later periods to reduce the processes of nature to a system of natural law. The schoolmen sought to disclose and define the laws of religion; modern scientists strive to discover and formulate the laws of nature. Do not the learned volumes of the several and divergent theories of evolution, produced by modern speculative scientists, remind us somewhat of the varying theological compendiums of the schoolmen, despite differences in approach and materials? In their strenuous endeavors some of the schoolmen employed sciences then in embryonic existence, such as psychology and physics. Reason so highly esteemed by scholasticism remains to this day one of the instruments of science.

In Christian monasteries precious manuscripts were copied, and compendiums of grammar, rhetoric, dialectics, mathematics, astronomy, and music were prepared. Christian monks preserved and spread the culture both past and then current, and continued the classical tradition of education. Scholasticism gave to monasticism a new vigor which to a large extent culminated in such great universities as Paris and Oxford.

Religion and Modern Science

Roger Bacon, a Franciscan friar of the University of Oxford who labored in the thirteenth century, is by many considered the father of modern science. Bacon criticized the methods and tendencies of scholasticism and sought to reform the study of theology. His scientific experiments aroused such amazement among his contemporaries that many imagined that he was in league with the Evil One and that with the aid of this sinister agency he had made a brazen head and imparted to it the gift of speech. He had a consummate knowledge of natural causes and their effects. He wrote works on medicine, geometry, chemistry, astronomy, cosmography, music, to say nothing of Latin, Greek, and Hebrew grammars, or philosophical and theological treatises. He was a scientific experimentalist. He appealed to common sense, inward and outward experience, and an accurate knowledge of facts. The adoption of his method has revolutionized the world. He was actively interested in the improvement of horological devices and optical instruments, had an insight into principles of chemistry regarded as fundamental today, and investigated the power of steam. He persevered in a truly scientific spirit despite persecution and the prison cell. Although his discoveries and inventions were condemned as "suspicious novelties" and his books suppressed, the work of this monk was recognized and appropriated by later generations.

Galileo, who flourished during the closing years of the sixteenth century and during the first half of the seventeenth, advanced and established the scientific method and temper. His well-known experiment from the Leaning Tower of Pisa demonstrated the law of falling bodies which is that all bodies fall at the same rate in a vacuum and at a velocity proportional to the length of time. He had challenged the authority of Aristotle, who had without experimental validation maintained otherwise. For nearly two thousand years Aristotle's followers had accepted and promulgated his false assumption. The act of putting Aristotle's claim to an experimental test was considered a gross disrespect for authority, which, to state it mildly, shocked the fathers. The pugnacious scientist furthermore seems to have aroused the ire of the ecclesiastics because he openly sought to discredit the doctrine of the infallibility of the Bible. The scientific achievements of Galileo were numerous and many of them significant. Not the least of his contributions was the establishment of the fact, with the cooperation of Kepler, that the earth rotates on its own axis and that it and the other planets revolve about the sun. Copernicus in his day had revived this doctrine which was asserted centuries before by Aristarchus of Samos, but neither had succeeded in submitting convincing supporting evidence. Galileo's outstanding achievement was the invention of the telescope, for the use of this instrument made additional progress in astronomy possible.

John Wesley, the outstanding religious reformer in England of the eighteenth century, voiced an appreciation of speculative science, of which the majority of the people called Methodists are as yet unaware. That he was a constant student of medicine and published two volumes of prescriptions is common knowledge. It is also quite widely known that he was fascinated by the experiments of Benjamin Franklin and was among the first to explore the therapeutic properties of electricity. His work entitled *A Survey of the Wisdom of God in Creation, or a Compendium of Natural Philosophy* merits a larger circle of readers than it has hitherto attracted. In this work Wesley, leaning heavily for his science on John Francis Buddaeus of Jena, Germany, expounded a form of theistic evolution about eighty years before Darwin published *The Origin of Species.* Anticipating opposition, Wesley indicates that the evidences for evolution which he presents will probably be rejected as false by the uneducated or inattentive reader. He describes the gradual progression of the works of God from vegetation to the polypus, from the bird to the quadruped, from the ape to man. He sees in the ostrich, which has the feet of a goat and runs rather than flies, a link which unites birds to quadrupeds. He considers the ape a rough draft of man and interposes a prodigious number of connecting links between the two.[6] It is clear that this churchman, theologian, and evangelist, like St. Augustine centuries before him, believed in the compatibility of the theory of evolution and a religious interpretation of the world.[7]

The rise and dissemination of the spirit of inquiry and research of the Italian Renaissance formed the effective beginnings of the substitution of the experimental method for as-

[6] Scientists do not hold, as Wesley did, that man has directly descended from the ape, but that both have evolved in divergent lines from a common ancestry.

[7] St. Augustine and his younger contemporary, Gregory of Nyssa, interpreted the Genesis account of creation in the light of Aristotle's doctrine of evolution. Creation as described in Genesis was potential, completed objects and forms gradually arising from chaotic material. Augustine in his *De Genesi Contra Manichaeos* declares that the world and its products were brought into existence not by events separated by time intervals but by an unbroken series of causes operating throughout countless ages. He held that the Biblical statement that heaven and earth were created by God in the beginning should not be interpreted literally. In the beginning God produced the seed as it were from which all things were ultimately and only after long periods of time derived.

sumption and disputation. A scientific and industrial revolution was the ultimate outgrowth of this new attitude and procedure.

The Church and Science

An important gift of the Church to science consists in the number of outstanding scientists whom she has educated and stimulated. Although she has too frequently rejected as either futile or dangerous or both the demonstrable findings of her scientific sons, the Church has both directly and indirectly enormously expanded the range of science. To call the roll of the illustrious churchmen who have furthered science is to mention the most important names of the formative period of modern science. Roger Bacon, Galileo, Copernicus, Francis Bacon, Newton, Faraday, Herschel, all beacon lights of science, were churchmen, either clerical or lay. If we call to witness the most illustrious scientists of our own generation, as Professor Robert A. Millikan has done, we shall learn that nearly all profess the Christian faith, and are identified with some branch of the Christian Church.[8] These men read the Bible for religious instruction and inspiration and investigate nature for their science, and sincerely believe that both Jesus' way of life and the processes of the natural order have one and the same purposeful, wise, and good Being as their author and consummation. The vast majority of scientists of standing would subscribe to the words of Pasteur, which are inscribed on his tomb: "Happy is he who carries a God within him, an ideal of beauty to which he is obedient—an ideal of art, an ideal of science—an ideal of the fatherland—an ideal of the virtues of the Gospel."

If it be charged that official Christendom for centuries was arrayed against scientific progress, the indictment must be tempered by the just consideration of a fact too frequently ignored. It is folly to deny that organized Christianity did impede the growth of natural science. It is, however, shortsighted to speak of the warfare of Christianity against science

[8] *The Christian Century,* Vol. 40, pp. 778-783, June 21, 1923.

as though the Church had invaded the domain and attacked the personnel of science as an aggressor from without. The history of the Church and science admits of no such antithesis. The warfare was a civil strife. When the Church persecuted men like Roger Bacon, Galileo, and Copernicus, she was not laying chastising hands on men outside the fold but on sons within the household of faith. When we call the roll of the persecuted scientists one son of the Church after another passes in review! A part of the Church revolted against another part of the Church. Within Christian circles, despite the obstacles provided by obtuse and antagonistic prelates, the spirit of free investigation was born and nurtured a few hundred years ago. With or without its official sanction the Church promoted scientific progress.

It is often lamented that religious leaders have been and still are exceedingly critical of the findings and deductions of the scientists. Such criticism, as already conceded, has frequently passed through the successive stages of scorn, hostility, and persecution. But criticism *per se* is good for anyone who has a new doctrine to propound and propagate. The prospect of adverse criticism should induce the scientist to examine his data thoroughly and to verify his conclusions completely before he publishes abroad his findings. Churchmen have seen too many doctrines conceived, brought forth, and nurtured by science which were later relegated to the limbo of discarded opinions by other findings and more brilliant generalizations, to accept fresh scientific deductions without overwhelming demonstration and proof. Scientists now affirm that the once generally accepted nebular hypothesis is tottering on its foundations, that the ether not long ago considered a necessary postulate by physics is fictitious, that the law of the conservation of energy should be retired, that Einstein's inferences make a revision of Newton's interpretation of gravitation imperative. It is not only conservatism or the haunting apprehension that science may rob religion of some treasured value but also the fact that science as a growing enterprise adopts and discards theories at a startling rate, which prompts religious leadership to put scientific thinkers on the defensive.

Christian leaders who read the literature of speculative science know that within the domain of science itself there is at times confusion and bedlam. One recalls, for example, the existing divergent schools of psychology, and protagonists of each who are ready to fall with destructive intent upon the systems of the others. Current theories of evolution suggest another illustration. The process of evolution as a fact based on a convincing mass of supporting data is now generally accepted by intelligent men. It is not the fact but the method of evolution which is still the subject of disputation. Differences of opinion exist among scientists as to the principles and forces which govern the total process of evolution. Is the theory of natural selection tenable? Is competition or co-operation the determining factor in biological survival? Are acquired characters heritable? Are species differentiated by gradual accumulations of small variations transmitted by inheritance, or by spontaneous leaps and bounds? Which exerts the more fundamental pressure on organic evolution: heredity or environment? The religious leader may be pardoned for his refusal to identify the fortunes of the Church with scientific speculations which have not won the support of a large fraction of the scientists themselves and which may be retired by further investigation and generalization. The Church cannot afford to form scientific alliances which may embarrass her or leave her in the lurch. It has been asserted that the average life of a scientific theory is about seven years. Wisely, the Church does not propose to stand or fall by any scientific hypothesis.

Unfair criticism born of prejudice and ignorance, while indefensible, should be a challenge rather than a deterrent to science. We have been told that the blood of the martyrs is the seed of the Church. Should not the blood of the scientists be the seed of scientific progress? Causes which are persecuted flourish; they command attention and investigation, they arouse the spirit of chivalry and attract adventurous followers. Woe unto him by whom offenses to science come, but science is in respect to persecution no more entitled to immunity than the Church. One dares to venture the declaration that the martyrology of the Church is far more extended than that of science.

Finally, religion puts scientific discovery and invention to constructive uses. The ethical regulation and socialized utilization of the marvels of applied science are imperative if our civilization is to continue to exist and realize its potentialities. More, not less creative religious idealism in actual operation is a primary necessity in an age of science like ours. So great are the strides of contemporary applied science that the prophet of idealism is disquieted lest our practical scientific applications have outrun our moral control.

In order to protect and preserve itself, in order that it may continue to unfold its possibilities, science must seek the co-operation of religion, must live and move and have its being in an atmosphere that will make the mechanical world it has created safe. For example, science itself has created such effective agencies of destruction that another war among the leading nations will destroy civilization and its scientific achievements. The religion of Christ cultivates that unity of aim, that consciousness of our common humanity, that spirit of co-operation without which the statesman is unable to organize the world for lasting peace. To keep from being entangled in and destroyed by its own technique science must share a comprehensive appreciation of the total range of human experience. It must add to itself the values by which the noblest of men have lived.

CHAPTER VIII

THE RISE AND DEVELOPMENT OF THE PSYCHOLOGY OF RELIGION

THE psychological investigation of the structure of religion and its function in human relationships had its inception at the beginning of the present century. Its development throughout the ensuing period has been rapid and continuous. The psychology of religion is a young but vigorous science. It is, as will be presently indicated, an American product. European students of religion grasped its significance and implications, imported it, and have added to the gathered lore of American scholars. During its still brief history, this science has brought forth a voluminous literature, developed research techniques, and made contributions to religious culture.

Two items claim attention: first, the philosophical and theological teachings which constitute the background of the psychological study of religious living; second, the researches and conclusions of the man with whom this science originated and the contributions of those who, following in his train, developed it during the dozen subsequent years.

European Forerunners

American psychologists who were pioneers in the investigation of religion had European precursors. Among those who prepared the way for the specialized psychological study of religion Hume, Comte, Kant, and Schleiermacher merit special consideration. In his volume bearing the suggestive title *The Natural History of Religion* and published about the middle of the eighteenth century, Hume sought the beginnings of religion in primitive man's conflicts and vicissitudes. He contended that religion originated in the emotions of fear and hope evoked by the clash between the needs of early man and the hostile course of nature. The imagination peopled the

122

world with gods whom man strove to placate and whose co-operation he solicited.   It is difficult for us to realize how radical the inferences of Hume seemed to his readers who were, of course, unfamiliar with our psychological theories and classifications.

Following the path which Hume had broken, Comte expounded the doctrine of the sociological origin and nature of religion.   He held that primitive man unconsciously created first fetishes and later gods.   He conceded reality only to the data of religion which can be subsumed under the categories of science.   He evolved the philosophy called positivism.   He excluded from the content of his world-view everything but natural phenomena or the properties of facts of perception and their relations.   All inquiry into causes both final and immediate he regarded as futile.   He included only what is scientifically and as he supposed therefore positively ascertainable.   Since Deity is not given to the senses Comte drew the doubtful conclusion that the existence of God is an illusion if not a delusion.   What he called the religion of humanity should displace theism; love for one's fellow-man, he taught, rather than belief in an imaginary God, should motivate the good life.   His sociological studies and findings contain valuable contributions, but positivism is marred by the defects which characterize modern humanism.   Taking their cue from Comte, Mill and Spencer advocated the doctrine of the unknowability of God.

The outcome of Hume's influence on Kant was far different and philosophically more constructive.   Aroused from his "dogmatic slumbers" by Hume's work, Kant proceeded with gusto to demolish the revered traditional arguments for the existence of God.   But Kant did not stop once he had exposed the fallacies of the stock reasons advanced for the validity of theism, for he replaced the defective logic of the theologians and philosophers with a moral argument.   Kant had a profound respect for the moral law within man.   He defined religion as the interpretation of moral obligations as divine commandments.   He gave morality a theistic guarantee.   He postulated God, freedom, and immortality as the ground of the good life.

Kant and Comte were both stimulated by Hume, but the philosophical end-results were antithetical.

Schleiermacher, a German theologian, made a fresh approach to the religious life, which is more psychological than philosophical. He reacted violently against the intellectualistic interpretation of the nature of religion. Hegel had maintained that "religion is absolutely true knowledge," and "is the region of eternal truth." [1] Schleiermacher, setting himself against such intellectualism with all the vigor he could summon, contended that the domain of religion is neither thinking nor acting, but intuition and feeling. He declared that the consciousness of God which imparts moral power emanates from the feeling of absolute dependence. [2] Schleiermacher, one is inclined to believe, was more nearly right than those who magnified religious knowledge and doctrine, for the emotions as incentives of conduct are stronger than reasoned conclusions. Although his conception of the core of religion was one-sided, as any strong reaction against an opposite extreme is likely to be, and many psychologists of our day so far from restricting the essence of religion to any one mode of human nature make it a function of the whole personality, it was warm, vital, and productive and, as such, forms a point of departure for further analysis and synthesis.

Starbuck

Edwin Diller Starbuck, disciplined in philosophy and empirical psychology and inspired by the desire to devote his life to religious problems, entered Harvard University as a graduate student when the previous century was drawing to a close. This brilliant and adventurous student was destined to create the specifically psychological approach to the interpretation of religious phenomena. With the rather timorous support of William James, his teacher, Starbuck prepared and circulated two questionnaires, one on the conversion experience and one

---

[1] Hegel, Georg Wilhelm Friedrich, translated by E. B. Speirs, *Philosophy of Religion,* Vol. 1, p. 90 (London: Kegan Paul, Trench, Trübner & Co., 1895).
[2] Schleiermacher, Friedrich, translated by John Oman, *On Religion,* pp. 26-118 (London: Kegan Paul, Trench, Trübner & Co., 1893).

on gradual growth in religion, and psychologized the mass of data which he collected.   The work of Starbuck definitely began a new epoch in the history of the study of religious experience.   He transferred his researches to Clark University, where his method and its results aroused so much active interest that within a short time a number of fellow-graduate students, to say nothing of President G. Stanley Hall, were engaged in the psychological investigation of religious experience.

In 1899 Starbuck published his findings under the title *The Psychology of Religion,* the first elaborate volume of its kind.[3] Conversion as the outstanding phenomenon of the period in many large evangelical groups was the coign of vantage from which Starbuck surveyed Protestant religion.   Conversion, he concludes, is predominantly an adolescent phenomenon.   It becomes necessary when the self that ought to be stands over against the self that is, and the contrast is painfully vivid.   In early adolescence fear of death and hell, conviction of sin, and social pressure are determinants of the conversion experience. In later adolescence the altruistic motive, a desire to realize a moral ideal, and a response to positive religious teaching are the active forces that sway the personality.   Starbuck distinguishes three types of conversion: the positive or volitional type, the negative or self-surrender type, and the spontaneous awakening type.   The religious life of mature persons who have been converted in adolescence does not markedly differ from that of those whose religious development has been free from abrupt transitions.

In his analysis of cases of religious growth not including conversion Starbuck discovered four increments in the experience of the individual as a child: first, an attitude of uncritical conformity to religious surroundings; second, a relationship of intimacy with Christ or God; third, the absence of fear and the presence of love and trust; fourth, an early de-

[3] Articles antedating the Starbuck volume were published by G. Stanley Hall, A. H. Daniels, J. H. Leuba, E. D. Starbuck, and G. A. Coe.   Starbuck's book won international recognition at once and was translated into German.

velopment of the sense of right and wrong. During adolescence a process of clarification and intensification occurs; there is a new insight into the meaning of religion; ideas of God, religious observances, and morals assume a fresh significance; a rich emotional response is made to the world of values. Belief in God is central. With the passing of the years belief in personal immortality is intensified. Tenets held to be nonessential are discarded in the course of time and religion as an inward life makes progress.

As the originator of the thoroughly psychological approach to religion Starbuck recognized the limitations of the scientific procedure. He conceived it to be the task of the psychologist to collect the factual data, to analyze and classify them and to discover the laws which govern religious behavior, but he did not presume to pronounce upon their ultimate ground or intrinsic nature. Furthermore, the psychologist, he maintained, should study religion as it is lived by the individual. The investigation of religion as a racial experience is of value, but should be undertaken by anthropologists and sociologists.

Starbuck's ability to create techniques of inquiry, his exhaustive researches, his brilliant application of psychological principles, the impetus he imparted to the investigation of uncultivated areas, the catholicity of his appreciations, all conspire to make his labors in the psychology of religion monumental.

Coe

Meanwhile George Albert Coe had been making a psychological study of religious awakening, conversion, the technique of revivalism, adolescent difficulties, divine healing, and the meaning of spirituality. In 1900 his volume *The Spiritual Life,* in which his investigations and conclusions are reported, was published. The practical application of this book to the religious nurture of youth was immediately recognized by Christian leaders.

Coe makes much of physiological disability as a determinant of the characteristic emotional and intellectual conflicts of youth. Unrest, discontent, morbid introspection, worry, indecision, bad temper, and susceptibility to sexual delinquency are all symptomatic, Coe declares, of nerve fatigue. General mental confusion, which is the resultant of defective religious teaching, frequently overstrains the nervous system of the adolescent. Coe exhorts parents and teachers not only to provide guidance in the formulation of an adequate philosophy of life, but to restore the health of the distracted adolescent through rest, proper diet, and wholesome recreation.

Coe's chief contribution as reported in this volume is his investigation of the relation of temperament to the form or mode which religious experience assumes in the individual. He undertook the task of determining why some people experience a dramatic conversion and others who put themselves into the same attitude of will fail to achieve a like result. He made an intensive and in part experimental study of seventy-seven young people, the majority of whom were college students, who had had positive religious training and were mentally and physically normal. Coe discovered that those whose expectations of a sudden and colorful conversion were unrealized constituted a group dominated by the intellect and marked by quick and intense reactions. The persons whose anticipations were satisfied were those controlled by feeling, and characterized by either slow and strong, or quick and weak responses to situations. Individuals of each group were hypnotized in order that the relative degree of suggestibility might be ascertained. The hypnotic experiments demonstrated that the persons who expected and experienced striking conversions were the more susceptible to social suggestion. Furthermore, those who were subject to such phenomena as visions, voices, vivid dreams, hallucinations, and other forms of automatism to which no religious significance was attached were predisposed to startling religious experiences. Coe learned that the psychological combination most favorable to dramatic religious phenomena consists of a wealth of emotion, imagination, suggestibility, expectation, and a general tendency to automatism.

Coe was wise enough to seek the permanent value of a religious experience not in a temperamental mode but in ethical change for the better, loyalty to principle, the spirit of service, and devotion to the kingdom of God. Needless anxiety and even antagonism to religion are the bitter consequences of an attempt to induce experiences which are foreign to one's mental constitution.

Although the later investigations of Jung, Hinkle, and others have yielded a more refined classification of personality types, Coe's general inferences for religious culture have stood the test of time and further application.[4]

James

In 1902 William James published his fascinating volume, *The Varieties of Religious Experience*. He brought to bear upon the religious quest of the individual a mind enriched by psychology and philosophy, a remarkable understanding of what is supremely vital to human beings, and the mastery of a literary style which enabled him to express his reactions with clarity, vigor, and grace. The material which James treated was in large measure derived from recorded cases of personal religious belief and behavior. In two exceedingly suggestive chapters on conversion James drew freely upon the stores of data and knowledge contributed by his former pupil Starbuck.

James divides religious persons into two groups, the healthy-minded and the morbid-minded, and proceeds to describe the spiritual processes whereby typical specimens of each are unified and adjusted. The healthy-minded individual is so constituted that he achieves unity by disregarding or by denying the existence of depressing elements of life. The morbid-minded man is the "sin-sick" soul, the one who is burdened by the stern realities of failure, disappointment, and injustice, and if religiously disposed, seeks deliverance from evil and the unification of the anguished self through conversion.

[4] In his volume *The Psychology of Religion* (Chicago: University of Chicago Press, 1916), Coe discusses such topics as racial beginnings in religion, the genesis of the idea of God, mental traits of leaders, religion and the subconscious, conversion, the religious revaluation of values, religion as discovery, mysticism, immortality, and prayer. In this work Coe identifies religion not with any specialized or new set of values but with a "revaluation of values that makes us individuals and organizes us into society" (p. 68). Religion involves the completion, unification, and conservation of all values of life.

His discussions of immortality, ultimate reality, and other related values are heavily weighted with his own philosophy. His personal mystical predisposition comes to the fore. Mysticism, its nature and effects, is his major concern. Like Starbuck, James makes much of Schleiermacher's contention of the centrality of feeling in the religious life. His conception that God may enter human experience via the subconscious has been the subject of considerable debate and the occasion of much confusion.

Uncomplimentary reference has often been made to James' citation of so many extreme cases of religious experience that the total impression which his book creates is that religion is an abnormal possession and venture. That James did actually associate pronounced religious attitudes and behavior with the more morbid personality types cannot be truthfully denied. The relatively stable and undramatic religious life of what are called the normal varieties of personality seem not to have intrigued his consideration. On the other hand, the reader should bear in mind that James held that the abnormal is an exaggeration of the normal, and as such enables one to perceive data not sharply defined and clearly discernible in the ordinary instances of the same larger classification.

Pratt

In 1907 James Bissett Pratt, a thinker of precision and balance and one of the most constructive of the pioneers, published his treatise entitled *The Psychology of Religious Belief.* In this volume Pratt presents illuminating discussions of the nature of belief, religious belief among primitive peoples, belief in India, belief in Israel, Christian belief, the development of belief during childhood and youth, and belief in mature life. He describes and enforces the intimacy of the relation which emotion sustains to belief.

As against those who assert that belief in God is valued merely or largely as a means to practical ends, Pratt maintains that religious persons prize and seek God not so much as a giver of things desirable but as a companion. His investigation of religious persons of intelligence disclosed that in so far as God is treasured as a dispenser of benefits, it is as the giver of such gifts as moral courage, insight, peace, and consolation. Pratt learned that the majority of men resort to prayer not primarily in order to obtain tangible favors but in order to come into direct fellowship with God. Among educated people the petitional prayer for special concessions is falling more and more into disuse, while the mood of worship and the desire for co-operation with God are growing. On the whole, belief in the existence and friendliness of God transcends the will to use him for utilitarian purposes.

Ames

Edward Scribner Ames, in his book *The Psychology of Religious Experience,* published in 1910, advanced and refined a sociological interpretation of the origin, nature, and function of religion. His point of view derives from the work of Comte, reflects the then contemporary social application of religion by men like Walter Rauschenbusch, Washington Gladden, and Josiah Strong, and is profoundly influenced also by the contributions of Harald Höffding. In his great volume *The Philosophy of Religion,* published in 1906, Höffding propounded the thesis that religion centers in the conservation of values. Religion, he holds, is identified not with this or that value only but with man's entire range of evaluational attitudes.

Making Höffding's position a point of departure, Ames developed the proposition that religion is the conservation of social values in their most ideal and intensified forms. Social values are not static but dynamic and change throughout the successive stages of religion. Ames drew his inferences mainly from anthropological data.

Ames concludes that God is a symbol or objectification of treasured social values which mankind has evolved in the course of cultural development; or at best the spirit which animates a socialized group, akin to the spirit which characterizes a college—an inference to which many of the best minds do not subscribe. Again, he argues that the individual has no significant appreciation of social relations and consequences before he is nine years old and that persons belonging to the earlier age group cannot be truly religious. The modern program of religious education controverts the theory and demonstrates that the consciousness of social values in their simpler applications can be engendered in children in the earlier ages.[5]

Ames' proposition that biological drives are of paramount importance is hardly sustained by the culture of advanced groups in which self-imposed future ideal ends are pursued at the cost of life itself. More consideration should be given to the fact that the prophet, so far from being determined to conserve social values precious to his contemporaries, actually proceeds to demolish them and to replace them with other ideals for which he is prepared to suffer. Furthermore, the reader is left in doubt as to just what are the specific "higher" social values.

One feels that Ames has abstracted some essential elements from the deepest experience of mankind and that the residuum is not religion but humanism. His positive contribution to the evaluation of religion is his emphasis on dynamic social relations as objectives of religious devotion.[6]

Stratton

In 1911 George Malcolm Stratton published *The Psychology of the Religious Life,* a notable volume. The main contribution is a study of the conflicts arising within the religious personality. The religious life is for the most part portrayed as an arena in which contrasting not to say contradictory emotions, ideas, and motives compete. Gloom and cheer, narrowness and breadth of sympathy, appreciation of and contempt for human life, imitation and originality, trust and jealousy, the ritual of

---

[5] See Coe, George Albert, *A Social Theory of Religious Education* (New York: Charles Scribner's Sons, 1917).

[6] Irving King, in his *The Development of Religion* (New York: The Macmillan Company, published also in 1910), submits anthropological data and arrives at substantially the same conclusions presented by Ames in his *The Psychology of Religious Experience.* Religion is an attitude, King declares, an attitude which includes an emotional cognizance of values, an intellectual predisposition to accept or reject them, and a tendency to react to them in some manner. Religion does not differ generically from many other evaluational attitudes. "The religious life is this social life in one of its phases" (p. 88). Religious ideas and acts are not analogous to the social and economic life of a people, for they are themselves an organic part of the life of the social group.

religion and the religion of ritual, acceptance and renunciation of the world, the immanence and transcendence of God, and other opposing pairs are presented and analyzed with appreciative insight. Stratton's thesis is that the central characteristic of religion is inner tension induced by antithetical forces. In support of his point of view he assembled an impressive array of data drawn from anthropology and the sacred literature of representative religions.

One may be inclined to doubt the finality of personality conflicts in religion. The principle of the balance of opposites, the possibility that contrasting emotions, or conceptions, or incentives to action are often dual expressions of a substratum of idealism, the probability that no single mood or concept can adequately comprehend a complex attitude, should receive a sufficiency of investigation and clarification. Perhaps contradiction is as potently present in science and art as it is in religion. Nevertheless, in lifting the element of conflict into prominence Stratton has labored in an area of importance to theologians and psychologists and of great utility to pastors and religious educators.

Leuba

In 1912 James H. Leuba published an important book entitled *A Psychological Study of Religion*. In this volume Leuba presents studies of the scope of the psychology of religion, the origin of magic and religion, and the relation of religion to morality, mythology, philosophy, and psychology.

Leuba's interpretation of the factual data of religion is influenced by the world-view of stark humanism. He contends that all gods, including the Father-God of Jesus, are the products of the creative imagination of men. He accounts for the persistence of the belief in and the worship of objectively nonexistent gods in terms of the practical advantages which the religious attitude entails, such as confidence and hope. He supposes that the mystical core of religion is reducible to the mental processes of the theist himself.

Leuba's main contribution to the understanding of religion is his stimulating conception of the respective sources and methods of magic and religion. He maintains that magic and religion differ in origin, nature, and procedure, that man may resort to both in the face of the same emergency, and that some of the oldest magical practices probably antedated religious behavior.

Summary

A survey of the first dozen years of the historical development of the American school of the psychology of religion, cursory and fragmentary as it may be, recounts amazing progress in the understanding of the religious response to the universe. The various contributions of the seven pioneers introduced not only possesses individual and independent worth, but in the aggregate constitute a respectable body of theory and empirical knowledge, and serve as points of departure for fresh investigations. Starbuck, with whom the thoroughly psychological study of religion had its inception, contributed an empirical investigation of conversion and of religious development without crises; Coe contributed an examination of the relation of temperament to the mode in which a religious experience expresses itself; James contributed a psychological and philosophical interpretation of religious mysticism; Pratt contributed a treatise on the nature, function, and varieties of religious belief; Ames contributed an anthropological and sociological theory of the beginnings, growth, and significance of religious behavior; Stratton contributed a description of conflicting forces in the religious consciousness; and Leuba contributed a comparison of the origin, quality, purpose, and technique of both magic and of religion.

The problems attacked by these pioneers are both numerous and vital, theoretical and practical, scientific and speculative. Many of their findings have stood the test of further research, some of them have been retired by more exact and refined analyses, and still others have been modified in the light of fresh knowledge and wider experience. The pioneers laid the foundations upon which a long succession of followers have built.[7]

[7] The bibliography which this work presents includes the contributions of the majority of these subsequent investigators.

CHAPTER IX

METHODS OF INVESTIGATION

THE psychological study of religious personality in order to be true to itself and to realize its potentialities must continue to foster the scientific spirit. It must not abandon the scientific approach and technique. It must be candidly realistic and critical, and cultivate a penchant for accuracy and suspension of final judgment. In order to be scientific, the psychology of religion must rely on observed facts of experience rather than on an opinion-structure upheld by self-consistent argumentation. It can extend its domain only by fidelity to facts and the willingness to go where they may lead.

The scientific procedure includes the following six steps: the gathering of a mass of pertinent facts, the analysis of the facts, the comparison of the facts with like known phenomena, the classification of the facts, the deduction of a formula, principle, or law from the facts, and the prediction under what conditions like facts may be expected to arise. The six steps may be reduced to four—collection, collation, generalization, and prognostication. Analysis, comparison, and classification may conveniently be subsumed under collation. Generalization may include the formulation of a new hypothesis which will most adequately interpret the related facts, or overthrow or modify or confirm an existing hypothesis. In addition, an hypothesis is a guide in further research. The thoroughness with which the scientist develops a project depends on the extent to which he elaborates the successive stages of the inclusive procedure. The psychologist who investigates religious personality, if he proceeds scientifically, like the physicist or biologist, accumulates suitable data, organizes it, draws an inference, and indicates the circumstances under which a result may be repeated.

The scientific study of religious personality is a co-operative enterprise. Imbued with the spirit of science, the psychologist is eager to labor with others, to share his findings, and to submit his processes to properly qualified individuals for suggestions and criticisms. He is more concerned with the advancement of the psychological exploration than with his own aggrandizement. Free exchange of method, experience, and materials prevails among men who are devoted to the search for truth.[1]

The main specific methods which are adopted in the psychological study of religion are the following eight: The questionnaire, the biographical, the re-creative, the documentary, the observational, the survey, the experimental, and the evaluational. The regular steps of the general scientific procedure to which reference has already been made may be taken in the application of any of these particular methods of research. Not that all special methods, which will be discussed, are of equal value in the acquisition of scientific information and control of personality. Again, one method may be more fruitful than another in the investigation of a given religious phenomenon.

The Questionnaire

The oldest method employed is the questionnaire type of investigation. A list of questions is carefully prepared and sent to persons whose reactions are thought desirable; the responses obtained are analyzed and classified. Starbuck's pioneer and monumental work on conversion and religious growth is based on materials secured by questionnaires.[2] Other early investigators adopted this method with varying degrees of success. Leuba, for example, made use of it in his study of belief in immortality and God.[3]

---

[1] When I was a graduate student engaged in researches in the psychology of religion Professor J. B. Pratt, to whom I had occasion to write, volunteered to lend me, a stranger, a mass of prayer data his own students had gathered, for use in the preparation of a treatise. Years later when I first met him personally I referred to this act of generosity. Quite characteristically, he had completely forgotten it.

[2] Starbuck, Edwin Diller, *The Psychology of Religion* (New York: Charles Scribner's Sons, 1899).

[3] Leuba, James H., *Belief in God and Immortality* (Chicago: University of Chicago Press, 1921).

The defects of the questionnaire method are readily recognized and recorded. Lapse of memory, unconscious exaggeration or suppression, suggestion, lack of spontaneity and descriptive inability may conspire to defeat the attempt to secure trustworthy accounts of religious belief, experience, and behavior. The psychologist himself encounters difficulty in accurately introspecting his motives, attitudes, and other emotionally suffused mental states. Personality is studied by personality; the psychologist and the object of his investigation are not static but self-active moment by moment, and in all probability no device for the elimination of the human equation can be invented.

Some of the ordinary defects of this method of investigation can be remedied by giving specific directions to the subject. The avoidance of ambiguity in formulating questions tends to make for greater reliability of response. Requesting the same information in several questions variously phrased serves as a check. Personal conferences or correspondence with respondents whose replies warrant further examination leads to confirmation, explication, or correction. Furthermore, the reactions can in many cases be tested by comparison with data derived from other sources.

The questionnaire method has undergone a process of refinement which has made it a more dependable instrument of research. Various revised forms are now employed with gratifying success. A few examples will suggest the nature and value of the improved procedure.

The multiple-choice questionnaire offers the subject a number of statements relative to the same topic, for one of which he is to indicate a preference. Example: Place a check after the statement with which you are in accord:

(1) God has a body like a man's,
(2) God is an impersonal force like electricity,
(3) God is personal and has his abode far beyond the planet which we inhabit,
(4) God is consciously in all creation,
(5) God is superpersonal,
(6) God is the ideal of goodness personified.

The true-false questionnaire consists of a series of statements to each of which the subject reacts either positively or negatively. Example: Read each following statement carefully and underline *Yes* if it is true and *No* if it is not true.

(1) Pilate's wife said, "Beware the Ides of March." Yes No
(2) St. Paul wrote the Epistle to the Galatians.   Yes   No
This form of the questionnaire has been widely used in tests of religious knowledge and in the study of beliefs and opinions.

The cross-out questionnaire, especially effective in determining the subject's emotional attitude toward meanings symbolized by words, submits a list of terms with the request that a line be marked through all which involve the element indicated by the investigator. For example, he may direct that all words in the following series which affect the subject disagreeably be crossed out: Jesus, Jerusalem, Judas, Adam, devil, sin, salvation, theology, prayer, thief, Christian, baptism, faith, forgiveness.

The completion questionnaire is composed of a narrative interrupted by blank spaces in which the subject supplies data in accordance with his knowledge or opinions. Example: The Bible is a library consisting of ——— books, ——— of which constitute the Old Testament and ——— the New.

The verbal association questionnaire presents a list of words to each of which the subject reacts with the first word that enters his mind. Example: stimulus word, hell; possible reaction word, heaven; stimulus word, Satan; possible reaction word, evil. These and other devices, although not instruments of unerring precision, have largely displaced the older cumbersome direct-question outlines.[4]

The discriminating use of the more refined question list has yielded a mass of substantial information. Betts, for example, collected the responses of seven hundred ministers living in or near Chicago to a set of theological propositions. The

[4] For a more extended list of question forms and tests which may be employed in investigating religious relations consult Watson, Goodwin, *Experiments and Measurements in Religious Education* (New York: Association Press, 1927). A technique for the study of religious attitudes is supplied by Thurstone, L. L., and Chave, Ernest J., *Attitude Scales* (Chicago: University of Chicago Press, 1929).

data received showed that on the whole 84 per cent believed in the resurrection of the body, 80 per cent in the doctrine of the Trinity, 71 per cent in the Virgin Birth, 68 per cent in the occurrence of miracles as events contrary to natural law, 64 per cent in the efficacy of prayer for rain, and 47 per cent in special creation as described in the Book of Genesis. Lutheran pastors held these tenets most generally, the Methodist and Congregational ministers believed in a smaller number of them.[5] There is no valid reason why the usefulness of the refined questionnaire method or the relatively high degree of reliability of its results should be disputed.

The Biographical

The biographical method centers in the analysis and comparison of the religious histories of individuals written either by themselves or others. The method is a sort of case study writ large. Autobiographies contain many spontaneous confessions of religious experience of which the psychologist may avail himself. The mystics and religious geniuses have been more prone than other personality types to record their inner struggles, defeats, victories, depressions, ecstacies, doubts, and beliefs. The autobiographical confessions of St. Augustine and St. Teresa are classic instances.[6] Other outstanding religious personalities have left behind them letters and diaries which are invaluable sources for the investigator.[7]

Biographies written by objectively minded scholars rather than by persons with a blinding excess of admiration for their subjects have unlocked rich storehouses of psychological data. The indiscriminate or exclusive use of the biographical method results in an exaggerated, not to say abnormal, exhibition of the religious life. Even the saints, carried away by their emotions, a sense of the dramatic, and a measure of egotism,

---

[5] Betts, George Herbert, *The Beliefs of Seven Hundred Ministers and Their Meaning for Religious Education* (New York: The Abingdon Press, 1929).

[6] See his *Confessions,* and *The Life of St. Teresa of Jesus,* by herself, also, *Letters of Saint Teresa,* translated from the Spanish and annotated by the Benedictines of Stanbrook (London: Baker, 1924).

[7] For example, see *John Wesley's Journal,* edited by Nehemiah Curnock (London: Robert Culley, 1909).

have mixed fact with fiction in their letters, diaries, and memoirs. Of course the psychologist is deeply interested in the world of imagination in which the subject has his being, but alloyed literary output, since it is at all times difficult and often impossible to separate the fancied from the real, is a treacherous source of objectively factual material. The investigator should take into consideration that it is the exceptional rather than the ordinary religious person who is inclined to submit a literary dissection of his experiences. The religious life of the average man is not, as a rule, striking enough to be autobiographically recorded.

The Re-creative

What might be called the re-creative method of study has been applied by a number of psychologists. The nerve of the method is an effort to reconstruct, with the aid of anthropology, social psychology, and genetic psychology, early man's religious beliefs, attitudes, and behavior. The study of the origin and significance of religious ceremonies, rites, creeds, and cults and their modern successors falls within the scope of this procedure. The data expressive of prehistoric man's religious interests are collected, interpreted, and organized. The religious customs and concepts of the most primitive people now living are objectively analyzed. The religious and other responses of the child are carefully examined, the supposition being that there are correspondences between the mind of a child and the mind of prehistoric man. With such materials the historical imagination seeks to re-create the social conditions under which our primitive ancestors lived, the origin and function of religion and its differentiation and early development. In the light of the construct, modern religion is assayed.

The re-creative method has been employed by such prominent investigators as Ames, Stratton, King, and Leuba, to whose contributions references have been made. Although the approach has enriched our appreciation of primitive religious culture and has added to our understanding of the historical beginnings and the nature and function of religion, its usefulness is limited by certain serious impairments. Our objective sources of information of prehistoric peoples are still so meager that complex inferences drawn from them are likely to be spurious. To say the least, it is difficult to know whether the deductions are actually warranted, for the dead cannot rise to confirm or reject them. The clash of opposing theories of early religious phenomena bears witness to the difficulties one encounters in the application of this method. The parallels which the scholar draws between extant primitive peoples and prehistoric primitive peoples exist within the realm of possibility or probability rather than within the realm of direct verification. The anthropological approach is too unreliable to yield adequate criteria for the appraisal of the mature and refined types of religion. That primitive man's mind is reflected in the growing child entangled in a modern environment seems, furthermore, to be an assumption rather than a scientifically grounded deduction. Incidentally, the materials and interpretations identified with this method are sociological rather than psychological. They constitute what might be termed a speculative sociology of religion. Nevertheless, the method and its results cannot be ignored in an attempt to account for racial religious origins.

The Documentary

One may make sacred literatures—the Bible of Christianity, the Five Kings of Confucianism, the Canon of Virtue of Taoism, the Vedas of Brahmanism, the Three Baskets of Buddhism, the Zend-Avesta of Zoroastrianism, and the Koran of Mohammedanism—the data of psychological study. Stratton has made extensive and excellent use of the sacred writings of leading living religions. In his important study of opposing forces in the religious consciousness, and especially in his investigation of the place of anger in morals and religion,[8] appropriate citations from authoritative religious documents supply him with an abundant grist for his psychological mill. The recorded experiences and teachings of the personal founders of religions and of their chosen disciples, despite the di-

[8] Stratton, George Malcolm, *Anger: Its Religious and Moral Significance* (New York: The Macmillan Company, 1923).

vergent interpretations of successive generations of followers, are venerated as unique and binding by the major portion of mankind, serve as courts of ultimate appeal, and give to religious bodies a measure of historical continuity. Originally, a sacred book is not the creator but the product of a religion.

The Bible of Christianity, not to allude to other sacred writings, contains masses of psychological materials which are as yet unexplored. A systematic psychological exegesis of the Old and New Testament would revive and enrich the study of the Bible. Studies have been made of the psychology of the inspiration of the Scriptures, of the Old Testament prophet and the priest, of New Testament accounts of conversion, the cure of disease, demon possession, the gift of tongues, and types of religious personality, but there is still much land to be possessed. Hebrew legends, epics, hero tales, historical narratives, and wisdom literature, although not neglected, are packed with psychological implications which await further development.

The Observational

The method of personal observation applied unobtrusively and with the maximum elimination of bias and prejudice provides first-hand knowledge of specific forms of religious behavior and the conditions under which they are evoked. If one desires to make an objective study of the technique of the professional evangelist, the obvious procedure is to attend camp meetings and revival campaigns as an observer. The investigator studies the way in which the evangelist conducts the meeting, takes notice of the various items upon which he relies for the effect he endeavors to produce, such as the hymns announced, the prayers offered, the message proclaimed, and the special mechanics used to induce individuals to make an immediate public religious decision. The observer is attentive to the dominant ideas expressed, the emotions aroused, the motives appealed to, and the principles of mass psychology applied.

Various forms of religious and semi-religious practices lend themselves to the observational method of research. It is especially applicable to the study of group behavior. Immediately following the World War a recrudescence of occultism swept over vast sections of the population of several countries. I attended performances of ouija board operators not as a participant but as an interested spectator. The observations made were later psychologized and with the consent of the manipulators given publicity. Others made personal investigations of spiritistic seances and of the speaking with tongues in religious assemblies and kindred occult phenomena. Public gatherings can be visited with profit by the student of the psychology of religion if he exercises discretion and does not permit his presence to vitiate his purpose. For several years I have been an interested observer of revival meetings conducted by Negro evangelists in the colored sections of Chicago. I discovered that the meetings vary in emotional intensity and moral effect. Some Negro revivalists control the emotions of their audiences and are powers for righteousness; others strive for what can be called an emotional orgy. Among people depressed by poverty and ignorance, emotional religious intoxication may be a type of compensation.

The observational method affords a personal contact with the subjects investigated, which possesses a freshness and fascination nothing else can supply. One sees the forces of religion in actual operation in their accustomed setting. Books cannot take the place of life itself, although they may throw light upon human experience and teach the investigator what to seek and how to find it. Individuals, breathing and living, directly and seriously engaged in a religious quest for reality and personality realization in the midst of the trials, temptations, and vexations of daily life, constitute an opportunity for research which the psychologist dare not forfeit.

The Survey

Various types of social surveys may be made for the purpose of inaugurating changes which will quicken and spread religion. A particular phase of the religious life of a community or a local church may be surveyed. For instance, an investigation may be undertaken to determine the number and kinds of religious denominations represented in a given area of population. Another form of survey consists of historical researches. Dr. Kincheloe has studied the successive phases through which dying churches pass.[9] A third type of social survey is illustrated by the systematic examination of interrelated community conditions and activities and their bearing on the task of the churches. The part which the churches should play in the community may be estimated in the light of the nationalities of the population, housing conditions, public utilities, health measures, industrial and commercial activities, recreational facilities, educational opportunities, and philanthropic and ameliorative provisions. A fourth kind of survey is inclusive in its scope. All aspects of a local church may be canvassed, or every religious agency in a community explored in detail, and the findings assembled.

One or two representative types of religious surveys may be introduced as illustrations of the method as a whole. Under the direction of Professor Athearn a survey of seventeen church buildings in Malden, Mass., was made.[10] The purpose of the project was to show the extent to which the location and physical equipment of the several churches in the community aided or restricted their function. The service value of the church buildings was determined by the use of a score card. The perfect score for the six different phases considered was 1,000 points. The First Baptist Church, for example, was allotted 751 points. The building is situated at the inter-

[9] See Kincheloe, Samuel C., "The Behavior Sequence of a Dying Church," *Religious Education*, Vol. XXIV, No. 4, 1926, pp. 329-345. In this article the author traces the progressive steps in the decadence of a specific church as follows: The church began as a mission, it developed a thriving Sunday school, it was deprived of lay leadership through deaths and removals, children of incoming immigrants were won and in due time became leaders, church forums and weekday activities were promoted, the church applied for and received material aid from the home missionary board, dissension over the causes of the pending church crisis broke out among the members, a disposition grew to glorify the past and the sacredness of the building, a small group bore the burden of responsibility, volunteer workers from training schools came to the rescue and finally dominated the church, the old building was sold and converted into a bottling works, the congregation rented a hall, play and recreation were stressed, finally the church was dissolved.

[10] Athearn, Walter S., *The Malden Survey* (New York: George H. Doran Company, 1920).

section of two main streets of the city and is in close proximity to the public library and the high school. The auditorium is attractive and worshipful. The parish house contains a large number of separate classrooms and a serviceable kitchen.

In 1920 a company of from twenty to thirty surveyors investigated the religious education of Protestants in the state of Indiana.[11] A vast body of valuable information was accumulated. The object of this state-wide survey was to obtain the facts which would provide direction in formulating denominational, state, and national programs of Christian nurture, suggest improved methods of measuring and conducting the processes of religious development, and contribute guidance to local churches and communities in designing adequate buildings, determining budgets, and testing results. Indiana was selected for this survey because the state is centrally situated in our country, has a variety of physiographical and occupational conditions, has progressive educational leadership, and includes in its total population more than 900,000 Protestants. Important general conclusions and recommendations were offered. For example, it was discovered that the major problems of the organization and administration of religious education are centered in the small church schools. The religious leadership of the state was urged to give immediate expert attention to the small church school as a distinct educational problem.

In 1924 the Institute of Social and Religious Research began to publish the findings of city-church surveys. Realizing that churches in great numbers are governed by accident, chance, and error, competent surveyors have undertaken the investigation of local churches themselves and of the communities in which they are at work. The parish minister and his associated lay officials who are mindful of their responsibility may desire a survey of their entire church, or an intensive investigation of particular aspects of its work, or serviceable informa-

[11] Athearn, Walter S., Evenden, E. S., Hanson, W. L., Chalmers, William E., *The Religious Education of Protestants in an American Commonwealth*, Volume 1 of the Indiana Survey of Religious Education, 3 volumes (New York: George H. Doran Company, 1923).

tion about the racial and religious affiliations of the surrounding population. Without the creation and operation of elaborate machinery the interested leaders of the local church may themselves make the type of survey which is required. Books which offer guidance are available.[12]

The Experimental

The experimental method is applicable to the study of religious personality. Broadly considered, experiment is controlled observation for the purpose of discovering some unknown fact, effect, or principle. The experimenter and not the subject determines the test conditions under which the process is conducted. Ideally the experimenter should be able to isolate and govern at will and in turn each component of the situation studied.

The laboratory type of experimentation in religion has to date not proved successful. The laboratory procedure so far from engendering or deepening the consciousness of religious values actually tends to depress or inhibit it. The psychologist cannot at will and under laboratory conditions create or analyze a conversion experience. Religious attitudes, responses, and emotions are not aroused by the imposition of the formal laboratory technique upon the subject. Furthermore, the order of meanings, values, and standards which plays the stellar rôle in the religious life is not amenable to the apparatus of the laboratory.

On the other hand, experiments in religion in their natural setting may be conducted with success. An evangelist may by repeated trials ascertain to what sort of hymns an audience predominantly consisting of persons of a certain cultural stratum will react with the responses he desires to receive. A preacher may experimentally discover the type of sermon which ministers most effectively to the religious needs of his constituency. The religious educator, by putting various possibilities to the practical test, may outline the most fruitful program of Christian nurture for a given age group in the

[12] For example, Douglass, H. Paul, *How to Study the City Church* (New York: Doubleday, Doran & Co., Inc., 1928).

church school. The pastor in the course of his intimate work with individuals may learn how most effectively to guide the delicate process of religious adjustment in a crisis. The devout soul may learn what to pray for and how to pray through the intelligent practice of the prayer life. A man may determine for himself under what conditions the resources of the universe for the enrichment of personality may be made immediately available.

One may, for example, insist that if God is objectively real and is interested in us there should be some way of ascertaining his existence and concern. Trout refers to a teacher of religion who advised a student who desired assurance of the existence of a sympathetically attentive God to stand alone under the open sky on a moonlight night, look up at the stars, and pray, "God, if there be a god, make thyself known to me." [13] The teacher declared that if the student would follow directions he would experience the responsive presence of God. The young man took the advice of his teacher and in due time reported that the experiment performed in the mood of reverent inquiry had resulted in a certainty of a revelation of God. Trout wisely suggests that if several persons, sincerely desirous of the same experience, follow his example, the negative as well as the positive results should be recorded and studied. It is evident that the results of what may be called free experimentation, if they are to possess scientific value, must be obtained by a sufficient number of persons of critical but constructive intelligence.

The foregoing suggests the importance of a "control" in experimentation. A test of honesty by a carefully devised method is given to a company of unsuspecting school children taking an examination in one of their regular studies. The dishonest children are then isolated from their trustworthy mates. The experimenter now endeavors to ascertain what effect a series of informal talks on honesty will have on the cheaters. The dishonest children are next divided into two groups, the two being as much alike in moral character and

[13] Trout, David M., *Religious Behavior*, p. 477 (New York: The Macmillan Company, 1931).

numbers as it is possible to make them. The talks are given to only one group of cheaters. Next the same tests already applied are again surreptitiously given to both groups of the dishonest. The results obtained from the two groups are compared. The group from which the talks were withheld constitutes the control. If the results from both groups are the same—if, for example, the two show about the same measure of improvement—the legitimate inference is that the talks were not influential. If the group to which the talks were given shows moral betterment and the other registers no progress, the improvement may be attributed to the talks.

Not that the psychological laboratory has no bearing whatever on research in religion. Laboratory investigations of psychological processes which enter into recognizable religious experience are constantly being conducted. The degree of suggestibility of individuals representing various personality types, as Coe learned, may be experimentally determined and a correlation between the findings and responsiveness to a variety of religious appeals established. Requisite prearranged laboratory tests disclose temperamental predispositions such as the relative control of the subject by feeling, thought, or action, and make possible a prediction of the mode in which the religious impulse will be discharged. One may investigate the relation of intelligence, experimentally measured, to the religious convictions, attitudes, and practices of the subject. It is evident that all sorts of comparisons of the experimentally amenable psychological phenomena with religious relationships may be instituted, although the religious integration of personality is not achieved by a laboratory exercise.

The Evaluational

The method of critical evaluation, although the last to be described in this survey, is not the youngest technique of research nor the least important to be employed by the psychology of religion. Adopting this method, the investigator analyzes, compares, and appraises the findings and theories of others, adds to the gathered acceptable lore his own insights and factual data, and finally with these materials and principles weaves a fresh pattern.

One plunges into the tangled jungle of the unexplored literature which the psychology of religion has produced. A bibliographical study is made. The critical processes are brought to bear upon the pages of the books read, author is compared with author, contrasting conclusions are examined and weighed, the positive contributions of the various writers are assimilated, psychological and philosophical predispositions are recognized. Old facts are scrutinized in a new light. A fresh point of view is established. Original ideas and investigations are incorporated. Elements both old and new are combined into a complex but ordered whole.

Critical evaluation as a method extending the scientific knowledge of religion is incalculably productive. Apart from it, each contribution would be isolated and unrelated. The method associates the findings of various investigators in such a way that the significance of each for the others is disclosed. It brings to light problems which would otherwise not emerge. Discrepancies in the report of an individual investigator or among several scientists provide a psychological problem. For example, Starbuck and Coe are almost in accord in their calculations of the average age when conversion is experienced. Although working at the same time and making use of the same method, the average age which Leuba's materials indicate is considerably older. Another and more recent investigator, Clark, has drawn the conclusion from his sources of information that the average conversion age has been lowered and is less than that recorded by Starbuck and Coe. How can the difference between Leuba on the one hand and Starbuck and Coe on the other be reconciled? How to account for the differences between the three and Clark is a problem which the evaluation method creates. Any type of investigation which formulates problems, raises questions, arouses doubt, stimulates further inquiry, and makes a fresh synthesis imperative possesses merits which the student of religious personality cannot forego without loss.

CHAPTER X

CURRENT SCHOOLS OF PSYCHOLOGY AND RELIGIOUS PERSONALITY

THE purpose of this chapter is to present the leading implications for religion of the central principles of representative modern schools of psychology, such as structuralism, functionalism, behaviorism, Gestaltism, and a variety of theories which emphasize dynamic aspects of personality. We shall seek answers to such questions as the following: What insights into the character and function of religion do variant theories of personality afford? In what respects do the several psychologies differ in their appraisals of the religious life? Is religion rooted in the very texture of personality?

In order to avoid the misunderstanding to which the psychological treatment of religion is always exposed, it should be made clear once more that genuine religion is regarded as involving always a relationship to an objective divine Reality. It is not a mode of self-communing, and its significance cannot be exhausted, though it may be illumined, by analyzing psychologically the mental processes and relationships involved. Religion is man's apprehension of, and surrender to, an active Purpose in the world of human relationships, a Purpose greater and other than himself which, in proportion as he rightly responds to it, transforms and regulates his conduct, and unifies and completes the self. Religion thus defined touches the deeps of personality and transcends creedal statements and institutional organization, though these are normal intellectual and social expressions of the religious attitude.

The peculiar difficulties which beset psychology are in large measure the sources of the divergent schools which have developed in Europe and America. The materials of psychology are subtle and elusive and, therefore, difficult to collect, examine, understand, and classify. Variant interpretations of the same data are almost inevitable. Furthermore, psychology as an experimentally grounded science is only about sixty years old. The organization and stabilization of any branch of science occupies an extended period of time. Again, the personal equation is prolifically operative, for psychologists, like the men who labor in other specialized sciences or in the arts, are not absolutely objective in their approach and infallible in judgment.

Structuralism

Edward Bradford Titchener, a young Englishman and a former student of Wilhelm Wundt in Leipzig, began his career as a psychologist at Cornell University at the turn of the present century.[1] He founded and promoted a school of psychology variously known as existentialism, introspectionism, and structuralism. Since several psychologies originating either in America or Europe are in conflict with the principles of structuralism, the core of this school should be made our point of departure. The subject matter of psychology, Titchener maintained, is experience depending on a living organism. Structuralism is primarily concerned with the nature of experience as distinguished from performance or behavior. It endeavors to disregard meanings and everything else beyond the experience that is being studied. The appellation "structuralism" derives from Titchener's attempts to reduce consciousness to its primary elements. Titchener concluded that every idea, every emotion, every sensation is complex. Since every experience is a compound it is the task of the psychologist to analyze each process into its constituents. Titchener distinguished three basic experiences: sensation, affection, and image. It will suffice for present purposes to refer to his theory that a sensation is composed of characteristic elements of perception welded by their associations. As a structuralist Titchener strove to

[1] Titchener, Edward Bradford, *An Outline of Psychology* (New York: The Macmillan Company, 1896); *Experimental Psychology, Qualitative Instructor's Manual, Quantitative Instructor's Manual, Quantitative Student's Manual* (New York: The Macmillan Company, 1901-05); *A Primer of Psychology* (New York: The Macmillan Company, 1898); *A Textbook of Psychology* (New York: The Macmillan Company, 1909).

discover the fundamental units of sensation and how they combine to constitute various types of consciousness.

Titchener's psychological theory is often called introspectionism, especially when his method of studying mental processes is the subject of inquiry. He maintained that introspection which is scientifically valid can be practiced only by those who have subjected themselves to rigorous and specialized preparation. He repudiated the notion that solicitous preoccupation with one's own thoughts and feelings is scientific. He was fully cognizant of the difficulty of dependable observation of fluctuating mentality, of singling out for examination a process enmeshed with other personal experiences, of concentrating the attention on the contents of consciousness rather than on the external objects involved in the situation. At its best, scientific introspection is experimental. Titchener's monumental manuals of experimental psychology attest his confidence in this type of procedure. A scientific experiment—i.e., one that is accurate, controlled, and systematic—enables one to isolate, vary, and repeat an experience. The purpose for which psychological laboratories and instruments are provided is the careful study of mental phenomena, the clear description of the findings, and the discovery of laws underlying consciousness.

William James, with his usual brilliance, argued that the problem of the "brick and mortar" psychology, as structuralism was often called, is a manufactured problem since the existence of fundamental elements and a cohesive is an assumption.[2] The structural elements are not given in experience, and if they are unreal the psychologist is under no obligation to discover or posit something which fuses them into synthetic formations. Granting, for the sake of argument, that the formations of experience are compounded of simpler elements, the theory of association as the "mortar" is, in the opinion of many psychologists and philosophers, vulnerable. It is evident that

[2] As a psychologist James defied classification. He did not found a school. He was more than an eclectic, for his original additions advanced the science of psychology. Many of his insights anticipated the findings of later experimentalists. See James, William, *The Principles of Psychology*, 2 volumes (New York: Henry Holt & Co., 1890).

the implications for religion of this school are, to say the least, negative.

Functionalism

Several schools of psychology originating in either America or Europe have combated the theories of Titchener. In 1894, James Rowland Angell, a young man twenty-five years old, and John Dewey, ten years his senior, began their work at the University of Chicago.[3] In the course of time they evolved a school known as functionalism. Unlike Titchener, who devoted his energies to the dissection of processes, these two men explored and stressed the relation of mental operations to the adjustment of the individual to the world in which he lives. Functionalism is primarily concerned with the part which the mental life plays in the survival and self-realization of the individual. Although it is not exhaustively and systematically expounded in any works of its originators, it gives point and direction to the subject matter of their major books. Neither Dewey nor Angell intended to found a new school. Opposition directed against them made defense and differentiation from the Wundtian and Titchenerian tradition imperative, and lifted functionalism into prominence.

Functionalism inquires, How do mental activities conserve or enhance one's welfare? What is the consequence to the individual? It is evident that such questions cannot be answered by deliberately abstracting mentality from its natural setting and subjecting it to analysis, but by studying the operations in their environmental circumstances. Utilities so far from being banished from the realm of psychology were made the criteria of value. The enterprise of the psychologist was subordinated to its practical reference. Functionalism is rooted in the acquisition of experience and in its utility in guiding conduct or adaptive behavior.

Functionalism leans toward applied psychology. The con-

[3] Angell, James Rowland, *Psychology* (New York: Henry Holt & Co., 1904); *Introduction to Psychology* (New York: Henry Holt & Co., 1918). Dewey, John, *How We Think* (Boston: Heath & Co., 1910); *Human Nature and Conduct* (New York: Henry Holt & Co., 1922).

sideration of adjustments and adaptations of the biological organism of man to his environment, and of psychological processes in the setting in which they actually occur almost inevitably led to various direct and practical applications. It induced Dewey to institute in the field of education sweeping reforms designed to bring into more effective association the curriculum of the school and the totality of the pupil's interests. Psychological operations are the activities of beings who are swayed by purposes and therefore mentality cannot be dissociated from its conditions and consequences. Consciousness is the instrument whereby an adjustment to a novel situation is made. The learning process is facilitated by the pressure of the problems the solution of which contributes to the enrichment or preservation of life. Taking their cue from Darwin that mental operations are useful to living creatures in their struggle for survival, the functionalists have exploited the utilities of psychological activity.

Functionalism regards the mind as an instrument in the molding and remodeling of the environment to the needs of mankind. Experience is the interaction between the organism and the physical and social environment. Consequences both actual and anticipated become stimuli for behavior and determinants of conduct. Activity which is creative, which furthers the adaptation of the individual to his circumstances, is identified with intelligence. Instrumentalism, as this theory of mind is called, has but little to say about the nature of creative intelligence. Its answer to the question, What is the mind? is vague. Mind as such is simply a tool. It is a product of nature's experiments in evolution by which a living organism may attain its ends. Although an instrumentalistic conception of mind is in accord with the utilitarian spirit of the age, there are still those who at times engage in a critical investigation and dispassionate interpretation of personality, not for the sake of deriving a "cash value" from the enterprise, but in order to determine the nature and quality of mental activities, and their relation to one another and to the whole of which they are parts. And beauty is still its own excuse for being. Some entities and experiences stand in their own right and do not require the support of the biologically useful.   The army of seekers after wealth, power, and material conveniences is admittedly vast, but there yet remains a company of disinterested lovers of truth and beauty.

Functionalism has placed at the disposal of the psychology of religion a principle or a point of view which has been exceedingly fruitful.   It has stimulated inquiry into the part which active religion plays as the rallying center of personality. Studies have been made of the manifold ways in which religion actually functions in human relationships.   Catching the spirit of functionalism, psychologically trained investigators have explored religion, not as a discrete and detached phenomenon, but in the cultural setting in which it is effective.   They have raised and with some measure of success answered the question, What are the personal and social consequences of the religious attitude?   Attention has been directed to the purposes which religion serves, the goals it erects and seeks to reach, the emotional satisfaction it induces, the sense of security it imparts, the significance with which it invests life, the character building values it possesses, the bearing which it has on the conservation of the human organism, and the implications of it for the reconstruction or the creation of social institutions.   The functional approach examines and appraises the ramifications of the religious response to the universe.   Religion in actual practice works.   It is justified by its results. Not that the functional estimate is entirely commensurate with all that religion implies.   Content and structure as well as performance and result, validity as well as practicability, the transcendental as well as the phenomenal, must be embraced in a comprehensive study of the religiously integrated personality.

Watsonian Behaviorism

A vigorous if not virulent protest against both structuralism and functionalism and all their works proceeded from John B. Watson.[4]   Titchener, as we have had occasion to remark, was not scientifically occupied with performance but with subjec-

4 Watson, John B., *Psychology from the Standpoint of a Behaviorist* (New York: J. B. Lippincott Company, 1919).   *Behaviorism* (New York: W. W. Norton & Co., 1925).

tive states and processes. His method was that of disciplined introspection. Watson rejected the structuralist's mode of procedure as lacking in objectivity and reliability, and denied the validity of most of the concepts of traditional psychology. Watson reacted against the concept of consciousness which functionalism espoused, and declared that to obtrude the mental is to cling to the superstition which gave birth to the erroneous and vicious notion of a soul. He made behavior interpreted in terms of the conditioned reflex, already experimentally explored by Russian scientists, the keystone of a school of psychology.

Orthodox Watsonian behaviorism is an organic and mechanistic theory of man and animals. Physiology, strictly speaking, investigates the functions of individual parts of the body, such as the hands, stomach, and eyes, but behaviorism has to do with the activity of the organism as a whole. The proper subject matter of psychology is behavior, and the method is objective and controlled experimentation. Watson claims that the sum total of organic activity consists of organizations of component processes and is ultimately reducible to specific stimulus-response connections. The mechanical reaction of the organism to external and internal stimuli is the basic postulate of behaviorism. Emotions are not specializations of feeling, are not "mental," but are bodily reactions involving chiefly the glandular system and the involuntary muscles such as those of the blood vessels and the intestines. Specific behavior which conserves or furthers the welfare of the organism is called intelligent. We arrive at intelligence by way of previous automatic responses variously conditioned and organized. Thought is a motor setting. Muscular habits acquired in actual speech result in implicit or internal speech, which is thought. When subvocal talking is absent, thinking may occur in terms of manual and visceral operations. Thinking is thus reducible to purely physiological processes. A so-called higher mental activity is, in the final analysis, a compound of modified or arrested reflexes.

The warfare which orthodox behaviorism wages against metaphysical concepts which it is alleged render an impartial examination of a human being difficult, if not impossible, would be more justifiable if the behaviorist did not interpose his own philosophical affiliations. Behaviorism is frankly mechanistic. It has much to say about the elaboration and integration of reflexes, but relegates mind or self as so much rubbish to the void of outgrown superstitions. Quite undismayed by the magnitude of its major premise, behaviorism attempts to reconstruct the science of psychology without reference to anything but physiological energies and measurable mechanical processes.

Watsonian behaviorism pours unmeasured contempt upon religion, grossly misrepresents its origin and true nature, and is resolved to exterminate it. Religion, it is affirmed, had its origin among clever persons who were too indolent to work with their hands. They unscrupulously devised means for the control of others. They learned to dominate the less intelligent through fear. They gained elaborate control over others through the invention of signs, symbols, ritual, and the like. The medicine men, as these charlatans were called, succeeded in accomplishing their purpose: they did not have to do manual work and enjoyed the best of everything. As the control of the medicine men became organized, religions and temples were evolved. Fearsome gods were created; in fact, God is a group or national medicine man.

The behaviorist who runs true to form, Watson continues, seeks to replace religion by experimental ethics based on objective methods. He predicts that the time will come when experimental ethics will determine the manner of living which best furthers the growth and the adjustment of the individual. Behavioristic ethics will decide whether it is best, from the standpoint of adjustments, to have one wife or many wives, prohibition or no prohibition, no divorces or divorces, a family life or never to know our own fathers and mothers. He appears to assume that the ethical experience and precepts of the revered teachers of humanity have to date been futile.

Gestalt Psychology

A third and more constructive reaction against structuralism and also one of the chief opponents of behaviorism is the

German school called, for lack of an exact English equivalent, the Gestalt psychology. Max Wertheimer and Wolfgang Köhler, both at the University of Berlin, and Kurt Koffka, now a research professor at Smith College, created this school and have succeeded in giving it prominence and recognition.[5] Structuralism, we recall, attempts to reduce states of consciousness to basic units, and to reveal the laws underlying the combining of elements into more elaborate processes. The core of the Gestalt psychology is, negatively, the criticism that the atomistic approach to mentality is fruitless since in an analysis of experience the essential something escapes; and, positively, the affirmation that only in the comprehension of a situation as a unified whole is an understanding of it made possible.

The constitution of the mind is such that it achieves appreciation through native synthetic activity. When we observe our world we see not bundles of elements, but definite objects like stones and trees and hills. The term Gestalt, although not easily definable or translatable, refers to a configuration or pattern of experience. Configurational structures are inherent in perception, thought, and action, and give these order and value. The development of perception, imagination, memory, and reason consists in the expansion of native patterns in increasing variety and complexity.

The distinction between object and environment, between figure and ground, is by the Gestaltists considered essential in the process of perception. The object seems to have outline and form, but the background appears like extended space; hence, the object or figure is more likely than the background to capture the attention. When his mother bends over his cradle the baby, according to the Gestalt psychologists, does not see a mere collection of points, does not experience clusters of sensations, undistinguished from their surroundings, but perceives a mass of color standing out from its background, a

---

[5] Köhler, Wolfgang, *The Mentality of Apes* (New York: Harcourt, Brace & Co., 1925); *Gestalt Psychology* (New York: H. Liveright, 1929). Koffka, Kurt, *The Growth of the Mind* (New York: Harcourt, Brace & Co., 1924).

figure which in time he comes to recognize. Not that he at first sees her face accurately, or knows what it is. The all-important thing is that he sees the face as a visual unit and thereby begins the project of familiarizing himself with its special characteristics considered in their relation to the totality.

The constitution of the mind is such that it achieves appreciation through native unified activity. Whistler's portrait of his mother makes its intended appeal when it impresses itself as a totality upon the observer, but its potential effect is vitiated when it is dissected and each segment dissociated from the rest. When one looks at this masterpiece one may observe in rapid succession the cap, the features in repose, the hands resting in the lap, the gown and other details, but it is all these together and each with reference to the others which create a totality which makes one see in the figure one's own mother symbolized. An object of perception is other and more than the mere sum of its parts; from the unified combination of related processes there issue a unique quality and significance.

The implications of the Gestalt psychology for religion are varied and weighty. The emphasis which this school places upon meaning and purpose supports the religious evaluation of the world of nature and man. Religion invests the ordinary occupations and concerns of human life, such as labor and play, education and politics, marriage and parenthood, with a peculiar inner significance. When religion has atrophied, these things lose their supreme import. Purpose initiates, outlines, regulates, and sustains action. The continuation of the routine of living becomes monotonous if not actually depressive when it is no longer animated by a religious purpose. When the tiresome is incorporated in a pattern of relationships tedium vanishes. To regard the details of living in the light of an aim religiously sanctioned is to be actuated by a relation which is intellectually stimulating, ethically productive, and emotionally satisfying.

It follows that religion has its being in a complex of relationships. It moves in a resisting medium the conquest of which quickens personality, arouses to activity its deeper-lying strata, and makes explicit its constructive possibilities. Religion thrives within a frame of reference. Nothing is religious which at the same time is not something else. Commerce could not maintain itself as such apart from buying and selling, banking and transportation, to say nothing of production. Religion, analogously, is so interwoven with life that it cannot be dissociated from it without loss of existence. It is as if one inquired which detail of a given masterpiece constitutes it a work of art. Religion cannot be itself in isolation from life, but exists in all that is of moment to a human being. It is not this thing alone, nor that, which constitutes religion, but the regulation of the sum of one's patternized reactions by a sense of Reality. Religion is not a separate or separable entity, but an approach to the universe, an approach which is enmeshed in the context of life. It functions in a total set of conditions in which it is inescapably entangled. The peculiar properties of religion are functions of the totality to which it lends significance. The atomistic or analytic approach is unreal and destroys the essence of religion. Meanings and purposes are inextricably involved in the relationships which men foster, and are, therefore, not amenable to abstraction from life or reduction to constituent elements without forfeiture of quality.

The pedagogical applications of the Gestalt school are exceedingly profitable. Christian nurture should give due consideration to the principle that unified wholes are the data of perception. The practice of transmitting the contents of the Bible, apart from the life affairs of moment to the learner, has failed to motivate Christian conduct. The Gestalt psychology supports the progressive principle in Christian education. The meeting of actual life-situations considered as functional units, by appropriate principles directly applied, is the most effective procedure of Christian culture. In this procedure the living Word again becomes flesh. Creative or progressive religious education proceeds within a framework of experience and, rejecting the atomistic approach, utilizes life-problems as wholes.

Dynamic Psychologies

While schools to which reference has been made were coming to the fore, a group of psychologies centering in instincts, impulses, motives, urges, and drives developed. A wide variety of theories possessing this common feature may be subsumed under the caption of dynamic psychology. Strange bedfellows are brought together by this comprehensive classification, including McDougall with his goal-seeking or hormic emphasis, Woodworth with his stress on drives, Freud with his theory of repressed infantile sexuality, Adler with his concept of the will to power, and Jung with his attempt to unite in a new formation the central teachings of Freud and Adler. However much each one of these psychologies differs from the others, all are grounded in motivation and its consequences.

Of the various aspects of human nature the hormic psychology regards purpose as fundamental. According to William McDougall, the chief advocate of this emphasis, purposive activity involves the perception of a situation, the prediction of the results to be obtained, the actual pursuit of an end, and satisfaction when the goal has been reached.[6] While knowing and feeling are genuine facts, the will to live and achieve is primary. He stoutly resists the conception that the influence of reason in human conduct is primary. A fundamental of McDougall's theory is that the instincts and the instinctive tendencies are the prime movers of activity, including intellectuality. Each of the seven instincts which he lists is associated with a specific emotion; for example, pugnacity with anger, and flight with fear. The emotional and the instinctive are thus brought together in a relation of dynamic intimacy.

The hormic psychology, stressing goal-seeking as the center of personality, supports the age-old religious conviction that at the heart of the universe purpose pulsates. McDougall's viewpoint implies the reality of ethical and religious principles which cannot be discarded without irreparable loss.

[6] McDougall, William, *Introduction to Social Psychology* (London: Methuen & Co., 1908) ; *Outline of Psychology* (New York: Charles Scribner's Sons, 1923) ; *Outline of Abnormal Psychology* (New York: Charles Scribner's Sons, 1926).

Robert S. Woodworth, also, is engrossed in reasons why people do things, in the springs of action, in motives.[7] Psychology, Woodworth declares, has occupied itself chiefly with the mechanics of mental processes, with the problem of how we think or how we learn or remember, and he proposes to devote attention to dynamics, to the problem of why we engage in psychic activity. In pursuing the ramifications of his task he inevitably makes what he himself calls the workings of the mind the field of investigation. Drives are accorded a place of prime importance in his system.

He differs with McDougall in including such native capacities as aptitudes and gifts in his list of dynamics. These drives, Woodworth maintains, lie outside the realm of instincts. An individual who is musical is responsive to certain materials in his environment, and it is this native readiness which makes him eager and efficient in developing the mechanism or technique for the realization and expansion of his particular gift. The native aptitudes are related to the intellectual rather than to the emotional or to the conative phases of human nature, but they are, nevertheless, potent spurs of appropriate activity.

Woodworth is not a finalist. He does not take sides in the controversy between introspectionism and behaviorism, for he utilizes the data provided by both. He freely concedes the incompleteness and the tentativeness of the science of psychology, and is a student of the problems of the workings of the mind rather than the defender of a closed system.

Woodworth's contention that the instincts are not the only spurs to activity but that interests rooted in other areas of personality, once they have become established and gained momentum, are powerful drives, is of the utmost significance to the psychology of religion. As has been stated in the discussion of the nature of religion the psychologist maintains, on the basis of his resurvey of human nature, that man is not endowed with a religious instinct which functions without guidance when the appropriate stimulus is applied. Man is

[7] Woodworth, Robert S., *Dynamic Psychology* (New York: Columbia University Press, 1918); *Psychology* (New York: Henry Holt & Co., revised edition, 1929).

not incurably religious in the sense that he is endowed with an instinct identified with a complex of religious emotions. Woodworth's dynamic psychology shows that religion as a developed capacity or a deliberately cultivated drive is as influential a determinant of outlook and conduct as any instinct in man's native equipment. Furthermore, it emphasizes by inference the necessity of surrounding growing personality with the religious culture from which it may utilize what is needful for the good life.

The psychology known as Freudian psychoanalysis revolves, according to the recent re-thinking of its promulgator, Sigmund Freud, about three dynamic concepts—the id, the ego, and the superego.[8] Although the latest reformulation of this theory has not yet been developed in every detail, the leading principles and many of their ramifications may be discerned with sufficient clarity to make the system as a whole comprehensible.

The id corresponds to the notion of the unconscious, that realm of personality which is primitive, non-moral, obscure, and imperious. It includes the sexual urge, and the tendencies which the individual has suppressed. The core of personality is the libido or the sexual instinct. The libido and the social order are in conflict.

A negotiator, an intelligent agent—namely, the ego—develops; its function is to cope with external situations and effect adjustments. The ego is the mediator between the id and reality or environment. It is an extension of the id. The ego is gifted with perception, requires knowledge, and possesses the ability to manipulate the environing forces. Self-love is the result of the id's being infatuated with the ego.

The superego is the fiend in the complexity of human nature. The superego is organized about the adopted standards of the individual. It is unenlightened, infantile, and arbitrary. The

[8] Freud, Sigmund, *Psychopathology of Daily Life* (New York: The Macmillan Company, 1914); *A General Introduction to Psychoanalysis* (New York: Boni & Liveright, 1920); *The Ego and the Id* (London: The Hogarth Press, 1927); *Autobiography* (New York: W. W. Norton & Co., 1935).

superego develops when the child accepts as mandatory the obligations and prohibitions imposed upon him by his parents. Its components are derived from the confused and highly emotional moral and aesthetic emergencies of childhood. The superego inflicts punishment upon the individual himself when its dictates are set aside. It demands satisfaction in terms of remorse or expiation for deeds which the doer does not even consciously condemn.

That conflicts both numerous and disintegrating arise within such a framework of codes at variance with one another and with the outer world is inevitable. Thwartings, anxieties, fears, designed accidents, and self-castigations are the consequences of the contrary currents of such a psychic pattern. The basic dynamic concepts of psychoanalysis are sexuality, infantile experience, and repressions.

Freudian and other investigations disclose that an impulse or event subconsciously buried or forgotten may, if it is of sufficient importance to the individual, be dynamic enough to influence attitude or conduct. A young woman who had lost the remembrance of the impressions which the mode of worship of the Episcopal church made upon her as a young child could derive so little benefit from the nonliturgical services of the church with which she united that she resolved to sever connections and entirely to abandon church attendance. One day, however, by force of circumstances she attended divine worship in an Episcopal church. Here the lack which she had felt for years was supplied. In all probability the impact of the Episcopal church upon her early years became an active subconscious need which in her adulthood could be fulfilled only by a resumption of the liturgical type of worship.

The dynamic psychology of Freud has important bearings on religious education, and the diagnosis and therapy of personality difficulties. The reality of consciousness, the significance of early religious impressions, the possibility as well as the urgency of adult reconstruction, the sublimation of crude human impulses, and the catharsis of confession have staged a creative revolution in education and religion. Psychoanalysis has provided a technique for the solution of personality adjustment problems.   The religious worker who utilizes the psychological approach to his task, adapting Freud's principles, recognizes in the maladjusted individual the following progressive steps: a drive, a thwart, flight or hatred, guilt, and anxiety.   Taking into account the contributions of Adler and Jung as well as those of Freud, the skilled counselor observes the following stages in the therapy of the morally defeated individual: recognition of the source of maladjustment, desire for the reintegration of the self, release from the sense of guilt, personality reconstitution, and a consequent renaissance or effective style of life.

Freud became estranged from Alfred Adler and Carl G. Jung because they proposed to modify his teaching of the centrality of sexuality.   Although Freud gave to sexuality a signification broad enough to include the whole pleasure life of the individual, a meaning embracing such simple practices as bathing and smoking and such complex developments as religious ceremonies and political and social institutions, or perhaps because of his extreme extension of sexuality, these men were alienated and proceeded to blaze new trails.   Both contend that sexuality is only one form in which personality expresses itself.

Adler stresses the will to power.[9]   According to him, sexual details illustrate and illuminate a deeper principle which is the urge for completeness, security, status, and superiority.   Adler's theory that the impulse to excel is the central motivating force of personality is weighted with numerous implications for religious culture.   The desire to be superior may condition a disjunctive or conjunctive form of philosophy and behavior. If the fundamental urge to exercise power is socialized, the individual is faithful in the stewardship of his abilities and possessions.

If the will to power is antisocial, or conflicts with one's competencies, or is obstructed by the environing culture, one

[9] Adler, Alfred, *The Neurotic Constitution* (New York: Moffat, Yard & Co., 1917); *The Practice and Theory of Individual Psychology* (New York: Harcourt, Brace & Co., 1924); *Understanding Human Nature* (New York: Greenberg, Inc., 1927).

may become mentally disordered. For example, overcompensation among women for limitations imposed by a world controlled by the men often takes an intensified and exaggerated form known as the masculine protest. One type of woman smarting under the disadvantages of living in a social order ruled by the men adopts a masculine rôle. This woman becomes ambitious and energetic, she attempts to excel her brothers and other men in their vocational and recreational activities, she evades the responsibilities of wifehood and motherhood. Another type of woman assumes a negative attitude, an attitude of supine resignation. This woman is subservient. She may induce neurotic symptoms which serve her purpose. She exhibits a helplessness and clumsiness designed to arouse sympathy for her. A third type of woman, feeling condemned to be an inferior being, openly lauds the privileged position of the men. A woman of this kind sings the praise of the men as the doers and achievers. By way of revenge for her subordinate status she shifts responsibilities of all sorts upon the men. Under the guise of recognition of masculine superiority she exclaims, "Only the men are competent to do thus and so." With rare penetration Adler has described these three types, the origins of the outlook and attitude of each, and the various forms of overcompensation for the ensuing sense of inferiority.

In this volume repeated use is made of Adlerian concepts, terminology, and teaching. At this juncture only one or two implications for religious living of Adler's theories and findings will be suggested. The socialization of personality which Adler stresses is an objective of Christian culture. The several varieties of the masculine protest are heeded by a religion which teaches the common fatherhood of God and the universal human fraternity. As St. Paul says, "There can be neither Jew nor Greek, there can be neither bond nor free, there can be no male and female; for ye all are one man in Christ Jesus." [10] In a true church there is no clash of the

[10] Galatians 3: 28. St. Paul's admonition to women to keep silent in the church meetings and not to pray with uncovered heads may be regarded as concessions to social custom and expediency rather than as an essential of the gospel as he understood and preached it.

sexes. Men and women are united in building the kingdom of love on earth. So far from rivaling one another, the one sex complements the other in a co-operative enterprise. Adler's exposure of the points of friction between men and women in their unsocialized state and the dangers inherent in overcompensation should give the religious leader guidance. Real Christianity in practice offers women as well as men reconciliation with life by guaranteeing them sex equality.

Jung incorporated the divergent basic conceptions of Freud and Adler in a unique synthesis.[11] The motive of sexuality or that of the will to power seemed to Jung to be an inadequate dynamic explanation of the behavior of all people. The fundamental principles of neither, he holds, is capable of universal application. The chief source of personality difficulty is the fact that circumstances have kept the individual from doing and being what he prefers. The victim of environmental conditions is in the course of time frustrated, unhappy, and socially maladjusted. Obviously the Jungian specialist seeks to aid the consultant in the discovery of buried and unfulfilled longings, and to guide him in the planning of a life which will be more satisfactory. Jung has been particularly successful with persons in middle life, for it is in that period when repressed desires are most potent.

In his doctrine of psychological types of personality Jung recognizes and at least in skeletal form preserves both the Freudian and the Adlerian teachings. He reasons that the individual who is motivated primarily by sexuality is occupied chiefly by the love-object, and that the attention of the person who is activated principally by the desire for superiority is largely engaged by his own concerns. The former is an extrovert, the latter an introvert. We do not comprehend the salient point of Jung's typology if we do not clearly understand that the classification is determined not so much by what one is supremely interested in as by why. A salesman may be either an extrovert or an introvert. If he engages in the sale

[11] Jung, Carl G., *Psychology of the Unconscious* (New York: Moffat, Yard & Co., 1916); *Psychological Types* (New York: Harcourt, Brace & Co., 1926).

of goods chiefly in order to enhance his own reputation by winning the plaudits of his fellows, he is an introvert. On the other hand, if he sells an article in order to achieve an effect in the outer world, if his life energy expends itself predominantly in the acquisition of wealth for its own sake, he is an extrovert. It is evident that some individuals may be swayed by the extrovert principle on one occasion and by the introvert on another; in fact, they may be controlled by either form of motivation in a given situation. Since many persons are consistent representatives of neither type, it has been found expedient to embrace the characteristics of both types in a composite classification called ambiversion.

Jung's analytic psychology has given religious workers a classification of personalities which reveals the folly and danger of proceeding on the assumption that all human beings are alike in needs, preferences, disposition, possibilities, and ways of reacting to stimuli. The extrovert and the introvert do not express their religious idealism in the same manner. The division of humanity into extroverts, introverts, and ambiverts naturally suggests a more elaborate classification of personalities. Further and further refinement of classification is bound to lead to the conclusion that in the final analysis the vast majority of human beings cannot be pigeonholed as pure types. In fact, the varieties within each category are numerically coextensive with the individuals who come within its purview. The principle of individual variation suggests that it is a primary function of the religious counselor to encourage each personality to develop its own particular capacities, and to approach every case of religious conflict in accordance with its own intimate characteristics. The qualities of individuality are the inalienable possessions of every person.

It has often been alleged that Jung teaches that God exists and that man has a soul. The God he introduces is, however, not the God of Christian tradition, and the soul he describes is not the self which is the conscious center of human experience. The God of Jung is a composite of the forces which drive us to the realization of our highest ideals. The soul or psyche, Jung teaches, is a racial unconsciousness, a collection of archaic remnants, a complex of primordial images which have drifted from a mother sea of crude figures into the mind during our dreams or abnormal mental states.

Conclusion

A brief comparison of the main tenets of the schools of psychology to which references have been made, together with their respective implications for the religious life, will recapitulate the findings of the present investigation. Structuralism, which is our point of departure, being an attempt to reduce mental processes, without regard to their significance, to their constituent elements and to trace their fusion into combinations through experience alone, offers little support to religion and is psychologically and philosophically presumptuous. An integrating agency, a self, is a fundamental religious belief. Functionalism as opposed to structuralism investigates mentality in its environmental context and stresses the part which consciousness plays in the adaptation of the individual to the world in which he lives. Its evasive or nebulous attitude toward the nature of mind leaves religion in the lurch. On the other hand, the application of its central principle makes prominent constructive personal and social consequences of religion. Watsonian behaviorism, which rejects structuralism but adopts some of the points of functionalism, would exclude from the science of psychology all except stimulus and response. It is a physiological interpretation of man. Its philosophical affiliations are mechanistic. Its insistence on experimentation, if not carried to extremes, is wholesome and should encourage the validation of religious truth in actual practice. Gestaltism abjures the atomistic approach on which structuralism places its reliance, and yields the primacy to the comprehension of units. It stresses integration rather than analysis. While not as utilitarian as functionalism, Gestaltism observes mental life as a network of relationships. Religion, since it is synthetic, appreciative, and lives in a frame of references, derives support from the Gestalt school. The several varieties of dynamic psychology are based on motivation in its manifold forms. Purposive psychology, which inquires why people react, rather than how, is an ally of religion. The clinical dynamic psychologies of Freud, Adler, and Jung have added to our understanding and therapy of the adjustment problems of individuals. The bearing of confession, prayer, conversion, religious instruction, and other procedures of the church on the development of personality is now more intelligently appreciated.

Despite radical differences in standpoint, each of these psychologies in at least some of its characteristics bears witness to the human urge to achieve unity of personality and enrichment of experience. Structuralism implies that these common goals are reached through experience as such, functionalism through the development of the utilitarian properties of mind, behaviorism through appropriate conditioned behavior, Gestaltism through the situational and synthetic approach, the dynamic schools through various arrangements of life including purposeful control of the instinctive and emotional equipment, the resolution of conflicts between impulse and accepted standards, and the socialization of the will to power. Now the consistency and enlargement of personality are two basic ends of the religious attitude. In diverse manners current schools of psychology lead us to the threshold of religion.

PART TWO

RELIGIOUS EXPERIENCE AND PERSONALITY

CHAPTER XI

RELIGIOUSLY INTEGRATED PERSONALITY

In ordinary speech the word "personality" is used in a confusing variety of senses. One of the most frequent significations which it is intended to convey is that of attractiveness. In a letter of recommendation to a school board an administrative officer of a normal college may say of a candidate for a teaching position, "She is a young woman of good health, neat appearance, character, ability, and personality." In such a context personality clearly means the combination of qualities which make one charming and magnetic. From the standpoint of individual psychology personality includes not only whatever of social graces and winsomeness one may have, but also health, appearance, character, and ability. In general the psychologist speaks of personality as the entire being of any individual, the sum total of his organic and mental possessions and functions both acquired and inherited.

Personality at its psychological best is a human organization in which integration and unity have been achieved. An organization is a union of parts functionally related to one another in such a manner that the whole has a distinct character and serves a definite purpose. Organizations differ, it is patent, in complexity of structure and in the ends which they serve. A broom is a relatively simple organization consisting of two things, a brush and a handle to which it is attached, and is applied in the removal of particles from floors, carpets, rugs, and other surfaces. The use of a broom stirs up dust which is detrimental to health and which settles upon the walls and the articles of furniture in a room, is laborious, and is not entirely effectual. It occurred to an ingenious mind that certain objectionable features of the broom might be eliminated or minimized. The carpet sweeper, a more highly organized broom, was invented. A revolving brush under a cover sweeps the particles upon shelves. The use of the contrivance reduces the energy requirement and disposes of the hazards of flying dust. On the other hand, at least one toilsome operation was not performed by either the broom or the carpet sweeper. In order to bring to the surface the embedded dust it was necessary to remove the rugs from the floor and to apply a carpet beater. Somebody invented a device which combines in one mechanical whole the essential functions of the broom, the carpet sweeper, and the rug beater—the vacuum cleaner. By means of suction this still higher form of organization removes the deeplying dust, and by means of a stationary brush catches lint, string, and other loose materials on the surface of the rug. Dustless beating and sweeping are accomplished in a single operation. It is conceivable that an inventive person may increase the number of functions performed by the vacuum cleaner now used in the home. The brush and the handle are factors common to the three implements, the broom, the carpet sweeper, and the vacuum cleaner. A plying movement is a constant principle in the use of each. Each one is a consolidation of related parts which more or less effectively serves a purpose.

In the realm of biology organization ranges from the relatively simple structure and activity of the unicellular species to the intricate organism and competencies of man. He, too, is a union of components. The extent and quality of personality organization is determined by three things: environmental influences, native equipment, and the governing philosophy of life. The three determinants are the raw materials from which character is fashioned. That they cannot be sharply distinguished in all their ramifications must be evident to anyone who has attempted to trace the relation of any one to the other two. The three constitute an indivisible and indissoluble whole, but each in turn may be abstracted from the others and characterized.

Environment

Environmental forces, the surrounding conditions under which one lives, contribute more to the making of personality

than the ordinary observer is inclined to suppose.   Man is
profoundly affected by the outstanding characteristics of the
geographical area in which he develops personality.   Climate,
for example, stimulates or depresses potentialities of human
nature.   Life in the two frigid zones of the globe is strenuous
but relatively simple, and therefore personality is organized
in terms of elementary relationships.   What with the heat
and prodigality of the vegetation, personality in the tropics is
generally indolent, sensuous, and relatively economically carefree.   It is in the temperate zones that man has evolved the
most elaborate personality patterns.   In Europe and North
America an industrial civilization based on scientific invention
has revolutionized man's mode of living and left its impress on
personality.   The effect of climate can be observed in the change
which personality undergoes when a man leaves the zone in
which he has lived and takes up his abode in another.   A typical
American Midwesterner, energetic and ambitious, who migrates
to the torrid zone becomes in the course of time, and often
despite resolutions to the contrary, phlegmatic and slovenly.
Influenced by the climate, to say nothing of the impinging
social forces, he exhibits a pronounced tendency to "go native."

The social environment in which the individual is enmeshed
is the major determinant of personality.   Our social inheritance
is a conglomeration of such factors as language, literature, religion, occupational opportunity, standards of morals and de-
portment, habits of thought and action.   In fact, personality
develops in a social context.   The infant is so dependent on
others of his species that it is practically impossible to imagine
how he could survive in isolation from them.   If by some
miracle he could maintain his existence and grow up he would
be void of so many competencies associated with adult personality that we could call him subhuman.   He would have no
articulated language tool, his thinking would be restricted to
the simplest relations, his talents for the most part would be
undeveloped, he would experience unidentified urges originating
in the gonads, but would have no sexual life, he would wear no
clothing, he would have no religion, no morals, no marked
aesthetic appreciation.   When the contributions of the social

order are abstracted from personality one is amazed at the debt to the environing culture.

The varieties of culture patterns lay the foundations for different standards of excellence. For example, the person who has learned to appreciate European musical masterpieces, the works of composers like Bach, Beethoven, and Brahms, will find Chinese music thin, harsh, and grating, if not positively excruciating. The Chinese, steeped in his art inheritance, takes no aesthetic pleasure in European styles of music. Aesthetic appreciation is not an inborn category which functions without learning or in any art situation, but is a capacity which is developed through exercise in a cultural setting.

Our conception of what constitutes occupational success is similarly derived from our social inheritance. The American Indian who has been relatively uninfluenced by the white man's idea of success teaches his children to do many things with their hands, to do them all well, and to do them with a generous expenditure of time and effort. The Indian's standard of success in the routine of living reflects an observable type of cultural tradition which takes pride in manual dexterity. We Americans intentionally or otherwise give our children the distinct impression that success in the world's work consists in doing a few things well, in doing them with brain or machine, and in doing them quickly and for the largest possible amount of pecuniary gain. In a highly competitive industrial social structure such a standard of success is a normal resultant.

Furthermore, the vocational predicament of myriads of our workers in industry severely restricts the expansion of personality. The employee in many a factory is not allowed to converse freely with other toilers during working hours; he performs a single mechanical operation times without number and day after day, often he does not know how what he does is related to the finished product; he has no opportunity to exercise such distinctively human functions as initiative, reflection, and self-expression. He must seek elsewhere during his leisure periods for stimulation and for an outlet for the competencies which constitute him a personality. Mass production by means of complicated machinery has made the reduction of the daily number of hours of work in industry economically imperative and thereby shortened the period of personality mechanization, but it itself does not provide positive opportunities for, and guidance in, the development of human potentialities. In an industrial order which is highly specialized the vocational life of the toiler offers but little inspiration and direction for self-realization. The church and other community organizations must supply the deficiency as best they may through programs for leisure time.

The insight and outlook of personality does, then, vary with the kind of social forces which play upon human beings. To be sure, social patterns change and new combinations are made from old materials, but no man can completely escape the environing culture. The social rebel, the man who revolts against the transmitted and generally accepted order, is stimulated by his environment. He too lives and moves and has his being in a complexity of social forces. He makes use of the major part of his social opportunities, of the products of society, of the techniques which an industrial order places at his disposal in order to overthrow that part of the social structure of which he disapproves, and to replace it with the pattern he champions.

Heredity

To submit what purports to be an exhaustive list of the inherited components of personality would be a hazardous undertaking. Our knowledge of original human nature must transcend its present limitations before we may with confidence venture to enumerate all the specific possessions and functions with which nature has endowed man. Nevertheless, a few which are of special importance for the organization of personality may be introduced.

One thinks first of all of the organism. Each of us has a body with certain characteristics, such as the color of the skin and eyes, the texture of the hair, the shape of the head, weight, and the form and size of the trunk and limbs. Some people are lank, thin, and tall. Others are muscular and well-proportioned. Still others are relatively short, stout, and thick-set. The bodies of many do not conform to any one of these patterns.[1] That the person whose body is well developed and proportioned possesses an initial advantage in the organization of wholesome personality seems to require no elaborate argumentation. Mere size produces effects; the presence of a large man overawes many small men. Some men have strong faces, others have weak faces. Appropriate physical types are selected for various parts of a stage play. Who has seen a fat and bald-headed leading man in a drama of romantic love? The size, proportion, and development of the organism sustains a relation to the building of a personality which is more determining than many have suspected.

No sharp line of demarcation separates the mental and the physical functions. The correlation of the two is so intimate that the one affects the other. Conflicts may be occasioned by bodily singularities. A sense of inferiority has been implanted in many a boy whose red hair has been made an object of ridicule by his schoolmates. A man of short stature is likely to add to himself a compensatory cubit such as speaking in a loud tone and with a dogmatic attitude. Conflicts induced by other than organic elements profoundly modify bodily functions. Anger suspends the process of digestion and prepares the body for an attack. The inseparability of the body and personality is indicated by the systems of organs and activities which compose the biological basis of man, such as those of metabolism, reproduction, sensitivity, conduction, and motility.

The endocrine glands constitute a biological system which provides the groundwork for various personality qualities. These internal glands—the pineal, pituitary, adrenal, thymus, gonad, and thyroid—pour secretions into the blood stream which in turn carries them to all parts of the body with consequent changes in the activities of different organs and in the

[1] This classification of human beings has been ably advanced by Paul Edward Kretschmer in his *Physique and Character* (New York: Harcourt, Brace & Co., 1926). The first type he calls the asthnic, the second the athletic, the third the pyknic.

personality as a whole.[2] The active chemical principles of the glandular secretions have been called hormones, but now they are more accurately termed autacoids. The thyroid and the adrenal glands play such conspicuous parts in personality development that they together with the pituitary body may well be selected from the group of endocrines for brief comment.

The thyroid is situated at the base of the neck; in fact, it rests on the trachea like a pair of spectacles on the nose. Its secretion, the active ingredient of which 60 per cent is iodine, appears to regulate the speed of brain activity. If an excessive amount of thyroxine, the thyroid autacoid, is produced, the mental activities are accelerated, the imagination runs riot, the pulse rate is increased, and irritability and emotional instability occur. Reduction in the size of the gland, by surgical or other means, often restores the affected individual to normality. The underfunctioning of the thyroid gland brings about dryness and brittleness of skin, nails, and hair, and a general retardation of both mental and bodily processes. This condition may be corrected by taking thyroxine obtained from sheep, or a remedy manufactured from coal tar products.[3] The normal strenuous person marked by rapid perception, strong volition, and an abundance of energy may be endowed with an active thyroid gland.

The adrenals are two small glands located on the kidneys. Ordinarily the adrenal secretion which enters the circulatory system acts as a tonic for the heart and muscles. When an anger stimulus attracts the attention, the adrenals begin to secrete rapidly, heart action is strengthened, the liver releases stored sugar, thus supplying the muscles with energy, and the digestive processes are inhibited. In short, the body is quickly prepared for violent action. An excitable individual may be one whose adrenal glands are over-active.

The pituitary gland is lodged in the bony cavity at the base

---

[2] See Berman, Louis, *Glands Regulating Personality* (New York: The Macmillan Company, 1921). Crile, George W., *The Origin and Nature of the Emotions* (Philadelphia: W. B. Saunders Company, 1915).

[3] Stieglitz, Julius, Editor, *Chemistry in Medicine*, pp. 232 ff. (New York: The Chemical Foundation, 1928).

of the brain. It consists of two lobes, the anterior and the posterior, with connecting tissue. The hyperfunctioning of the anterior lobe is supposed to produce giantism by stimulating the growth of the skeleton.[4] The posterior lobe exercises a tonic influence on the smooth muscles, and furthers the conversion of glycogen into sugar. Furthermore, many endocrinologists claim that the pituitary body promotes the secretory action of other glands. Convinced that it controls the functions of the thyroid, the adrenal, and the gonads, some have called it the master gland. The amount of its autacoid is small but reputedly potent.

Several other glands affect the behavior of the individual in characteristic ways. There is a high degree of probability that chemical substances produced by the endocrine glands and conveyed in the blood stream to the different parts of the body are among the significant organic elements which outline the several types of personality. Many leading psychologists are, however, by no means convinced that personality as a whole can be reduced to the activity of the glandular system. It seems to be established that the amount of secretion varies with individuals and with corresponding personality effects, and that organisms differ in their readiness to arouse the glands to increased activity. That the endocrine system influences bodily growth, metabolism, and reproduction, is a regulator of the vigor of reactions, and thus provides emotional predispositions must be conceded. When the endicrinologist prepares the groundwork for a change for the better in the habits and attitudes of an individual, human purpose and competency dominate the enterprise.

The native endowment of man includes reflexes such as sneezing, crying, gagging, coughing, winking; craving and irritations such as hunger, thirst, itch, tickle, and cramp; sensations[5] such as sight, hearing, smell, touch, taste, temperature,

---

[4] Medical literature contains records of giants ranging from 8 feet 3 inches to 9 feet 2 inches in height.

[5] Three kinds of sense organs are involved in our normal biological inheritance: the distance receptors or the group receiving impressions from the external world, the contact receptors or those receiving impressions from

balance, and probably weight and pain; instincts such as fear, anger, affection, self-preservation, self-expression, and gregariousness; and fundamental urges such as those for social intimacy, excitement, adventure, safety, recognition, power, and the avoidance of the disgusting or dangerous.[6] It is evident that inborn competencies, functions, impulses, and urges enter into the formation of personality with profound significance. Cravings, sensations, instincts, and basic desires interact; if they are antagonistic to one another they induce conflicts, but if they are congenial they support one another in a sort of conspiracy.

The bearing of intelligence on personality organization should be stressed. Intelligence is an inborn capacity which is developed through purposive experience. The measure of intelligence is the number and kind of things one is able to learn, especially on the level of the higher mental processes. The chief features of intelligence are the ability to discern in a new requirement the essential elements and their implications, and the ability to effect an appropriate adjustment. Intelligent activity involves memory, imagination, responsiveness to relations, judgment, and initiative. It differs from knowledge as mere information, and from talent which is the development of a specific capacity. Knowledge is acquired, intelligence is a general ability of the personality effectively to apply knowledge.

The potential degree of the intelligence of the individual is native and unalterable. The quality of intelligence remains constant throughout the life of a person; the stupid child becomes a stupid adult; a capable child becomes a capable adult. Educational advantages are of no avail when inborn capacities are deficient.[7] Training can only convert capacity into

---

things in contact with the body, and the internal receptors which report what is going on within the organic structures.

[6] For a brief discussion of the dominant wishes see Stolz, Karl R., *Pastoral Psychology*, pp. 32 ff. (Nashville: Cokesbury Press, 1932).

[7] Tests which measure various competencies of personality have been devised. See Catalog of the Test Service Division of the Psychological Corporation, 522 Fifth Avenue, New York, N. Y. The results of any kind of test are valid only for the particular function or ability explored. Perhaps the subject's use of words is the best single indicator of the quality and development of his higher mental processes.

ability.   Against stupidity even the gods battle in vain, a German proverb declares.   No matter how diligently the dullard may attempt to train himself, no matter how many opportunities for self-improvement he may have, the fertilized ovum, barring injury to the brain after birth, from which he developed contained determinants of limitations which he cannot remove.   On the other hand, a native capacity for intelligent responses to novel situations will remain latent unless it is made actual by practical application.

The distribution of intelligence is patently uneven in all species in which it can be traced.   A dog is more intelligent than a rabbit, but both individual rabbits and dogs vary in intelligence.   Man is more intelligent than the dog, but men display perhaps even greater variation.   The degrees of intelligence which characterize human beings may be scientifically ascertained.   Techniques of mental measurement have been devised and refined.   The tests given all ages of people have been so standardized that the results are reliable and pedagogically applicable.   What is called the intelligence quotient, generally abbreviated to IQ, is the mental age of the person tested divided by his chronological age.   The IQ of an individual of just average ability regardless of his age is 100 per cent.   If a child's mental age is 12 and his chronological age is 10, his IQ, disregarding the decimal point, is 120, and he is therefore rated as superior.   His IQ indicates that he is two years in advance of his chronological age, and has acquired knowledge and skill 20 per cent faster than the average child does.

The distribution of intelligence quotients in the general American population is as follows:

IQ	69 and below	2%	feeble-minded
IQ	70 to IQ 89	23%	dull
IQ	90 to IQ 109	50%	normal
IQ	110 to IQ 129	23%	superior
IQ	130 and above	2%	gifted

The average IQ in the grade school is 100, in high school

115, in colleges of the highest rank 130.[8] The child in grade school with IQ 120 is far above the average, the same person in high school is still above the average; in college, however, this person is below the average. The IQ has remained constant, but the situational requirement has been progressively increased.[9]

The person marked by breadth of knowledge, sympathetic understanding of others, wide range of skills and diversity of interests is cultured and resourceful. He not only adjusts himself with minimal effort and emotional friction to his surroundings, but in addition molds parts of the environment to his own desires. He can make organic functions such as sensation and instinct the servants of his will. The implications of intelligence for the moral and religious attitudes of personality are decidedly far-reaching. Although the correlation between a high IQ and good morals is not inexorable, the intelligence of criminals confined in penitentiaries is approximately as low as that of the general male population mustered by the army draft during our participation in the World War. The correlation between high intelligence and ethical responsiveness is much closer than that which exists between physical health and morals. Bodily health is as good among delinquents as it is among law-abiding citizens living in the same community. The relation between a high IQ and the critical evaluation of religious concepts is positive. On the other hand, students in college who receive the lower grades are likely to cling to primitive religious ideas which were acquired during childhood. Sects which stress the intellectual elements of religion attract some of

[8] Hollingworth, Harry L., *Psychology, Its Facts and Principles,* pp. 479, 480 (New York: D. Appleton & Co., 1928).

[9] Among the factors which tend to encourage individuals to respond to their full capacity to intelligence tests the following are of special importance: the friendly attitude of the tester, the prime physical condition of the subject, emotional poise, freedom from distraction, the use of the cultural pattern of the subject, familiarity with the English language in the case of a foreigner. An excellent handbook for use in connection with the Stanford revision of the Binet tests is Terman, L. M., *The Measurement of Intelligence* (New York: Houghton, Mifflin & Co., 1916). A more recent analysis of the technical problems is Thorndike, E. L., *The Measurement of Intelligence* (New York: Teachers College, 1919). See also Pintner, Rudolph, *Intelligence Testing* (New York: Henry Holt & Co., 1923).

the relatively few individuals who achieve distinction in science, art, industry, or business. On the whole it is evident that intelligence contributes to the enlargement, enrichment, and efficiency of personality, is likely to impart a definite momentum in the direction of morally and socially sensitive conduct, and is predisposed to censor inherited concepts of religion and conduct.

The Integrative Principle

The interaction of man and his environment produces or develops a wide range of interests. Growing experience in a social matrix places at our disposal resources from which we select the possiblities which seem important and desirable and convert them into interests. It is obviously impossible for the individual to respond to and assimilate all of the innumerable incitements which proceed from the enveloping culture. Choice is imperative. Some potentialities are overlooked or deliberately sacrificed. Consolidations of impressions and capabilities occur. Interests are formed.

An interest may be described as a system of active dispositions which is deliberately cultivated and to which one is devoted. We readily recognize such observable interests of normal people as the economic, the political, the social, the philosophical, the aesthetic, and the religious. Not one of these interests is reducible to a single or simple principle or function, but is a complexity of components correlated by a dominant idea or value. Wishes, drives, impulses, and capabilities shape and modify interests. The desire for security, for example, may dominate the economic interest; the will to power, the political. The interests hold the attention and determine the directions in which vital energy flows. The quality of personality depends on the number, variety, and value of the interests which are fostered.

The interests of organized personality constitute a hierarchy in which each occupies its proper place and is subordinated to a central control. An inclusive and dominating desire, sentiment, or ideal acts as an integrating agency. The ruling principle may be roughly compared to a traffic policeman who stands on duty at the intersection of streets and directs the flowing tide of motor vehicles and pedestrians. It holds the interests together in a relation of coherence and subserviency.

Personalities may be divided into three types—the unintegrated, the integrated, and the disintegrated. The unintegrated group consists of those whose interests have never been co-ordinated by a master principle. In such cases the components of personality may be good severally, or bad, or intermixed, but they do not constitute a working whole with a character of its own. Unintegrated individuals constitute an identifiable personality type. To what extent the unintegrated adult is responsible for his condition is difficult to determine. There is a strong likelihood that in many instances the unintegrated state exists not because the individual has no capacity for integration, but because for some reason he prefers to remain unintegrated. He may be too indolent or too indifferent to exert himself. Lack of integration may be part and parcel of adult infantilism. On the other hand, multiple dissociation may be native—that is, it may be reducible to characters in the germ plasm from which the individual has originated. To what degree, if any, is such an inborn psychological pattern alterable? Only further scientific experimentation in the modification of representative personality types can supply the answer to this perplexing question. Those whose mental constitution is such as to make integration under ordinary conditions practically impossible may be considered sub-normal. The unintegrated person is not necessarily void of the religious interest; in fact, in the procession of interests religion may be a lively interest although it does not dominate the other constituents of personality. It is detached from that of the other interests.

The integrated group is composed of those whose processes are ordered and regulated by a governing objective. It would be difficult to submit a complete list of the central illuminating and organizing principles from which a choice may be made. The concepts about which men order their lives are not only legion in number but vary tremendously in moral quality. Psychologically, the personality of a criminal may be as well integrated as that of a saint. The criminal's interests are nurtured and controlled by his antisocial conception of what is most worth while. The confirmation of his personality, if it is unified, is such that he absorbs opposition and thereby prevents disorganization. As we put it, he runs true to form. The possibility of paying the death penalty for his crimes is by him regarded as one of the necessary perils and risks of his career. He is quite self-consistent and his behavior is predictable with a high degree of certainty. In this psychological respect all integrated personalities, the bad as well as the good, are alike.[10] The quality of the regulating principle and the extent to which it is effective determine a man's value to society and his own independent worth.

Not that integration is in any case complete. The extent to which a personality is integrated is perhaps most clearly demonstrated by the way in which a crisis is met. The higher the degree of integration the greater facility with which obstacles, conflicts, aversions, and adversities are removed or assimilated. No matter how finely attuned to the central theme a personality may be, there are always some discords. Areas of minor influence are dissociated from the master control, but so long as they do not seriously impair the harmony of the personality as a whole, integration exists. Furthermore, the wholesome personality is constantly undergoing a process in which progressively higher integrations are achieved. The reconstruction of personality in accordance with fresh insights is an evidence of mental and moral health. The reorganization of personality, paradoxical as it may seem, is the first stage in the recentering of it on a higher level. The individual, for example, whose life is ordered by self-complacency is in need of decentralization as a preliminary to reorganization with a more productive point of reference. Integration at its best is on the one hand not total and on the other not static but progressive.

A large proportion of persons are members of the disin-

---

[10] Although this is true psychologically, it is not valid in the larger and philosophical sense. If we are living in a morally undergirded universe, the antisocially integrated personality is not in accord with basic principles. The soundest integration implies harmony with cosmic forces.

tegrated group. The reference is to those who have not maintained the stage of integration reached. When the organizing agency collapses or is repudiated it is as if the traffic policeman had withdrawn from his post. The strong but reckless and selfish drives, released from control, collide with the tender and considerate interests, and confusion, conflict, and dissociation occur. If the disruption of personality is serious, thinking is irrational and irrelevant, the emotional responses are spasmodic, unstable, and variable, and behavior is unco-ordinated and unpredictable.

In many cases the process of disorganization is a resultant of a philosophy of life based on unreality. The inadequate leading concept is effective so long as its validity is unchallenged by a comparatively uneventful course of life. When one's guiding principle gives way under the special strains of an emergency, the personality is disrupted. In a crisis, fictions, shams, illusions, and unrealities are ruthlessly exposed, and the personality they have hitherto supported is reduced to disparate segments, some of which clash. The assumption is false that what the individual believes in and is guided by is of no consequence if only he is sincere.

An allusion to an experiment in the limitations which mark the power of a false impression to affect personality will provide an analogy. The experimenter gives the subject a glass of colorless and deodorized spirituous liquor, conveying the positive suggestion that the fluid is only water. It is possible for the subject to consume just so much liquor which he believes to be water before he, to his own amazement, begins to experience and exhibit a state of intoxication. It is conceded that the quantity of alcoholic content required to induce intoxication is greater in such a case than when it is known that a spirituous beverage is being drunk and the normal reaction is anticipated, but the deception does not indefinitely postpone the natural effects. After all, alcohol is not water.

Similarly, one may cling to an erroneous centralizing concept and be sustained by his faith in it until it is overtaken and shattered by a crucial experience. For instance, a devout person may make a defective conception of God as a helper in time of need a vital part of his life. He assumes that in response to his petitions God will alter or suspend the course of nature, if only he exercises implicit faith. In an hour of desperation his supplications are unanswered, the special favor expected even at the cost of the disturbance of the equilibrium of nature is not forthcoming. If the disappointed petitioner does not rationalize the prayer failure, the central tenet of his philosophy is overthrown and the religious disintegration of personality occurs. What one believes in as supremely important does make a difference.

Religion rooted in the realities of personal experience is a co-ordinating and controlling interest. It embraces all other interests, including the political, economic, social, aesthetic, and philosophical, in one comprehensive dynamic whole. It refines and regulates the various psychological systems which compose the hierarchy of personality. The instincts, fundamental wishes, and abilities are governed by the master interest. It enables the person to throw all of himself into the enterprise of the good life. Religiously organized and stabilized personality appreciates symbolism, color, incense, architecture, ritual, pageantry, and other accessories of worship, combining them in a synthesis, in a total impression. The conviction that the universe is purposeful, that every individual has a place in the total scheme of things, and that the striving for goodness, insight, and beauty is a basic obligation of human nature strongly motivates the religious integration of personality. From this point of view religion is the progressive organization of personality with a dynamic sense of an ultimate reality as the center of reference. The Christian religion may be defined functionally as the progressive integration of the component interests of personality with an expanding dynamic sense of the rallying center which Jesus disclosed and interpreted as ultimate reality. The life of the genuinely religious man is not a jumble of discontinuous and meaningless occurrences. It is ordered and worthful. The religious interest supplies the values and goals which invest life with dignity. The religious interest grounded in enduring values, in verities that survive the shock of life's vicissitudes, and made centrifugal, is after all the most effective integrating force.

St. Paul is an outstanding example of religiously motivated and regulated personality. Identification with Christ and unswerving loyalty to his service gave to the apostle's life unity, meaning, and power. The centrality of the religious interest is disclosed in statements of his like the following: "It is no longer I that live, but Christ liveth in me." [11] "For though we walk in the flesh, we do not war according to the flesh . . . bringing every thought into captivity to the obedience of Christ." [12] "For the love of Christ constraineth us." [13] Persecution, loneliness, misunderstanding, and deprivation, although not easy to endure, could not demolish the religious foundations of Paul's life and shatter his personality. He was cast into prison more than once, five times he received forty stripes less one at the hands of the Jews, thrice he was beaten with rods, he was shipwrecked three times, he suffered hunger and thirst, cold and destitution, the treachery of false brethren and the defection of his converts, but none of these nor any combination of them was able to separate him from the love of God.[14] "I can do all things in him that strengtheneth me," [15] is a testimony which reveals the dynamic cohesive of the personality of the Church's greatest theologian, missionary, pastor, and administrator.

[11] Galatians 2: 20.
[12] 2 Corinthians 10: 3-5.
[13] 2 Corinthians 5: 14.
[14] 2 Corinthians 11: 23-29.
[15] Philippians 4: 13.

CHAPTER XII

SIN AND TEMPTATION

Sin and temptation are prominent elements in the theology of a religion of ethical redemption. Theological problems connected with them, such as original sin and freedom of the will, lie outside the scope of this inquiry and therefore need not be discussed. Although psychology is able to throw some light upon these perplexing and persistent issues, the present purpose is to describe various mental exhibitions of temptation and to indicate how sin affects personality. Suggestions for the accumulation of moral reserve and resistance will be derived from a psychological interpretation of temptation, surrender to evil overtures and the personality consequences of sin.

The Concept of Sin

The story of the fall of man as recorded in the Book of Genesis, although not to be understood as strict history or science, is in its underlying psychological principles true to the probable experience of the human race and to the actual experience of the individual sinner. Its psychology of sin and temptation is fundamentally sound, although modern science teaches that our early ancestors, so far from having lived a carefree existence in a garden, emerged from a state of savagery characterized by a fierce conflict of opposing brute forces. It is evident that at some point in social evolution, no one knows exactly when or how or where, the first transgression of what was interpreted as the will of the Controller of destiny occurred. When man revolted against his judgment of religious obligations, however elementary his power of moral discrimination may have been, he fell under conscious condemnation. There is no warrant in Genesis for the assumption that the first persons were created morally perfect and that their act of disobedience plunged them from the highest pinnacle of virtue to the lowest depth of degradation. Adam and Eve are described as undeveloped persons living a life of the simplest relations whose outstanding characteristic was the gift of speech. Their innocence was that of ignorance, which can become virtue only when subjected to trial and proved. When the test was applied they willfully failed to sustain it. Ignorance rather than virtue must be ascribed to our primitive ancestors who lived before the perception of moral values evolved. With the growth of the ability to reflect, personal and social effects of behavior were scrutinized, appraised, and predicted, and the distinction between the good and the bad arose in the mind of man.

Sin is a theological concept and as such designates behavior which is at variance with or neglectful of what is construed as the will of God. The consciousness of sin emerged at a relatively advanced stage of the evolution of culture. When taboos, customs, and codes of behavior were identified with the commands of God the possibility of sin originated. When mankind reached progressively higher levels of religious insight the antisocial quality of sin was correspondingly recognized. Conscience approving social judgment makes mandatory what is regarded as right. When justice is a religious requirement and injustice is condemned in the name of religion, divergent paths of rightness and sin are at least relatively plain. Sin is a moral defect for the existence of which the responsible personality is accountable to God. The Westminster Shorter Catechism declares that "sin is any want of conformity unto, or transgression of, the law of God." God alone can impute sin to man, and he only has power to forgive it. When Adam and Eve fell they disobeyed an ordinance of God. The penitent psalmist confessed to God: "Against thee, thee only, have I sinned." [1] Sin is thus more than an offense against the social order, or one's own best interests; it includes either or both and as a religious prohibition is also and essentially an affront to God. It follows that sin can be exculpated by God alone.

[1] Psalm 51: 4.

Sin presupposes a standard of excellence and comparison, the adoption of a goal to which all other purposes are subordinated as of lesser value and urgency. Sin implies the presence of an ideal higher than the promptings of natural impulses. The moral ideal is not a biological inheritance, but is developed and religiously sanctioned and enforced through human experience within the cultural environment. The highest excellence is disclosed in the control of the individual by an ideal of conduct which is for him indubitably right and obligatory, but which arouses the hostility of his less enlightened or more impious contemporaries. In order to be effective as a norm, the system of moral principles believed to receive cosmic support must crystallize as a master sentiment and as such be authentic and binding. Deviation from the authoritative mandates of God is sin. Psychologically, sin is, then, the disturbance of the equilibrium of the personality by an attitude or act inconsistent with the accepted standard. The disruption of the unity of the self is an indication that ideal and conduct are incompatible. Shame, anxiety, and guilt accompany this condition.

The Jew believed that the law as recorded in the Pentateuch was divinely inspired instruction, and that God rewarded those who kept it and penalized those who broke it and then did not resort to the appointed means of atonement. No distinction was made between the ceremonial and the moral requirements of the law by the generality of the pious Jews. The Old Testament prophets, however, did exalt social justice, compassion, and mercy above the exactions of the sacrificial and legal statutes. In other words, what was regarded as sin by the priestly cast was rejected as nonessential if not as an encumbrance by the prophetic order. A mind sensitized by the teaching and spirit of Christ would doubtless consider the violation of any of the ten commandments sinful, with the possible exception of the fourth literally interpreted.[2] It would rate as contrary

[2] The Christian Sunday as a day of rest, worship, and special effort to extend the Kingdom sprang spontaneously and directly from the spirit of Christ which animated his early followers. There is no suggestion in the New Testament that the Jewish Sabbath was transferred from Saturday to Sunday by the apostolic church.

to the Christian way of life such things as contempt or hatred for a fellow man, disabling anxiety, lustful imagination, hypocritical condemnation of the minor character defects of another, and exhibitionism in the form of vulgar display of piety. Sin may, besides, be pride and murder, gambling and drunkenness, boasting and laziness, waste and greed, dishonesty and the coveting of another's spouse. No complete catalogue of specific sins can be made which will be approved by all men, since what is sin to one might not be sin to another.

The division into sins of commission and sins of omission is consistent with the psychology of ethics. "To him therefore that knoweth to do good, and doeth it not, to him it is sin." [3] In the description of the universal and final judgment of mankind, which Matthew's Gospel introduces, men are doomed to punishment not because they lied, or stole, or committed murder, or contravened any other prohibition of common morality, but because they were callously indifferent to ordinary human need.[4] It is not sufficient to refrain from actual injustice, dishonesty, or hatred; refusal to promote justice, act honorably, and love one's neighbor is sin in its most insidious and deadly guise. Absence of virtue is sinful, for Christian conduct is not so much a complication of negations as a program of affirmations.

The all-inclusive sin according to the dominant current of the New Testament teaching is the rejection of the love of God especially as made manifest in the character and redemptive work of Christ. Godlessness in the quite literal sense of acknowledging no Determiner of destiny, of having a world-view without a central cosmic intelligence and unifying agent, of recognizing no responsibility to anything beyond human personality and no moral values aside from temporary whim or passing expediency, is the essence of sin however much men of ethical fervor and insight may diverge in their conceptions of what forms of psychic events and details of behavior constitute specific sins.

[3] James 4: 17.
[4] Matthew 25: 31-46.

Temptation

Sin may be regarded as a correlative of temptation. Theologically speaking, temptation may be defined as an incitement to sin by the presentation of motives which are alluring or plausible. Sin is not a necessary outcome of temptation. It is no sin to be tempted.

The process of temptation is set forth and illustrated with remarkable clarity and vigor in the story of man's first transgression as recorded in Genesis. The tragedy of Eden is repeated in the moral defeat of the modern man who obeys an impulse condemned by a religiously enlightened conscience. The temptation to which Eve and Adam succumbed includes in its various bearings the main psychological components of the fall of millions of human beings. The Bible story presents the incentives and conditions which issue in the act of sinful disobedience. It introduces a series of occurrences in which one recognizes the presence of impulses or drives, enticements, conflict, rationalization, overt response, inferiority, and attempted transference of responsibility. Most, if not all, these events occur whenever an individual surrenders to the temptation to deviate from the set pattern of conduct.

The sight of the forbidden fruit in the garden of Eden was a stimulus, but as such it had no invincible power to compel action. It was the occasion but not the determinant of sin. Eve saw that the fruit was good for food, a delight to the eyes, and the means of acquiring a knowledge of good and evil.[5] The inducement to eat of it was a combination of the desires for creature comfort, aesthetic gratification, and superknowledge. Three powerful impulses joined forces and made a concerted appeal.

The sensuous appetites contributed their full measure to the total situation to which Eve finally succumbed. It must be conceded that the sensuous elements in man's nature provide the background for a large proportion of his immoralities. Man's intercourse with and knowledge of the universe are mainly dependent on the operations of his sensory apparatus. It is, how-

[5] Genesis 3: 6.

ever, the wrong use of the sensuous promptings and instincts and never the proper employment of them that is sinful. Eve's perception of the properties of the attractive fruit was no sin. On the other hand, a divine command had restricted the area within which the couple could act with impunity. "Thou shalt not eat of it," was the express prohibition of God.[6]

The appreciation of the beautiful is one of man's noblest competencies, but when, as in the Genesis narrative, it imperils the religious integration of personality it is subtle temptation. To thrill to the sheer loveliness of nature in its various forms is not an adequate substitute for obedience to the will of God. The close relation which religion and aesthetics may sustain to one another often renders this aspect or form of temptation difficult to distinguish from a divinely sanctioned prompting.

Eve, furthermore, thirsted for godlike knowledge. She wanted to know good and evil. According to the sequel the fruit of the prohibited tree produced the effect predicted by the serpent; the eyes of the couple were opened, but the knowledge acquired, so far from bringing happiness, induced guilt, shame, and terror. The desire for knowledge with the power and prestige which it confers, rightly motivated and directed, is praiseworthy; but when it obscures the obligations of duty, it is an insidious type of temptation.

Eve yielded to a complication of impulses. The major temptations today, as in the Genesis account, are appeals to self-gratification at the cost of moral stamina, to the desire for knowledge, pleasure, status, fame, and wealth. Pride and false ambition, malice and envy, and scorn of the object of religious worship are deplorable concomitants of the surrender to the incitement to selfishness.

A conflict arose between Eve's desire for self-indulgence and the known obligation to obey God, between powerful impulses and the approved religious ideal. The awareness of frustration and bafflement was irritatingly present in her mind. The disagreeable sense of being thwarted was the conscious accompaniment of the neural blockage of an intense desire clamoring

[6] Genesis 2: 17.

for satisfaction. She was moved by the challenge of the forbidden. The temptation stimulus cast its spell upon the woman and made her increasingly avid for choice food, aesthetic gratification, and godlike knowledge. The longer she looked at the singular tree the more difficult it became to dismiss its allurements from her mind. Two strong forces of opposing qualities contended for the mastery of Eve. Psychologically, the side which won and held the attention was victorious.

A process whereby justification for the projected act of disobedience was attempted ensued. In the Genesis story the serpent, malevolent and crafty, raised a question intended to confuse Eve, "Yea, hath God said, Ye shall not eat of any tree of the garden?" [7] The woman, not to be misled immediately by such flagrant misrepresentation, replied that permission had been granted to eat of the fruit of all trees save that of the one in the midst of the garden. As if to end the machinations of the serpent, she added, "God hath said, Ye shall not eat of it, neither shall ye touch it, lest ye die." [8] Quick to discern a fresh approach, the serpent flatly denied that death would be the result of disobedience and insinuated that God's motive in threatening them with capital punishment was to keep Eve and her husband from becoming like gods who know good and evil. The suggestion that God was chargeable with selfish intent captured her imagination and lowered her resistance to the serpent's wiles. Having heard what she wanted to believe, the deluded woman gave the tree her undivided attention and, excluding all contrary ideas and principles from her mind, gave way to the pressure of temptation.

The Hebrew accepted the story of the fall of man as literally true. He believed that the serpent owes its present method of locomotion and the enmity existing between it and mankind to its complicity in man's first sin. The Hebrew did not regard the serpent in the garden as a symbol but as a visible and actual agent in the enticement of the woman. It must be acknowledged that in millions of cases the temptation stimulus is reinforced and intensified by the influence of an enticer. Many a

[7] Genesis 3: 1.   [8] Genesis 3: 3.

man would not surrender to sinful promptings if he were not
urged and abetted and even cajoled or dared by an unscruplous
companion. Now and then a tempter is shortsighted rather
than vicious and is himself persuaded that the course of action
he is advocating is commendable. When Peter attempted to
dissuade Jesus from subjecting himself to future hostility, suffering, and death Jesus properly rebuked him, saying, "Get
thee behind me, Satan." [9] There is no valid reason to suppose
that Peter deliberately tried to persuade Jesus to abandon his
ideals. The evident purpose was to induce Jesus to adopt the
Messianic rôle which would be in accord with Peter's own conception. In various forms and impelled by divergent motives,
abetters like the serpent in Eden, co-operate with one's potent
desires which are contrary to acknowledged religious principles.

The serpent may be given a subjective signification. It may
represent one mode of the self divided by the conflict between
impulse and obligation. It may symbolize disapproved desire
as opposed to religious requirement. The personality may subjectively dramatize the temptation with such graphic portrayal
that two beings, as it were, contend with each other, and advance argument and refutation until the one self prevails. The
form in which the temptations of Jesus in the wilderness were
cast is explicable in terms of an internal drama in which he as
the beloved Son of God and Satan as his antagonist played the
leading parts.[10]

What should be a realistic attitude toward temptation, a candid recognition of ugly facts, an analysis of the situation into
its components with an exposure of fallacy and treachery, is
too often nothing more than a process of rationalization. An
attempt to justify one's proposed misconduct usually precedes
capitulation to the blandishments of temptation. Specious arguments are adduced in order to appease the injured sense of right.
A pitiful effort is made to bring the projected misdeed into
harmony with the moral sanctions of the individual, or to
keep reprehensible impulse and standard apart, and thus forestall personality disruption. Eve evidently resolved to believe

[9] Mark 8: 33.   [10] Matthew 4: 1-11.

that God had issued his commandment because he was jealous of her and Adam, and deeply resented the possibility that in at least one major ability they might become like himself. No doubt she maintained that it was her bounden duty to eat of the forbidden fruit, for is one not under sacred obligation to enjoy the good things the Creator has provided and to know life as it really is? Not to eat of the luscious fruit would be a sin! A superficial sense of rectitude is deliberately cultivated. With self-deception, delusion, pious fraud, and guiding fiction the susceptible individual drugs himself into an at least temporary state of moral insensibility in which, like a weary man yielding to sleep, he succumbs to temptation. Of course if the previous acceptance of a constellation of religious demands has created a fairly constant condition of moral sensitiveness, such a shallow attempt to transform sin into virtue, a prohibition into a positive obligation, is likely to prove abortive.

A recoil from the misdeed committed is in the circumstances the normal reaction. Misconduct once stripped of its disguise of goodness breeds a sense of inferiority, condemnation, and alienation from God. When the consequences of sin are made mainfest, the individual realizes that he has been duped by the allurements and false promises of temptation. Sin as defined by an ethical religion like Christianity is not only an offense directed against God, but is also an antisocial act and a betrayer of the guilty personality. One is left in the lurch by the temptation which prevails. A realization of personal degradation overcomes the fictitious vindication of the transgression. The anticipated delights, advantages, privileges, and immunities of sin are in many instances not forthcoming or are outweighed by the tortures inflicted by an outraged conscience.

When the individual is compelled by the conflict raging within him to admit that a wicked deed has been done he may attempt to exonerate himself by disavowing the responsibility. That the act in question is a sin is not denied, but accountability for it is disclaimed. The blame is shifted. A scapegoat is found or created. An effort was made by Adam and Eve to relieve inner tension and to escape penalty for disobedience by evasion of reality and attempted transference of guilt. In re-

sponse to the divine call, "Where art thou?" Adam, shrinking
from the confession of the whole truth, alleges that he is afraid
of God because he is naked. Brought face to face with his sin,
Adam, instead of acknowledging culpability, casts the blame
upon the woman and indirectly holds God himself ultimately
responsible. "The woman whom thou gavest to be with me,
she gave me of the tree, and I did eat," [11] is his cowardly repudiation. Questioned in her turn by God, Eve likewise displays an unrepentant and dishonest spirit, maintaining, "The
serpent beguiled me." [12]

The repudiation of blame for one's errors, faults, and misde-
meanors is an almost automatic response of the undeveloped or
infantile adult. One of the most dependable characteristics of
mature personality is the assumption of blame for reprehensible
conduct. The individual who has not outgrown childhood inclinations and illusions repudiates personal responsibility for
misbehavior with the uncritical spontaneousness with which an
arm is raised to ward off a blow. The scapegoats they present are a variegated assortment. Chance, heredity, environment, misunderstanding, and the deceptions and malign practices of others are among the more common scapegoats upon
which men naïvely would lay responsibility for misconduct.
Like Aaron who renounced complicity in the idolatrous worship
of his people by explaining to the indignant Moses that from
the gold cast into the fire the objectional calf without further
ado emerged, many with childish simplicity attribute their de-
fections to a nebulous casual agency denominated fate, or pre-
destination.[13] The disposition to ascribe to an irrelevant or at
the most to a secondary or contributing cause what should be
referred to the perverted will of the individual himself is typical of all who refuse to face themselves with candor.

Effects of Sin

The consequences of sin are so numerous that it is impossible to submit a complete list. Typical results comprehend the
disruption of the poise and peace of the personality, self-

---

[11] Genesis 3: 12.   [12] Genesis 3: 13.   [13] Exodus 32: 24.

castigation, lacerating memories, the destruction of health, propagation of moral evil by imitation and suggestion, the continuance of social effects after sin has been abandoned, and the loss of moral sensitiveness.

When they heard God walking in the garden in the cool of the evening, Adam and Eve in a panic of fear sought to escape the divine presence by hiding among the trees. The victim of sin is overtaken by a feeling of anxiety, incompetency, failure, and impending disaster. The world of wish-phantasy collapses under the pressure of the realities of religion and the sinner is buried beneath the ruins. Sin is a disorganizer of personality. The psychological effects of an aroused conscience such as inner conflict attended by fear, guilt, and despondency are not to be ignored. The ghost of forebodings haunts the chambers of the convicted soul.

The awareness of personal sin is sometimes accompanied by a disposition to exact from the tortured self an expiatory penalty. Consequently "accidents" are subconsciously designed, or the individual deliberately exposes himself to situations in which he proposes to suffer for wrongdoing. Now and then one encounters a child who is seemingly motivated by a veritable itch for chastisement and despite the repeated warnings of his elders persists in a series of provocations calculated to precipitate the desired punishment. Such forms of self-castigation are evidently prompted by a subconscious endeavor to appease the outraged sense of moral values, and thereby to restore the internal harmony and peace of the personality.

Admission of guilt and exercise of faith in the clemency and power of God through Christ issue in the Christian assurance of divine forgiveness and the shattering of the sinful impulse. In the process of reclamation a system of religious principles crystallizes and assumes control of the personality or, if it has already been enthroned, is so strengthened that it extirpates the specific sin which has been the point of friction. Certain consequences of sin, some within the self and others outside it, some physical, others mental and still others social, persist despite forgiveness and deliverance.

The memory of wrongdoing in the distant past may haunt

one and induce a lasting feeling of unworthiness. St. Paul remarked, "I am the least of the apostles . . . because I persecuted the church of God." [14] The recollection of former dereliction need not be morally depressing, but may become the source of a quality of humility that arouses sympathy for others who fall. On the other hand, the guilty past may be revived to terrorize the remorseful but impenitent soul. When King Herod heard of Jesus and his message and mighty deeds, he was so terror-stricken that he imagined that John the Baptist whom he had beheaded had arisen from the dead to torment his murderer.[15] Many a modern sinner is thrown into consternation by a reminder of unforgiven sin.

Not all physical results of sin are removed by repentance. If one has been deprived of an arm or an eye in the service of iniquity religious rehabilitation will not replace the lost physical member. If the bodily constitution has been ruined in the pursuit of evil, moral reconstruction will not necessarily restore health, although there is in many instances a direct and positive correlation between good morals and health. In its coarser varieties sin is especially destructive of bodily energies.

Disregard for the moral order is a prolific source of human misery and calamity. Although the theory that the misfortunes which befall us proceed in every instance from sin as judgments of God is untenable, it is an observable fact that many of our afflictions are directly traceable to the inexcusable ignorance, the hatred, and the avarice of man. An earthquake or a tidal wave which devastates a city is no longer generally interpreted, as it once was, as the penal consequence of the sins of the inhabitants, nevertheless the actual disconcernible outcomes of irreligious and evil behavior are too numerous and awful to be discredited.

Sin displays a pronounced tendency to perpetuate and disseminate itself both in the individual and the group. One sin breeds another. "He who steals, also lies," is a German

---

[14] 1 Corinthians 15: 9. In Ephesians 3: 8 St. Paul remarks that he is the least of all the saints, but since the genuineness of this epistle is disputed the confession should not be pressed too hard.

[15] Mark 6: 14.

proverb which is psychologically true. Eve tasted of the forbidden fruit, "and she gave also unto her husband with her, and he did eat." [16] In a closely-knit social order sin spreads from one person to another with amazing rapidity. One man imitates another. The one misleads the other. In the course of time a collective although unconscious tendency to sin which impinges upon us all was evolved. Our responsiveness to the behavior of others coupled with a native inclination to selfishness and greed makes it easy for sin to lure and beguile us. Sin is in the human stock, is transferred from one generation to another as a social inheritance, and its consequences both personal and social are too devastating to be flouted. It is so prevalent and powerful that it has assumed the proportions of a collective menace which exerts a constant pressure upon the individual.

The social effects of misdeeds are likely to continue long after the sinful inclinations themselves have been eradicated. It is impossible to trace all the ramifications of sin, and to undo the harm they have wrought. To be sure, a reclaimed individual may counteract some of the social results of canceled sin; but many of the outcomes, especially those which have gained considerable momentum, will continue to extend their malign careers. Transgression releases forces and entails consequences many of which are active and multiply after the sin itself has been uprooted in the originating personality.

Sin which is persisted in deadens moral sensibilities. The reflex action of ethical evil is in general subversive of the nobler aptitudes of man. The disruption and demoralization wrought in human personality by sin, together with man's alienation from fellowship with God, are frequently represented as a form of death in the New Testament. "The wages of sin is death." [17] Men living in the flesh are spoken of as "dead through trespasses and sins." [18] "Sin, when it is full-grown, bringeth forth death." [19] The final fatal award of a life of willful disobedience, the end of the sum total of depravity, is death as the

[16] Genesis 3: 6.
[18] Ephesians 2: 1, 5.

[17] Romans 6: 23.
[19] James 1: 15.

separation of the individual from God. Sin permitted to rule robs the personality of ethical sensitiveness, which is a major competency of normal human nature. Repeated and constant refusal to respond positively to appeals to confess sin and seek deliverance from it creates a condition of moral callousness than which nothing can be more calamitous.

Overcoming Temptation

The foregoing analysis suggests ways in which one may successfully cope with a temptation. The progressive steps in the enticement and downfall of the sinner, as has been indicated, embrace the arousal and support of powerful impulses or drives of human nature, the conflict between impulse and ideal, the rationalization of the intended behavior, the actual performance of the misdeed, the ensuing consciousness of betrayal, guilt, and inferiority, and the frequent repudiation of personal accountability. Many temptations are personality crises of such magnitude that the effectual mobilization of spiritual resources is the precondition of victory. Modes of procedure can be devised which will sustain the personality sincerely resolved to be true to its sense of religious realities in the face of the allurements of evil.

The first safeguard to be mentioned is the constant and deliberate cultivation of religiously integrated personality. A tremendous "gravitational" pull of firmly established and approved moral habits occurs when one is incited to open dubious channels of motor discharge. Ingrained standards offer neural as well as ethical resistance to opposing forces. Correct moral decisions may become habitual and almost automatic. In fact, Christian character renders the rise of some forms of temptation improbable. The man who is accustomed to tell the truth is seldom really tempted to lie, for prevarication is inconsistent with principles which govern his manifold relationships. Should an occasion arise on which he contemplates the fancied advantage of a lie, discriminating religious convictions are likely to crystallize into veracity without delay. Conscience is kept alive and effective by a ceaseless process of religious nurture.

Preoccupation with constructive interests is another effective preventive of moral corruption. If Eve had eaten her fill of the delicious fruit of the other trees in the garden, she would have had no appetite for the prohibited fruit. Those whose minds are occupied with worthy projects seldom have either time or energy for misdeeds, but Satan still has work for idle hands. If St. Paul's admonition to hold in mental focus the things that are true and honorable and just and pure and lovely and reputable is heeded, temptation will have but small opportunity to assail and capture the imagination.[20] The law of the motor discharge of the mental content is pertinently applicable. The idea which commands the attention tends to express itself more or less automatically; hence the mind should be richly furnished with the imagery of the approved. As a man thinketh, so is he.

It is expedient to retire with all possible haste from a temptation stimulus. The longer Eve lingered near the forbidden tree, gazed at its fruit, and argued with the serpent, the more she became confused and intrigued. If the nature of the instigation to evil is social, withdrawal from the situation may elicit the jeers and hostility of others; but persecution is less costly than moral lapse. Joseph, declining the overtures of Potiphar's wife, escaped from her attempted embrace and fled the premises.[21] St. Paul's exhortation, "Be not deceived: Evil companionships corrupt good morals," [22] is worthy of acceptance.

If the incitement originates within the personality, subjective flight may be achieved by changing the object of attention. A special effort may be required to divert the attention from the fascinations of evil, but the feat can be accomplished as multitudes bear witness. A counter attraction, an adequate substitute for the temptation either subjective or objective, should claim the attention. In fact, the susceptible person should not expose himself needlessly to situations with a strong temptation appeal. Unnecessary hazards should be scrupulously avoided.

[20] Philippians 4: 8.
[21] Genesis 39: 7-12.
[22] 1 Corinthians 15: 33.

Temptation is most readily overcome in its incipient stages, especially if it involves such passions as anger, envy, malice, greed, and lust. The intense emotions referred to as passions are powerful instigators of action which is at once irrational and disorganizing. A passion narrows the field of consciousness to such an extent that corrective possibilities are excluded from consideration. Once a passion is unleashed, the personality is swayed as by an irresistible force. He who succumbs to it sacrifices judgment and acts on impulse and without regard for consequences. It is significant that the individual who has been the victim of a passion of his own, may remark in retrospect, "I was beside myself," or "I was not myself," and thereby indicate that his behavior was like that of a person under the control of an extraneous and evil spirit, that he was as one possessed by a species of madness. When the wise man feels a passion arising within him, realizing that if he harbors it, it will precipitate misconduct, he slays it in its incipience by the heroic exercise of self-control. Any form of temptation is most easily disposed of in its nascent period. To dally may be finally to compromise.

The exposure of the treachery, fallacy, and deceit of a temptation situation is essential to successful resistance. The prudent man refuses to be hoodwinked by the seductions of evil. Satan does not always appear in easily recognizable form, but often in the guise of an angel of light bearing a message from God. It requires clarity of perception to discern evil masquerading as good, and to distinguish the better from the best in a critical moral exigency. Jesus, who was "in all points tempted like as we are, yet without sin," [23] had sufficient moral courage and insight to overcome the insidious suggestion to compromise his ideals by conforming to the then current conventional standards.[24] An attitude consisting of emotion and volition is not sufficiently critical and realistic to set the individual free from the tyranny of the plausible. Emotion dulls the judgment and obscures the vision. A certain degree of objectivity and detachment coupled with a suspension of

[24] Matthew 4: 1-11.   [23] Hebrews 4: 15.

action enables the intelligence to weigh alternatives and to envisage the outcomes of various possibilities.

Of the means of grace at the disposal of the individual struggling with temptation none is more effective than prayer. Psychologically, prayer is a form of personality control. One outcome of prayer may be the clarification of an issue and the emotional reinforcement of the sense of moral values. Prayer as interaction between man and the Determiner of destiny may be resorted to at any time and place by him who is desirous of preserving his integrity. No specific locality or hour is a prerequisite of efficacious prayer, only the attitude of humility, trust, and expectancy. He who prays for help or guidance presupposes that the angels are on the side of right, that honor, decency, justice, and mercy are in accord with the spirit of the universe. The one who earnestly desires the support of love, wisdom, and power other and greater than human will not be disappointed.

CHAPTER XIII

THE RECENTERING OF PERSONALITY

THERE are three ways in which religion may organize or reconstitute personality—gradual growth, spiritual illumination, and conversion. An increasing number of individuals are undergoing a continuous development in religious insight and behavior. Many who from childhood are God-conscious and zealous in the discharge of what they conceive to be their religious obligations, at some definite time experience a more or less dramatic enlightenment which establishes a new goal in the pursuit of which they put forth their energies. Others undergo a change in point of view and conduct so radical that it is most appropriately called a rebirth. In such cases a powerful system of religious forces reconstructs the self. It is not easy to distribute all forms of religious organization among these three categories, but unmistakable instances of each can be found in abundance. The cultural environment in which the individual is entangled is perhaps the most influential determinant of the general variety of integration which he consciously or otherwise adopts.

When an individual is moved by an intense and dominant desire to relate himself to the Controller of destiny interpreted by Jesus, there are stirrings and strivings, inner growths and connections, incitements and interactions which are not amenable to our present methods of scientific analysis. It is impossible to demonstrate how much of religious recentering is of God and how much of man, for the process as a whole is a unified one, an experience in which the divine and the human co-operate. It is a joint creation. The outcome of divine love is conditioned by man's response, and apart from the invasion of human life by God no sound religious integration of personality occurs. May we not infer that an individual has responded to divine promptings when he has reorganized his powers about a higher standard of behavior?

Gradual Growth

Multitudes experience successive and progressive integrations from childhood and throughout the formative years without emotional upheavals or deep conviction of sin, and never lose the consciousness of being God's children. The course of religious living is unbroken although it requires depth and an enriched content with the passing of the years. Integrations of personality in accord with Christian beliefs and practices are accomplished without abrupt transitions. The renewal of character is constant and continuous.

Edward Everett Hale, eminent writer and preacher, is an excellent specimen of what has been called the "once-born" or the "gradual growth" type of religious orientation and organization. In an article published in 1890 Dr. Hale enumerates and briefly describes the formative influences to which he was largely indebted. He alludes to work, days spent in the open, the lessons in give-and-take learned in the public schools and college, a liberal share of disagreeable duties, writing for the press early in life, personal intercourse with men of active intelligence, and birth into a home where religion was simple, reasonable, and positive. In his reference to the last of the seven conditioning forces, Dr. Hale states that his life was free from religious struggles and crises, and remarks: "I always knew God loved me, and I was always grateful to him for the world He placed me in . . . my relations with God, whose child I am, were permitted to develop themselves in the natural way." [1] He believed that a child who is early taught that he may live with God will have at hand infinite strength for the conquest of difficulty.

As one might anticipate, a study of the personal histories of those whose lives from childhood have been progressively integrated in terms of Christian attitudes discloses identifiable underlying preconditions.[2] Development in a wholesome religious

---

[1] Hale, Edward Everett, "Formative Influences," *The Forum*, Vol. X, pp. 64 ff. The last section of this article appears in Starbuck's *Psychology of Religion*, pp. 305, 306. James quotes from this part in *Varieties of Religious Experience*, pp. 82, 83.

[2] See Starbuck, Edwin D., *Psychology of Religion* (New York: Charles Scribner's Sons, 1899).

atmosphere is the basic determinant. The mediation of the
Christian spirit through the application of a creative program
of religious nurture is essential. The teaching of doctrines
which cannot stand the test of reflection and the realities of
life must be avoided. God should be presented as a father of
love and grace and not as a harsh judge ready to consign even
little children to perdition. Faith and doubt must be so balanced that doubt does not lead to religious disorganization but
to fresh insight and Christian progress; faith which is adequate steadies the personality but does not render it static.
Religious practices such as prayer, church attendance, the study
of the Bible, the growth of virtues and graces, social service
and reconstruction, and the support of the missionary enterprise, must be fostered according to the expanding understanding and capabilities of the growing individual. Character defects must be uprooted in their incipient stages. Life-needs
must be met as they emerge in the trend of living by religious
principles. It is imperative that there be no extended period
of estrangement from God in the development of personality.
Thanks to the increase of intelligent devotion with which Christian nurture is being promoted in our homes and churches, the
cases of gradual growth are multiplying. "That the child is to
grow up a Christian and never know himself as being otherwise," is, as Bushnell insisted it should be, the guiding principle in Christian nurture.[3]

The term "conversion" is not appropriately and accurately
applied to the gradual growth method of Christian development. Since the individual has never known himself to be
anything but a Christian, and his personality at no time has
suffered disorganization through the abandonment of Christian
life as a whole, and he can recall no datable transition from a
condition of disloyalty to Christ to one of loyalty to him, the
concept of growth rather than that of conversion designates
this form of religious awakening and progress. Life in many
cases is a progressive series of almost imperceptible integrations

[3] Bushnell, Horace, *Christian Nurture,* p. 10 (New York: Charles
Scribner's Sons, 1846).

of insight and goodness rather than divided into the two opposing periods of alienation from and reconciliation to God; hence development may be said to characterize the continuous type of experience, and conversion the moral crisis type.

Spiritual Illumination

The course of religious experience may be intensified emotionally, given fresh channels of motor discharge, and enlightened by the acceptance of new or reconstructed principles. The transformation is not characterized by an antecedent consciousness of specific wrongdoing with a corresponding burden of guilt, but by a poignant sense of insufficiency and incompleteness. Its essence is a change of direction or rapid advancement within the kingdom of religious values rather than a passage from without into the religious realm. A want is supplied, a truth apprehended, a responsibility assumed, a sacrifice made, a deeper consciousness of cosmic relation attained. One becomes a better religious being through a nonmoral crisis. Psychologically, a new synthesis of the resources of the personality is formed, a synthesis which makes the individual more confident, more victorious, more socialized, more assured of the divine favor.

The individual may realize that what he has hitherto in all sincerity interpreted as the true service of God, is in sharp conflict with a new ideal which has made an irresistible appeal. The very foundations of the form of religion on which he has depended for salvation may be threatened with destruction by the appreciation of the fresh sense of divine obligation. Such was the situation of Saul who became Paul. Placing his reliance on the keeping of the law as expounded by the Pharisees, Saul was religiously nerved to extirpate the religion of Jesus by persecuting the followers of the Way. In the crisis which occurred before the gates of Damascus, Saul implied that he had, against inner conviction, for a long time denied the lordship of Jesus.[4] Salvation by faith in the redemptive work of God through the agency of Christ is made the rallying point in

---

[4] Compare Acts 9: 1-19; 22: 3-16; 26: 9-18; Galatians 1: 13-16.

the reorganization of his personality, and the cause he once despised and sought to exterminate he now advances with intelligent zeal and astonishing success.

The conversion of St. Paul was not marked by a breaking of the power of canceled sin, nor by a rescue from a course of degradation and shame, but by a complete transformation of point of view and purpose. One religious system was discarded and another enthroned in its place. The Christian philosophy of life had, despite his efforts to convince himself to the contrary, obtained his approval and had become a point of tension in his mind. Whenever it emerged into awareness and demanded recognition and allegiance, he repressed it, and thereby consigned it to the subconscious where it increased its divisive activity. Unable to endure the inner conflict longer, he at last faced compelling reality and surrendered himself to all that the new outlook implied. Self-surrender removed any remaining obstacles to the functioning of the developing idealism, and made it regnant.[5]

An experience of intense spiritual illumination and uplift reorganized the life of Martin Luther. His early years were spent in a pious home where discipline, judged even by the standards of that stern age, was severe. Religion was a major influence in his life as a schoolboy sheltered in the friendly home of Frau Ursula Cotta and as a student at the University of Erfurt. As a youth he began the work of each day with prayer. His early training and religious environment led him to regard God as a stern judge ready to condemn a poor mortal to everlasting torments unless placated by strenuous efforts to make reparations for sins committed and to obey the divine commands. Like many of the most faithful servants of God throughout the centuries, Luther had a deep sense of his own unworthiness. The illness of himself and the violent death of a friend multiplied the weight of his burdens.

"What can I do to win the favor of God?" was the question the answer to which he had been seeking for years. As

[5] For a discussion of the relation of temperament or personality type to the form of religious experience consult Stolz, Karl R., *Pastoral Psychology*, Chapter V (Nashville: Cokesbury Press, 1932).

an Augustinian monk he strove by fasting, labors, humiliations, devotion to the discipline imposed by the monastery, and appeals to the Virgin and the saints, to win the peace which his heart, troubled by his petty shortcomings, so ardently craved. At last the hour of illumination and fulfillment arrived. In Rome, to which he had been sent on a mission by the order of which he was a member, he was shocked by much that he saw and heard. Laboriously climbing the stairway on' which Pilate was believed to have presented Jesus to the Jewish mob, the words of St. Paul, "The righteous shall live by faith," [6] resounded through his soul in trumpet peals. The revelation of salvation not by his own efforts but by faith in Christ wrought a complete change in Luther's point of view, brought him a sense of deliverance and peace, and laid the foundations upon which he was destined to build the Reformation in Germany.[7]

The religious reintegration of John Wesley was in its essentials akin to that of Luther. Carefully, even strictly educated in the rectory home by his mother, Wesley as a child made religion his chief concern. As a schoolboy he hoped to be saved from the wrath to come by not being so bad as other people, by having a regard for religion, saying his prayers regularly, going to church, and reading the Bible. As a youth he set apart an hour or two each day for religious retirement. He received the communion twice a week. He was on guard against sin in word or deed. He was a leading spirit of the Holy Club at Oxford, that band of valiant seekers after a godly life. Young Wesley visited the prisons, assisted the poor, and ministered to the sick. He omitted no form of self-denial he deemed lawful. An unsuccessful religious mission at Savannah in America and the imminent danger of death during a storm at sea on the homeward passage, intensified Wesley's inner turmoil and his desire for peace.

Peter Böhler, a Moravian, instructed him in the way of salva-

---

[6] Galatians 3: 11; Romans 1: 17.

[7] For a fuller account of Luther's religious progress see Walker, Williston, *The Reformation,* pp. 79 ff. (New York: Charles Scribner's Sons, 1900).

tion by the renunciation of his dependence on his own merits and by a living faith in Christ as God's appointed redemptive agent. In London, on a memorable occasion, the New Testament method of salvation became a personal experience. An entry in his diary records the eventful transaction: "In the evening I went very unwillingly to a society in Aldersgate Street, where one was reading Luther's preface to the *Epistle to the Romans*. About a quarter before nine, while he was describing the change which God works in the heart through faith in Christ, I felt my heart strangely warmed. I felt I did trust in Christ, Christ alone for salvation; and an assurance was given me that He had taken away *my* sins, even *mine*, and saved *me* from the law of sin and death." [8] No tongue can tell, no pen describe the moral, religious, and social consequences of Wesley's central experience of deliverance from internal conflict. From childhood he had served his God according to his lights, but salvation by faith experienced as an adult became the dynamic of a personality that has altered the destiny of millions.

In the case of both Luther and Wesley, who became the spiritual descendants of St. Paul, the hour of religious illumination and inspiration was preceded by years of groping toward the enthronement of a new ideal of personal assurance of salvation, a process of incubation largely subconscious, the growth of a more emotionally satisfying and morally cohesive self. When the new system of principles was mature enough to take command of the personality, it precipitated a revelation of itself about which the components of personality crystallized. The functioning of an approved and effective religious control released tension and evoked elation.

Conversion

Conversion, strictly speaking, is the fruit of repentance and leads to regeneration. Repentance signifies a change of heart,

---

[8] *The Journal of the Rev. John Wesley, M.A.,* Vol. I, pp. 475, 476, edited by Nehemiah Curnock (London: Robert Culley, 1909). Some authorities believe that what was actually read on this occasion was Luther's preface to his commentary on the Epistle to the Galatians.

a re-evaluation of one's moral habits, and, positively, an altered attitude toward what is regarded as supremely good.
Conversion consists of the actual process of the reconditioning
of personality in the light of the new insight implied in repentance. Regeneration may be thought of as the total reorganization of personality, with faith in Christ and devotion
to the will of God as the integrating principles.

The conversion type of reintegration includes a renewal of
one's disposition, and a change in belief, attitude, and behavior.
It is supported by powerful convictions. It presupposes a hu-
miliating awareness of actual personal sins of commission and
omission and an oppressive sense of culpability. It entails a
turning point, a moral crisis which separates the past from the
future, a new departure. A formation of religious principles
supplants the consolidation of ideas and interests fallen under
condemnation, and takes active charge of the personality. A
new sense of cosmic aid redirects human energies. As a form
of personality reorganization conversion is, negatively, the abandonment of a false center of reference, and, positively, self-
realization guided by the order of religious reality. "Old
things are passed away: behold, they are become new." [9] In
the New Testament conversion is often associated with faith,
or the committal of the self to the redemptive work of God
through Christ.[10] Recentering accomplished, the peace which
passeth all understanding disperses the demons of gloom and
depression and floods the personality with joy, hope, and assurance of oneness with God.

St. Augustine's cataclysmic and radical change of disposition
and character may be cited as a case in point. His "Confessions," written about ten years after his baptism in 388 A.D.,
contains a detailed account of the critical hour that witnessed
his conversion. He was the child of mixed pagan and Christian parentage. The father, a surly and volatile character, forbade his Christian wife Monica to train their son in the principles of her faith. He was not baptized in infancy or childhood. Nevertheless, Augustine appears to have been taught

[9] 2 Corinthians 5: 17.
[10] John 3: 16; Acts 16: 31; Galatians 5: 6; Romans 3: 26; Hebrews 11: 6.

the rudiments of the form of Christianity then current in Northern Africa. He took seriously a magical conception of prayer; but when his petition to God that he be spared being beaten at school was denied, his faith in the efficacy of prayer was shaken. There is evidence that he did not become a student of the Bible until he was a young man, although from his childhood he had an insatiable thirst for knowledge. Since he was a youth of promise his father, who was not a man of abundant means, gave him an excellent education at the cost of considerable self-sacrifice. In due time Augustine practiced the profession of a rhetorician and as such won wealth and renown in such cities as Carthage, Rome, and Milan.

In his youth Augustine fell away from the teaching of his mother. In his adolescent years he became a profligate and a sensualist. In Milan he came under the spell of Ambrose, a preacher of rare power, and a commanding intellect. One day in a garden, bowed down with a burden of bitter contrition, he heard a voice, as of a boy or girl, prompting him repeatedly, "Take up and read." He interpreted the admonition as a divine command to open a volume of the apostles and to read and apply to himself the first passage he should see. Obeying the impulse, he secured the volume, opened it, and in silence read verses which seemed to have been written by St. Paul expressly to him: "Not in reveling and drunkenness, not in chambering and wantonness, not in strife and jealousy. But put ye on the Lord Jesus Christ, and make not provision for the flesh, to fulfil the lusts thereof." [11] The peace he had for years sought in vain, now was his portion. Instantly all gloom was banished by a light, as it were, infused into his heart. He was now in possession of that supreme good for the sake of which he desired all other eternal values. Sin had abounded in his life, but grace now wrought in him the more abundantly. The effects of this momentous transformation, which he experienced at the age of thirty-two, are incalculable, for he became a theologian whose influence is active in the Church of to-day.

[11] Romans 13: 13, 14. See *Confessions,* Book VIII, Chapter 12.

Conversion includes three identifiable successive stages—the recognition of the reality of personal religion and its correlative, the conviction of moral inferiority; the acceptance of deliverance from sin by faith and its concomitant self-surrender; a dynamic consciousness of oneness with God or the functioning of a new center of personality.

When the prodigal son faced with candor the devastating situation which his waywardness had precipitated and recalled the home where there was "bread enough and to spare," "he came to himself." When he clearly perceived and acknowledged the moral madness to which he had succumbed he had already, in a sense, begun to transcend it. The appreciation of his plight was the first step in the total process of deliverance and restoration. The painful awareness of the contrast between what was and wha should have been, between his status as a herder of swine and his rightful position as a son in his father's house, induced in him the penitent attitude. "Father, I have sinned against heaven and in thy sight," is his admission of sinfulness, perversity, and inward disharmony. So far from attempting to justify his invasion of the far country of freedom from restraint, he had the courageous self-knowledge that leads to moral rehabilitation.

Psychologically, conviction of sin and its attending sense of guilt may be described as a consciousness of inferiority.[12] The recognition of the antithesis between the defective character and the realizable moral ideal gives birth to the awareness of inferiority. A sense of inferioriity does not, however, inevitably constitute the initial stage in deliverance from sin and culpability; the individual may allow himself to be so overborne by it that it only increases his weakness and helplessness. A yielding to the subtly disintegrating influences of admitted inferiority undermines character, evokes the divisive and destructive emotions of anxiety, fear, apprehensiveness, and in-

[12] In many cases converts to Christianity exhibit moral conduct which is not in keeping with the teaching of Jesus. Such instances are the outcome of the unchristian environment within which the subjects have been reared and morally conditioned. A post-conversion experience, the resultant of which is moral renewal in accordance with Christian standards, is a desirable sequel.

duces a series of recurrent moral lapses. Such a course may arouse remorse and, as in the case of Judas, may culminate in a frame of mind in which the gift of life proves to be too burdensome to be borne.[13]   On the other hand, there is a constructive form of inferiority conviction, a form which acts as a spur to personality reintegration. A sense of moral inadequacy and guilt which occupies the attention and is under the control of the will to be reconditioned, is normally purposive and creative. It is a feeling of insufficiency and culpability which, as in the case of Peter, although arousing mental anguish and self-condemnation, leads to forgiveness, reparation, and amendment.[14]

Faith in the redemptive work of Christ expressing itself in self-surrender marks the turning point of the process of conversion. A disquieting sense of undoneness and yearning for freedom from sin and for the possession of peace and moral power are the antecedents of the acceptance of salvation by confidence in God's love. As the condition of inner turmoil and conflict continues, the desire for moral cleansing and victory is intensified and monopolizes the field of consciousness. Nature's method of healing a breach in consciousness is to widen it. The maturing of a new center of personality is not the product of a moment, however sudden and dramatic its projection into consciousness may be, but is a complex process requiring considerable time, the development of new channels of motor discharge, and the atrophy of old neural paths and connections. One longs for the new life, leans out toward it, strives for it, and expects to have it. A crisis occurs. At last the seeker in his extremity feels that further striving for the desired end is useless, ceases to struggle for character renewal, surrenders himself to the forces surging through his personality, and to his surprised relief experiences an assurance of pardon and deliverance from sin and a consciousness of fellowship with God or Christ. Cessation of conscious effort to achieve salvation resolves the conflict between the rejected old dominant pattern of life and the newly developed

[13] Matthew 27: 3-5; but compare Acts 1: 18.
[14] Mark 14: 66-72; John 21: 15-17.

forces ready to command the personality. If the will is exercised in the direction of the reintegration of the personality until the foundations of the old life crumble and dissolve, the seeker in a supreme venture of faith commits himself to the new order of reality subjugating and harmonizing his being. The act of surrender, whether it be accompanied by a state of emotional indifference or despair, is the crucial step in the complex of reconstructive activities. It is facilitated by a belief in a God who loves and welcomes the sinner.

The third stage, which is the sequence of the preceding developments, brings the subject release and exhilaration. The reliance of the individual on the cosmic life when the conditions are auspicious, relieves tension, unifies consciousness, and evokes a sense of deep peace. Relaxation, rest, joy, and satisfaction attend the functioning of the new self.[15] A coherent and harmonious system of religious purposes is enthroned, and seeks to establish its reign and strengthen the moral energies united in its service. Order is brought out of the dark chaos of personality. Voices and visions, if the individual is characterized by a vivid imagination, a wealth of emotion and a general tendency to automatism, may give the experience added significance.[16] There may be bodily lightness, weeping, and shouting. The world of nature which once seemed prosaic may now be glorified; every wild flower nodding in the breeze may be a censer swinging in the vast temple of God.

Conversion is regarded as a transcendental event, an event which is authoritative and in which the grace of God has been authentically mediated, an event which is not the outcome of

[15] In evangelical denominations assurance of salvation is a normal resultant of a sound conversion. Evangelicalism offers the conscience-stricken person who turns to God in Christ with faith, complete and unmediated salvation. Catholicism can make no such inducement, for it assumes the necessity of repeated sacrifices of the mass. The Catholic sacramental system appears to rest on the conviction of the continuous need of expiation for man's sin. See Howley, John F. W., *Psychology and Mystical Experience,* p. 11 (London: Kegan Paul, Trench, Trübner & Co., 1920).

[16] The kind of voices and visions which accompany conversion reflect the religious environment and upbringing of the subject. A Catholic in a spiritual crisis may have a vision of the crucifix or hear the voice of the Virgin. The contents of the automatism which a Protestant experiences are derived from the characteristic concepts and mental imagery of his apperceptive mass.

merely human striving but one in which the power of God has played upon the subject.[17] Love for God in Christ is a normal outcome of release from the power of evil, and the consciousness of divine favor. In gratitude and love the life interests are subordinated to Christ as the object of chief loyalty. Once the theoretically accepted Christian order of life was an external pressure, a restraint imposed from without upon protesting human nature; now it is an inward compulsion to which willing obedience is accorded.[18]

Groups in Need of Reclamation

According to statistics compiled by Clark, the percentage of persons undergoing conversion has been constantly declining during the past thirty years. Of the 2,174 individual instances of religious awakening investigated by Clark, only 147 or 6.7 per cent are recognizable as definite crisis cases. Of the remainder, 1,437 or 66.1 per cent are cases of gradual growth.[19] Although the increase in the number as well as in the percentage of gradual growth cases is gratifying, one is disposed to inquire whether the number of conversions should not be multiplied. Surely thousands in our country stand in need of that radical recentering of personality called conversion. The day of the periodic emotional mass evangelistic appeal may be far

[17] For more extended discussions of conversion consult the following: Starbuck, Edwin D., *The Psychology of Religion,* Part I. (New York: Charles Scribner's Sons, 1899); James, William, *The Varieties of Religious Experience,* Chaps. VI-X (New York: Longmans, Green & Co., 1911); Coe, George A., *The Psychology of Religion,* Chap. X (Chicago: University of Chicago Press, 1916); Underwood, Alfred Clair, *Conversion: Christian and Non-Christian* (New York: The Macmillan Company, 1925); Sanctis, Sante de, *Religious Conversion,* translated by Helen Augur (New York: Harcourt, Brace & Co., 1927); Clark, Elmer T., *The Psychology of Religious Awakening,* Chaps. II, III, VIII (New York: The Macmillan Company, 1929); Pratt, James B., *The Religious Consciousness,* Chaps. VII, VIII (New York: The Macmillan Company, 1930); Lang, L. Wyatt, *A Study of Conversion* (London: George Allen & Unwin, Ltd., 1931).

[18] An individual may dethrone the governing system of Christian principles and enthrone a system of irreligious principles. Such a radical change may as a whole include the approval of an ethically unsound body of concepts, the intrenchment of the new order and self-commitment to it with subsequent unification of personality. The reversion is most properly called a counter conversion.

[19] Clark, Elmer T., *The Psychology of Religious Awakening,* pp. 47 ff. (New York: The Macmillan Company, 1929).

spent in the majority of our communities, but the need of bringing the message of redemption to defeated and depressed individuals was never more urgent.

In the four incomparable parables of the lost sheep, the unpossessed coin, the prodigal son, and the scornful elder brother, Jesus, in defense of his associations with disreputable elements, introduced his hearers to four classes of people in desperate need of reclamation.[20] These familiar parables are freighted with profound insight into the circumstances and dispositions of various groups of persons gone wrong as well as into the redemptive passion of God.

The lost sheep represents those who through obtuseness and improvidence are overtaken by moral ruin. A sheep, obeying its instincts or inclinations, which are simply natural rather than censurable, strays from the fold, becomes confused, and loses its sense of direction. Heedless men yielding to the promptings of unwise but scarcely downright vicious impulses are morally lost. In order to be accounted lost it is quite unnecessary to plumb the depths of degradation; negligence and willful stupidity create moral havoc sufficient to make redemption imperative. The representatives of this class of sinners are individually as well as collectively somewhat deficient in understanding and will power, but they are intelligent enough to be held to accountability for their behavior. Only when they are sought and guided by ambassadors of Christ who possess the courage, sympathy, perseverance, and intelligence of a good shepherd, can they be reclaimed.

Another class of frustrated persons is vividly depicted in the parable of the lost coin. Those who comprise this class, like the unpossessed coin, are the victims of uncontrollable external circumstances. The coin, subject to the laws of physics, fell from its place to the earthen floor of a modest home, and rolled into a crack or a dark corner or under an article of furniture. It was not responsible for its situation. One is reminded of the helpless millions doomed to lives of economic and moral wretchedness by social conditions for the existence

[20] Luke 15: 1-32.

of which they are not accountable.   One recalls children cursed by incurable hereditary diseases, by arduous toil, by the greed of degraded men.   One considers the submerged masses in the slums of our cities, precariously existing on the verge of starvation and destitution, without hope or agreeable prospects, and condemned to sordidness and vice.   One thinks of those who are denied the material necessities in a land of actual or potential plenty.

Some who are submerged by a degrading environment are resigned to their lot and without complaint take their miserable existence for granted; others are embittered by their wretched situation and nurse a sense of injury and hopeless resentfulness.   Poverty is a common, direct source of crime.   Economic deliverance and the reconstruction of debilitating social conditions do not make the religious rehabilitation of underprivileged personality inevitable, but they do afford it the opportunity without which conversion is exceedingly difficult if not impossible.   The broom of drastic social action guided by the candle of intelligence can play a necessary part in the moral recentering of persons defrauded of elementary human rights by forces from the clutches of which, unaided, they are powerless to extricate themselves.

The third type of defeated humanity is introduced in the moving tale of the prodigal son.   Like the willful wastrel in the parable, many want "to see life," to feel an exotic thrill, and therefore cast aside all irksome inhibitions, heedless of possible personal or social consequences.   Like the prodigal son whose request for an immediate share of his father's property was granted and whose proposal to leave home encountered no obstacles or reproaches, thousands of the privileged classes of society are in possession of the means and the opportunity to gratify their determination to wander into the far country of moral unrestraint.   Like him, many come to grief.   Brought to his senses by the normal resultants of waywardness, many a prodigal both ancient and modern has become mindful of benefits once too lightly esteemed, and has resolved to return to the father's house, to confess with shame his inexcusable delinquency, to acknowledge the just forfeiture of his sonship, and to sue for the lowly status of a servant in the home. The stinging awareness of moral madness is most likely to overwhelm the profligate upon whose childhood years the influences of a religious home have played. In his case conversion consists in the revival and enthronement of the early religious affinities, habits, and beliefs. His defection is not the product of a sluggish or dull intellect nor of evil surroundings from which he cannot escape, but of perversity compounded of a lack of appreciation of his advantages and an impatience of the restraints of ordinary decency.

The fourth class of persons in need of conversion is characterized by the attitude of the elder brother toward both his father and the returned prodigal. The son who remained at home and was in several respects a model young man was consumed by inordinate pride, moral exclusiveness, and priggish superiority. He exemplified the prudential virtues of industry, honesty, frugality, and sobriety, but he was a stranger to mercy and charitable judgment. He refused to welcome his brother and displayed a jealous and rebellious spirit when his father personally entreated him to participate in the festivities in honor of the reclaimed youth. Sullen, melancholy, and joyless individual that he was, he nevertheless complained that his father had never prepared a feast for him and his friends. He disowned his brother, remarking, "When this thy son was come," and proceeded to drag out the details of his disgrace and infamy. The father sought to soften the attitude of the austere and obdurate son, to induce him to conquer his jealousy, to subdue his captiousness, and to forsake his ingratitude. How hard it is for the respectable and reputable man to realize that, steeped in merciless self-esteem, he is actually lost! The reconditioning of such a one is not impossible although the assumption of his own rectitude makes it difficult.[21]

In his own inimitable method of presentation Jesus introduces and characterizes four types of lost humanity and God's concern for their rescue—the impulsively and obtusely negligent, the underprivileged cursed by debasing inheritance or en-

---

[21] Compare the parables of the prodigal son and the elder brother with the parable of the Pharisee and the publican in Luke 18: 9-14.

vironment or both, the thrill-seeking, and the dutiful but uncharitable and harsh. Each class presents an opportunity for comprehensive evangelism and personal service. Each is present in practically every community. Although each requires an approach in accordance with its particular features, the primary necessity of all is the adoption of a higher center of personality control, in short, evangelical conversion. The Church is a life-changing agency if it is true to its spiritual head, and as such must seek and find the lost sheep and the unpossessed coin, the wayward son and prideful elder brother.

CHAPTER XIV

METHODS OF PERSONALITY CONTROL

RELIGION has adopted various methods for the conversion of primitive and antisocial impulses, instincts and tendencies, drives and interests, into constructive and ethical action. In addition the insight and inspiration of Christianity produce new recognizable character values. Christian education recognizes the almost innumerable implications of faith in God for the cultivation of soundly integrated personality. In the development of Christian personality, which is the most delicate and difficult achievement of which an immature individual is capable, religion radiates to every mental function and permeates each mode of experience. Both objective and subjective occurrences are brought under the control of the Christian ideal and given momentum and direction.

In the course of its development religion has either devised or adopted identifiable techniques for the regulation of human nature. Five representative methods may be selected for special consideration—sublimation, selection, substitution, disuse, and creativity. These modes of personality control, as will directly appear, tend in many instances to overlap. A given personality function may be refashioned or discarded or created by more than one of the specific techniques which the religious personality employs. In order to facilitate an examination of the regulatory value of religion each method may be disengaged from its complicating context, but it should be borne in mind that in actual operation several techniques may support one another.

Sublimation

Darwin, in a two-volume work, shows that plants and animals now serviceable to man are transformed wild types.[1] Dogs

[1] Darwin, Charles R., *Variation of Animals and Plants under Domestication* (London: Murray, 1868).

are but reclaimed wolves, jackals, and kindred untamed animals. The intimacy of connection which exists between breeds of dogs and wolves has been vividly set forth by Jack London in his popular story, *The Call of the Wild*. The tame rabbit is the direct descendant of the common wild rabbit. The several species of pigeons, although dissimilar, such as pouters, carriers, and tumblers, are all the products of man's domestication of a single original wild species, the sudden variations which occurred at rare intervals under domestication being the points of departure for new species. What is true of the domesticated animals is likewise true of the domesticated plants. Grains, vegetables, fruits, ornamental trees, and garden flowers are cultivated offspring of wild forms. From raw materials types useful to man in a wide variety of ways have been derived. Today the geneticist is still further improving our fauna and flora by experimental methods.

Dr. Heiser reports that the enforcement of the law against head-hunting in the Philippines was difficult. The white man's usual method was to shoot the offender. He and his associates changed the underlying form of rivalry. They introduced athletics. The strongest men in equal numbers, from two rival villages, engaged in the game of tug of war. In these contests the tribesmen sublimated the violent emotions which formerly had been given an outlet in bloodshed.[2]

In many cases religion by a process of refinement converts a physiological impulse, a crude instinct, or a misdirected desire into a socialized force or a more acceptable personal characteristic. Hunger and thirst manifest themselves solely on the vegetative level in the infant; on the sensorimotor level an appetite for muscular activity, sights, sounds, tastes, and smells clamors for satisfaction; on the reflective level there is a longing for insight and wisdom; on the religious level one craves for identification with the spirit of the universe. Jesus, it is of interest to observe, employed gustatory terms in one of the

[2] Heiser, Victor, *An American Doctor's Odyssey*, p. 136 (New York: W. W. Norton & Co., 1936.).

most significant of the beatitudes, "Blessed are they that hunger and thirst after righteousness: for they shall be filled." [3]

Fear is a response in terms of a painful consciousness accompanied by a tendency to flee or to be rooted to the spot, which religion may either intensify or transmute into more refined attitudes.   Multitudes living in a naïve cultural environment are periodically terrorized by a belief in the existence of a material hell, the malevolent activity of ghosts and hostile spirits, and the imminent end of the world.   Many a sensitive and conscientious but unenlightened person has been tormented into insanity by the conviction that he has committed the unpardonable sin.   That religion has made abundant use of fear as a persuasive to piety and conformity to inherited customs and precepts even a cursory reading of nothing more than a section of the history of the Church will disclose.   Nevertheless, fear has likewise been the raw material which religion has transformed into the successive stages of awe and reverence.

Awe may be described as fear mingled with respect.   The normal reaction to the awesome is not flight or the paralysis of locomotion, but an appreciation of its superiority or magnitude coupled with a sense of one's own inferiority.   Fear is not altogether absent, but it is modified and in large measure subdued by the consciousness of the extraordinary.   Awe is aroused when one grasps as a whole an object which transcends the ordinary standards of comparison, accomplishment, or measurement.   One may experience awe in the presence of either the inanimate or the animate, of stars or a person invested with superlative powers.

Reverence is a further refinement of fear.   It is more intense than awe and is invariably engendered by the recognition of great worth or merit in others.   It is disinterested veneration directed toward one who is spiritually elevated and exemplifies ideal qualities.   It is likely to induce the mood and attitude of worship.   A desire arises to win the approval of and to serve the existence which inspires reverence.   Fear unrelieved of its

[3] Matthew 5: 6.

terrors may move a votary to placate or appease a wrathful deity or drive the worshiper into servile subjection, but reverence is marked by the double sense of unworthiness and ethical love.   Awe culminates in a realization of the grandeur or glory of the instigating object, but it does not lead to a humble dedication of the self to its will.   The religious sublimination of fear reaches its most advanced and creative stage in the attitude of reverence.   Fear is disjunctive, reverence is conjunctive. Solemn wonder, wholesome esteem, submissive deference, and a measure of trepidation, which characterize reverence, are powerful integrating components of the religious attitude.

Anger is another emotional reaction which the religious consciousness utilizes and often socializes.   The anger response is a disagreeable emotion combined with a strong impulse to destroy the instigating circumstance or agent.   It may prompt the individual to defend his property and rights and to overpower an antagonist.   Anger frequently expresses itself in the taking of revenge.   Retribution may be delayed; a person who has been insulted or outraged may not retaliate at once, but bide his time and when the conditions are auspicious pay the score.   A teacher was requested by a former student to recommend him for a desirable position, but the teacher, recalling that the student years before on a public occasion on the campus had made light of him, refused to comply with the request.

Anger transformed by the religious attitude may become superiority or righteous indignation.   Instead of permitting anger to discharge its violence in acts of retaliation or destruction the individual may stand on his dignity.   Moved by self-regard, one may successfully resist the temptation to destroy or hate the anger-inducing person or thing.   One rises above the taking of revenge or the poisoning of the self by the virus of hatred.   The actual application of the principle of vindictiveness affords momentary primitive relief and satisfaction, but instead of decreasing evil in another, generally multiplies it. Self-mastery which refuses to yield to the savage impulses aroused by anger throws an adversary who has not anticipated such conduct into confusion, shames him, gives his ire time to cool, affords him an occasion for reflection, and robs him of the fleeting intoxication of meeting force with additional violence. There is a moral strategy in self-discipline which restrains a man from falling upon an offender in the fury of rage and with deadly intent, a strategy which the world has been slow to understand and even more reluctant to practice.

Anger socialized becomes moral indignation. Perhaps St. Paul appreciated the value of socialized wrath, for he exhorts his constituency to be angry and to sin not.[4] According to the New Testament records the fiery indignation which repeatedly impelled Jesus to resort to invective or drastic action, was evoked by those who oppressed the poor, the outcast, the ignorant, and the defenseless. It was in each case detached from self-interest. An affront to himself did not induce Jesus to display anger and its works. His anger was kindled by and directed toward those who, despite their superior advantages, opposed truth and mercy, and he did not hesitate to stigmatize them as hypocrites, blind guides, fools, and whited sepulchers. Consumed by indignation and moved by a sense of social justice, Jesus overthrew the tables of the tradesmen who had degraded the house of prayer into a refuge of thieves, and drove them forth with blistering denunciation. In him anger was converted into righteous aggression.

Pugnacity which generally, but not always, includes anger is one of the strongest impulses which one endeavors to subordinate to the Christian ideal. Combativeness enabled the human species to emerge victorious in the desperate struggle for existence which characterized the period of savagery in the evolution of society. Pugnacity had its rapid development, if not its origin, in the jungle where primitive man had to fight bloodthirsty members of his own species as well as wild animals, or perish. Pugnacity crosses other elemental impulses. Man like other sentient creatures may fight in self-defense, he may fight for food or for a mate, he may fight to save his progeny from injury and death. Even play and self-assertion may assume the form of fighting.

A fundamental impulse like pugnacity, once it has gathered

[4] Ephesians 4: 26.

sufficient momentum, is difficult if not impossible to extirpate. The annihilation of this drive would render the individual passive and negative. On the other hand, pugnacity may be permitted to exercise itself without irksome restraints. It may be made the ruler of the house. No regulations may be imposed upon it, no boundaries indicated beyond which it may not go. An uncontrolled active predisposition to fight invariably results in personal degradation or antisocial conduct, or both. Permitted to flourish and express itself without curb or check, combativeness becomes the instrument of evil. The savage resorted to the arousal and unhampered indulgence of it whenever he was provoked to anger by an adversary. Modern man in warfare achieves the same temper and with like consequences. It is a matter of profound regret that leaders of the people have in the name of Christianity repeatedly effected a recrudescence of violent hatred discharged in the wanton destruction and brutal slaughter of war.

It is possible to repress pugnacious tendency. A conscious effort may be made, not to eradicate it, but to snub it whenever it manifests itself. It may be forced into the subconscious region of personality whenever it seeks conscious recognition and realization. The repressed impulse, since it is denied conscious control, turns upon itself and leads a surreptitious subconscious existence. No longer amenable to the will, it may "bore from within" and create a pathological disturbance.

There is yet a more excellent way, the way that Christianity at its best selects. Pugnacity may be neither submerged nor given free rein, but disciplined and subordinated to human welfare. It may be directed into ethical and social channels. It may be pressed into the service of the common welfare.[5] The primitive force may be subjected to noble aims and expressed in constructive achievements. There is no necessary and therefore honorable vocation in which the God-given militant impulse cannot be profitably employed. The lawyer may fight against iniquity and for justice, the teacher may fight against ignorance and for culture, the physician may fight against dis-

---

[5] See William James' famous essay "The Moral Equivalent for War," *Memoirs and Studies* (New York: Longmans, Green & Co., 1912).

ease and for health, the washerwoman may fight against dirt, the civil engineer may fight against the unfavorable works of nature and bring them under subjection to human welfare. Pugnacity may take an almost incalculable number of creative forms.

A constant pressure of righteous indignation is to be brought against the powers of injustice. He who subdues an evil renders both the community and the offender a service. Goodness should be aggressive. St. Paul was the leader in a conflict waged against a movement to impose Jewish rites upon Gentile Christians. In his campaign for freedom from Jewish legalism, Paul did not employ military weapons, but placed his sole reliance on moral and religious influence.[6] At a later time in the course of his ministry, realizing that the good life is a perpetual struggle against evil, he described the Christian in the imagery of the soldier fully armed for the fray.[7] At the close of his career he delivered his valedictory, exclaiming, "I have fought the good fight."[8]

In this respect the Christian faith as it was proclaimed by its founder and propagated by his most illustrious early follower is unlike such living world religions as Buddhism and Islam. Since it advocates the progressive abstraction of all desire, as the panacea for the misery and pain of human existence, Buddhism at least theoretically precludes the exercise of pugnacity. As a religion of tranquil detachment it cannot reconcile aggression with its conception of the good life. On the other hand, Islam, in its attempt to convert or slay, unfettered the belligerent drive. Allah, swayed by a warlike and vindictive disposition, coerced his followers into merciless conflict with all who refused abject submission to his will. Christianity, pure and undefiled, would neither uproot the will to fight, give it destructive expression, nor submerge it below the level of awareness, but transform it into an effective instrument of good will.

Curiosity is such a potent determinant of intellectual as well

[6] Acts 15, Galatians 2. [7] Ephesians 6: 10-20.
[8] 2 Timothy 4: 7.

as motor activity that religion must needs take it into account and utilize it. Curiosity is a species of hunger. Like the normal appetite for food, curiosity when gratified is no longer felt. It can be most easily quenched by an immediate and positive response, and is readily intensified through alternating partial satisfaction and suspended expectation. Curiosity is not an exclusive human function. Although fish possess a relatively low grade of intelligence, they are impelled by curiosity to nibble at the bait extended by the angler. Cows, evidently spurred by mingled curiosity and fear, will alternately approach and retreat from a person standing with outstretched hand in a pasture. It manifests its presence in the interminable series of questions which the young child asks his elders. Little children, motivated by curiosity mingled with acquisitiveness, reach for the moon. Curiosity supported by desires for recognition and excitement has driven men into the frigid zones in search of the poles. It leads people to investigate the cosmic ray, the evidences for evolution, the systems of the philosophers, the history of civilizations long extinct, and the structure of the atom.

In the field of religion curiosity raises questions, some of which nobody has as yet been able to answer to the satisfaction of even an enlightened minority of mankind. Why do the innocent suffer although a just God orders the affairs of the universe? Why did God permit moral evil to enter humanity? Where are the beloved dead? What is the metaphysical relation which subsists between God and Christ? There is no reason to suppose that, so long as religion continues to be a major interest of mankind, questions like these, prompted by curiosity reinforced by life problems, will not be asked. Curiosity, perhaps, reaches its culmination in the effort to communicate with the dead, in spiritism.

Selection and Emphasis

The vast majority of our mental experiences are not simple and unmixed but complicated. Impulses, instincts, drives, attitudes, and emotions, so far from being reducible to one sole constituent, are each compounded of various processes and states. Melancholy, for instance, is a relatively simple mental experience, yet it is a combination of sadness and sweetness, a combination, by the way, to which many persons surrender themselves ecstatically because they derive pleasure from it. The regulatory activity of religion may unite in a new synthesis the congenial or moral elements of a compound, and disregard the disjunctive components. The quality of an attitude may be determined by the aspect which religion makes dominant.

Love is a consolidation of such components as self-regard, jealousy, sex attraction, co-operation, and sacrifice. Self-regard is a basal principle in the survival of the individual. In its crudest form it is sheer selfishness, an attitude which impels one to employ others as a means to an end, and to acquire and retain, at any cost to society, material or other advantages. It is ruthless individualism. In the religious relation evidences of selfishness can be detected, such as prayer circumscribed by one's own needs and desires. On a higher level self-regard assumes the form of an intelligent self-interest. Present advantages and immediate gains are sacrificed to greater future inducements. Bread is cast upon the waters in the expectation that it will return as cake. A person may apply for membership in a church, for social or business reasons, or make a large subscription to a good cause in order to enhance his status in the community. Receiving still further refinement self-regard may become self-respect. One scorns the unworthy as something beneath one's dignity. An increased sensitiveness to reputation may be deliberately fostered. It is evident that self-regard in any one of its several possible manifestations is a qualifying ingredient of love.

The element of jealousy may be conspicuously potent in the total love relation. Jealousy tends to explode itself in destructive anger and hatred. In some cases jealousy is a manifestation of fear charged with wrath—fear of being deprived of a prized or coveted possession. Moved by envy, Abel kills Cain, the sons of Jacob sell their brother Joseph into slavery, the elder brother in Jesus' incomparable parable refuses to welcome and receive the returned prodigal. If jealousy is an active component, love is selfish.   Love may be so possessive that, as it were, it surrounds its object with tentacles and absorbs it to extinction.   In religion it takes the form of resentment against those who despite their unworthiness have won the divine favor.   Jonah, typifying the Jewish nation, is jealous and sulks because Jehovah has compassion upon the repentant Ninevites and withholds the predicted destruction of a great city.   Jealousy may be a spur to devotion.   St. Paul is of the opinion that in time the Jews, made jealous by the salvation accorded the Gentiles by God, will turn to Christ in penitence and faith.[9]

The sexual instinct may be numbered with the constituents of love.   Love may be so governed by sexual appetite that it culminates in carnal satisfaction.   Personality which is sexually centered evaluates all contacts and opportunities in terms of immediate or eventual sexual gratification.   Love may exhaust itself in sexual identification with its responsive object. On the other hand, the sexual impulse may be discharged in any one of several approved socialized forms.   In its sublimated state it may express itself in the welfare of little children, the care of the sick, and the relief of the poor.   It may manifest itself in the parental protective relationship.   Its irradiations may include the conjunctive attitudes of sympathy and altruism.   Trees and flowers provide an analogy.   The roots, the trunk, the branches, the leaves, and the flowers engage in a conspiracy to produce seeds.   Fruits and seeds which man finds not only edible but also palatable are love foods.   Milk is a love drink.   In its symbolical ramifications the sexual urge may be released in the production or appreciation of poetry, fiction, sculpture, and other art forms.   In fact, it may find expression in any socially useful activity.[10]   Evidently the quality of love is in part determined by the rôle which the sexual instinct plays in the life of the individual.

Co-operation is a characteristic feature of the love which

[9] Romans 11.

[10] For an example consider the poem "Anne Rutledge" by Edgar Lee Masters, *Spoon River Anthology*, p. 184 (New York: The Macmillan Company, 1916).

Christianity enjoins upon its following. Co-operation among human beings as an active principle of common welfare is, as it were, foreshadowed in the realm of nature. Various parts of a flower co-operate in transferring pollen from the stamen of one blossom to the stigma of another. Brilliantly colored petals attract the notice of bees, tiny flowers grow in clusters and are thus collectively more easily detected, nectar is offered as a reward to the carrier of pollen, white petals are seen by insects infesting the night, perfume lures the insects that cannot see. The seeds of a co-operative plant, like the thistle, being equipped with wings or parachutes, are widely distributed by the wind. The principle of co-operation is equally operative among animate specimens of creation. Such insects as ants, bees, and wasps which exist in colonies or swarms possess a survival probability which the individual, feeble and defenseless in its isolation, lacks. Such individually weak creatures as sparrows can maintain themselves only in flocks.

Why love as a religious obligation includes and magnifies the attribute of co-operation is obvious. It is in co-operation rather than in competition that the well-being of the individual in the group is assured. The voluntary co-operation of the resourceful who could at least for a time profit materially by ruthless competition can be elicited only by an affection for the less privileged members of society. In a highly technological social system where production of material necessities exceeds consumption co-operation becomes economically and politically mandatory. When co-operation is the outcome of coercion rather than affection and free will it may be socially expedient, but it is not a typical form of religious behavior. When coercion ceases or is abolished by superior force the co-operation which it has imposed upon unwilling men is withdrawn. The love which a tender-minded religion like Christianity makes central provides an adequate basis for enduring, expanding, and flexible varieties of co-operation.

The refinement of love under the influence of idealism reaches its culmination in intelligent self-sacrifice for the good of another or society. Self-sacrifice is the hero in the play which love stages.   To surrender one's identity in order that a larger value may be preserved or created is the summit of Christian love.   Sacrifice that is needless or is not commensurate with the consequences fails to secure the approval of the judgment of the discriminating individual although it may arouse his appreciation of the kindly disposition which prompted it.   The time, place, circumstances, motives, and methods associated with a sacrificial act of love are all positively or negatively significant.   To know the due occasion for a supreme expression of ethical love requires intelligence of a high order.   The Christian religion, as the annals of its sacrificial leadership show, is not content with an idle gesture springing from an undistinguishing, although generous, heart.

Love is, then, a fusion of a variety of mental processes and impulses including self-regard, jealousy, the sexual instinct, co-operation, and sacrifice.   The quality of love as a compound is conditioned by the ingredient which the personality has made integrative.   If the principle which governs the personality as a whole is sordid and individualistic, self-regard in terms of selfishness, jealousy in terms of destructive exclusiveness, and sexuality in terms of its cruder manifestations are potently active in the love relation, but co-operation and sacrifice for ethical welfare are conspicuously absent.   If the Christian outlook and insight regulate love, co-operation and sacrifice motivated by affection and directed by intelligence are given the pre-eminence.   In addition, self-regard as self-respect, jealousy for the welfare of another rather than of him, and the parental and aesthetic aspects of the sexual instinct are cultivated.   In brief, an ethically sensitive religion sees to it that in a consolidation like love the socially profitable components are embraced and active and the more primitive impulses are subordinated and refined.

Substitution

In many cases religious control is exercised in a process of substitution whereby an unworthy response is displaced by sanctioned behavior.   A young child denied the possession of a watch or relieved of it may not create a scene but engage in a compensatory smile. If a child is playing with a sharp knife, the parent may offer him an apple as a substitute. The principle of substitution is applied by the religious personality to various circumstances, but especially to situations in which contradictions and antitheses figure. Negations are canceled by affirmations as darkness is dispelled by light. "Perfect love casteth out fear." [11] Error may be expelled by truth, vice by virtue, dishonesty by honesty. The center of attention and the direction in which energy is expended are shifted from the undesirable to the commendable.

Substitution differs markedly from sublimation. In the course of sublimation a crude or antisocial impulse is given a form of discharge in harmony with the ideals of the individual. In the process of substitution a desire or function is deliberately uprooted and supplanted by another with which it has had no affiliation.

Mutually exclusively opposites afford the clearest examples. Rivalry within the Church universal has kept alive differences and antagonisms which otherwise would have perished long ago. The overchurched condition of many of our smaller communities and the persistent refusal of responsible denominational officials to correct the evil is the direct outcome of a union of unchristian traits of which rivalry sanctioned and incorporated in the name of religion is a potent motive force. Co-operation which is impelled and directed by a sincere devotion to the cause of Christ for which all the branches of the Church professedly stand, can supplant the spirit of rivalry and its melancholy works.

Disuse

Under the influence and guidance of the religious motive many character defects are subjected to the atrophy of disuse. Reprehensible practices are no longer countenanced, but simply discontinued. No effort is made to provide substitutes for them, they are just no longer countenanced. Denied exercise, the unsanctioned drives wither and perish. Alco-

[11] 1 John 4: 18.

holism may be abandoned at the dictates and by the power of religion without the aid of a substitute like coffee or carbonated water.   The personality supported by religious resources is purged of a habit that contradicts one's sense of fitness.   Disuse liberates from unworthiness and inferiority rooted in moral delinquency.   It makes possible improved modes of personality integration.   Native impulses can best be subordinated to a religious ideal by the cultural process of sublimation, but disuse is an effective means of release from habits, desires, and purposes which have no redeeming features.

Creativity

The principles of sublimination, selection, substitution, and disuse do not exhaust the resources of religiously integrated personality in its quest for the good life.   The mind that was in Christ is accepted as the anticipated goal of religious aspiration.   The concept of reclamation from evil does not comprehend in its entirety the function of Christianity as the integrative agency of wholesome personality.   The eradication of the roots of inquity is to be accompanied or followed by the growth of the fruits of the Spirit.   Positive resultants of various methods of religious control have been indicated, but the cultivation of specialized conjunctive experiences and character values should receive its due measure of emphasis.

Other means of religious reconstruction and growth are supplemented and completed by definitive creative activity.   The constructive and progressive practice of productive Christian principles sustains, if it does not also originate, a passion for truth, a love for the beautiful, and the graces such as good will and courtesy as well as such homely virtues as honesty, industry, and frugality.   St. Paul, bearing in mind the creative power of Christianity, says: "The fruit of the Spirit is love, joy, peace, longsuffering, kindness, goodness, faithfulness, meekness, self-control." [12]   The fertile Christian personality strives to realize the purpose of God in the extension of the kingdom which Jesus founded.   A tranquil gladness is the

[12] Galatians 5: 22, 23.

prevailing accompaniment of the experience of progressively higher forms of Christian creativity.

The core of Christianity which is that God in Christ has invaded humanity with unique power is not a biological inheritance, nor an inborn revelation which all members of each succeeding generation possess, nor an instinct that functions of its own accord. It is a dynamic self-impartation of God to those who are prepared by faith to receive it. The Christian integration of personality involves not only the methods of sublimation, emphasis, substitution, and disuse, but also a distinctive moral creativity without which the individual would lack some of the experiences and attributes characteristic of a dynamic faith in God.

Only by the constant and intelligent exercise of the creative religious control over his primal urges and inclinations can man maintain the progressive stages of spiritual culture which the Christian ideal entails. Left to themselves, animals and plants derived from wild forms either perish or revert to the primitive types. It is significant that the most improved domesticated animals cannot long subsist when thrown back into the state of nature. A sheep, for example, thus relegated would soon fall an easy prey to ferocious carnivorous beasts, or the inclemency of the weather. When domesticated animals, forced to obtain their food by their own efforts and exposed to competition with other and more savage creatures and to the rigors of an inimical climate, do actually survive they tend to assume the characteristics of the parent stock. Pigs, when permitted to run wild, if they do survive, acquire the shape of body, the length of muzzle and legs, the thick bristles, the dark color, and in some cases the tusks of the original wild species. The application of these references from biology to human nature and its spiritual domestication is obvious.

"Watch and pray,"[13] for human nature tends to revert to barbarism, if not to savagery, with its colossal selfishness. Unceasing vigilance and cultivation are the price of Christian

[13] Matthew 26: 41.

character.   Such means of grace as worship, prayer, confession, repentance, amendment, Christian fellowship, and sacrificial service, which support and direct the religious reintegration of personality, cannot be discarded without danger of retrogression.   Faith-union with God so enriches the subsoil of personality that the seed of the gospel germinates and in due course bears an abundant harvest of the characteristics which adorn the true Christian.

CHAPTER XV

BALANCED RELIGIOUS PERSONALITY

FOR centuries students of human nature have recognized three major phases of mentality—thinking, feeling, and doing. All psychological occurrences are reducible to these basic modes. Not that every mental event is easily classified, for thought, emotion, and behavior interpenetrate and tend to merge. For instance, when the individual is engaged in the process of thinking, action internal, overt or incipient, and emotional states are involved to some degree. Nevertheless, at a given moment of experience one psychic mode is likely to predominate.

In which mode is religion primarily centered? Hegel sought the essence of religion in the realm of truth, Schleiermacher in a feeling of dependence, Kant in the voluntaristic strain in personal relationships. Is it possible to reconcile these divergent positions? Does an inquiry into the nature and function of religion as it is lived by earnest, intelligent, and good persons disclose a preponderance of any one phase or a creative synthesis of all three?

The Nature of Thought

The psychologist traces the development of cognition in the individual throughout the successive stages of sensation, perception, imagination, memory, conception, reasoning, and judgment. The physiological correlative is the central nervous system which consists of the brain together with twelve pairs of cranial nerves, and the spinal cord with thirty-one pairs of spinal nerves. Aristotle maintained that thinking is communing with one's self. Thinking implies the consciousness of relations, the weighing of evidence, the balancing of alternatives, the consideration of probable outcomes, the evaluation of situations and experiences. Analysis, antithesis, and synthesis, Hegel declared, outline the development of a process of rigorous thought. Thinking is the play of events by means of such

240

symbols as words and images.   Creative thinking, as a rule, occurs when the ordinary course of events is challenged, when one tries to surmount a barrier in the field of forces.   A turning point is a spur to thought.   Ideas are natural occurrences and as such are representations of details in a larger context or reaction system.

Thinking develops relatively late in the child.   The infant reacts and feels, but does not think.   At birth the cerebral hemispheres, the physiological correlatives of reasoning, are undeveloped.   Judgment is perhaps the most complicated mental process of which human beings are capable.   The last function to emerge in the evolution of consciousness, it is the first to succumb when the mind degenerates.   In fact, few men are capable of independent and dependable reflection and the majority of such do not exercise their ability to the utmost.   Most of us do not attempt an adjustment to a novel situation by abstract reasoning, but resort to the utilizing of known patterns, to the following of clues, and to the performing of experiments.   We interpret outcomes after they have been made manifest rather than anticipate them in productive imagination.   Inventions, for example, are as a rule not the creations of a logical train of thought but are hit upon more or less by repeated attempts to bring various elements into an effective relation.   It is said that Thomas A. Edison, following such a procedure, invented the incandescent electric lamp.   One evening when he was in his laboratory he took particular notice of a bit of lampblack in his hand.   It occurred to him that this might serve to complete the form of illumination he had in vain been attempting to contrive.   He cut off a short piece of cord, charred it in the fire, then put the crude filament into a glass globe, connected the combination with an electric current, and his long-desired light flashed into existence.

Values of Religious Thought

It would be exceedingly difficult to imagine a form of religion void of thought.   No religion without an intellectual content could develop its potentialities and be transmitted from generation to generation.   The personal founder of each of the great living religions, to say nothing of the others extinct or extant, promulgated a more or less coherent system of concepts and precepts. Religions differ widely in the cogency of their thought structures. On the other hand, the tenets of a religion other than one's own would be more convincing than they actually are if one were familiar with the cultural tradition in which they are rooted. Each religion has a characteristic if not an indigenous theology or ideology.

No more than a cursory reading of the history of the Church is necessary to disclose the importance which the Christian religion in its major branches has attached to thought. The Scriptures, to go back to the primary document of the Church, exalt intelligence and judgment. Hosea attributed to ignorance of the true God the depths of degradation to which his contemporaries had sunk. "My people are destroyed for lack of knowledge," [1] he cries out in Jehovah's stead against the delinquent leadership. In the book of Isaiah the gracious invitation is extended: "Come now, and let us reason together, saith Jehovah: though your sins be as scarlet, they shall be white as snow." [2] The prophet Habakkuk predicts the dawn of a new era when "the earth shall be filled with the knowledge of the glory of Jehovah, as the waters cover the sea." [3] Jesus himself was called rabbi, or teacher. He could think with such swiftness and clarity that time and again he immediately exposed the fallacy in the position of an adversary and silenced him. He was a man of ideas. He had a message. Jesus developed his capacity for rebuttal and argumentation and made it an amazingly effective instrument of his ministry. He attached importance to knowledge. Dying on the cross, he prayed, "Father, forgive them; for they know not what they do," [4] and thus made the ignorance of his persecutors the plea for their forgiveness. The ministry of Jesus from its beginning to its close is supported by teachings which one may reject but cannot ignore.

The personality and teaching of Jesus have received repeated

[1] Hosea 4: 6.   [2] Isaiah 1: 18.
[3] Habbakuk 2: 14.   Compare Isaiah 11: 9.
[4] Luke 23: 34.

and diversified systematic intellectual formulation at the hands of a vast succession of theologians. The very genius of Protestantism, the individualism which it at least in theory supports, originates theological disputation, schisms, and consequent confusion. Now and then individual Protestants, wearied by the conflict of the teachings of the sects, seek refuge in an authoritarian church where there is uniformity of theology.

A liberal infusion of the pale cast of thought into religion has its recognizable advantages. In the first place, ideas are definitely related to ideals. An ideal is an idea of achievement adopted as a goal. Again, knowledge, other conditions being auspicious, makes the conscious performance of duty possible. Virtue in the highest sense is impossible without knowledge. Furthermore, teaching is a medium by which the concepts of religion are transmitted to children and other persons. The success of the missionary enterprise and the program of religious culture depends in considerable measure on instruction, for a religion cannot be effective in the life of the individual who is ignorant of its principles and objectives. Granted that in every religion there is a mystical core, an element that defies intellectual dissection, an adequate understanding of the doctrines and behavior requirements is an indispensability. Finally, reflection and judgment play a necessary part in the application of ethical principles to particular situations as they arise in the course of personal or group experience. Jesus decreed little or no specific moral legislation, but promulgated generalities such as ethical love and self-respect, and relied upon men to exercise intelligence in giving them concrete and definite expression.

Perils of Intellectualism

On the other hand, certain perils are likely to beset the emphasis on cognition in religion. If the intellect were the taproot of ethics, knowledge of our duties would suffice to build character. Most men have more moral light than moral power. A moral code apart from emotional appeals lacks effectiveness.

Thought crystallized in a historic creed is a statement of

theological beliefs rather than a summons to moral action. The great creeds that have come down to us from the distant past and are still being recited by millions arose in periods of theological controversy, and although they include doctrines accepted by all Christians they were primarily designed to incorporate the beliefs which had divided the Church. It is possible to assent to every article in a traditional creed without direct personal committal to a single deed. One may be as theologically orthodox as Satan is reputed to be and remain almost as far from the kingdom of God. A creed as a body of doctrinal affirmations may be cogent, but the acceptance of it as true does not necessarily produce the good life. The implications for daily life of the articles of a formal theological creed are seldom developed.

Most men are incapable of a valid critique of religious ideas. The majority lack the theological and philosophical background essential to an analysis and appraisal of the concepts of religion. Quite aside from this lack, the fact is that but few men are endowed with a capacity for abstract reasoning. Theological concepts are too subtle and elusive to be grasped, compared, and evaluated by the average man. In most cases, inherited ideas of religious relationships are uncritically accepted or rejected. A reliance on tradition or external authority rather than on conclusions independently arrived at is characteristic and general. There is a strong and widespread tendency among deeply religious people to rest content in an almost mechanical assent to the body of inherited religious tenets as absolute truth.

The individual who is preoccupied with his own intellectual processes is likely to be an observer and critic of others rather than an active builder of the kingdom of God on earth. Standing aloof from the swift current of contemporary social, economic, and political affairs, he may analyze and deprecate its confusion and futility, but refuse to lend a hand in purifying and redirecting it. His interest in religion if not negative is primarily doctrinal. He is predisposed to be a theorizer who conceives it to be his mission to expose the fallacies and failures of those who are engaged in the reconstruction of the social order. To be sure, he serves as a disturber of the self-assurance of the extrovert, and as such exercises a function useful within narrow limits. His besetting sins are likely to be the sins of omission rather than the sins of commission. He does not seem to realize that to know the good and not to do it is the deadliest of sins. Reserved, detached from practical enterprises, and meticulously critical, he possesses insight but lacks the passion and the will to participate in the world of overt action.

The Nature of Emotion

That the religious approach to the spirit of the universe is heavily charged with emotional experiences as compared with the philosophical or scientific approach requires no lengthy disquisition. A religion void of emotion would be an anomaly. Religion has placed a unique reliance upon non-rational experience.

The term "feeling" is generic rather than specific and as such signifies an elementary, conscious, unanalyzed, and subjective condition. Feeling is the awareness of either pleasantness or unpleasantness. The quality of feeling is relative. What is pleasant to one person may be unpleasant to another. A rainy day may occasion pleasantness in the mind of a farmer whose crops need moisture, but unpleasantness in the minds of a group of school children whose plans for a holiday in the open are ruined. Here as elsewhere the law of diminishing returns operates. If it rains for several days, the dismal likelihood of the destruction of the farmer's crops will dissipate his sense of pleasantness and induce the feeling of unpleasantness. Since the rain has interfered with the original plans of the children, the teacher may give them special privileges in the schoolroom such as the playing of favorite games and the impromptu dramatizing of stories, with the result that unpleasantness yields to pleasantness. Pleasantness and unpleasantness depend on the individual himself, his outlook, his bodily state, his desires, his necessities, and other personal considerations. Since what is meat for one individual is poison for another, feeling is highly subjective.

All emotions are specializations, or extensions, of feeling. Woodworth's definition is so suggestive that it merits favorable consideration. He says, "An emotion is a conscious stirred-up state of the organism." [5] The organic condition involves a multitude of reverberations in the autonomic nervous system, such as changes in digestion, circulation, respiration, and glandular secretion. Although the array of emotional patterns is almost infinite, most psychologists are convinced that there are only a limited number of primary emotions. The present tendency is to regard the vast majority of the emotional states with which everybody is familiar as degrees, nuances, and combinations of a few elementary emotions. Allport, for example, concludes that fear, anger, and love are the major emotions. Fear is recognizable, he points out, in the attitudes of awe, reverence, bashfulness, surprise, wonder, suspicion, loathing, and anxiety. Anger plays a part in hatred, jealousy, envy, remorse, resentment, reproach, and scorn. Love is an ingredient in grief, pity, sorrow, gratitude, fascination, and, possibly, humility.[6] Primary emotions are biologically inherited and as native states of mind are not learned or acquired although they are aroused by experience.

An emotion entails organic preparation for some type of overt or consummatory behavior. Fear impels one to withdraw from or avoid the presence of a stimulating situation interpreted as dangerous. Anger moves one to vindicate censured deeds, to humiliate an adversary and render him helpless, and thus to enhance one's own status. Love induces an individual to identify himself with the object of his devotion. The overt expressions of many emotional derivatives and fusions are not so specific, and therefore not so easily observed and reported, but in all probability they do occur unless impeded or suppressed.

[5] Woodworth, Robert S., *Psychology*, p. 119 (New York: Henry Holt & Co., 1921).

[6] Allport, F. H., *Social Psychology*, p. 95 (New York: Houghton Mifflin Company, 1924). See Hollingworth, Harry L., *Psychology, Its Facts and Principles*, pp. 491 ff. (New York: D. Appleton & Co., 1928), for classification of affects, emotions, and instincts proposed by Warren, Dunlap, McDougall, and Seashore.

No distinguishable set of religious emotions has been disclosed by the scientific study of human beings. An object of worship may instigate or evoke fear or love, but that emotion as a state of mind does not differ intrinsically from fear or love aroused by any other sort of stimulus. The incitement has for the individual a religious significance and the personality may give the emotion a form of discharge which is religiously meaningful. Fear may move the devotee to placate or appease the divinity by ritualistic performance or reformation of conduct; love may impel him to enter into communion with the object of adoration and to exceed its formal requirements. It is only in some such sense that we can speak of religious emotions with any measure of precision.

Adler's classification of the emotions under two divisions, the conjunctive and disjunctive, is valuable.[7] The conjunctive emotions as Adler conceives them are those which unite men, promote good will, and engender and intensify the social consciousness. Specific emotions which belong to this group are joy, sympathy, and modesty. Since modesty does not always bring the individual into closer relationships with his fellow men, but sometimes leads him to withdraw into himself, it is not invariably socializing. The disjunctive emotions, as one would anticipate, are antisocial in their character and effects. Anger, sadness, disgust, fear, and anxiety constitute this division. The classification has profound implications for the development of the religious life.

Benefits of Emotion

The conjunctive emotions not only foster the social spirit and hold men together, but contribute also to the organization, stability, and unity of the individual in whom they arise. They play an important part in religiously integrated personality. Reverence, loyalty, ethical love, hope, and faith, especially when sanctioned and directed by a refined form of religion, are conjunctive attitudes, in which the emotions of joy, sympathy, and modesty are more or less recognizable. The

[7] Adler, Alfred, *Understanding Human Nature,* pp. 265 ff. (New York: Greenberg, Inc., 1927).

disjunctive emotions are divisive, disorganizing, and destructive personal as well as social forces. The emotions of anger, sadness, disgust, fear, and anxiety, individually and collectively, are ingredients in such disjunctive attitudes as jealousy, despair, remorse, hatred, and scorn. The classification of the emotions and attitudes introduced is not absolute. Joy, for example, may be unholy, and sorrow, or sadness, may be godly. "Hope deferred maketh the heart sick," [8] in other words the conjunctive attitude of hope repeatedly shattered may give way to the disjunctive attitude of despair. In the light of such a change from a conjunctive to a disjunctive state, or *vice versa,* Adler's statement that emotions are "psychic movements which possess a definite time boundary" is pertinent.

At least two major advantages or benefits accrue from the religious appeal to the emotions. In the first place, the non-rational is a source of truth. The mystic testifies that only when thinking and doing have ceased does the receptive personality hear the unspeakable words of God. Jehovah's exhortation "Be still, and know that I am God," [9] is psychologically and religiously justifiable. The faith on which religion takes its stand is vindicated by the inspiration and insight it affords and by the accomplishments to which it gives birth. It is demonstrable wisdom to trust the self's invincible surmise in the face of unknown and uncharted exigencies. Account for it as we may, what we can apprehend exceeds what we can comprehend. Confidence, loyalty, reverence, and love at their best are not irrational, but they do at times transcend the logic of reason and bring into being new relations and transformations. Apart from such emotions and attitudes certain meritorious possessions and experiences could not be our portion. In the process of progressive personality integration they are indispensable functions.

In the second place, emotions make ideas of action vivid and urgent. Emotionally toned ideas naturally seek concrete overt expression. Ideas associated with our loves and hatreds, our admirations and repulsions, are powerful determinants of con-

[8] Proverbs 13 : 12.   [9] Psalm 46 : 10.

duct. The mere intellectual comprehension and sanction of ideas lacks volitional pressure. A certain Christian leader delivered a series of lectures on an adequate community program of religious education before an intelligent audience in a small American city. The hearers were lavish in their acclaim of the program expounded, but were dumfounded when the lecturer proposed that the principles advocated be at once practically applied by them in the life of the community. Intellectual approval was not sufficient to arouse sluggish wills to activity. If the lecturer's proposals had induced in his auditors an intense emotional support as well as intellectual assent, inertia and conservatism would have been overborne. To communicate or engender sufficient enthusiasm to make ideas effective motor forces in the lives of others is the perpetually herculean task of the educational leader. It is possible to be so intellectually prim and correct as a speaker or a hearer that the springs of emotion dry up and the will atrophies.

Perils of Emotionalism

An excess of emotion is perilous. It is a matter of common observation that emotions may be divorced from volition. Emotional states do not always lead to right conduct and fruitful service. The preparatory reactions which occur in the organism are inevitably present, but the consummatory behavior, the overt act, may be omitted. The novel-reader or theatergoer may shed copious tears over the trials and wrongs inflicted upon an imaginary character, but remain callously indifferent to the relievable tragic conditions in which actual persons in the community are known to be entangled. The emotional experience may be cultivated for its own sake. In fact, a melancholy enjoyment of emotions aroused by the harsh realities of life is by no means uncommon. A morbid examination of the emotions is frequently the consequence of such a preoccupation. The habit of detaching conjunctive emotions from their natural consummatory tendency robs personality of stamina, and makes it flabby and impotent. The individual pulls himself up by the roots, so to speak, in order to examine his ethical growth. A deliberate effort is often made to induce and maintain an emotion of religious certainty severed from conduct. A fundamental requirement of a religion which includes ethical obligations is an indissoluble union of emotion and volition.

The reduction of the power of criticism through the emotional control of personality is equally pernicious. When the passional sways the individual the rational is held in abeyance. The emotionally unstable are easily victimized by all manner of religious delusions and frauds. Many spurious cults do not go into the highways and byways, seeking the degraded or the confused or the indifferent who are outside the Church, but focus their proselyting efforts on those members of the Church who live in their emotions and are therefore uncritical and prone to adopt almost any vagary that masquerades in the name of religion. Specious ideas of life and religion imposed with an assumed authority by the charlatan inflame the emotions of the highly suggestible person and render him intellectually defenseless. Recently I attended a meeting of earnest but naïve persons, in which by means of exhortation, instrumental and vocal music marked by repetition and rhythm, the clapping of hands, and the swaying of bodies in unison, several individuals, the majority of them women, achieved a state of emotional intoxication, fell to the floor, rolled from side to side, groaned and muttered. It was assumed that such phenomena duplicated the Pentecostal experience of the infant Church, which is recorded in the second chapter of the book of Acts.

An undeviating blind loyalty to a sect, the doctrines and practices of which are questionable, is quite as reprehensible as a procession of passionate attachments to an assortment of debilitating cults. Although the New Testament contains much that is difficult to understand, it includes also a body of teachings which can be grapsed by persons of even mediocre intelligence and which should serve everyone who professes to be a Christian as a standard of comparison in matters of worship, doctrine, and conduct. The adoption of an objective norm of excellence tends to curb excesses and uproot excrescences.

Varieties of Action

The dictum of William James that "all consciousness is motor" has become axiomatic. Movement within and without the organism is the correlate or sequence of every conceivable kind of thought or feeling. Sensory impression and motor expression are two aspects of a single normal mental occurrence. Emotions, instincts, and drives possess prodigious propulsive power. Ideas serve as stimuli for overt action with which they have been associated. Even the most abstract idea, let us say a philosophical concept, cannot arise in the mind without motor reverberations in the organism. Recall the posture, the muscular contractions, the facial contortions, and the other motor exhibitions of Rodin's statue, "The Thinker." The law of motor discharge operates throughout the entire gamut of the mental life.

Reaction is the basic property of all organisms, from the most elementary to the most complicated. The unicellular structure reacts to its environment, encloses food particles, absorbs suitable pabulum, and forfeits its identity in the division of the organism. Although not consciously purposive, its responses serve the ends of self-preservation and reproduction. As organisms in the course of evolution are progressively refined in structure and function, the range of motor responses is correspondingly widened. In man the culmination is reached in active devotion to a chosen ideal that defies self-regarding motives.

At least four types of action are observable—involuntary, random, impulsive, and voluntary. Involuntary action is mechanical and unattended by awareness unless impeded, and serves a specific purpose. The eyelid reflex and the dilation or contraction of the pupil are involuntary. Learned actions which are habitual and proceed automatically once they are initiated, like writing, speaking, and walking, may be called secondary involuntary actions. Random movements are aimless and without definite end-results. The free arm and leg motions of an infant in the cradle belong to the group of random actions. Impulsive action occurs spontaneously and consciously but without forethought, as when one strikes another who has aroused in one a paroxysm of anger. Voluntary action involves deliberation, emotional strain, decision, and effort. The desire to gain an ulterior end often motivates voluntary action. The result is at least in part imagined. Since it is a sheer impossibility to respond to all the multitudinous stimuli which play upon us, choice or selection is imperative. I may voluntarily wink in order to demonstrate that I can perform that operation, or in order to attract the attention of another, or in order to drop a friend a hint. Intended action, planned action, action in spite of internal conflicts and directed against external obstructions, action in the face of public misunderstanding, disapproval, and hostility, action prompted by an ideal of duty is voluntary action of the highest order. Conation in religion is intimately associated with conduct, the propagation of the faith, and social welfare.

The Primacy of Response

The voluntaristic mode of mentality is given the palm in the precepts and example of Jesus. The primacy of behavior is clearly avowed in many of his recorded statements. "My meat is to do the will of him that sent me, and to accomplish his work." [10] "Not my will, but thine, be done." [11] Jesus established a kinship which transcends the biological and sociological ties of family when he declared, "For whosoever shall do the will of God, the same is my brother, and sister, and mother." [12] The affective consciousness, dissociated from sanctioned behavior patterns, imparts a false sense of security which endures for a season, but is shattered when a man stands face to face with his ultimate destiny. "Not every one that saith unto me, Lord, Lord, shall enter into the kingdom of heaven; but he that doeth the will of my Father who is in heaven." [13] Jesus identifies his own purposes with the will of God and makes them normative for his followers in the closing affirmations of the Sermon on the Mount: "Every one therefore that

[10] John 4: 34.
[11] Luke 22: 42.
[12] Mark 3: 35.
[13] Matthew 7: 21.

heareth these words of mine, and doeth them, shall be likened unto a wise man, who built his house upon the rock." [14]

Moral action leads to the clarification of religious beliefs and is at the same time a pragmatic test of their validity. "If any man willeth to do his will, he shall know of the teaching whether it is of God." [15] The challenge with which Jesus confronts Matthew the tax collector, is not emotional or theological but essentially volitional: "Follow me." [16] Matthew's preliminary ideas of religion will be refined and his emotions quickened and redirected through fellowship with Christ. Evidently Jesus, line upon line and precept upon precept, taught that the center of religious personality is responsiveness to the divine will as he disclosed, interpreted, and lived it. It is said that Horace Bushnell, tortured by doubts about his religious status, finally applied the ethical test in a self-examination. He raised the questions, "Am I now in the right? Do I consent to be right, to live for the right, to make sacrifices for the right?" He could answer the questions in the affirmative with an approving conscience and therefore concluded that he was a child of God. In after years he used to call this moral self-support, and the sense of certainty which it aroused, his conversion. Moral reaction to the acknowledged will of God was his criterion of true religion.

Thought and feeling were determinants of behavior in a succession of events in the mission of Jesus. It would be contrary to the records of his life to assert that neither beliefs nor emotions instigated action which possessed special significance for him. It is patent that the perception of human need that he could meet evoked not only his compassion but also purposive effective action. Motor response was grounded in emotion and directed by intelligence. A leper appealed to him for deliverance from his malady, and "being moved with compassion, he stretched forth his hand, and touched him, and saith unto him, I will; be thou made clean." [17] We read that Jesus had compassion on the multitudes that had followed him into a barren country, and healed their sick and fed the hun-

[14] Matthew 7: 24.   [15] John 7: 17.
[16] Mark 2: 14; Luke 5: 27.   [17] Mark 1: 41.

gry.[18] Having seen with his own eyes the economic abuses which were perpetrated in the court of the Gentiles of the temple, and heard with his own ears the din of vociferous trading that rendered worship a mockery, Jesus is filled with righteous indignation that impels him to direct action against the vested interests.[19] In all his efforts to lead men into a transforming experience of God, to free men from moral corruption, to deliver them from physical disability, and to combat injustice, it is certain that the affective states and cognitive processes were prominent.

Insufficient Action

Action apart from directive thought, although suffused with conjunctive emotions, may be impulsive and therefore detrimental. An unreflective act may spring from a kindly and generous heart, but its consequences may harm the recipient. Overborne by a wave of sympathy one does that which might have remained undone if the possible outcomes of the act had been clearly envisaged. Moved by pity, one may give a beggar the gift which he requests, and thereby witlessly contribute to his further delinquency. Works without knowledge do more harm than most of us realize or are willing to admit. Sentimentality is a dangerous attitude.

On the other hand, a cool head may dictate a course of action which is undeniably profitable but does not satisfy the emotional requirements of the situation. Social service rendered impersonally is seldom entirely sufficient. Man does not live by bread alone. "The gift without the giver is bare." A student scandalized his parents with the report that he had recently taken a homeless man to his apartment and given him shelter there for the night. They intimated that he would have met the demands of the case if he had paid for the stranger's lodging at a hotel. "He required the personal touch," was the defense of the student. Personal interest, concern, understanding, and fellowship are necessary concomitants of social work which is most effective.

[18] Mark 6: 32-44; Matthew 14: 14-21. How Jesus fed the multitudes is irrelevant in the present context.
[19] Mark 11: 15-17; Matthew 21: 12, 13; Luke 19: 45, 46.

Conclusion

Thinking, feeling, and doing, interlocking and working together, constitute a whole with a unique vitality and quality. Each mode in its creative form contributes to the unification of personality. Ideas make ideals and intelligent action possible. Conjunctive emotions are sources of wisdom and invigorators of ideas. Behavior expresses, clarifies, and tests ideas. When any basic function is dissociated from the others the balance of personality is disturbed. Ideas apart from emotion are likely to be ethically barren. Emotion severed from critical thought is likely to be maudlin and morally weakening. Volition apart from judgment is likely to be misdirected. The three modes of mentality are not independent components, but constitute an organized totality.

Although each mode as a creative function is essential to balanced personality, the degeneracy or paralysis of volition is the most disrupting. The religiously integrated personality is not an equilateral triangle, each side of which is, by definition, exactly as long as either of the other two; thought, emotion, and action are not on a parity. Wholesome personality is more accurately symbolized by a right-angled triangle, of which the hypotenuse or the longest side is volition. The master passion of the religion of Jesus is expressed in the twofold aspiration of the model prayer, "Thy kingdom come, thy will be done on earth as it is in heaven." The cause of the kingdom is thus interpreted as the realization of a divine purpose in accordance with an ideal eternal pattern. Effective citizenship in the kingdom of God is motivated by good will and guided by intelligence.

Love is the dominant attitude in the Christian arrangement of life. Some man will inquire, "Is not love primarily an emotion?" No doubt attitudes and practices have been associated with Christian love which have been more repellent than attractive to wholesome personalities. Misconceptions of the meaning of love as advocated in the New Testament are perhaps rooted in the multiplicity of relations which the English word "love" signifies. The meaning of the English term ranges from sexual attraction between human beings to the sacrifice of one's life for an ideal or an unpopular cause. The Greek language in which the New Testament was originally written includes several words each of which symbolizes a specific affective attitude, and for which there are no exact English equivalents. The Greek word *philia* means an attachment prompted by feeling and sense to almost anything, and the Greek word *agape* means an attitude of good will directed toward another by choice. *Agape* is employed also to denote God's love for man.[20] The two Greek words are as a rule rendered by the word "love" in our English translations. *Agape* is consistently used by Jesus and Paul to indicate moral excellence.[21] It is essentially a reaction word. It entails thought and affection, but the criterion of the attitude which it symbolizes is intelligent selfless behavior. The term "ethical love" approximately expresses the signification of the Greek word. It is this form of love which, as Paul says, "beareth all things, believeth all things, hopeth all things, endureth all things." [22] In his evaluation of the Christian graces, faith, hope, and love, Paul yields the primacy to love, *agape,* and well he may, for love not only involves faith and hope but transcends them as a moral and social dynamic.[23] He says it is the greatest of the gifts of the Spirit.

The conative, the affective, and the cognitive phases of religion interpenetrate. Balanced religious personality develops a conjunctive emotional attitude toward cherished values, and undertakes an intellectual but constructive criticism of its own beliefs. It reacts to the affective and cognitive relations. When a gap between a felt human need and its religious satisfaction occurs, powerful emotions are engendered and sway the personality. It is also within this situation that creative theological thinking, if ever, arises. An appropriate overt response, a reaction which supplies the pressing need, completes the triad of basic functions of personality.

[20] John 3: 16; Romans 8: 37; 2 Thessalonians 2: 16; 1 John 4: 11, 19, and many other references.
[21] Matthew 5: 43 ff; 19: 19; John 11: 5; Galatians 5: 14; 2 Corinthians 11: 11; Romans 13: 8, and other passages.
[22] 1 Corinthians 13: 7.
[23] 1 Corinthians 13: 13.

CHAPTER XVI

PRAYER IN A UNIVERSE OF LAW

PRAYER is either the grossest form of superstition or the culmination of wisdom. It is one or the other. There is no other verdict. When we trace its history we discover that prayer has been a creative practice in the lives of millions whose character and intelligence claim our respect. In view of its honorable career in the development of religious personalities, prayer cannot be dismissed with a contemptuous gesture.

Prayer was the most intensive mood and activity in the experience of Jesus. Prayer quickened his intelligence, sustained mental health, and guided his sacrificial ministry.[1] His incomparable manhood could not have been supported by a false and illusory religious practice. Face to face with grim realities, the personality founded on self-deception and error collapses. The numerous constructive consequences of prayer, not only in the life of Jesus but also in the lives of millions of the humble and the nameless, should make one hesitate to consign it to the limbo of discarded stupidities.

Prayer is a personal experience, not a philosophy or a theology. To be sure, any given type of prayer practice reflects the individual's world-view. Prayer as such is, however, a psychological and religious reaction pattern, rather than a self-consistent and cogent system of thought. Prayer as experience is primarily an active relationship between the individual and a power other and greater than himself, a power which he acknowledges as the solicitor of single-minded loyalty. It is the means whereby the human personality catches the spirit of the universe. At its best, prayer is man's supreme venture of faith, his whole-hearted response to the impact of God. It is a method of human adjustment to destiny. Psychologically considered,

[1] For survey of the prayer life of Jesus see Bundy, Walter E., *The Religion of Jesus,* pp. 189 ff. (Indianapolis: Bobbs-Merrill Company, 1928).

257

prayer is a clarifier of ideals, an arouser of the conjunctive emotions, and a director of volition. Prayer purges the personality of incompatible elements and promotes attitudes and habits which are in accord with the established master motive or a newly gained religious insight.

The mere repetition of pious phrases or the formal statement of a wish is, of course, not prayer. The saying of prayers is to be distinguished from genuine praying. Unless prayer springs from a personality aflame with desire and supported by faith in the aggressiveness of the universe, it is but an exercise which affords ideas oral expression and clarification. Imagine the consternation which would be created by the answering of the prayers thoughtlessly offered daily by millions! The momentum of habit, the compliance with a vague undefined impulse or a dim sense of obligation is, one is inclined to suppose, the originating condition of myriads of prayers which are as futile as the practice of magic. True prayer demands the individual's best, his concentrated attention, his most intensive thinking, self-control, and patience, and the adventurous spirit.[2]

The range of prayer objects is almost, if not entirely, co-extensive with the needs and yearnings of human beings of various degrees of religious insight and attainment. A study of the prayer life of college students, for example, discloses petitions for success in examinations, sufficient money for the continuance of their education, an invitation to the junior promenade, the winning of a football game, election to membership in a fraternity or sorority, a happy love affair, vocational opportunity after graduation, personal comfort in sorrow, the reinforcement of moral attitudes, the elimination of evil habits, a sense of relationship with God, the cure of disease, the dis-

[2] The technique of problem-solving prayer may or should include the following successive steps: the realization of a situation to be met, a period of exposure of the self to the impact of God, the definition of the issues involved, a search of one's experience for a solution, the exploration of profitable experiences of others, an analysis of possible outcomes of the solution or solutions discovered, a choice of outcome, the integration of the chosen outcome with the religious idealism of the personality. Bishop Brent, as an aid to effective devotions, wrote prayers in his own hand, revising many of them until they met with his approval. See Brent, Charles Henry, *With God in Prayer*, pp. 11, 12 (Philadelphia: George W. Jacobs & Co., 1907); *Adventures in Prayer*, pp. 11 ff. (New York: Harper & Brothers, 1932).

persion of loneliness, and the welfare of others. It would be exceedingly difficult to make a complete list of the specific favors, concessions, and experiences which men seek to obtain through prayer.

An inclusive classification consists of two groups of prayers, the subjective and the objective. The subjective group comprises those prayers the answers to which are resident within the individual himself, and the objective group comprises those petitions and intercessions which are intended to influence other persons or to effect changes in the external world. The subjective forms of prayer resultants are integral constituents of the personality itself, the objective consequences are independent of and exist apart from the praying individual.

Subjective Prayer

Subjective prayers may be subsumed under two divisions— the centripetal and the centrifugal. The centripetal section embraces the petitions and the devotional attitudes and exercises which enrich the self through an addition or accession. Suitable pabulum is absorbed. The praying individual is receptive, a value or principle is adopted which creates a higher integration of personality. Peripheral ideals are appraised and emotionally internalized and thus made dynamic. Centrifugal prayers, on the other hand, are characterized by expulsive power. Internal pressures of various kinds are released. An intrusion is banished, a haunting memory is released, a distasteful desire is afforded escape, an evil habit is broken, an impulse repressed but not at variance with conscience is permitted to express itself. Centripetal prayers are psychosynthetic, centrifugal prayers are psychoanalytic.

Centripetal Types

The prayers of aspiration, consecration, submission, guidance, and communion with God are representative centripetal varieties. The prayer of aspiration springs from a motivating appreciation of an ideal as a goal of endeavor. The core of it is an ardent desire for the elevated. In devotional mood the individual aspires to be just, merciful, and in harmony with the divine purpose as he understands it. The vision of practical idealism tends to give life an impetus toward a more exalted formation of the functions of personality. The prayer of aspiration steadies vagrant impulses, reinforces the moral attributes, summons the energies for ethical expression, and thus contributes to the stability and self-consistency of religious personality. The consequent coalition of the functions of the individual presents a solid front to the array of evil forces which attack the moral integrity of the self. The aroused religious consciousness joins together ideal and conduct in a unitary relation.

A high-school girl offered the following prayer of aspiration in the church school after the class of which she was a member had studied the closing years of St. Paul's life: "Dear heavenly Father, give us the strength and will-power of Paul. Reveal to our minds a definite object toward which we shall always work, an aim and desire such as gave Paul the strength and fire to accomplish what he did. Forgive all our excuses for shirking in your work and put a spark into our hearts to do great things for you. In the name of Jesus Christ our Saviour. Amen." [3]

The prayer of consecration is a religious exercise in the course of which the federated powers of the personality are subordinated to acknowledged duty. Only dedication to what the individual regards as a sacred obligation can avert the disorganization of personality. Consecration to an ideal of unselfish and intelligent service socializes human beings. A clear conception of what one should be or do creates a sense of dissatisfaction which only the triumph of idealism can dispel. A tendency to drift with the current, to cling to the past, and native moral inertia all yield to the prayer of consecration. Self-committal to a noble purpose opens a new channel of motor discharge. It gives the energies a fresh outlet. In the prayer act one's mission is clarified, the consciousness of obligation deepened, the sense of urgency fostered, and the challenge

---

[3] Shaver, Erwin L., *The Project Principle in Religious Education*, p. 274 (Chicago: University of Chicago Press, 1924).

of recognized obligation accepted. When the decision to obey the call of conscience has been made, inner tension is released and equilibrium restored.

Jesus had a pivotal experience when he was baptized by John. Luke records that when Jesus was praying the Holy Spirit descended upon him and a voice proclaimed him the beloved Son.[4] In baptism Jesus committed himself without reservation to the task of establishing the kingdom of God. In the prayer of consecration his convictions became explicit and were consolidated. Dedicating himself to God's will which was progressively defined in due course, Jesus was vouchsafed a dramatic certainty of divine approval and an initial empowerment for his mission.

The prayer of submission reconciles one to grim and insurmountable realities. Do what we can to escape them, disaster and tribulation sooner or later overtake us. Anguish and death are impartial, relentless, and inevitable. We cannot avoid an attitude of some kind toward the misfortunes and calamities which compose an essential part of each life. Christianity cultivates a wise submission to the unavoidable disagreeable, a firm trust in the ultimate triumph of justice, and an unwavering confidence in the persistence of moral values.

Prayer does not relieve us of all burdens, but it does infinitely more when it helps us to bear what cannot be moderated or discarded. It constructs a personality that rises above the vicissitudes which are the lot of even the best of men. St. Paul prayed thrice for the removal of a thorn or stake in the flesh, a form of physical disability which was an obstacle in his missionary labors. Although his petition as such was ungranted, he was given the courage and patience to endure his cross, and became the greater man for the discipline of suffering. "My grace is sufficient for thee: for my power is made perfect in weakness." [5]

Submission assimilates, to the conservation of the religious attitude and the unity of the consciousness, the adversities which life entails. There is no catastrophe over which the prayer of

[4] Luke 3: 21, 22.   [5] 2 Corinthians 12: 9.

submission cannot be victorious. The incorporation of tribulation in the program of living calms a distracted mind and averts the blight of a disrupted personality. The prayer of submission in its truest form does not habituate the individual to surrender to obstacles which should be removed, but enables him to accept with gratitude such gains as life may grant and to witness the collapse of cherished prospects or possessions without being wounded beyond recovery. It teaches him to collect the fragments of a shattered hope and to weave them into a fresh design of beauty, devotion, and love. It is a type of mental control which facilitates resignation to impending doom or deprivation. A young clergyman once remarked that if his child were stricken by a fatal malady he would still pray, not that the infant's life be spared, but to find comfort in the hour of sorrow and strength to bear bereavement with dignity and poise. Socrates face to face with martyrdom remarked, "My dear Crito, if it thus pleases the gods, so let it be."

The answers to prayer for divine guidance range all the way from the calming of an excited mind which enables the petitioner to make the requisite adjustment by the usual processes to an inward illumination which possesses the force of a divine revelation. Mental poise acquired through prayer is in many instances the condition necessary to a proper accommodation of the person to a situation. The late Rev. W. A. Sunday used to claim that prayer aided him in the first ball game he played in after his conversion.[6] At a critical point in the game a fly came toward him in the field. He ran with all his might and petitioned God to help him catch the ball. He looked over his shoulder, saw the ball near, reached out his hand and caught it. Perhaps the prayer inspired Mr. Sunday with confidence which, in turn, induced effective motor control. The scattered energies were collected and made to function as a victorious unit.

Often when the individual is entangled in a complication requiring the choice of one of several possible courses of action, the prayer for guidance results in a correct appraisal of the different potentialities and in a wise selection. A wisdom,

[6] Cited in Pratt, James B., *American Journal of Religious Psychology and Education*, Vol. IV, p. 58.

wrought in the inward parts, emerges into consciousness and is incorporated in one's practical philosophy. A student in the final year in the theological seminary was faced with the necessity of making a difficult decision. He was invited to a pastorate in a large city. A church in a frontier town sought his services. He was offered an opportunity to do graduate work in a university and thus to specialize in a socially useful field. Which of the three opportunities should he embrace? For weeks he was tortured by indecision. He had a desire to do what would best further the Kingdom. One evening he attended an informal reception given to the senior class by one of the seminary professors. After an hour or two of games and other forms of diversion, the students gathered about the piano and sang hymns. Without further preliminary or announcement the professor offered prayer, petitioning that each senior might be sensitive to the striving of the Spirit and find his place in the grand strategy of the kingdom of God. The young man felt that the prayer had special reference to his quandary, although he had not taken counsel with this or any other member of the faculty. In the course of the prayer graduate study was clearly indicated as the opportunity which he should embrace. His mind ceased to weigh the reasons pro and con for each of the other possibilities, certainty flooded him, and the decision, once made, partook of the nature of the inevitable. In the months that followed he could not visualize himself doing anything but graduate work for the next few years. Perhaps what had germinated and been maturing in the deeper strata of his being was integrated with his determining system of values when he gave the petition addressed to God by the professor a personal application.

The prayer of communion centers in the cultivation of the very heart of religion. The greatest achievement of prayer is the God-consciousness which rests the spirit of man, satisfies the craving of the soul for fellowship with deepest ultimate Reality, and imparts to the whole of life an impressive significance. To be sure, it is the apprehension rather than the comprehension of God that is the product of the prayer of communion.

Difference of opinion prevails as to the nature of the experience of God. Persons who are quite absorbed by effects in the external world and whose evaluation of experiences, possessions, and outer events are generally in pragmatic or utilitarian terms, are inclined to believe that God is apprehended in the clarification and deepening of right purpose and in corresponding moral action. Religious persons who are introspective and introverted, who rely on faith and intuition, who appreciate meanings and interpretations, who like solitude and are given to meditation, and who are artistic, as a rule crave a direct, unmediated fellowship with God. A mystic writes: "I cannot imagine how religious persons can live satisfied without the practice of the presence of God. For my part, I keep myself retired with him in the fund or center of my soul as much as I can; and while I am so with him I fear nothing, but the least turning from him is insupportable." [7] This form of the devotional life exhibits a definite tendency to move within the area of spiritual appreciation and to culminate in itself. The emotional tone of the experience of God is that of wonder, adoration, fascination, awe, and reverence.

Centrifugal Types

The centrifugal group of religious exercises includes the prayers of confession and praise, and petitions for ethical betterment and for the cure of disease. In each instance prayer is, psychologically, a means of purging the self of an element which is incompatible with the master sentiment in control, or of liberating a restrained impulse which is consequently adjudged worthy.

Oppressed by a sense of guilt and regret, the individual may engage in the prayer of confession. An unconfessed and unforgiven moral lapse or a questionable desire creates a mental disturbance which only confession and possible amendment, restitution, or reparation can quell. The anguish of spirit which the guilty one endures originates in reminiscences of reprehensible conduct or attitudes or the realization of present

[7] Brother Lawrence, *The Practice of the Presence of God*, p. 32 (Philadelphia: American Baptist Publication Society, 1908).

character defects. The distracting element infects the mind like a splinter in the flesh. To persist in denying the irritation recognition is merely to increase its power to disorganize the personality. Many nervous disorders have their genesis in experiences either forgotten or remembered which are contrary to the moral standards of the sufferer. In fact, the unconfessed determinant, subconsciously active, may manifest itself in pathological symptoms which seem to have no connection with the moral scruples of the victim. It is evident that the prayer of confession, when it brings to clear consciousness the underlying causal circumstances, is a form of mental therapy. Confident that God is compassionate, the person may in prayer re-enact with the original emotional excitement the details of the disquieting scene which has become a point of tension within him, and consequently experience profound relief and be mentally restored at once or soon. If the prayer of confession is made as soon as reprehensible impulses are entertained or even concretely expressed, pathological complications are forestalled.

When the confessed event is a mere memory, and no amends can be made, the conscious reinstatement of the offense with a painful emotional accompaniment, together with faith in the forgiveness of God, is of itself sufficient to cleanse the self and to restore its equilibrium. An evil habitual practice which is permitted to emerge into awareness may stand convicted before the tribunal of conscience and be sentenced to die. Petitional prayer may then be made in order to eradicate what has been condemned. If the fault is not deeply rooted, has not acquired a firm grip, and the moral constitution is vigorous enough, it may perish at once in the flame of indignation and repulsion which confession kindles. Conscience may neither approve of nor denounce certain inclinations and drives, but demand that they be modified. Crude trends may be transmuted into acceptable forms of self-expression through petitional prayer.

Contrite confession of evil is normally followed by a sense of divine forgiveness, the breaking of the power of sin, and fellowship with God through Christ. Unless wrong is admitted and repudiated there is neither forgiveness nor moral cleansing. The awareness of personal sin daunts courage, undermines confidence, and frustrates effort. So long as the person cleaves to the culpable and refuses to renounce it, he alienates himself from goodness and separates himself from God. Only admission of personal guilt and amendment, if the latter be possible, can restore the severed relationship between man and God. A profoundly sound psychology underlies the experience recorded by the psalmist, "I said, I will confess my transgressions unto Jehovah; and thou forgavest the iniquity of my sin." [8]

The psychology of the prayers of praise is akin to that of confession. The process of psychoanalysis is discernible in both confession and praise. There is, however, a difference between these forms of the prayer life. Confession liberates from repression a culpable desire or painful memory. The content and outcome of the prayer of praise are different. Praise releases an impulse fully sanctioned by conscience. The urge afforded devotional expression is not an unholy compulsion and as such to be condemned, but an ennobling force which can accomplish its mission only when set free. Praise turns on self and enriches the source from which it flows.

Two types of devotion comprise the prayers of praise, adoration and thanksgiving. God is adored for what he is and thanked for what he does. Adoration and thanksgiving are closely connected in the prayer of praise, and they weave themselves into the total pattern of the devotional life. The contemplation of the attributes of God, his power, wisdom, and benevolence, induces in us the attitude of adoration. The prevailing emotional tone of the mood of adoration is that of awe and reverence. Prayer is a natural outlet for the appreciation of the sovereignty and goodness of God. The urge to adore and worship God, when denied its normal mode of discharge, may create at least a temporary internal religious conflict.

The prayer of thanksgiving springs spontaneously from sensitiveness to the benevolence of God. It is a favorite form of

[8] Psalm 32: 5.

the devotional exercises of devout men. It implies such a degree
of awareness of the graciousness of the universe that Lessing
may in truth declare, "A single grateful thought toward heaven
is the most perfect prayer."   When the individual rehearses
and acknowledges the manifold benefits which have been be-
stowed upon him he is disposed not only to thank God but also
to make petitions and intercessions. St. Paul exhorting, "With
thanksgiving let your requests be known unto God," [9] senses
the relation which exists between gratitude and petitional
prayer. When thankfulness sways the personality, faith in the
universe is strengthened, and holy courage and venturesome
assurance support the prayer life.

The psychological basis of the prayer of praise is, then,
the recognition and appraisal of the nature and love of the
Determiner of destiny. The impulse to adore and thank God
is released in the prayer of praise. Adoration or thanksgiving is a liberation of devotional promptings, a liberation not of
a condemned desire but of an urge religiously induced and approved, a liberation which augments reverence for and confidence in God.

Epictetus, speaking of the divine blessing, exclaims: "Ought
we not, both in public and in private, incessantly to sing hymns
and speak well of the deity, and rehearse his benefits?—What
else can I a lame old man do but sing hymns to God? If I
were a nightingale, I should act the part of a nightingale, if
a swan the part of a swan; but since I am a reasonable creature it is my duty to praise God. This is my business. I do
it, nor will I ever desert this position so long as it is vouchsafed
me; and I exhort you to join in the same song."

The prayer for moral betterment, sincerely and persistently
made, is effective. Evil habits are eradicated through prayer.
A conflict between a sensitive conscience and a questionable pro-
pensity may be avoided by keeping the two separate, or by
lowering the standard which governs conduct. The ethically
responsive individual can do neither; until the opposition between idealism and misconduct is obliterated through the tri-

[9] Philippians 4: 6.

umph of the moral attribute and the expulsion of culpable desire, guilt and other exhausting emotional accompaniments castigate the wrongdoer.   Only when the appropriate adaptive response is made to the moral requirements of the self as a whole do confusion, frustration, and depression yield to relaxation and serenity.   The expulsive power of the prayer for moral cleansing effectually disposes of the internal clash of unsanctioned impulse with moral obligation.   When faith in petitions for betterment is exercised, a subconscious growth of self-discipline occurs, and when the individual feels that conditions are ripe he casts himself upon the world-life surging within and closes the old channel of discharge.

Any effective disposition of the crass urges and bad habits is to be commended although religion is the most potent form of personality control one may adopt.   Religious teaching induces a desire for improvement without which ethical progress is never consciously undertaken.   There is no adequate substitute for religion as a creator of deep desire for emancipation from moral ignorance, from the antisocial functioning of the instincts, and from the dominance of all that degrades.   Again, religion in its organized form protects the individual who has been delivered from his baser inclinations and practices.   The Church endeavors to make moral relapse difficult.   It strives to conserve its results.   The Church as a fellowship imparts moral inspiration, promotes the devotional life, and provides constructive social outlets.   Extreme humanism and such psychological means as post-hynoptic suggestion apart from religious motivation can, it should be gratefully acknowledged, accomplish much when the will for deliverance from evil is present; but since it is a response to the highest we can dream or know, the strategy of the petitional prayer for purity in the inward parts is unique.

The prayer for the cure of a bodily or mental disorder is centrifugal.   Many seek and actually find relief from disabilities which lower vitality, undermine efficiency, and generate depressing emotional states.   Nothing could be more firmly established than the efficacy of prayer in the healing of certain maladies.   Fixation of the attention, faith in the power appealed to, and a response, largely subconscious, are recognizable psychological features of the prayer for the restoration to health and its answer. The petition which holds in mental focus the idea of recovery excludes from the field of awareness contrary conceptions. Expectation of the cure is indispensable to the answering of the prayer. A bodily or mental cure which is anticipated with confidence is likely to ensue if it is within the bounds of possibility.

It should be borne in mind that disorders originating in mental conflicts or organic lesions are not cured by ignoring them or expelling them from the attention, but by recognizing their existence and attacking them with weapons which science has forged and placed at our command. A form of faith cure which in principle and practice willfully disregards the roots of a disease may check the symptoms and thus afford temporary relief. A relapse is inevitable. On the other hand, a derangement the seat of which is the creative imagination may be cured by the rigid exclusion of the idea of disease and the concentration of the attention on the idea of health.

The attempt to define the scope of effective prayer for the healing of disease is incautious. When life in the providence of God has run its course, the prayer for restoration is unanswered in the sense that the object of the petition is denied. If prayer could always cure us, few of us would ever die. It is appointed unto every man to depart this life. To affirm that prayer is directly effective in the healing of functional disturbances, but only accessory in the cure of organic disorders, is to utilize a classification of diseases which, in the best medical opinion, admits of no such sharp line of demarcation in numerous instances. The distinction is far from absolute. It is, of course, reasonable to deduce that prayer alone will not remove a bullet embedded in the flesh or set a broken bone, although it may further an attitude which makes such misfortunes easier to bear. Submitted proofs for the validity of the cures of so-called test cases of this sort of organic disorder have been uniformly exploded by critical investigation. On the other hand, it has been abundantly demonstrated that prayer possesses therapeutic value in the treatment of many ailments subsumed under the category of nervous disorders.

Dr. Jones gives an account of restoration to health through a religious experience, which merits careful consideration.[10] He states that years of strain as a missionary in India resulted in several nervous collapses before he sailed for America on furlough. Before his return to India and afterward, despite several extended rest periods, he suffered several additional collapses. Although his health was shattered, the call to service resounded through his spirit. In Lucknow while engaged in prayer a Voice seemed to inquire, "Are you yourself ready for this work to which I have called you?" He replied, "No, Lord, I am done for." The Voice said, "If you will turn that over to me and not worry about it, I will take care of it." Dr. Jones accepted the challenge; a deep peace took possession of him, and the tides of new life surged within him. He was so uplifted that for days he scarcely knew he had a body. He worked incessantly without weariness. Nine years later he testifies that there has been no recurrence of the nervous disorder, and that throughout the long interval his health has been excellent. He supposes that this experience may be psychologized, but rejoices in the abundant life, bodily, mentally, and religiously, which in its totality transcends analysis. He adds that all that he had to do to secure the higher life was to take it as a gift.

Objective Prayer

Objective prayers, as has been observed elsewhere, are those the answers to which occur outside or beyond the petitioning individual. One seeks to produce changes in other people or in the world of nature through prayer. Objective prayers may accordingly be subdivided into two groups, the personal and the impersonal. Intercessory prayers, hortatory and instructional prayers, and petitions for the substance or service which others may contribute are typical forms of the personal objective subdivision. Petitions for rain or sunshine, for a bountiful har-

[10] Jones, E. Stanley, *The Christ of the Indian Road,* pp. 18-21 (New York: The Abingdon Press, Eighth Edition, 1925).

vest, deliverance from the dangers of a storm, the preservation of crops from hail, a safe journey by train, ship, or airplane, are specimens of the impersonal group. The psychological mechanism which supports the personal objective prayers is social suggestion. The impersonal petitions are designed to affect the processes of the world of chemistry and physics.

Personal Objective Types

Intercessory prayer which is offered by intelligent persons is not by them supposed to be a means of reconciling a vengeful deity to those who oppose his will. It is prompted by a genuine concern for the well-being of others, by a desire that others adjust themselves to what is interpreted as the purpose of God. Intercessions such as those for religious reintegration, the healing of disease, moral improvement, and divine guidance are answered when those whom they are calculated to influence co-operate. So long as the individual for whom one prays does not respond, whatever the reason may be, intercession cannot accomplish its major mission.

Many social prayers have a didactic, hortatory, or inspirational purpose. Although formally addressed to God, they instruct and admonish men. They widen the outlook of the subjects and supply comfort and encouragement. Their appeal to those who respect the claims of religion is especially strong. When such petitions are associated with fundamental urges, determining drives, and treasured intimate experiences their effectiveness is augmented. A prominent clergyman in a radio prayer petitioned God to touch the heart of a boy mentioned by name who had left his home for parts unknown, and to move him to return to his sorrowing mother. The boy heard the prayer, and, conscience-stricken, notified his mother at once of his whereabouts, and told her that he would return to his home as soon as possible.

Frequently requests are made for the prayers of others for the furtherance of a project with a public appeal. Those charged with the responsibility of conducting a socially valuable undertaking secure the support of responsive and competent people. In memory of George Chase Christian, a citizen of Minneapolis, Minn., an institute for the study of the cause and cure of cancer was opened in the University of Minnesota in 1925. On the Sunday nearest the opening the regents of the university and the medical staff of the institute requested the prayers of the churches for the future development of this enterprise. The form of prayer, which was distributed in large quantities in the churches, read: "O God, who declarest Thy almighty power in showing mercy and pity to all who call upon Thee, and who revealest to men in each new discovery, a part of Thy truth: remove with Thy grace, we pray Thee, the dullness of our blinded sight, and grant a new vision to all those who serve Thee in their search for the cause of cancer and its cure. Lighten their darkness, O Lord, we beseech Thee, and mercifully direct them into Thy paths of knowledge and truth; grant them the realization that through Thee all things are possible; pour upon them the abundance of Thy inspiration; and finally lead them to the attainment of victory, that the scourge of cancer may be ended, and that we, being freed from this burden of fear, may live continually in the love and service of Thine only Son, our Saviour Jesus Christ. Amen."

Many petitions for things within the gift of others, such as money and time, are answered by informing other people of the existing needs and the reliance on prayer to supply them. The measure and nature of the responses are conditioned by the generosity and material resources, or the intelligence, willingness, and capabilities of those who hear the petitions or otherwise obtain knowledge of them.

Certain orphanages and other charitable institutions have for years been maintained by officials depending solely on prayer to provide the necessary funds. No money for the support of such commendable organizations is directly solicited. The nature of such benevolent causes and the knowledge that the managers rely on prayer as the prompter of generous impulses constitute a subtle but powerful social summons. It is difficult to imagine a more productive conspiracy of conditions.

The petition for the personal participation of others in the work of the Church or any other worthy enterprise is about the most effective appeal that can be made. The prayer for laborers in the fields of good causes ready for harvesting has all the force of an indirect solicitation, and as a form of social suggestion constructed by religious and humanitarian interests, arouses the noblest in men. Social pressure directly applied often induces resistance. Prayer which refers to a need, and petitions God to move to appropriate action those who are able to meet it, is a type of influence which times without number has been rewarded with the desired outcomes.

Often a coincidental happening is deliberately so adapted that it is construed as the desired specific answer to a petition. A little girl told her mother, who was in straitened circumstances, that since the children at the church school had noticed that her shoes were badly worn she had requested the heavenly Father who cares for us to give her a pair of new ones for next Sunday. When Saturday night arrived the impoverished mother had been unable to buy the shoes for which her little girl had prayed. The child said her bedtime prayers as usual, but added a special plea for the shoes. Seeing her mother disturbed, the little girl said, "Don't cry, Mother; God will bring me shoes." After sleep had overtaken the child, ten dollars from an unexpected source arrived. The mother hastened to a near-by shop, purchased the shoes, and before retiring placed them where the child would see them in the morning. On awakening, the child saw the shoes and gleefully exclaimed, "God did bring my shoes!" The incident illustrates a human tendency to answer prayer by adjusting flexible conditions.

In some cases the responding self has knowledge that petitions were offered, in others the contributing self has no such conscious information. In a multitude of instances the persons whose co-operation has been secured received the necessary data through the ordinary channels of communication. What is the psychological interpretation of the countless prayers answered by persons wholly unaware that they were made?

In the first place, the part which coincidence may play should be given its due weight. The concurrence of events having no causal connection is not only possible but actually inevitable.

In a world prodigal in the nature and variety of its circumstances and occurrences coincidences which may be interpreted as answers to prayer are bound to arise.

In addition, the investigator has recourse to the possibilities of unrecognized stimuli, telepathy, and direct impressions proceeding from God to sensitive individuals.[11] Many scholars are disposed to distribute the transference of unknown prayers to their respondents among these three, assigning some to subconscious reactions to stimuli too delicate to be perceived, others to telepathic activity, and the remainder to the immediate intervention of God.[12]

It is a demonstrable fact that although one may be unaware of receiving any message through sense-perception, the subconscious may take into account imperceptible stimuli. Our behavior and outlook are influenced by innumerable impressions subconsciously gleaned. The range of the sensibility of personality is far more extensive than that of clear consciousness. We respond to more stimuli than we consciously perceive. Religious interest may be expressed in a look of concern, a warm handshake, or between the lines of a letter. When the petitioner or intercessor and the subject associate under ordinary circumstances and no conscious effort is made to influence the latter, the conditions for the answering of the prayer are auspicious. The outcome of prayers not directly communicated is relatively dependent on the competency of the petitioner to radiate subtle indications of his religiously supported desire and on the receiver's capacity to interpret the delicate effects and his ability to react to them.

Believers in telepathy assert that one mind may read the thoughts of another without the ordinary means of communication. If this contention can be supported by an unshakable body of evidence, the telepathic impression of a person by a petitioner will have to be conceded. It is, however, at the pres-

---

[11] Believers in occultism may affirm that in some cases the petition is transmitted by a co-operating spirit to the earthly individual it is designed to control.

[12] For experimental evidence of subconscious responses to imperceptible stimuli, see Stolz, Karl R., *The Psychology of Prayer*, pp. 142-148 (New York: The Abingdon Press, 1924).

ent stage of the investigation of telepathic phenomena venturesome either to affirm or deny such a means of lodging a prayer in the mind of another. It is expedient to keep an open mind and reserve judgment. At present the supposition of telepathic prayer transmission is held in abeyance.

That the humanly unmediated prayer may be conveyed to its proper destination by direct divine action is a logical inference if we believe in the existence of a resourceful God. The question that may be raised is, "Is it necessary for God to attain his ends by imparting information by the method of immediate inward illumination or revelation?" If the answer is in the negative, this method of divine operation while still possible is improbable. If the answer is in the affirmative, it would still be impossible to determine to a finality whether a given response to prayer was directly inspired by God or indirectly by intimations subconsciously acquired and elaborated. The mystical transmission of a prayer cannot be analyzed by scientific methods and instruments. It lies beyond the domain which psychology successfully explores, and as such is subject matter for the philosopher and theologian. The conviction that when a social prayer touches the will of God he often influences the person whom the entreaty is designed to move, without reference to the usual avenues of intercommunication, is, then, compatible with the Christian doctrine of God, but not an experience the validity of which can be determined by the science of psychology.

Impersonal Types

Impersonal objective prayers are being made by a rapidly diminishing number of people. To be sure, some still assure us that, impelled by the faith of a petitioner, God halts if he does not actually disturb the orderly processes of nature. Most men are, however, disposed to give a negative answer to the following questions: Is prayer efficacious outside the range of personal and social relationships? Does prayer infringe upon or suspend the laws of nature? Does the scope of prayer include the realm of physics and chemistry as well as the sphere of morals and religion?

It should be conceded that lapse of memory, unintentional exaggeration, coincidence, and the accommodation of a petition to an event which resembles the answer desired are human tendencies. The psychologist observes expressions of human nature which escapes the notice of the believer in impersonal objective answers. On the other hand, it is sheer scientific dogmatism and bigotry to assert that prayer answer outside the ramifications of personal functions is absolutely impossible. Many events of nature once supposed to contravene the laws of physics and chemistry have disclosed their connections and been linked with other uniform sequences. Although defying our present scientific methods of analysis and current classifications, certain objective answers may in time be associated with laws which we shall discover.

Men who pray for rain in a season of protracted drought are right in their assumption that God is interested in our daily bread for which Jesus taught his friends to pray. Although God as father is by no means indifferent to the physical necessities of his children and prayer for rain is often immediately followed by a down-pour, we cannot be absolutely certain that rain would not have fallen if special prayer for it had not been offered. There is no known test by which the issue can be decided. The prayer for rain and other recurring phenomena of nature is confusing. Furthermore, God lets the rain fall upon the unjust who pray not, as well as upon the just who pray.

To confine prayer to personality relationships is to forestall perplexity. Prayer as a method of enriching personality does not necessarily involve the external physical world. Many a sensitive but misled individual has been unable to unlearn that God can be persuaded to abrogate the laws of the impersonal world, without an unfortunate and needless loss of confidence in the validity of religion itself. The indiscriminate believer in impersonal objective prayers is likely to involve himself in contradictions and inconsistencies. A farmer reported to a skeptical friend that in answer to his prayer an approaching hailstorm divided and passed by his field of ripening grain on both sides. The friend mildly inquired whether it was ethical to pray a hailstorm upon the farms of neighbors. A few weeks later the farmer, dejected and discouraged, returned to his friend. He explained that, a few days before, hailstorms had destroyed his crops. The friend could not resist the impulse to inquire, "Didn't you pray?"

It is more religious and in harmony with the divine will to adjust ourselves to the laws of nature than it is to try to set them aside by the power of prayer. Instead of praying for rain, why not irrigate the arid regions, plant trees to modify the atmospheric conditions, and apply the principles of dry farming? Instead of trying to deliver themselves from a plague of grasshoppers by means of prayer, intelligent men are plowing under the larva and preventing the propagation of the noxious insects. Instead of relying solely on prayer to arrest the ravages of an epidemic of typhoid fever, they submit their drinking water and milk to scientific analysis in order that they may combat the malignant scourge at its source. They appropriate the skill of the surgeon to set a broken bone or to extract a bullet embedded in the flesh. They consider the employment of natural means to attain material ends an obligation which should not be shifted to where it does not properly belong. God himself is creatively active in natural processes, and it is therefore positively sinful to be unwilling to conform to his established order.

If one is impelled by a changed world-view or unsatisfactory experience to discontinue impersonal objective petitions, varieties of personal and social classifications, as well as the centripetal and centrifugal forms of subjective prayer may still be offered with gratifying effects. After one has abandoned the prayer for rain in the expectation of moving God to grant a miraculous downpour, intercessions for the welfare of others, inspirational, hortatory, and educational petitions, and pleas for co-operation or substance, if somehow they are lodged in the minds of willing and competent persons, can be presented at the throne of grace with desired consequences. Instead of petitioning God to convert a desert into a garden of roses, the intelligent man may, in the prayer of confession, unburden a spirit tortured with unholy memories or impulses, let his soul soar with the wings of the prayers of adoration and thanksgiving, break the hold of deleterious practices, and cure various types of ailments through the prayer of faith.   When the individual has lost confidence in the power of prayer to protect fruit trees in a critical stage against the usual ravages of a severe frost, he may still with the utmost assurance offer the prayer of aspiration and thereby reach a higher level of personality integration, offer the prayer of consecration and thereby dedicate himself to the implications of a fresh out-look, offer the prayer of submission in the day of tribulation and thereby absorb an otherwise disrupting experience, offer the prayer for guidance and thus sensitize conscience and uni-fy life in terms of duty or manifest destiny.

CHAPTER XVII

WAYS OF PUBLIC WORSHIP

SOONER or later every intelligent man discovers that he must worship something or some one, a superior existence to which he can give himself wholly, and in which he loses himself only to find himself enriched. Of and by himself a man is insufficient. Since it is a complex of many religious attitudes and processes, worship is difficult to define, but its nature as profound reverence for God and its place in personality integration may be suggested. An adequate description of worship and its ramifications would occupy volumes; hence only a few selected phases can be presented here. This discussion will occupy itself chiefly with worship in Protestantism and will be restricted to group as compared with private worship.

The Essence of Worship

In worship the warm inner life of man goes out in reverence, adoration, homage, love, and praise to an active God, and as a result the individual is moved to participate in the purpose of God, to pursue truth, goodness, and beauty as expressions of God, and especially to appreciate God for his own sake. Worship is a quest for communion with a responsive ultimate reality, the prevailing emotional accompaniment of which is compounded of awe, reverence, fascination, love, and gratitude. In the worship experience one recognizes the presence and power of God, appropriates his proffered benefactions, and is moved to obedience to his will. It is essentially the adoration of God. The worshiping individual is swayed by a power greater and other than himself and to which he surrenders in the mood of adoration. The essence of the act of worship is the creation or the intensification of the attitude of veneration. Furthermore, we adapt ourselves through worship to our environment as a whole and in such a manner as to receive the inspiration and support of God.

279

Worship is infinitely more than an aesthetic thrill. It transcends the mere appreciation of the beauty of a sunset, the balance and rhythm of a well-worded litany, or the appeal of majectic music. The attitude of worship itself is more fundamental. Aesthetic contributions are made or duly evaluated as such by persons who do not by deliberate acts of their own worship God. Only when the individual through the appeal of beauty senses ultimate reality does aesthetic appreciation partake of the quality of worship.

Worship is more and other than theological reconstruction. The theories and findings of science have successfully challenged certain traditional tenets and practices of the Church. In various quarters of the Church, doctrines have been reinterpreted and restated in the light of the methods, spirit, and results of scientific research. The historical approach to the study of the Bible, to specify but a single instance, has been gaining ground and its provable conclusions have strengthened the foundations of the Christian faith. On the other hand, it must be confessed that there is but scant nourishment in theological controversies in which branches of the Church are embroiled, for people seeking comfort in sorrow, freedom from moral delinquency, and inward peace. However imperative and important an adequate philosophy of life may be, the majority of men are burdened with cares, vexations, and obligations which are remote from abstract argumentation and debate, but which worship can relieve or impart the requisite courage and patience to bear. A cogent system of Christian theology as an intellectual achievement does not release all the resources of personality.

The transformation of the institutions of ordered society in accordance with the teaching of Jesus must be prosecuted with increasing intelligence and vigor, but the successful application of his social principles would not be a satisfactory substitute for personal religious experience. The intelligent reconstruction of the social structure may be inspired by a dynamic worship experience, but various deeper private issues of the multitudes are not met by the program of the reformer. If poverty, ignorance, and disease were banished, the millennium would not be present with us, for the spirit of man would still crave a unique enrichment, and the sin-sick soul would continue to plead for deliverance from its thralldom. The crosswork of internal conflicting desires, ignoble emotions, and unholy thoughts cannot be disposed of by economic security, ample leisure time, an equitable supply and distribution of modern luxuries such as the motor car and the radio set, and the settlement of international disputes by peaceful arbitration. Worship has social implications which we are under sacred obligations to develop, as will be pointed out in due time, but it remains as true today as it was centuries ago that man liveth not by bread alone. The word that proceeds from the mouth of God, the word of comfort, the word of forgiveness, the word of peace, the word of assurance that we are his, as well as the word of social obligation is heard when man is bowed in reverence, humility, faith, and responsiveness before the throne of God. Often a laudable effort to better the world such as participation in a crusade to end war serves as a diversion or an escape from inward tension and keeps the individual from achieving a higher integration of freedom from defects of character and the resolution of antagonistic impulses. There are depths of human personality which the cult of social service cannot fathom and nourish. There is no adequate substitute for worship.

Perfunctory church attendance should not be confused with worship. The inference from the remarks of ministers as well as laymen of many divisions of Protestantism is that being present at the Sunday morning service, singing parts of a few hymns, placing a coin or weekly offering upon the collection plate, listening to a sermon if it is interesting enough to capture one's attention, and shaking hands with the preacher who has during the final hymn made his way to the rear of the church constitute the worship of the Eternal. Such confusion is disastrous. Some of the items enumerated may when rightly employed induce or intensify the worship mood, but the mechanical observance of an order of service does not engender a celebration of the value of God. Listless and artificial exercises are inimical to the spirit of worship.

What often passes for worship in the church school reminds one of the enthusiasm of a luncheon club, or the zeal of a political rally, or the cheering of college students at a football game. In many church schools a person whose function is akin to that of a cheer leader at an athletic contest tries to inject vim into the assembled pupils and teachers. He exhorts the audience to sing with a will. He and his following imagine that the singing of inane songs with gusto and the use of a stereotyped form of service distributed by a denominational publisher constitute worship. Such a performance is a travesty. It lacks the inwardness which proceeds from an appreciation of majesty and goodness of God and the response to his initiative.

Vitalizing worship maintains or furthers adjustment to an environment in which God is the determining power. The worshiper feels consciously inferior, insufficient, defective as he stands in the presence of God. Forgiveness follows contrition and confession. Peace floods the worshiper and thanksgiving fills his being. Prayers for the welfare of others spontaneously flow from the heart at one with God. Such attitudes as reverence, awe, love, gratitude, joy, and peace are the concomitants of worship. The goodness, wisdom, and purpose of God are not only contemplated and extolled, but actually appropriated to the measure of the capacity of the worshiper. The glowing personality radiates intelligent good will to all men and is prepared for constructive social action.

The outward elements of worship such as ecclesiastical architecture, classical music, devotional preaching, liturgies and litanies, rites and symbols are, when rightly employed, aids to the dynamic experience of God, but are not indispensable. The church edifice is not the only place where a person may worship. A woman remarked that not long since while riding on an elevated train in New York City she had a life-changing vision. Sometimes an individual comes face to face with God in the jostling throngs of a city street:

"Where cross the crowded ways of life,
    Where sound the cries of race and clan
  Above the noise of selfish strife,
    We hear Thy voice, O Son of man!"

Another touches ultimate Reality in the solitude of the hills or fields:

> "O Sabbath rest by Galilee!
> O calm of hills above,
> Where Jesus knelt to share with thee
> The silence of eternity,
> Interpreted by love!"

One may effectively worship in solitude. The individual may retire from the presence of others and engage in solitary interior worship. Worship may take the form of meditation, whether the individual be alone or one of a group, a form void of ritual, sensory representation, or sacraments, but marked by adoration and the dedication of the will to the Infinite. Thoughts, mental imagery, attitudes, and emotions which are of the essence of worship may be deliberately cultivated by the individual who has temporarily withdrawn from his group. God is the inspirer of burning adoration and disinterested oblation whether the individual engages in public or private worship. Individuality and social relationships interpenetrate.

Worship is disinterested although it furthers the growth and enlargement of personality. A prayer may or may not be disinterested. Prayer and worship overlap, but they are not entirely equated. The core of worship is adoration of the Eternal which leads to self-oblation. Thankfulness gives way to the awe-struck sense of the glory, majesty, holiness, and infinite love of God. Worship is the way in which we as finite beings acknowledge objective Reality. It neutralizes our preoccupation with the succession of desires to which we are subject as human beings. Meek admiration, humble recognition of the cosmic mystery, apart from self-regard, advances one in religious insight and virtuous life.

Response to the divine initiative as the conscious worship of transcendent Reality is expressed by four historic means: ritual or liturgy, symbol or image, sacraments or visible deeds connoting or conveying unseen realities, and self-dedication.[1] As Evelyn Underhill elucidates, these four instruments of

[1] Cf. Underhill, Evelyn, *Worship,* pp. 20 ff. (New York: Harper & Brothers, 1937).

worship possess characteristics in common.   First, they are marked by a social quality.   They make it possible for men to worship together, to experience the same emotions, and to engage in the same activities.   Next, they place at man's disposal the means of responding to God by a rich complexity in which the whole of human nature is concerned.   The personal and the social, the visible and the invisible, the manual and the contemplative, thought and speech, the rhythmic and the free, habit and attention, which are all representative of human nature, are involved in the historic ways of worship.

A religious ritual is a framework within which corporate worship may occur.   It is an agreed routine.   The ritual sense is conservative, it resists innovation and novelty.   It tends to become traditional.   The peril of ritualism is constancy to an inherited form at the cost of the soul of worship, the encouragement of the survival of ceremonies which serve no present purpose or have ceased to embody the living beliefs of the worshipers.   But formal worship is not necessarily divorced from living Reality.   Times without number the familiar phrases of the liturgy through their beauty, inherent power and connection with the past, induce in the worshiper the adoration of God.[2]

Symbols employed in worship vary in nature and effects. Words are intangible but meaningful symbols.   The crucifix and the ikon are visible representations which aid concentration and arouse appropriate thoughts and emotions.   The danger which waits on symbolism is the identification of the image with the reality for which it stands.   Used with discretion, the symbolic objects represent realities which ordered action or stately phrases fail to express.   If the worshiper is carried beyond the symbol to the world it is designed to suggest, he approaches Reality already on the way to meet him.

A valid sacrament, historically understood, actually conveys meaning and power from God to the worshiper by a material process.   Baptismal water cleanses morally, the bread and wine of the Eucharist feed and sustain the communicant, the

---

[2] Originally a liturgy was an order of service for the celebration of the Lord's Supper, but now almost any service book is described as liturgical.

sacrament of marriage unites in indissoluble bonds, the laying on of hands consecrates the candidate and confers upon him new responsibilities and rights. Sacramentalism opens channels through which the prevenient action of God may reach, refresh, and transform men. It arouses the mood of reverent adoration in the breast of the sincere worshiper. To be sure, the sacraments may be degraded by formalism, but he who would abandon them on that account is indeed shortsighted. The sacraments, properly administered and devoutly received, give to the order of religious values a cogency and vitality which is worshipful.

Worship culminates in self-giving to God. Self-oblation in its highest form is not motivated by fear or selfishness. It is not mere self-renunciation. It is the normal and ultimate expression of man's appreciation of the goodness and glory of God. It is the disinterested but concrete embodiment of the worshiper's adoration of God who has condescended to stoop to his weakness, to deliver him from the bondage of fears, and to speak to his soul. Self-dedication to God keeps worship from becoming a subjective and sterile emotional experience. It affords the attitude of adoration and humility an appropriate avenue of discharge.

The worship mood is induced in deeply religious personalities quite irrespective of the denominational channels through which the divine energy flows. A Protestant should be able to worship God in a Catholic church. An Episcopalian should be spiritually sensitive enough to respond to God in a Methodist church. A member of a liberal Congregational church in New England reports that recently he was so impressed and challenged by a Mormon service broadcast from the great tabernacle in Salt Lake City that his heart was strangely warmed within him, that he was vouchsafed the consciousness of God and received inspiration and courage to resume his daily round of obligations. The spirit of worship transcends sectarian ties.

In the final analysis provision for and the actual conduct of genuine worship is the most significant contribution of the Church to the citizenship of a republic or other form of political organization in which the Church and state are separate. The

Church together with its several arms is the only public institution in which we receive guidance in the approach to God. The avowed objective of our public school system is the development of good American citizens. To this end the public school teaches a variety of subjects. In addition, the moral virtues without which a state cannot long endure are both directly and indirectly taught in our public schools. Worship is a unique function of the Church. Under present legal provisions worship cannot be fostered in the public schools. Our citizenship will be deprived of the religious motives and moral sanctions which the consciousness of God implies, if the Church shirks its responsibility as the chief agency of worship in our republic.

Historic Types of Christian Worship

The range of types of worship in the Christian Church extends from the silent meditation of the Quakers to the elaborate services of the Catholics.[3] For the sake of survey and comparison we may recognize four types: the Greek Orthodox, the Roman Catholic, the liturgical Protestant, and the non-liturgical Protestant.[4] Each type has its characteristic emphasis, and each seems to appeal to a particular section of the Chris-

---

[3] For more extended accounts of the several types of public worship see Heiler, Friedrich, *The Spirit of Worship* (New York: George H. Doran Company, 1926); also Byington, Edwin H., *The Quest for Experience in Worship* (New York: Doubleday, Doran & Co., 1929).

[4] For a study of the liturgical values of the Psalter see Peters, John P., *The Psalms as Liturgies* (New York: The Macmillan Company, 1922). Psalms 100, 104-107, 111-118, 120-134, 135, 136, 145-150 were committed to memory by the Jews and were repeatedly used in the service of worship in postexilic times. When the daily morning sacrifice was offered in the Herodian Temple, a priest struck the cymbals and the Levitical choir sang the psalm of the day in three parts. At the close of each part the trumpets sounded three times, and the people prostrated themselves and worshipped. A second liturgical but nonsacrificial service followed later in the day. In the late afternoon another sacrificial-liturgical service, shorter but like the one in the morning, was held. Certain psalms were sung in connection with the celebration of the annual festivals such as the Passover, Pentecost, Tabernacles, and Purim. Psalm 130 was used on the Day of Atonement. Practically the same use of the psalms was made in the synagogue as in the Temple. The synagogue service occupied the place of the elaborate service of the Temple after the latter was destroyed. The law, the prophets, and prayer took the place of the sacrificial cultus of the Temple. The scheme of the services of the early Christian church was derived from the order of the synagogue worship. Consult the above, pp. 77 ff.

tian constituency. Whether cultural and religious background or the conformation of personality we call temperament determines the type in which the worshiper engages with the greatest profit is difficult to ascertain. The probability is that the majority of people who conclude that the form of worship which is a part of their religious inheritance is unsuited to their dispositions do not seek a more congenial type but merely disavow organized religion altogether. It is only the questing personality that, unsatisfied with the transmitted structure of worship, explores other ways of celebrating final reality.

The liturgies of the Eastern or Greek Orthodox Church assumed definite form in the fourth century, a fact which is cited with pride by the adherents of this division of Christendom. The liturgies of the Western Church developed new features long after those of the Eastern branch were crystallized. The rift between the Eastern and the Western churches began in the early centuries of the present era, although the final separation did not occur until the eleventh century.

The service of the Greek Orthodox Church is characterized by the spectacular and mysterious. The liturgical acts are impregnated with a sense of the glory and majesty of Christ and God. Such features as the radiance of myriads of lighted candles, and the dazzling silver and gold of the vestments of the priests dramatize the divine splendor, especially in the larger and more elegant churches.

The bread of the communion dipped in the wine is given on a spoon to the worshiper by the priest. The church baptizes the children of its members in infancy or early childhood and all baptized persons are admitted to the communion service. In the Lord's Supper the sinner is cleansed and purified, and God plants the assurance of immortality in his soul. The crown of man is the remission of sins and the gift of blissful endless life. This is the nerve of the Greek type of worship. The death and resurrection of Christ figure prominently. Accordingly, worship reaches its climax in the ornate and joyful Easter services. Preaching seems almost foreign to this type of worship. Both the Greek Mass and the Roman Mass are supposedly in strict accord with the precepts and example of

Christ which he gave his disciples on the last night before his crucifixion.

The core of the service of the Roman Catholic Church is the repetition of the sacrifice of Jesus in the Mass.[5]   Such events in the records of the life of the Lord as the incarnation, the crucifixion, and the ascension receive special consideration in the Mass at the appropriate time of the church year of Roman Catholicism.   The Mass is not a mere symbol of the sacrificial death of Christ; it is an actual renewal of it. Christ is truly present in the wine and wafers. In the communion man is united with God. The Mass consists of two essential acts. The first is transubstantiation, the miraculous conversion of the bread and the wine into the veritable body and blood of Christ when the priest utters the words, "This is my body" and "This is my blood." The kneeling of the officiating priest, the sign of the cross, the ringing of the bell are prescribed by the church. The second act is the sacrifice of the Mass which is made when the priest offers on the altar the bread and wine, as a repetition of Christ's sacrifice on the cross, as a real sacrifice of Christ to God. Mass is celebrated daily. Mass, whether it be High or Low, whether it consume about half an hour or an hour, is the main, almost the sole feature of Roman Catholic worship.   Confession to the priest and participation in the Mass once a year suffice to keep one in good standing in the Roman Church.

It is an active service. The priest is in motion almost constantly, making the sign of the cross, bending, bowing, using his hands in intercession or benediction, kissing the altar, elevating the bread or cup. These actions arrest and hold the attention of the worshiper. The worshiper also is active, changing his posture a dozen times in a quarter of an hour.

Between the main divisions of the Mass the notices, the requests for prayers for the dead, and the Gospel lesson are read in the vernacular of the people. A sermon, brief and practical, may be delivered. Some prayers offered by the priest as well as responses are clothed in the language of the worshipers.

[5] See Fortescue, Adrian, *The Mass* (New York: Longmans, Green & Co., 1914).

Of the liturgical Protestant denominations the Lutheran and Episcopal may be noted as outstanding examples. The service of worship in the Lutheran Church is conducted in accordance with an established form.[6] An altar with candles, a lectern and a pulpit, paintings of crucial events in the ministry and passion of Christ, and the clerical vestments of the clergy all contribute to the dignity and impressiveness of the Lutheran order of service. Worship centers in the preaching of the Word of God. According to some influential divisions of the Lutheran Church the sacraments are dead apart from the Word. The heart of the Lord's Supper is God's Word, his promise of the forgiveness of sins. The sentence of the institution of the Supper, "This is my body," is living language, a sermon on the divine forgiveness of sin. The Supper is the seal of the Word.

The worship is characterized by relative simplicity. As contrasted with the Roman Catholic type of worship, the language of the people is employed throughout the service, prayers for the dead are omitted, no petitions are addressed to Mary, the saints, the martyrs, and the angels. Incense is banished. Purgatory is not recognized. The doctrine of the universal priesthood of believers and their direct access to God dominates the theory and the method of worship.

The communion is administered only a few times a year. Transubstantiation, which is tenaciously held by the Catholic Church, is rejected. Consubstantiation, Melanchthon's doctrine of the actual presence of Christ with the bread and wine apart from physical transformation of these elements, is affirmed by the bodies true to the Lutheran historical tradition and discarded by other Lutheran groups. Both elements, the bread and the wine, are given the laity. Considerable latitude in the order and conduct of worship is allowed the individual church. Religious teaching, prayer, and praise are accorded the preeminence in the ordinary public service of worship. Instruction is exalted, for ignorance is the enemy of religion; devo-

---

[6] See Schaff, Philip, *The Creeds of Christendom,* Vol. III, pp. 3-73 (New York: Harper & Brothers, 1877).

tion and sincerity alone are insufficient, knowledge and truth must triumph.

The Episcopal or Anglican Church seeks to unite in its service elements of the Roman Catholic worship compatible with its own genius. The Episcopal Church is marked by a sensitiveness to beauty, seemliness, and order. It has a given creed and a stated ritual which are incorporated in the Book of Common Prayer, the first issue of which was introduced in 1549. Most of the controversies in the Episcopal Church have raged over forms of worship and proposed additions or amendments to the Book of Common Prayer. It makes much of its historical continuity and succession.

Holy communion occupies a dignified and important place in the worship of the Episcopalians. The "high" church wing, with its confessional, its priestly absolution, and its celebration of the Mass, is not far removed from Roman Catholicism. On the other hand, the "low" church division, while maintaining a stateliness of worship, is much more Protestant in form, doctrine, and outlook. It adheres closely to the Prayer Book. In many of the local churches communion is celebrated once a Sunday in a simple but impressive service. Prescribed selections from both the Old and the New Testament in harmony with the church year are read at public worship. In addition, every Sunday in the year has its appropriate collect, epistle, and gospel for the communion service. Responses are made by the people or the choir. On the whole the service is balanced and creates the distinct impression that its purpose is the cultivation and satisfaction of the worship mood. The sermon may be mediocre and the communion may not be administered, but the worshiper feels that it is edifying to praise God with others assembled for the same purpose, an act which deserves an attentive and reverent mind and an appreciation of beautiful liturgy.

The Methodist Episcopal Church, which derives from the Anglican communion, enjoins upon its ministers an established order of service and a ritual for the administration of the Lord's Supper and baptism, the solemnization of marriage, the ordination of deacons and elders, and the consecration of deaconesses and bishops. In this respect Methodism is liturgical. On the other hand, this denomination, like many others, lays upon the pastors of the local churches almost all responsibility for the content of the usual public worship of God, such as the selection of hymns, Scripture passages, and the sermon theme, and the composition of the prayers. To be sure, the Apostles' Creed and the Lord's Prayer are recited. The sermon has been the outstanding element of the Sunday services.

The nonliturgical denominations are too numerous to be mentioned by name in this context. In America there are probably more than 260 denominations, great and small, which are Protestant and nonliturgical. They range all the way from the Quakers, who in theory eschew a specialized ministry and the sacraments, to the Holy Rollers with their unbridled enthusiasm and emotional excesses. Between these extremes are such major bodies as the Presbyterian, Baptist, and Congregational, with their varying sense of decorum and orderliness in worship. Several influential and numerically strong denominations have radically modified or discarded their respective historical rituals. Such a highly organized communion as the Presbyterian, which to an appreciable extent determines the theological belief and ecclesiastical procedure of the local church, could not consistently refrain from giving public worship a measure of guidance. The Presbyterian denomination in America places most of the responsibility for the conduct and substance of public worship upon the minister, but it does advise him to take cognizance of the Book of Common Worship. A study of this manual occasions regret that its disuse is so prevalent among Presbyterian churches in America.[7]

In an effort to arouse or intensify the state of worship, many churches have borrowed devotional aids from liturgical bodies. Litanies, prepared prayers, the communion table in the sanctuary as the focus of the attention of the congregation, and other accessories of worship have been introduced. In order to attract larger audiences and to stimulate religious interest some churches devote services to particular causes or occasions.

[7] See Perry, William, *The Scottish Liturgy* (London: A. R. Mowbray & Co., Ltd., 1922).

Would not the appropriate observance by such churches of the most significant of the special Sundays in the ecclesiastical year of the Episcopal communion, in the long run, be more profitable than an increase in the number of such days as Father's Day and Flower Sunday? In a multitude of local churches the participation of the people in a carefully planned service has reduced the importance once attached to the sermon and magnified other items of public worship. It has been suggested that churches divide the Sunday service into separate periods any one or several of which may be attended by the worshiper. The program would consist of a unit of meditation, a unit of music, a unit of preaching, and a unit of discussion or instruction. The individual would be encouraged to select the parts which could most effectively minister to his necessities.

That there are unrealized worship possibilities in many of our social customs and practices a moment's reflection will disclose. Dr. Pratt calls attention to the potential religious values of the funeral service.[8] The disposal of the dead is a religious ceremony. Death startles us out of our complacent practical attitude. As a mysterious force which removes man from the earthly scene, death fills us with solemnity, impels us afresh to question the meaning of human life, and makes us aware of a lost moral perspective. The funeral service worshipfully conducted increases or corrects our religious beliefs, redirects or fortifies our ethical convictions, and arouses in us a desire for contact with that which is not subject to the vicissitudes of the world of sense experience. Other crises within or without the individual possess latent opportunities for worship.

The new emphasis on the technique of worship is freighted with perils as well as gains. A worship service as an artistic spectacle is likely to induce aesthetic ecstasy rather than religiously meaningful experience. Since Christianity is ethical and social, one test of the worth of the enrichment of worship is growth of both the ministry and laity in humility, kindliness, active participation in community enterprises which improve the common lot, and substantial support of the far-flung mis-

[8] Pratt, James B., *The Religious Consciousness,* pp. 304, 305 (New York: The Macmillan Company, 1920).

sionary cause. Does the reconstituted service bear these fruits? Does richly embroidered formal worship foster or diminish the prophetic vision and voice of the ministry? Is an order of service a drug which renders the worshiper tolerant or insensitive to the inhumanities and cruelties of the predatory group? Is the ornate and artistic form of worship so complicated that the worshiper is diverted from the simplicity, power, and appeal of the gospel of Christ? Does the service provide the worshiper adequate opportunity publicly to affirm his faith in God? Is it a fellowship of believers? Does the order of service in both substance and form express the genius of the Christian faith? Churches which have embodied in their public services various historic techniques and ritualistic features of great liturgical communions do well to ponder and avoid the perils of formalism to which they have exposed themselves.

Modern Worship Patterns

Public worship properly understood and participated in consists of a sequence of attitudes, responses, ideas, and purposes which further a higher religious integration of personality. To this end various orders of service have been evolved and amended from time to time in accordance with a change of specific aim or a clearer insight into the processes by which the controlling objective may be attained. We have already taken into general account types of worship which characterize representative branches of Christendom. Specific worship patterns have recently been devised for the several nonliturgical and the more flexible liturgical denominations. The contributions of Sperry, Vogt, and Sclater are representative and significant.[9]

It is obvious that it would be exceedingly difficult if not absolutely impossible to construct an order of service which would answer the felt needs of every worshiper in the average congregation. A company of worshipers might as individuals

[9] Sperry, Willard, *Reality in Worship* (New York: The Macmillan Company, 1925). Vogt, Von Ogden, *Modern Worship* (New Haven: Yale University Press, 1927). Sclater, J. R. P., *The Public Worship of God* (New York: George H. Doran Company, 1927).

be conscious of fifty different wants. No one worship pattern is comprehensive yet specific enough to solve all the diversified personal problems of a large group of worshipers. On the other hand, worship should be co-operative as well as collective. The categories of public worship may be spacious enough to minister to man's fundamental and constantly recurring spiritual necessities, such as the realization of the presence of God in human life, the forgiveness of sin, peace, and courage for whatever circumstances impose. In addition, heart speaks to heart, one individual subconsciously interprets another. The more numerous the worshipers in a sanctuary are, the closer they sit, kneel, and stand together, the deeper their fellowship will be. A rhythm is produced which unites them in thought, emotion, and expression. The worshipers are swayed by the dominant sentiment impressed upon them by the minister, are for the time occupied by the same set of ideas and react in unison to the divine impulse felt. In the prevailing common mood of confession, adoration, gratitude, and self-dedication the individual identifies himself with the congregation as a whole and receives the illumination and inspiration which he needs.

Vogt and Sperry working independently evolved similar worship patterns from the sixth chapter of the Book of Isaiah, which is an account of the young prophet's inaugural vision. Vogt distinguishes the following eight progressive steps in worship as the celebration of the whole of life and the praise of God: the preparation of the worshiper, a vision of the Lord of Hosts, the consequent humility of the individual, fresh religious vitality, recollection of the goodness of God and man's manifold obligations, illumination in terms of the challenge of a specific task, dedication to the service of mankind, and peace. That this scheme here and there, as in the final stage, is at variance with the recorded experience of the youthful Isaiah does not detract from the value of the formula as a whole. It is a union of psychologically graduated human responses to the progressive manifestations and purposes of God, a union which passes through the successive stages of contemplation, awe, repentance, forgiveness, appreciation of a specific duty as a divine command, acceptance of the commission of service, and peace which affords release from a crucial experience charged with intense emotion, a union which is more than the aggregate of its constituents and as such is characterized by a unique quality and potency.

Sclater's order of service applies what he appropriately calls the principles of alteration and ascension. Alteration in worship centers in a rhythmic movement between divine vision and human response. Man swings from his consciousness of the holiness of God to the consciousness of his own unworthiness, from the requirements of religion to his inability in his own strength to comply with them, from his acceptance of the forgiveness of God to an answering gratitude. Stimulus and reaction thus alternate. The nerve of the principle of ascension is a cumulative succession of emotions and attitudes. In the considered worship of God fear may yield to awe, awe to joy, joy to love.

The principles of alteration and ascension are applied in the two component parts of the service—the approach to God and the act of worship itself. Sclater's intricate pattern of worship is designed to direct the worshiper's attention to God and to himself in a progressively creative series. To this end the familiar instrumentalities of worship, such as prayer, passages of Scripture, hymns, anthems, the sermon, and the benediction are utilized.[10] Alteration and ascension evoke a progression of human responses to promptings interpreted by the religious personality as divine stimuli and unveilings. There are obvious points of similarity between the order suggested by the course

[10] In the summer session of 1931 conducted by the Presbyterian Theological Seminary, Chicago, a class of 34 men and 2 women, studying the psychology of worship, made a list of favorite hymns. Every member of the class, the majority of which were parish ministers, independently indicated in the order of preference the ten hymns which most appealed to him. In all 106 hymns were chosen. The ten most frequently selected are here listed with the number of preferences for each: "Faith of Our Fathers, Living Still" (14 times selected), "O Master, Let Me Walk with Thee" (13), "Holy, Holy, Holy, Lord God Almighty" (12), "O Jesus, I Have Promised" (8), "Dear Lord and Father of Mankind" (7), "O Love, That Wilt Not Let Me Go" (7), "All Hail the Power of Jesus' Name" (7), "Where Cross the Crowded Ways of Life" (7), "I Need Thee Every Hour" (6), "Spirit of God, Descend upon My Heart" (6).

of Isaiah's pivotal experience in the temple and Sclater's framework. They differ mainly in the sequence in which the several parts of worship are introduced.

The dominant attitude which wise leaders of public worship in our more or less informal types of services seek to induce is that of reverence. The attention of the worshiper is directed to the glory, majesty, moral perfection, power, and wisdom of God. We are to adore and praise God, but not because he would be jealous or vindictive if these honors were withheld. Psychologically when we reverence God we do not contribute anything to his welfare, but cultivate in ourselves the spirit of humility, dependence, and submission. It is evident that the leader cannot arouse reverence for God in the members of the group simply by exhorting them to be reverent. In order to become reverent the individual must foster that due sense of the attributes of God to which the natural reaction is one of reverence. The worshiper must realize that God and he are not equals, that between the two there is a gulf that can never be bridged, that the two are separated by differences that nothing can remove. Contemplation of the God of heaven and earth arouses a holy awe in the heart of the worshiper.

It is psychologically impossible to complete the mood of worship in a single concept or attitude. The appreciation of God as Otto and Sperry have so penetratingly declared instills in man not only a profound respect for the divine majesty but also confidence in the divine benevolence.[11] God is father as well as Lord of Hosts. Other experiences illustrate the sense of double quality. Autumn is a season of contrasting moods. The flaming foliage may remind a person of the passing show of life, of decay and death and fill him with sadness, but soon the riot of scarlet banners may transport him with joy. In one and the same individual the two opposite moods may alternate.[12] Similarly the holiness of God, his moral sublimity, his glory as expressed in nature, the mystery which is he, alter-

[11] Otto, Rudolf, *The Idea of the Holy* (London: H. Milford, Oxford University Press, 1923).
[12] Compare Bliss Carmen's poem "A Vagabond Song" with Edna St. Vincent Millay's poem "God's World."

nately overwhelm us and attract us, cast us down and lift us up, humble us and exalt us. Jesus himself bows in humble submission in the presence of the God of all beings, and stands before the Father with trust and joy. When he teaches his disciples to pray in this manner, "Our Father who art in heaven, hallowed be thy name," he unites the tender and the sublime in a synthesis of reverence. The true worshiper is conscious not only of the Lord shrouded in mystery, pavilioned in splendor, and girded with moral superiority, but also of the Father who knows that our frame is dust, who remembers that we are frail creatures of conflicting desires, whose property it is at all times to exercise mercy toward those who truly seek him. The principle of alteration is operative in a worship pattern the very texture of which is reverence and its implications.

The adoption of an order such as Sperry or Vogt have formulated or the application of Sclater's basic principles by churches without a historic and demonstrably effective liturgy would do away with the "opening exercises" and give to the public worship of God, point, continuity, impressiveness, and progression.

It is evident that other orders of worship marked by dignity, beauty, and inspiration may be devised by those who have the requisite gifts. It is suggested that the interested reader make the Lord's Prayer the basis of an original order. Let him reduce this model prayer to its components. Let him note that the familiar prayer begins with the reverential approach to the Father and ends with an ascription of dominion, power, and glory to God. Let him consider that between the introduction and the conclusion are the aspiration for the coming of the kingdom on earth in which the will of God reigns supreme, the general petition for the physical necessities, the cry for forgiveness with its implied confession and repentance on the grounds of the remission of the trespasses of others against us, and the reliance upon God lest we yield to temptation. Let him select Bible passages, hymns, anthems, collects, in accordance with the undergirding ideas of the different parts of the Lord's Prayer. Let him organize all the materials into a connected and unified whole. Let him take cognizance of the variations in emphasis which a worship pattern derived from so magnificent a contribution as the Lord's Prayer makes possible.

Worship as an End in Itself

In reply to the inquiry, why worship God? many pragmatic reasons may be given. Some have already been indicated in the course of the present survey. Reference has been made to such consequences of worship as moral self-diagnosis, release from guilt, correction of character defects, comfort in sorrow, reconstruction of personality, call to special service, and religious unification of the self. Worship lifts the individual above the worrying, frettings, and distractions which relegate the building of the Kingdom both within and without himself to a secondary place, if they do not vitiate it altogether. A balloonist in midascent, finding himself in a furious storm, may throw overboard the weights carried as ballast in order that his balloon may rise above the violence of the elements and remain for a season where it is calm. Analogously, the one whose life is lashed by circumstances which threaten to disintegrate personality may in the attitude of worship cast all care aside and ascend to a plane where security, serenity, and faith reign. That true public worship does have definitely recognizable consequences for personality none who is impartial in his judgment will be disposed to deny.

On the other hand, why seek to justify the public worship of God by its so-called practical results alone? Why strive to multiply the utilities of the adoration of God? Are not many experiences and possessions to be prized for their own sake? Are we under sacred obligation to regard our most intimate moments as means to practical ends? In developing the specific and definitive implications of public worship do we not expose this exalted experience to the danger of forfeiting a precious value? A rose is its own reason for being, and a poem, a sunset, a child, a symphony. An appreciation of sacred mystery possesses a quality which makes worship stand in its own right. Our reaction to the sublimity of God culminates in itself and is its own exceedingly great reward.

Dean Sperry calls attention to a bronze statue of a naked

Indian astride his standing pony, his hands raised to the Great Spirit, his head thrown back, and eyes lifted.[13] The sculptor's genius has recovered the fundamental posture of a human being come to rest, of one possessed of the peace which subsists at the center of sincere worship. The noble poise, the simple physical expressions, and the finality of the entire attitude of the figure proclaim not so much the practical consequences of religion as the self-sufficiency of the worship mood.

[13] Sperry, Willard L., *Reality in Worship*, pp. 63-67 (New York: The Macmillan Company, 1925).

CHAPTER XVIII

OCCULTISM AND PERSONALITY

THE occult includes spiritism, automatic writing, telepathy, clairvoyance, theosophy, numerology, palmistry, astrology, reciprocal dreams, apparitions of either the living or the dead, demon possession, glossolalia, witchcraft, reincarnation, faith cures, and kindred phenomena.[1] Volumes almost without number have been written on the methods and objectives of occultism, and the active interest in supernormal experimentation is mounting in our day. In both Europe and America societies for the systematic investigation of the several branches of unseen realms and extra-human relations have been founded.[2] The work being done by societies for research in occult phenomena should be studied by those whose interest in occultism extends beyond the references here made. In the present context, only a few typical varieties of supernormal experiences, representative forces which originate, support, and increase belief and participation in occultism, reported results and a tentative evaluation of the findings of the experimenters can be introduced.

Telepathy

The nature and scope of alleged or real telepathic occurrences may well claim more than passing attention. The conclusion underlying the doctrine of telepathy is that, under certain necessary conditions, thoughts and feelings are transmit-

[1] For definitions of these terms from the standpoint of occultism and an abundance of illustrative material consult Fodor, Nandor, *Encyclopaedia of Psychic Science* (London: Arthurs Press, Ltd., 1933).

[2] The Society for Psychical Research, 31 Tavistock Square, London, was organized in 1882. The American Society for Psychical Research, 15 Lexington Avenue, New York, was founded in Boston in 1885. The American Psychical Institute and Laboratory, 20 W. 58th Street, New York, was established in 1920. The British College of Psychic Science, 15 Queens Gate, London, was founded in 1920. The reports, journals, and books published by these and similar societies provide a plethora of case material.

ted from one individual to another by means for which the senses recognized and described by prevailing psychology are completely inadequate. It is maintained by upholders of this kind of occultism that telepathic transference is not affected by the distance between the sender and receiver in the same way in which seeing, hearing, and other sensations are limited by space. The fundamental contention is that the mind under auspicious circumstances may receive impressions distinct from the commonly known sense communications. Extra-sensory awareness of the mental states of another, his thoughts, his emotions, his plans, is called telepathy. Extra-sensory perception of physical objects such as conflagrations hundreds of miles distant is called clairvoyance.[3] The conclusion has been drawn that telepathy and clairvoyance are manifestations of a common underlying ability to perceive material objects or mental images without the use of the ordinary senses.

Of a group of 137 students and faculty members of a theological school present at a panel discussion of occultism, which I attended, 64 per cent expressed belief in the validity of telepathic phenomena, 26 per cent were in doubt, and only 10 per cent definitely declared that they lacked credence. It is safe to say that the majority of psychologists in our colleges and universities do not accept the submitted evidences for telepathic occurrences as scientifically trustworthy. They are inclined to reduce the reports of telepathic marvels to a hopeless jumble of suggestion, coincidence, chance, hallucination, illusion, subconscious impression, unreliable observation, defective memory, unintentional exaggeration, and fraud. They maintain that an unbroken chain of sensations, conscious or subconscious, as psychology has explored and tabulated them, intermediates every perception. On the other hand, Rhine claims to have established the validity of telepathy by a series of experiments evaluated by the mathematics of probability. His outstanding telepathist was George Zirkle. In 5,025 trials he averaged 10.7 correct guesses per 25 Zener cards when only 5.0 would have been expected on the basis of chance. Zirkle's telepathic score

[3] Rhine, J. B., *Extra-Sensory Perception,* p. 14 (Boston: Boston Society for Psychic Research, 1934).

was better when he and the sender were twenty-five feet apart and a wall separated them, than when the agent sat near him.[4]

Spiritism

Spiritism is one of the oldest forms of occultism.[5]   It is claimed that messages from the dead, received by the living, include memories and interests of human relationships which are identifiable as those of the personality patterns of the departed with whom the communication has supposedly been established.[6] The undergirding tenet of spiritism in its various manifestations is that the information transmitted from the realm of the dead is of such a character that it could not be fabricated by mediums or others, and that it is not amenable to the usual methods of acquiring knowledge.   It is said that rapport between the dead and the living is cultivated by various means including mediumship, ghostly sounds, and automatic writing.

It is a distinct characteristic of apostolic Christianity that it makes no provision for direct intercourse with the dead.   Spiritism flourished in ancient Egypt and was prevalent among peoples of Canaan who surrounded Israel.   The law of Israel sternly forbade spiritistic and allied practices.   No witch, necromancer, or other inquirer of the dead was suffered to live among the chosen people.[7]

King Saul sinned when, having failed to secure advice in a military crisis from Jehovah through priest, prophet, or dreams,

---

[4] *Ibid.*, pp. 91 ff.

[5] See Paton, Lewis Bayles, *Spiritism and the Cult of the Dead in Antiquity* (New York: The Macmillan Company, 1921).   A distinction between spiritism and spiritualism should be made.   The latter is a religion based on alleged communications with the dead; spiritism may or may not possess religious implications.

[6] See, for example, Lodge, Oliver, *Raymond* (New York: George H. Doran Company, 1916); Hyslop, James H., *Contact with the Other World* (New York: The Century Company, 1920); Richet, Charles, *Thirty Years of Psychical Research* (New York: The Macmillan Company, 1923), translated by Stanley De Brath; Myers, Frederick William Henry, *Human Personality and Its Survival of Bodily Death* (New York: Longmans, Green & Co., 1903); *Science and a Future Life* (New York: The Macmillan Company, 1901); Hart, Hornell and Ella B., *Visions and Apparitions Collectively and Reciprocally Perceived, Proceedings of the Society for Psychical Research*, Vol. XLI., pp. 205-249, May, 1933.

[7] See Exodus 22: 18; Leviticus 19: 31; 20: 27; Deuteronomy 18: 9-14; Jeremiah 27: 9, 10.

he consulted the witch at Endor. At his behest she professedly summoned from the realm of the dead Samuel through whom Saul learned his impending fate.[8] Swedenborg, whose personal system of occultism provided a presumably safe, orderly, and ethical approach to the loved departed, declares that the spirit that responded to the witch of Endor's attempt was not the spirit of Samuel but another spirit that impersonated him and thus deceived both the witch and Saul.[9] A literal interpretation of the Bible narrative does, however, quite plainly indicate that it was Samuel himself and not another who appeared at the memorable seance. The record contains elements which one encounters in modern seances such as a troubled man in disguise, a secret visit under the cover of night, a woman with a talisman or object of divination in her hand, and an attitude on the part of the seeker after advice or information compounded of anxiety, credence, and expectation.[10] One is inclined to doubt that the spirit of Samuel told Saul anything that a shrewd woman acquainted with the political and military situation in the land of the Hebrews could not have fathomed and ventured to predict. Was she a ventriloquist?

Startling spiritistic phenomena associated with mediumship are recorded by modern investigators of occultism. "Margery," the wife of Dr. L. R. G. Crandon, a Boston physician, is one of the outstanding mediums of our day.[11] It is reported that Margery's "control" is her deceased brother, Walter Stinson. He speaks and acts through his sister. Several years ago it was reported that Walter had made fingerprints of his own on proprietary dental wax which receives and retains impressions in fine detail. The genuineness of the finger impressions has been called into question. In fact, it is claimed that the fingerprints attributed to Walter are identical with those of a certain living man. In an attempt to identify them as those of Walter, since no digital impressions made by the earthly Mr. Stinson

[8] 1 Samuel 28: 3-25.

[9] Swedenborg, Emanuel, *Adversaria,* Part II, par. 5022.

[10] The talisman of the witch of Endor was perhaps a human skull.

[11] Margery Mediumship, *Proceedings of the American Society for Psychical Research,* Vol. XXII, 1933. For a record of the developments of the mediumship of Margery see Vols. XX-XXI, 1926-27.

are available, reliance is primarily placed upon the voice and message issuing from the medium, and secondarily, upon arm-like and fingerlike processes extending from her body.

Experiments have been made which supposedly demonstrate that the Walter voice affirming the genuineness of the finger-prints is not Margery's own, nor that of an accomplice nor produced by a physical mechanism, but a supernormal voice—namely, that of the late Mr. Stinson. It is said that at certain times a unique substance, called ectoplasm or teleplasm, deli-cate in texture, yet firm enough to impress a design upon plastic material, extends from various parts of the medium's body, but principally from the orifices. Sometimes the emanation is like a luminous vapor, often it solidifies and assumes the nature of elastic material; on one occasion it may be visible, on another invisible. The teleplasm is re-absorbed by the body of the medium. From Walter's statements and the extrusions from the body of Margery the inference is drawn that the wax finger-prints in question are his and were made by him through the control and manipulation of ectoplasm. Dr. McComas in order to show that what Margery does can be done by other and natural means and that Dr. Crandon should permit a more exhaustive investigation of her mediumship, conducted seances of his own in which an imposing Hindoo, duly in-structed, told the sitters the numbers and suits of cards selected in a dark room, rang a bell in a small box, was the mouth-piece of a control called Gogol, introduced an apparition, and created an atmosphere in which several felt psychic breezes.[12]

Strange noises are often interpreted as the antics or serious demonstrations of spirits. The story of the ghost haunting the rectory occupied by the famous Wesley family at Epworth, England, is widely known. At night and during family prayers knocks, groans, the rattling of pans and doors, and the howling of dogs disturbed the household. Samuel Wesley when urged by his friends to vacate the haunted rectory retorted that he would not flee from the devil but would let the devil flee from him. Mrs. Wesley wrote her son John, destined to become the

[12] See McComas, Henry C., *Ghosts I Have Talked With* (Baltimore: Williams & Wilkins Co., 1935).

outstanding religious leader of his generation, that she did not understand why these phenomena were permitted, since they evidently have no commission to give us information about the invisible world that would make us wiser or help us to avoid danger. Perhaps "Old Jeffrey," as the children in the rectory called the ghost, was answerable for John Wesley's belief in the objective reality of apparitions and witchcraft.[13]

We know that when a condition of suggestibility exists, water dripping from a tap into a bathtub or washbowl at night sounds like footfalls, the snapping of wires in door or window screens as a result of changes in temperatures or the cracking of old boards and timbers sounds like pistol shots reminiscent of murder or suicide, the audible breathing and snoring of cats, dogs, and other household pets sound like the groaning of a spirit in distress, and the whistling of the wind through small openings in walls or in other surfaces of a building sounds like the shrieking of an Irish banshee. Such noises proceeding from natural causes are heard in exaggerated form in a nocturnal or other stillness, and are misinterpreted by superstitious, anxious, alert, and imaginative listeners. Eye and ear illusions are common occurrences.

Now and then the investigator of the occult reads or hears a report of weird noises not so easily reducible to the sources to which the reference has just been made. One who writes under the pseudonym of Harlan Jacobs, but for whose competence and veracity reputable editors vouch, describes certain mysterious crashes heard by himself and wife during their four-months occupancy of a house on Cape Cod.[14] Passing by sounds like the impact of a cane upon a brick sidewalk, a sound like that of a newspaper swishing across the floor of a chamber although no such stimulus was discovered, and the sound of something like a rolling pin falling upon the floor and then

[13] Under the powerful preaching of Wesley, listeners on occasion would be seized by paroxysms in which, motor control suspended, bodily jerking would pronouncedly occur. So far from regarding these reactions to his message as the manifestations of the divine Spirit, Wesley attributed them to Satan's interference with his ministry, and therefore fulminated against them and rebuked the victims for interrupting his preaching and distracting his hearers.

[14] *Harper's Magazine,* November, 1934.

rolling across the room although no object was found, attention is directed to what Mr. Jacobs calls the Grand Piano Smash. One night in midsummer he and his wife while in the living room heard a deafening crash, a crash like that produced by a grand piano suddenly deprived of its legs, a crash which seemed to issue from the garage in the rear of the premises. An immediate investigation of the garage disclosed not the slightest evidence of a catastrophe or uproar. Subsequently the crash was heard several times. In September the lawyer of Mr. Jacobs, accompanied by his wife and daughter, arrived. The lawyer listened to the tale of the fearsome sounds with scouting skepticism. The three visitors occupied the front bedroom that night. The next morning the guests reported that in the night they had heard a terrific crash which so frightened them that the daughter was taken into the bed occupied by her father and mother. The host and his wife exchanged meaningful glances. For some unfathomable reason they had not on this occasion heard the Grand Piano Smash. The origin and nature of this peculiar phenomenon has not yet been satisfactorily explained.[15]

A friend introduced me to a woman in Cleveland, Ohio, who claims to be in communication with spirits and daily receives guidance from a deceased physician. The three of us sat in a well-lighted parlor. The performance was entirely subjective, so to speak; no objects moved their positions and no mysterious visible changes in the realm of physics and chemistry occurred. She closed her eyes and described what she saw in the spirit world. Some of her reports were either far from the truth or could have been secured from friends of mine. She did, however, mention the Christian name of my father and the disease of which he died. At the time I was thinking of something entirely different; hence, mind reading is either a very remote or an altogether false explanation of the correct statements made by the psychic.

[15] Conan Doyle in his book, *The Vital Message* (New York: George H. Doran Company, 1919), describes the checking of a noisy entity active in an old house in which in all probability a crime had been committed by an "earth-bound" criminal. Mr. Doyle writes that he made contact with the noisome spirit, prayed for it, exhorted it to rise to a higher plane, and was assured through a message tilted out at a table that it would mend its ways. Subsequently quiet reigned in the house.

The Ouija Board

One form of the ever-spreading occultism is the manipulation of the ouija board. This device consists of a flat surface bearing the letters of the alphabet, the ten numerals, "Yes" in the upper left-hand corner, and "No" in the upper right, "Goodbye" in the center below the numerals, and a small and generally heart-shaped structure, called the planchette, standing on short, smooth legs. The two operators, seated with the board between them, place their fingers upon the planchette, which glides about and spells out the answers to questions put by an operator or another to Ouija or some other power supposedly in control of the performance. Ouija is a trade-mark name, and a combination formed from the French, "oui," meaning yes, and the German, "ja," meaning, likewise, yes, the implication being that the planchette will answer in any language. The process is a form of automatic writing.

It may suffice for illustrative purposes to give an account of one of the many performances of the ouija board in which I was a participant. I select a typical session at which I was the only inquirer and at which a man and his wife who had developed considerable skill in the use of the planchette were the operators. John Smith, deceased, spelled out a willingness to answer questions. The dialogue in which one operator asked John Smith the questions I raised was recorded at the time as follows:

Question: John, do you know who it is that wants to ask you some questions?
Answer: Gentleman, heard him preach.
Question: Where did you hear him preach?
Answer: In the Methodist church.
Question: In what town?
Answer: G——
Question: Do you know how L—— (a professional mind reader) answers the questions put to her?
Answer: It is beyond my sphere.
Question: What do you mean by that?
Answer: Get the gentleman to make an explanation.

At this point I interrupted to explain that there is no Methodist church in G——. John Smith was further quizzed.

Question: Since there is no Methodist church in G——, how do you explain your statement?
Answer: All sects attend.
Question: Did you ever meet him personally?
Answer: Not that I recall.

At this juncture I tried to jog the memory of the "spirit" and requested the conducting operator to ask

Question: Do you remember meeting him in a hardware store at G——?
Answer: No, he must mean David.

Keeping as inscrutable and noncommittal as possible, I threw the operators upon their own inner resources, which in this case were extremely slender, although I did relent sufficiently to correct a wrong answer and try to stimulate the spirit's memory. I did actually meet the deceased in a hardware store, a few years before his death, as hinted, and had a lengthy conversation with him.

In interpreting the output of the ouija board performance or any other form of automatic writing, one should first of all take into consideration the observable tendency to ignore or excuse failures or mistakes. At the ouija board performances I have attended, the failures have been more numerous and important than the successes. Of course, some occultists account for wrong or unintelligible messages as the products of intruding mischievous or malicious spirits. When reminded of the failures, other believers in telepathy or spiritism intimate that the inquirer's skepticism or lack of mental concentration is responsible. The unbiased and critical psychologist regards the negative as well as the positive results as data which his science must recognize, investigate, and reflect in his report.

The contribution of chance and coincidence should not be ignored. The degree of probability is, of course, a quantity which varies with circumstances. When the questions put to the ouija board are answerable by "yes" or "no," in the long run one-half of the answers will be correct on the basis of chance alone. As regards coincidence it is well to bear in mind that the external world is so rich in the nature and variety of its events that correspondences between them and the output of

the ouija board are bound to occur.   It could hardly be otherwise.

Frequently the two operators of the ouija board will insist
that a message includes facts of which neither has had previous
knowledge.   Now nothing is more treacherous than memory.
We recall but very little of what we have actually experienced.
Experimenters in abnormal psychology induce hypnotic states in
which the subjects disclose data which they have been unable
to remember under normal conditions.   An individual may not
recollect his dreams of last night, but in the trance he will report them to the inquiring hypnotist.   At one ouija board performance I witnessed, an operator firmly maintained that he
had never known the given name of a person present, which
was correctly spelled out, until he was reminded that it had
been appearing in the newspapers for years.   Many results that
appear to the operator and others to be novel and unrelated to
normal experience are doubtless latent and potential memories
come to consciousness.

Furthermore, we respond to stimuli imperceptible to awareness.   The range of one's total sensory experience is far more
extensive than the range of impressions which are directly
recognizable.   It has been repeatedly demonstrated that we are
motivated by a multitude of subconscious registrations of which
we are ignorant.   We know more than we consciously know,
we hear more than we consciously hear, we see more than we
consciously see.   There is a subtle inclination to attribute a
definite response to unknown but subconsciously dynamic stimuli, to another individual at a distance, or to a spirit or other
unseen power.   It seems natural if not actually logical to refer
thoughts, feelings, and actions excited by sensory impressions
too delicate to be consciously noted, to sources outside the self.
Such reactions appear to be prompted by wills other than our
own.

Some of us are exceedingly sensitive to the signs of agreement or disagreement exhibited by the facial expressions and
bodily attitudes of others.   The lifting of an eyebrow, the aspect of the eyes, a smile, a trace of surprise or hesitation or
trepidation, a slight movement of the head, a little gesture of

the hand may all possess a significance to an operator of which he himself may be wholly unaware.[16]   Time and again, I have seen a group of unsophisticated persons bending over the ouija board and with breathing, facial signals and perhaps unintentional and inaudible whispering, so direct the performance that they unwittingly supplied the equally innocent operator with clues to the requested answers.   There is, furthermore, a noticeable tendency among operators to check up their results as they proceed.   Reactions by the questioner to important items of a message as soon as they are severally announced serve the performer as guides.

The ouija board is an admirable device for stimulating and bringing to the surface subconscious contents and elaborations. The manipulation of the planchette permits much skirmishing for clues and hints.   It is said that the spiritistic medium often experiences difficulty in submitting unusual names and dates. Having before them the alphabet and the numerals, and the planchette being given the range of the entire board, the ouija board operators have a chance to feel their way letter by letter or number by number.   If an answer to a question is not forthcoming within a reasonable length of time, an operator may consciously give the planchette a little start upon its mission. The success of the performance is materially facilitated by the contributions of two operators.   What the one cannot produce, the other may be able to supply.   To be sure, now and then a conflict between the two arises, which is likely to bring the planchette to a halt unless the one yields to the other.   The chief characteristics of a good operator are a reliance on impulse and feeling, an unwavering expectation that results will be obtained, and a high degree of sensitiveness to the outward signs and symbols of the inner mental movements of the inquirer and others present.   Although not everyone can become

---

[16] The skilled bridge player examines the countenances and behavior of his partner and opponents.   He judges the value of the hand of another by the way the cards are sorted and by the glances which fall upon them. Embarrassment or eagerness betrays the situation of an opponent or partner.   The analytical player considers the manner in which a card is placed upon the table or a trick is gathered up and governs his playing in accordance with his deductions.

a successful operator, the ouija board performance is considered a relatively simple form of occultism.

Automatic Writing

Involuntary composition with pen or pencil is often ascribed to the workings of the spirit world. The Reverend Dwight J. Bradley states that he has become deeply interested in certain occult phenomena as a result of the number and good character of those who accept them as valid, the quantity and apparent reliability of the findings of psychic researchers, and his own experiences in automatic writing.[17] On a certain afternoon in March, 1931, while he was composing a letter of condolence to the widow of a friend, he felt an urge to write something on another sheet of paper. The impulse was suppressed for a time, but when it became exceedingly insistent he obeyed it. For several subsequent days he seemed to be under the immediate control of the deceased to whose widow he had been writing. Apparently guided by his departed friend he repeatedly wrote what occurred to him. His hand formed words without conscious direction. Mr. Bradley is convinced that this writing is the output of a personality other than himself, in fact that it was inspired by his deceased friend. The content of the writing is characterized as both beautiful and important. It has impressed others who have been privileged to read it.[18]

The phenomenon of automatic writing is often produced by a subject who at the time has no knowledge of its contents. Sometimes the automatic process occurs during sleep or a state of drowsiness or trance. The declaration of Coleridge that he wrote "Kubla Khan" when asleep is credible. On the other hand, some are fully aware of the words as they are being written, but have no foresight of what is about to be recorded.

[17] *The Congregationalist,* September 22, 1932.

[18] In a readable book, *Thy Son Liveth,* letters automatically written by an American mother under the control of her son Bob, who was killed in battle, describe life in the spirit world. Bob lives in a camp with others of his regiment who were killed at the same time. Tenuous clothing is worn, a refined form of food is eaten, some sweethearting occurs, there is much laughter without a sense of humor. Each one carries out his inclinations, Bob, for example, continuing radio experiments begun on earth.

In facile automatic writing the motor response together with the impulse that originates and sustains it is more or less dissociated from the main stream of conscious activity. The orthodox psychologist affirms that a fragment of the writing personality, a segment independent of the central directive awareness, instigates and controls the automatic process.[19] The believer in occultism is equally positive that at least occasionally a mental ability not recognized by traditional psychology, or the influence of incorporeal beings, is expressed in the automatic performance and its contents.

Many who have never written automatically can learn how to do so with pencil, planchette, or other device. In some cases the ability has been spontaneously developed by holding a pencil upon a sheet of paper and immersing the conscious mind in the reading of an absorbing book. It is noticeable that invariably only those who have consciously learned to write for the ordinary purposes, engage in occult writing, and that subjects almost always record impressions or messages in languages which they normally employ. Words and phrases of unfamiliar languages, now and then appearing in the automatic recording, may be intrusions of subconscious linguistic deposits.

Originating and Sustaining Motives

What are the motives underlying participation in the different types of occultism? How do the methods and results of occultism minister to the religious life? What experiences do they precipitate or modify? Do they help people respond to the supreme reality called God? What do occult phenomena contribute to the religious integration of personality? In what frame of mind are the people who have sought a satisfying portion in occultism but have dismally failed in their quest?

Ordinary observation teaches that the desire for practical aid in crises incites persons in great numbers to consult mediums, clairvoyants, palmists, astrologers, and others supposedly endowed with superior insight and wisdom. Statesmen and

[19] See McDougall, William, *Outline of Abnormal Psychology*, pp. 235 ff. (New York: Charles Scribner's Sons, 1926). Also Prince, Morton, *The Dissociation of a Personality*, pp. 255 ff. (New York: Longmans, Green & Co., 1906).

industrialists as well as underprivileged and submerged individuals seek information or guidance through occult means. They apply for help in the conduct of a love affair, the making of profitable financial investments, the recovery of lost or stolen articles, the cure of disease, and the pursuit of vocational success. It must be conceded that many advisers quite apart from any occult powers they may or may not possess are skilled readers of character, penetrating discerners of social, economic, and political trends, and accurate diagnosticians of the personality problems of their clients. That such counselors are able to render their respective constituents important personal service none should be disposed to deny. A palmist asserts that she gives sorely needed help to patrons who are confused by their emotions or menaced by mental incompetence. It is not strange that the pressure of adverse circumstances combined with a lack of other trustworthy advisers motivates a multitude to appeal to practitioners of the occult.

The destruction of former social sources of confidence often leads to the utilization of the occult. In a day of political and economic chaos, numbers of men, having been deprived of a sense of security, in the mood of expectation approach various cults which promise contact with stable and invigorating realities. When the inherited cultural patterns are generally disowned or discredited, sensitive individuals may seek refuge in another order of obligations and meanings. New and more firmly established foundations for the enrichment of life become the objectives of questing humanity. The occult movement which is affecting European and American civilization is not a detached and sporadic phenomenon. The period of disillusionment which has followed the World War is inciting men to appropriate what seem enduring values existing beyond the ebb and flow of a disintegrating social structure.

Preoccupation with occult practices is in many instances a result of temperament, of an inborn impulsion to accept without much deliberation proffered real or illusory benefits. Those who find it easier to love and appreciate than to exercise critical determination are by nature inclined to occultism. The trustful emotional approach frequently occasions the misinterpretation of the marvels of occultism. The mere imposition of strictures upon occultism and all its works by the Church or any other form of social control is seldom an effective corrective. It is imperative that the Church learn how to minister directly to the necessities of those whose desire for identification with the ethically inspiring is combined with the hopeful, uncritical, and expectant disposition.

Impetuosity frequently results in active participation in occult movements. As compared with the plodding and cautious disposition, the hasty and erratic temperament becomes impatient with persistent and time-consuming efforts to answer the deeper questions of man's origin, nature, duty, and destiny. In order to make an effective appeal to the impulsive personality, any plan of procedure must promise immediate and substantial results. When an undisciplined mind attempts to penetrate the mysteries of human experience it is prone to assume that a precipitate method is the one which will be the most productive. Such impatience with patience is likely to eventuate in the oversimplification of complex problems and in superficial identifications where no causal relations exist. Occult experimentation seems to such a one to cast as rubbish to the void most of the gathered lore of the ages and to offer deliverance from the tentativeness which accompanies the statements of so many scientists and philosophers.

Dissatisfaction with sense data coupled with a desire to appropriate the values of a suprasensible order often issues in occult activity. The wonders which the microscope and the telescope reveal are by many regarded as temporal and therefore insufficient to sustain the spirit of man. The mere manufacture and distribution of marketable commodities do not always afford the imagination and the emotions adequate scope. The mind, restive in its involvement with the physical, seeks emancipation. Occultism promises an escape from the fetters which lifeless and soulless things have imposed upon the dynamic personality. It longs to enter the promised land of transcendentalism, that world of eternal verities which lies beyond the realm of material form and substance.

Sheer boredom often motivates occult experimentation.

When the type of religion acquired is a dull, prosaic, and stereo-typed way of life it is not strange that those who are already depressed by the commonplaceness of human existence turn in ennui to the more stimulating overtures of occultism. The systemization of industry and commerce with its associated mechanization of human beings fills many of its victims with discontent with their lot. The most distinctly personal at-tributes, such as creative imagination, initiative, inventiveness, and originality, are stifled by extensive regimentation. The lives of those who crave variety, change, excitement, and even hazard are rendered almost intolerable by the monotonous round of daily affairs. Denied adventure in the usual course of living, they may explore the diverting possibilities of oc-cultism. Experimentation in the occult becomes a type of compensation which supplies the savor of romance and melo-drama in an existence otherwise flat, drab, and unvarying.

Participation in occultism often emerges from bereavement and loneliness. The mourner frequently has a warm desire to communicate with the loved one whom the hand of death has removed from the earthly sphere. During the final illness of the deceased the relationship of intimacy between the two may have been intensified. Does the one gone before live? Is he a self-aware being, and does he know that his former intimates on earth mourn his loss and hold him in tender remembrance? It is only natural to desire a demonstration of the conscious ex-istence of the dead and their continued affection for us. Grief and loneliness may conspire to arouse such an intense longing for direct contact with the dead that the bereaved one is moved to consult a medium who is reputedly able to establish the de-sired communication. The sitter seeks the solace which the assurance of survival of the shock of death and the sense of the presence of the disembodied personality can bestow. Brood-ing over the departure of a lamented intimate, the sorrowing may by chance or design engage in automatic writing and thereby record impressions to which a mystical or unique sig-nificance is attached.

Reputed Products of Occultism

Occultism, as indicated, receives the ardent support of many who have either lost or never possessed confidence in the world of ordinary sense perception. Belief in the validity of occultism engenders or upholds the conviction that, after all, the universe, contrary to previous opinion, is flexible and vital rather than inert. The acceptance of the tenets of occultism undermines the assumption of the rigidity of the order in which nature and man have their being. The inference is that the mechanics of the universe are not absolute, final, and supreme. The line of demarcation between physical objects and spirit beings wavers. If spirits can be materialized, the physical may be but the veil of a creative order, the congealed energy generated by a dynamic reality. Occultism offers the assurance of security and imperishable worth to all who will adopt its technique and accept its findings. It teaches that the constitution of the universe is such that personality may expand itself and indefinitely preserve its identity. The dead live, one mind reads the thoughts of another apart from known sense mediation, lovers separated by distance meet in dreams which both simultaneously have, a magnetic leader in politics or religion is an ancient worthy reincarnate. Personalities are indestructible existences. They are destined to triumph over the vicissitudes of the world of physics and chemistry, over the limitations of the human body and its material environment, over time, space, and death.

The inference that occultism invariably leads to the acceptance or invigoration of a theistic philosophy of life is fallacious. It is possible to accept the phenomena of occultism for what its advocates declare them to be, apart from the cultivation of religious idealism. In fact, one may be convinced of the validity and genuineness of the evidences for conscious personal life beyond the grave, telepathic insight, apparitions, glossolalia, and kindred marvels, without being moved to acknowledge so much as the mere existence of God.[20] One may

[20] The distinguished philosopher John Ellis McTaggart believed in the survival of the self, but was not a theist. See his *Some Dogmas of Religion* (New York: Longmans, Green & Co., 1906); also *The Nature of Existence,* Vol. I (London: Cambridge University Press, 1921).

be a believer in the claims of occultism and continue to be an atheist. In China many a Buddhist or Confucianist worships ancestral spirits and in so doing is adopting a substitute for the outreach for God, the Spirit supreme. The conviction that the dead have demonstrated that they live and that they are reaping the consequences, blissful or baneful, of their earthly character antecedents, does not necessarily result in the religious integration of personality. The core of religion is not communication with the spirits of the dead, but commerce with God. Abraham, requested to send Lazarus to this world to exhort the five brothers of Dives lest they come to the place of torment, retorted: "If they hear not Moses and the prophets, neither will they be persuaded, if one rise from the dead." [21]

In some cases a fresh synthesis of religious verities, or at least the enrichment of an anaemic faith, is an outcome of the assimilation of elements derived from occult practices. A friend gratefully testifies that when his religious faith had been shattered an introduction to occult experimentation led to a new and far more fruitful appropriation of the principles of Christianity. In some instances the conclusion that occult powers exist and are subject to human control does actually provide the individual with a foundation for an initial transforming experience of God. It may culminate in a belief in the existence and potency of God, fellowship with him and the higher reorganization of human personality. Persuaded that through occult phenomena our contacts with one another and with the great company of persons throughout the ranges of the universe have been intensified and beautified in a boundless love, the individual may yield to the overtures of God.

Anticipated benefits are incentives and supports. The list of originating conditions implies such desired outcomes as practical advice or direct aid in a more or less critical situation, refuge in an enduring and more ideal order from crumbling social structures, escape from the tyranny of lifeless things, emotionally satisfying sources of confidence, immediate demonstration of the reality of the spiritual world, relief from

[21] Luke 16: 31.

the monotony of dull routine, comfort in bereavement, a stable rallying center in a universe of change, and the stimulation and enrichment of the religious attitude.   The objectives vary qualitatively in their respective contributions to soundly organized personality.   Assayed in the light of Christianity, all are not of equal value.   Such outcomes as escape from the thralldom of inert things, consolation in sorrow, the conviction of the continued existence of the self after death, and contact with a dependable center of reference in the midst of a succession of mutations can without exception be integrated with religiously grounded personality.   These are included in the philosophy of the evangelical communions.   Occultism differs from the Christian Church as a whole in procedure and claims.   For example, while the Church's assurance of life everlasting rests on faith ably supported by reason, spiritism boldly offers an objective demonstration of the survival of personality.   How much of the technique and findings of occultism the Church of tomorrow will incorporate, only further lapse of time can reveal.

The Trustworthiness of Occultism

That some occultists are charlatans who deliberately perpetrate frauds and victimize ingenuous and artless patrons is a melancholy conclusion that few impartial investigators will be inclined to challenge.   What is needed to disclose the factual data in some performances is not the technique of a psychologist but that of a detective.   Human nature is evidently so gullible that the most preposterous pretensions, if only they are advanced with melodramatic fervor, are widely acclaimed as verities.   The psychologist may be pardoned if he hesitates to accept as true the allegation of an individual that he is Elijah reincarnate and has power to exorcise demons.   The charitably disposed psychologist may infer that megalomania, a form of mental disorder marked by delusions of grandeur, rather than intentional deception accounts for the vagaries of such a self-styled wonder-worker.   On the other hand, it would be unscientific to ignore the work of honest and capable experimenters in occultism.   Their methods, aims, and results are materials for psychological investigation.   When the evidences for the mysterious demonstrations have been critically explored, is there a residuum of established fact?   If so, what is it?

Whatever may be the settled conclusions of those who are convinced that under certain conditions operators of the planchette are inspired and directed by a power not themselves or by mental competencies the existence of which is denied by most psychologists, I am persuaded that the output of the many ouija board performances I have personally observed or participated in is reducible to such phenomena as chance, coincidence, dormant memory, and the unconscious transmission and perception of unrecognized data.   Others will bring forward messages of a startling and mystical and mystifying nature, but to all such I can only say that what I myself have witnessed requires neither a telepathic nor a spiritistic explanation.   To maintain that no other investigator has collected data that orthodox psychology cannot reduce to its principles, would be an offense of presumption.   On the other hand, I have no psychological explanation of the information imparted to me by the amateur medium in Cleveland, Ohio.

In a fascinating volume Hamlin Garland claims that under test conditions he has heard the strings of a closed piano, has witnessed the movement of books and other small objects without contact by anyone, secured independent writing on sheets of paper two yards from the reach of the psychic, received messages on slates untouched by the psychic or himself, felt on his left arm the grip of a strong right hand darting from a cloud of vapor before the psychic's breast, and obtained on a sheet of paper the print of two large hands and on wax the print of the thumb which was neither that of the psychic nor that of any other person present.[22]   Mr. Garland accepts these and other phenomena as genuine.   He states that if his testimony concerning these experiences is of no value it is of no value concerning any other experiences he has had.   He is still seeking a satisfactory explanation of their production.   He

---

[22] Garland, Hamlin, *Forty Years of Psychic Research*, pp. 381 ff. (New York: The Macmillan Company, 1936).

still questions the identities of the manifesting forces or intelligences. He frankly dissents from the interpretations offered by many occultists. He is still, at seventy-five, an experimentalist, although he believes that the recorded phenomena are born of unknown human powers, that they are the products of mind controlling matter, and that they all originate in the seance room and not outside it. He is not convinced that these marvels have demonstrated conscious life beyond the grave.

It does not become the psychologist to assume a captious air when reliable investigators of occultism report phenomena which are excluded from the conventional classifications of his science. In fact, occurrences which allegedly transcend the ordinary categories of science should stimulate research rather than excite derision. If in the midst of all the chicanery, credulity, and morbidity of occultism there are shafts of light which are disruptive of present widely-accepted theories of personality, science must ultimately incorporate the new insights at least as points of departure for further experimentation. Only the finalist, who as such lacks the scientific temper, disposes of all the submitted evidence for the reality of occult findings with a dogmatic denial of its trustworthiness or an assertion of deliberate fraud. Open-minded skepticism is an indispensable attitude of the truth-seeker. The psychologist who is worthy of his profession welcomes fresh light upon the intricate workings of personality. Research in occultism should occupy a dignified place in the psychological curricula and laboratories of all great universities.

CHAPTER XIX

RELIGION AND MENTAL HEALTH

THE field of clinical psychology may be divided into two major areas—that of mental hygiene or psychoprophylaxis and that of personality reconstruction or psychotherapy. At certain points of contact the two overlap and are not easily distinguishable.

The aim of mental hygiene as fostered by the Church is the progressive and relatively uninterrupted development of personality through the surrounding of the individual with wholesome formative influences, the inculcation of proper standards of conduct, the growth of creative religious attitudes, and the correction of moral and mental defects in their incipient stages. Its function is largely preventive. It seeks to forestall an ineffectual mobilization and utilization of the resources at the disposal of the individual. It is the province of religious leadership to guide persons in releasing and making determinative the forces which enrich the self and preserve it from disintegration under stress. The principles and procedures of personality hygiene should be integrated with an adequate program of Christian nurture for the entire constituency of the local church.

Much of the work of the psychologically equipped religious leader is remedial. The number of unadjusted and disorganized persons in our country is tragically large, and ministration to broken lives is a delicate and intricate art. Identified with the Church or actively co-operating with it are such preventive and reconstructive agencies as child guidance clinics, family relations institutes, vocational direction bureaus, and leisure time clubs. The process of personality restoration includes psychodiagnosis or the scientific determination of the origin of a defect or deviation, psychotherapy or the removal or control of the deficiency, and prognosis or the forecasting of the probable course which a given case will take under specified conditions.

The goal of both hygienic and reconstructive procedures is normal personality. The normal individual keeps a clearly defined life-purpose in view. He examines himself so objectively that he detects and condemns his own faults and lays bare the sources of mischievous prejudices. He maintains a wholesome relationship with friend, mate, or child. He has a sympathetic understanding of the situations of other people. His vocation is socially useful. He pursues an avocation which is a satisfactory outlet for inner tension. He appreciates some form of art. He faces all emergencies bravely and does not expect special favors from life; his philosophy of life absorbs the griefs and tribulations of our common lot. He is free from disrupting emotional involvements. He possesses a sense of serene security in a world of drifting and shifting external events. His religion, so far from being a system of beliefs and practices added to the sum of the baffling, drab, and exhilarating experiences which we comprehend under the term "life," is a relationship with untimate Reality in which he evaluates things both seen and unseen and achieves his destiny.

The Field of the Religious Counselor

Those who are harassed by major mental disabilities form a large and tragic company. They require the specialized services of physicians, surgeons, and psychiatrists. About one-half of the total number of patients committed to insane asylums and similar institutions are the victims of alcoholism, drug addiction, syphilis, congenital idiocy, epilepsy, and arteriosclerosis of the brain. These pathologies have an organic involvement, although some of them like alcoholism originate in personality maladjustments. The other half of the institutionalized mental patients are afflicted with derangements the sources of which cannot be disclosed by any mechanical devices thus far contrived. To this group belong the paranoiacs who entertain delusions of grandeur and persecution, and the manic-depressives who are the prey of alternating moods of abject despair and apparently groundless elation, or of an extended period of the one or the other extreme, together with a lack of discernment and judgment. Since no organic defect or lesion is discoverable, it is assumed that the origins of these disorders are what we call psychological. The victim of schizophrenia, or dementia praecox, is emotionally indifferent, unresponsive to various stimuli, and lacks ambition and interest in life, although his passivity and apathy are at times interrupted by explosions of anger.[1] There is reason to believe that at least in some cases of this mental pathology an anatomic or toxic condition is determining.[2] The Church through its various arms of service may minister to the institutionalized defective groups, under the supervision of the specialists in charge.

The more or less independent service of the religious worker with psychological training, experience, and competency is obviously restricted to cases of minor mental aberrations, personality anomalies and singularities, moral delinquencies, ordinary social maladjustments, and religious conflicts.

It follows that the religious worker should know enough about the symptoms of the various psychoses to be able to recognize such disorders. He should realize that there are mental derangements the successful treatment of which is beyond his sphere and skill. He should bear in mind that he may do irreparable harm by undertaking the treatment of major mental pathologies. If in the course of his work with an individual he is in doubt, he should consult the physician or the psychiatrist. In many cases the religious leader should enlist the co-operation of the psychiatrist, the social worker, and the schoolteacher. The religious worker should develop his capacities through study, observation, and supervised experience and utilize his abilities to the fullest extent, but also recognize the limitations of his training and experience.

The range of tensions and minor pathologies is wide enough to put to the severest test the skill of the ablest lay counselor.

---

[1] For an excellent survey of mental disorders see *Manual of Psychiatry,* edited by Aaron J. Rosenoff (New York: John Wiley & Sons, Inc., 1927).

[2] There is reason to believe that some disorders regarded as organic are induced by psychic experiences. For example, hyperthyroidism with its associated mental pathologies is at least in some instances the outcome of an emotional shock or sustained tension.

Some persons stand in need of vocational guidance, others of religious reorientation, still others of the correction of moral blemishes, and many others of deliverance from a variety of emotional entanglements. Personality irregularities and immaturities include disloyalty to duty, day-dreaming which precludes purposive activity, oversensitiveness to slights, extreme defensiveness, groundless suspiciousness of associates and superiors, ill health without organic basis, over-tendency to accidents and errors, inconsistency manifested in double-mindedness or hypocrisy, intolerance of the convictions of others, irrational fears, marital incompatibility, parental fixations for children of the same or opposite sex, infatuations which can end only in frustration or disgrace, contemplated suicide, self-satisfaction with a low level of ethical achievement, doctrinal confusion, bereavement, and refusal to do battle for the right when due occasion arises.

The religious worker should not attempt the treatment of the psychotic, the one who is so mentally disordered that he imagines he is normal and other people pathological. On the other hand, the clinically prepared religious leader may with ethical propriety undertake the rehabilitation of the more tractable neurotics—i.e., persons who are aware that their energies are misdirected and futile. The neurotic is an individual who is socially maladjusted and personally distressed. The confirmed neurotic stands in his own light, he defeats himself, he nullifies any laudable intentions he may harbor. In every community persons lead lives of quiet desperation although they achieve a measure of vocational success, derive a modicum of satisfaction from their social relationships, and will never suffer a "nervous" collapse. The Church may minister to these with hope of success.

Illustrative reference may be made to representative problems of two classes of persons in need of guidance which the Church should supply—namely, to those of young people and to those of the unemployed heads of families. Many instances of servile surrender to unfavorable circumstances occur among adolescents. The majority of drifting young people of both sexes were pampered in childhood, and, now lacking ambition, are parasitic. Self-assertion and bluster are compensations for failure. A large number of cases of delusion are rooted in misunderstanding or self-deception: a girl may insist that another is trying to attract her beau although no such plot has been formed; a high school boy may really believe that his failure in an examination is not deserved but imposed by an unfair and prejudiced teacher. Lack of success in securing employment or in gaining status and recognition in one's occupation, or in winning the favor of a member of the opposite sex, may induce a chronic state of despair. Youthful delinquents who have willfully disregarded the teachings of the Christian home and Church, acknowledged as obligatory, are likely to suffer a paroxysm of anxiety. Conscience inflicts torture when its mandates are violated. Deferred marriages made advisable if not imperative by unfavorable economic conditions often result in relationships which are unsanctioned by the group to which the couples belong. Continued emotional depression, or prolonged engagements with their attendant hazards are concomitants of such unfortunate circumstances. These and other equally disrupting conditions with which young people contend constitute a legitimate field of service for the Christian counselor.

Unemployment of the breadwinner of a family, with its economic loss and enforced leisure, creates a multitude of personality tensions and domestic upheavals. Often the sense of inferiority which the unemployed man develops is manifested in passivity. Unable to pay the family bills, much less give his dependents coveted luxuries, he frequently remains at home for days and broods. If social agencies provide food, shelter, and medical care for his family, he is of course dethroned in his own eyes if not in those of others. Told that he is not to blame for his economic plight and that all who know him assume that he would work if only he could find employment, he continues to be dejected.

Another unemployed family man may express his feeling of inadequacy or bafflement in aggressive behavior. He may spend the little he does have or secures on himself and let charity associations support his wife and children. He may leave his family not with the intention of deserting his own but to seek employment in a distant place. Not finding a job, he in due course learns that it is easier to go from place to place alone in order to loaf and beg than if he were accompanied by his family, and thus little by little his contact with wife and children is broken and at last is not likely to be resumed.

In some cases wives nag their husbands and incite them to desertion or deeds of violence. A woman may vex her husband because she feels that he is less energetic and capable than his neighbor who is gainfully employed. The sense of frustration which torments wives and mothers is discharged in a variety of forms of vengeance. The wife of a man who had lost his position after serving a firm for thirty-three years, and whose daughter was thereby at a social disadvantage, only with the utmost difficulty restrained herself from throwing a stone through the window of the palatial home of her husband's former employer.

Sexual desire is often intensified. The seeking of sexual satisfaction as a compensation for vocational failure is common among the unemployed. Sexual appetite increases. Emotional tension is induced by a reluctant partner. Statistics disclose that the birth rate is higher among families of the unemployed than it is among families of the employed of the same social stratum.

Economic distress is not likely to bring the members of a family closer together if but little understanding, sympathy, and intimacy have pre-existed. When food is scarce, the house cold, the clothing shabby, and the children cry for ordinary creature comforts, mutual devotion, deep and substantial, is required to keep husband and wife together in the bonds of loyalty.

The specifically religious problems of various classes and conditions of people are legion. A religious difficulty is not necessarily a fault, a trial, a hindrance, or a disgrace. It may be the consequence of inadequate childhood training in the home and church. It is difficult if not actually impossible to compile a complete list of religious perplexities which disturb or disorganize personality. The study of science may arouse doubts about the validity and value of religious concepts once un-critically held. Unanswered prayer in a personal crisis may shatter the basic structure of the religious life. The exist-ence and the goodness of God, the deity of Jesus, the authority of the Scriptures, the immortality of man, the operation of a special Providence are among the prominent objects of un-certainty, questioning, and skepticism. The persistence of moral evil as well as unmerited physical and mental suffering raises philosophical problems of the first magnitude. Confu-sion as to the purpose of human life occasions much inner ten-sion and dejection. Many anguished persons have yet to learn that they can live heartily and wholesomely without being able to supply satisfactory answers to questions which have baffled the intelligence and tested the faith of generations of good people. Not that theological inquiries are useless and imperti-nent. As experience accumulates and personality matures and mellows, some doctrinal issues are decided at least to the indi-vidual's satisfaction, and others are held in abeyance without the loss of the religious control of the self.

It must be admitted that many ideas and practices trans-mitted to their constituencies by misguided religious leaders create mental conflicts rather than conjunctive attitudes. Not all that is said and done in the name of religion uproots men-tal disorders and promotes the development of wholesome per-sonality. What passes for sound religion often induces need-less fear, a groundless sense of guilt or superstitious practices, and ultimately produces such a measure of disorganization that the individual becomes the victim of a psychic pathology. For example, a wrong conception of sexual relations, fostered by organized religion, may produce conjugal infelicity. Defective religious teaching is a prolific originator of sexual conflicts with all the miserable sequels that such divisive circumstances entail. To cite another example, sons and daughters are in too many cases repressed by parental fixations which are regarded by those most vitally concerned as religious obligations. The ex-cessive love of a son for his mother, which excludes marriage, or the abnormal attachment of a daughter for her father, which makes her jealous of her own mother and keeps her from loving another man, is often erroneously commended as a singularly beautiful example of filial piety. A specious religion, it is evident, may exact serious penalties.

Diagnosis

The dual interpretation of the individual is helpful and cogent. Accordingly, the body is a biological machine which functions in and of itself something like an automobile. The physician works largely on this the physiological level. By means of drugs, surgery, and other agencies which are directly applied to or introduced into the organism attempts are made to restore health. The mind or the inner non-organic phases of personality uses the body as an instrument for the expression of its conscious or subconscious attitudes, impulses, wishes, and feelings. On this level of personality the clinical psychologist and the psychiatrist function. They help the disordered mind to summon its resources and to achieve a reorganization which retrieves mental equilibrium.

The organism reacts quite automatically to mental processes. A Jewish rabbi relates that although he has become the leader of a liberal congregation and has disavowed many of the traditions of his orthodox forebears he is still subconsciously and actually dominated by his early training. Of course the food taboos were sacredly respected in the house of his father. No pork was served. As a rabbi he resolved, as a matter of principle, to disregard the distinction between clean and unclean meats. Quite compatible with his professed emancipated beliefs, he bought a little pig and fattened it. In due course the pig was slaughtered and roasted in the rabbi's home. He and the members of his family ate it and expressed their appreciation of the taste and smell of roast pork. Not many minutes after the meal the revulsions implanted in the rabbi became embarrassingly active. He was nauseated and soon was unable to retain his food. The warm interior life of the rabbi ruled the organism much as he controlled his automobile. The practitioner in mental hygiene encounters numerous cases of neuroses such as hysterical blindness and psychic paralysis which are conditioned by incongruous behavior or secret and unsanctioned desires.   The counselor should constantly bear in mind the dual nature of the individual who appeals to him for aid, and that mental states, conscious or unconscious, profoundly affect man's physiological equipment.

The correct diagnosis of a defect and the reconditioning of the personality depend in most cases on the co-operation of the sufferer with a skilled counselor.   Self-help alone is difficult if not futile in the majority of cases of social maladjustment and internal conflict.   The condition of the individual is generally such that he is either too depressed to help himself or so deluded by escape mechanisms that he is unaware of his plight. In many instances the originating circumstances are subconsciously buried and the victims do not realize what are the roots of their irrational behavior.   An intimate friend or a treatise on personality singularities and aberrations may disclose defects with startling vividness, or a crisis may reveal the inadequacy of the existing mode of life, but in the greater number of cases the services of a competent psychological counselor should be requisitioned.   Sedatives or a vacation or the cheery advice to summon the scattered energies and to extricate oneself from a personality depression will not alone bring the needed relief.   Assistance in the reconstruction of purposes and attitudes is usually afforded by one who has had the appropriate technical training and clinical experience.

Perhaps the majority of those who are the victims of social maladjustments and harassed minds believe that deterioration of the nervous system is the seat of their disturbances.   They suppose that a neural disability, such as exhaustion or impairment of the nerves, is responsible for their disorders.   One reason for this common inference is the use of such misleading terminology as nervous breakdown, neurotic, and neurasthenia. It is safe to say that most neurotic behavior does not have the slightest connection with diseased nerves.   The origins of the major fraction of mental deviations are as remote from a defective nervous system as they are from any possible occurrence on the planet Mars.   To be sure, pathological cases exist in which a change in the structure of the brain, the spinal cord, and the nerves is the source of emotional instability and irrational conduct.   Emotional tension induced by thwartings is, however, the taproot of the majority of neurotic exhibitions.

Psychodiagnosis includes a variety of procedures designed to bring to light the determinant of the personality disorganization.   The first diagnostic measure upon which the counselor insists is a thorough medical examination unless the person has recently consulted a competent physician and been pronounced free from organic disease.   An obscure physical ailment, such as a mild inflammation of the duodenum, may originate such a mental aberration as an obsession to commit suicide, or the overactivity of the thyroid glands may produce extreme nervous irritability and emotional excitability.   Relatively few who are ill in body are mentally sound.   A repressed or clearly recognized social or internal conflict may give rise to debilitating emotional states and irregular conduct.   Often the case is so complicated that the co-operative services of physician, pastor, psychiatrist, and social worker must be requisitioned in order to lay bare the cause of the disorder.   Among the more specific diagnostic instrumentalities at the command of a skilled counselor are mental tests, personality assaying techniques, the intelligent observation of the individual's behavior in selected or typical situations, the study of the history and development of the case, the interpretation of significant events of childhood, the analysis of dreams, and the exploration of peculiar reactions, inhibitions, emotional tensions, and emphases.

The experienced worker with individuals ensnared in aberrations knows that in many instances the victim's explanation of the origin and nature of his ailment is erroneous.   Often the individual is positive that the disturbance is the consequence of willful disregard of religious obligation.   Sometimes he is mistaken.   A divinity student believed that he had committed the unpardonable sin.   Disconsolate and despairing, he brooded for days in the seclusion of his room.   He developed pronounced symptoms of a neurosis.   The efforts of his professors who visited him to convince him that he was innocent of the unforgivable transgression were futile.   The student persisted in his belief.   A mature fellow student who had seen service as a male nurse sensed the originating factors. He induced the sufferer to accompany him on long walks, to engage in wholesome forms of recreation, and to associate more freely with other students. Adopting the new regime, the obsession was soon dissipated. Lack of bodily exercise and social life, coupled with one-sided mental activity and an extremely sensitive conscience, rather than unatonable or unpardonable iniquity, had induced the distressful fixed idea. How essential common sense is in the diagnosis of personality anomalies!

In his zeal for rectitude many a parent, teacher, or pastor has overlooked the psychological origins of what seems to be unethical conduct. A critical study of the so-called lies of little children will illustrate and enforce the fact that the source and character of many personality deviations is psychic rather than ethical. It is unnecessary to postulate the doctrine of the total and inherited depravity of human beings or to assume the existence of an otherwise perverted will in order to account for most of the misinformation which the child imparts. Correctly understood, a lie is a willful deception, an intentional falsification, and of such a reaction the little child is less frequently guilty than an uninformed adult may suppose. Some of the child's misstatements are consequences of his inability to distinguish between the imaginary and the objectively real, between fact and fiction. The one is as valid to him as the other. From the third to the sixth year the child lives in a world of spontaneous productive imagination, a world of wonders, portents, and miracles. It would be amazing if all his statements were in accord with the logic of stern reality. Imaginative and lonely children often create mythical playmates. A little girl four years old evolved a playmate of fancy whom she named Charley. So real was Charley that often she insisted that a cover be laid for him at mealtime and that food be placed upon his plate. One afternoon when she was unable to fall asleep and take her daily nap she complained that Charley was screaming at the top of his voice and thus keeping her awake. Only one or two sources of children's lies have been mentioned, but they are typical enough to show the advisability of inquiring into the sources of what seems to be reprehensible. The same principle is applicable to adult behavior. When we know why some people have engaged in socially unsanctioned practices, we are not prone to condemn but eager to help.

Avoidance of Reality

Many persons either deliberately or unconsciously conceal the origins of personality disorganization. They do not face pertinent facts. They construct various types of escape from reality. Of the dozen or more specific forms of which the psychologist takes cognizance, a few which are representative may receive passing reference. One often flees from things as they really are by creating or utilizing a substitute formation. A novelist writes that he was a large and seemingly robust lad but his ironical inability to play any game well led him, in an effort to perserve his pride, to construct a world of unreality where he could be the hero. The habit of retiring into a world of fantasy grew constantly stronger and soon he lived almost entirely in the realm of imagination. Later he became a novelist, and the tragedy of his helplessness appears in his literary output.

Rationalization is one of the most frequent methods of escape from reality. It is a favorite form of self-deception by means of which one evades unpleasant facts and attempts to inflate the ego. Often rationalization assumes the form of excuses. Striking instances are found in Jesus' parable of exacting discipleship.[3] Having been bidden to a great supper, one man said he had bought a field and must needs inspect it, another that he had acquired five yoke of oxen and must test them, and still another that he had just taken a wife and therefore could not come. The excuses more or less plausible are rationalizations, attempts to circumvent the truth with pretense and rhetoric. Specious reasons are offered.

Another typical form of flight from the world of reality is the projection of criticism to others which is really applicable to ourselves, or the ascription of our faults to others and the assumption of virtues which we do not really possess. An

[3] Luke 14: 16-20.

aroused conscience is placated by projecting one's own misconduct to another or blindly believing that another is culpable. The story is told of two women, for years total abstainers, who were induced to indulge in champagne for the first time. Soon one exclaimed to the other, "You're drunk! You have two noses." Drunk herself, she accused her sister of her own lamentable state. Often an inner conflict is defended or deflected by assuming a sensorious attitude toward the acts of another. One may go so far as to deplore the mote in a brother's eye and to ignore the beam in one's own eye.

We are inclined to disguise a hatred, a wish, or an exhilarated state by substituting for ourselves others as the objects of the dominant emotions. This is called displacement. A man may suffer financial losses during business hours and later in his home make his wife the convenient object of his irritation. The wife, exasperated by the insinuations of her husband, may with a feeling of righteous indignation punish her child for a minor offense. If the husband has been promoted by his superiors or has done business at a substantial profit, he may in the bosom of his family praise his wife redundantly for a small favor. The wife, made happy by the compliments of the husband, may shower her child with extravagant rewards on the slightest pretext. The individual is unaware of releasing a disappointment or provocation by inflicting suffering upon the innocent, or of expressing joy by lauding or indulging others to excess.

The skilled diagnostician penetrates our subterfuges, exposes our shams, confronts us with the truth and with the reasons why we are evading reality and responsibility. He knows that the beginning of personality reconstruction is the exposure of cherished fallacies. Unless the individual is willing to examine the motives of his behavior and to repudiate the character defects or correct the mental deviations which have thwarted him, his case is hopeless. It is a function of the psychologically disciplined counselor to guide the neurotic in the discovery of the incentives of his irrational conduct often concealed in the mechanism of the subconscious, and in the attainment of a reasonable and acceptable goal. When the neurotic is fully persuaded that once the maladjustments and deficiencies constituting points of tension within him have been eliminated he will be happy and useful without either undue repression or harmful expression, he is prepared to co-operate with his counselor.

The first precondition to the correction of a mental and moral disability is the individual's frank recognition that he has been swimming not with but against the current of unselfish, serviceable, and wholesome living. He must freely admit that he has been trying to live in a private world, a world of his own creation, a world at variance with the dictates of conscience and the reasonable demands of society, a world of pretense and chicanery, a world in which he has been a fugitive from his own best self. He must concede that his problem is not an accident, but the inevitable result of false goals of endeavor and faulty techniques of living. He must take cognizance of the fact that the avoidance of tests of his ability has led to paralysis of will. Until he strips himself bare of all self-deceptions, no improvement in moral or mental health can occur. To realize his plight and to have a sincere desire for deliverance is already to transcend his limitations.

Psychotherapy

The person who has been in conflict with himself and others must be taught that the power to overcome obstacles grows through the conquest of life's allotment of disappointments, trials, and frustrations. If a careful medical examination discloses no organic defect, the individual should mobilize his mental and religious resources for the battle against the inner conflict and the outer maladjustment. Drugs, rest cures, and the like are merely palliatives, and do not correct the fundamental and determining point of view. They afford temporary relief by dulling memory or distracting the attention from the painful situation, but when their effects have vanished, the problem manifests itself in its acute condition. To temporize, poetize, and compromise is in the long run simply to intensify mental anguish and to multiply neurotic symptoms.

It is easier to be a religiously integrated personality than it is to be torn by conflicting motives, tortured by the consciousness of wrongdoing, and to be emotionally unstable. The wise and courageous sufferer resists the temptation to coddle himself, to lull himself into a false sense of security, and deliberately induces a crisis, a crisis in which the differences between the abundant life and the tottering existence are discerned with unprecedented clarity, a crisis in which he under God declares his emancipation from debilitating circumstances or faults, a crisis in which he begins to function in a new and approved pattern.

Clinical psychologists, psychiatrists, and social case workers employ at least twenty-five varieties of therapy. It will serve the present purpose to allude to half a dozen which may be religiously motivated and sustained—a reconstruction of the philosophy of life, assurance, catharsis, sublimation, worship, and identification with a worthy cause. In many cases several of these therapeutic agencies are united in an effort to cope with neurotic conditions. Overlapping treatment is often necessary.

The majority of persons suffering from curable mental disorders stand in need of an adequate philosophy of life, of life-giving convictions which will sustain them in their hour of perplexity. The common dictum solemnly announced as the quintessence of wisdom that it is not what one believes but what one does that is supremely significant, should be amended and qualified. Not that it is imperative that one construct an absolutely self-consistent system of philosophical concepts. It is, however, essential that a wholesome and satisfying world-view be adopted and that an attitude of trust in the spirit of the universe be cultivated. When life is not well buttressed internally, an adverse pivotal situation is likely to precipitate a collapse. We require a sense of the worthwhileness of life, a constant conviction that we are in league with cosmic energy, that we are engaged in an adventure in friendliness with God. Religious ideals lift us above the gross and transient elements, the ebb and flow of our personal fortunes. The life-belt of a pitiful delusion of heroism fails us when our ship of material ease and security has sunk, for only the ability to swim in the mid-ocean of a tested and trusted idealism can save us from mental and moral disaster. Religion supplies the background of encouragement and hope which makes life not merely tolerable but dignified, fruitful, and serene. It is the rallying center of the forces of personality. Psychologically, religion summons the vital forces and organizes them for victory over adverse circumstances. The only thing which can deliver a multitude of men and women from their bondage is a thorough religious conversion, a radical change in point of view and conduct.

Friendship, encouragement, and assurance are patent aids in the dissipation of a sense of inferiority engendered by misfortune or sorrow. An expression of brotherliness and understanding lends support and inspiration to a personality undergoing tribulation. A word of cheer and hope, spoken in due season, often removes an almost intolerable weight of insufficiency and releases inhibited gifts. The ministry of inspiration is sorely needed in the world of discouraged and thwarted men. A word of confidence in the moral integrity of a depressed individual or in his ability to overcome his defects may be the decisive factor in the reconstruction of his personality. Unless the word is spoken the individual may sink to lower levels of despondency or degradation. A Christian gentleman one day while taking his daily constitutional encountered a young man and his wife who were in distress. The husband, charged with diverting funds, had recently been dismissed by his employer. The gentleman halted, chatted a moment with the couple, and before he resumed his walk laid his hand upon the shoulder of the accused man and remarked, "I do not know the details of your situation, but I want you and your wife to be assured that I am your friend and that I believe in the days to come you will give a good account of yourselves." Not long afterward the gracious individual left the community and established himself in a distant city. He forgot the incident. Ten years later he returned. The man whom he had encouraged and who was now a prosperous merchant invited him to visit him in his office. The visitor was astonished when he was told by the merchant that the confidence expressed a decade before had imparted the courage to make a new beginning in business and to live down unsavory insinuations. "A word fitly spoken is like apples of gold in network of silver." [4]

Mental catharsis or confession is a form of therapeutics which Protestantism at long last has recognized and is utilizing. Without conceding the validity of all the doctrines and practices which are associated with secret auricular confession by an important branch of Christendom, Protestant workers are employing catharsis and related procedures with gratifying results.   The disturbing memory or drive is reinstated with intense emotional accompaniment.   The confession may be made to the one wronged if such an act is deemed necessary.   Restoration may be made where damage has been done.   An outraged conscience is appeased.

True confession is an excruciating experience, one that prostrates the personality in humility and shame, but which purges it of incompatible elements.   Potentialities emerge into powerful actualities when reprehensible habits or haunting and agonizing memories are faced and disposed of in accordance with the mandates of conscience.   Such a process differs radically from that of the individual who assumes a defiant attitude and exclaims, "I did the deed which a section of society condemns, but I am not penitent and under the same circumstances I should repeat it.   It was excusable and justifiable, therefore what does either man or God propose to do with me?"   How different is the confession of the one who prays, "God be merciful to me a sinner," or the revelation of faults to one another in order that the one may assist the other with advice and consolation, or the admission of guilt to a neighbor in order to effect a reconciliation with him.[5]

The sublimation of crude forces or their conversion into socially useful practices possesses a therapeutic value which the alert religious leader commends when the welfare of the personality requires such a procedure.   Not that all instincts and drives are readily transformed.   Hunger for food, for example,

---

[4] Proverbs 25 : 11.

[5] For a penetrating exposition of confession in the Church see Calvin, John, *Institutes of the Christian Religion*, Book IV, pp. 569-573, translated by John Allen (Philadelphia: Presbyterian Board of Publication, 1844).

cannot be sublimated. Food for the soul like poetry and music is no adequate substitute for meat and bread. The sexual instinct is not easily sublimated, although many have given it release in poetry, science, social service, and teaching. Sexual sublimation is not inhibition, but expression in an aesthetic, social, or useful parental activity which is in full accord with the ruling ideal of the individual. The distinction between the inhibition of a fundamental impulse and its refined outlet is pertinent. Furthermore, a stimulating, fruitful, and emotionally satisfying relationship which does not develop into courtship and issue in marriage may exist between a man and a woman. After all, men and women have much which is inspiring and stabilizing, quite apart from romantic love, to give to one another. This fact suggests an area in which men and women may seek and find constructive fulfillment on a non-romantic basis. The sublimation of other interests and impulses has elsewhere received attention.[6]

The implications of public worship for recovery from mental and moral deficiencies are various in cases in which religion makes a positive appeal. The hymns, prayers, Bible passages, the sermon, and the presence of the other worshipers in the congregation all conspire to minister to a mind confused and distracted. Some psychiatrists prescribe attendance at public worship. Worship may be a solace, a tonic, a challenge. It adds to life what is necessary in order that fuller self-realization, social usefulness, and inward peace may be acquired. The individual who is burdened by a sense of guilt may experience the pardoning grace of God. Diseased minds and perverted wills are often restored by keen ethical judgment, consolation, and redirection of the energies of the personality, which participation in public worship entails.

In the attitude and act of worship the participant becomes aware of his defects and delinquencies. Worship affords an opportunity for that kind of personality analysis which is the beginning of self-discipline and improvement. In the act of sincere worship the neurotic may experience a sense of the

[6] See pp. 224 ff.

reality of a good and merciful God that becomes a new rallying center for the scattered and misdirected energies. The worshiper may discover that he is the victim of a debilitating disposition or an unworthy obsession which arrests self-development
and hampers creative social relationships. The spirit of worship may induce an individual to cry out, "O God, deliver me
from my fault and grant that I henceforth shall lead an acceptable and fruitful life." Hatred against another may be eradicated, inner conflicts may be resolved, impatience may yield to
long-suffering, confidence may displace irrational fears, impul-
siveness may be supplanted by deliberative ethical judgment.
The association of a mind oppressed by removable limitations
with others who are soundly integrated exerts a constructive influence difficult to measure. Persons who are prone to anxiety,
distrust, and self-indulgence may find in a well-ordered service
of worship suggestions of faith, hope, love, and temperance.

The identification of the individual with a cause socially
useful contributes to his mental health. It may serve as compensation for bitter loss. To be sure, irksome and devastating
faults and defects must be bravely faced and eradicated rather
than evaded by the submersion of personality in distracting
activities. When employed in conjunction with other means it
contributes to the resolution of mental and moral conflicts. The
undertaking of worthy tasks not only collects and redirects the
energies, but also elevates the emotional tone. Morbid introspection, self-pity, loneliness, and kindred states are directly
curable by the absorption of the personality in a benevolent
cause.

The various forms of service which persons may perform
through the several organizations of the local church offer
not only an outlet for the altruistic impulse but also a remedy
for a multitude of emotional singularities that render the victim gloomy, querulous, and petulant. A young wife, whose domestic situation through no fault of her own is ghastly, earns
her living as a stenographer. She was ordained a deaconess in
the Presbyterian Church. Functioning in the capacity of a
deaconess during her free hours, she visits the sick, comforts
the bereaved, counsels the perplexed, and otherwise serves the

church and its constituency. As a deaconess she has made a host of friends, developed her own gifts, and so enriched her life that the life of the successful society woman is by comparison empty and eventless. Bitterness and disappointment, which are the natural accompaniments of her private lot, have been overcome by her parish work. What thousands need is not drugs or psychoanalysis or a vacation, but hearty, wholesome participation in the extension of the kingdom of God.

In diverse manners active religion furthers and contributes to the restoration of distorted minds. It generates in men a discontent with their unnecessary limitations and arouses their latent resources for personality rehabilitation or growth. The competent religious leader so stimulates persons that they discover and define their needs, opportunities, and responsibilities, face unpalatable facts with intelligent courage, and acquire or devise techniques for the mastery of crises which have developed in the course of their lives. The religious approach to perplexity or adversity is not the triumph of illusion over despondency, but the beginning of the dominance of experience by insight, courage, and inspiration. There is no conflict between a sound psychological and a wholesome religious approach to the solution of a personality problem. In fact, the process of adequate counseling is not complete until the individual has been led into the meaning and experience of a form of religion which gives him confidence in the universe and creates harmony among his experiences.

CHAPTER XX

RELIGIOUS MATURITY

IT is life's crowning achievement to be grown up religiously as well as physically. St. Paul vividly indicated the cleavage between immaturity and maturity when he wrote to the congregation at Corinth: "When I was a child, I spake as a child, I felt as a child, I thought as a child: now that I am become a man, I have put away childish things."[1] Certain attributes and habits which characterize childhood should be outgrown with approaching adulthood and the responsibilities of maturity assumed. In the course of time personality should reflect the distinctive qualities of a developed religious outlook.

To be sure, Jesus declared, "Except ye turn, and become as little children, ye shall in no wise enter into the kingdom of heaven."[2] From the trend of the ministry of Jesus it is evident that he did not propose to make immaturity the goal of the good life. Religious maturity as the objective of discipleship is prominent in his teaching. Aside from certain attributes of the normal child the Kingdom is inaccessible, and the maturing of personality impossible. The conditions of growth are resident in the child, such as sensitiveness to the wonder and mystery of the universe, a sense of security and confidence in the world, and an attitude of good will toward other persons. The childlikeness which Jesus commends and makes a precondition of citizenship in the Kingdom is leagues apart from childishness.

Adjustment to Reality

The adult who is religiously mature faces the realities of life and copes with them to the best of his ability. Most failures in the conduct of life are attributable to a lack of the mobilization of the resources both potential and actual which

[1] 1 Corinthians 13: 11. [2] Matthew 18: 3.

are at the command of the personality. Magic-seeking, the rubbing of Aladdin's lamp, and the trusting in luck have no place in the life of the mature Christian. Face to face with an emergency, he relies on prayerful planning, initiative, resolution, and effort. In the developed personality religion functions as vision, inspiration, power, and co-operation with God.

In the presence of harsh facts the immature adult resorts to self-deception, evasion of duty, subterfuge and wish-phantasy. He is a shirker; he demands special concessions from life, and expects the universe to waive its laws in his behalf. The religion of immaturity is at once an escape from reality and an opiate which drugs its victim into a false sense of security. Refusal to recognize the existence and implications of disagreeable facts is an indication of mental, moral, and religious inferiority. That there are forms of religious belief and behavior which encourage their adherents to rationalize, pretend, daydream, temporize, and transfer responsibility is all too tragically evident on almost every hand. To condone social evils which should be eradicated in the name of humanity, on the ground that God in his own good time will remove them with a supernatural gesture is to permit a specious piety to triumph over judgment and righteousness.

The religion of adult infantilism disguises disagreeable reality with irresponsible rhetoric and childish illusions. A false respectability calls a lie a terminological inexactitude. Stealing is referred to as kleptomania, a disability for which the ordinary thief is not responsible. A man who habitually acts the bully may induce in himself a sentimentally pious consciousness of rectitude by recalling with tears his mother's prayers. In fact, many harsh experiences are gilded with artificial elegance of language. When a bank fails and the depositors lose ninety per cent of the funds lodged with the institution, the directors declare a "dividend" of ten per cent. All such efforts to conceal unpalatable circumstances or excuse patently flagrant conduct are symptoms of tragic immaturity.

That Christianity taken in earnest has inspired men to confront and solve their personality problems and to combat the social evils of the period, no one who is conversant with the history of the Church will be disposed to deny. So far from reducing religion to an escape mechanism, many heroes of faith "subdued kingdoms, wrought righteousness, obtained promises, stopped the mouths of lions, quenched the power of fire, escaped the edge of the sword, from weakness were made strong. . . . Others were tortured . . . had trial of mockings and scourgings, yea, moreover of bonds and imprisonment: they were stoned, they were sawn asunder, they were tempted, they were slain with the sword: they went about in sheepskins, in goatskins; being destitute, afflicted, ill-treated, . . . wandering in deserts and mountains and caves, and the holes of the earth." [3] Men like Wesley and Booth were incapable of holding before the oppressed multitudes the prospect of bliss beyond the grave as an everlasting reward for patient submission to rampant injustices on earth. Instead of employing religion to drug the minds of the tractable into subhuman insensibility to their lamentable lot, these and other leaders let faith in God kindle the flame of righteous indignation and launched crusades against entrenched wrong.

The tendency of human beings to substitute phantasy for stern fact is accentuated by an infantile type of religion. In fact, almost any reaction may assume the nature of an escape or defense. Scientific research and experimentation may be a flight from a tortuous fact to a world of desire, or be a form of shirking, just as truly as drunkenness or daydreaming. Sermons condemning the present social order with its evils may, like the descriptions of a blissful hereafter, be a substitution of fancy for reliable thinking. In fact, the fiery emotional attack may be prompted by the reformer's half-conscious sense of guilt. Many indulge in contradictory principles in order to be wealthy, popular, and powerful. The inner spirit is in conflict with outward demands. It must be admitted that multitudes of religious people are deluding themselves. An emotional experience to which religious significance is attached often takes the place of directive thinking or strenuous effort.

Petitional prayers the answers to which would entail viola-

[3] Hebrews 11: 33 ff.

tions of the order of nature are addressed to the heavenly throne by many who demand personal concessions and special favors. Dr. Harry E. Fosdick refers to a woman who demanded that the construction of a subway in New York City be abandoned because the blasting agitated her canary. In the name of religion, the immature would live in a world of irresponsible optimism, seeing loaves of bread where there are only stones and making trial of God by casting themselves from the pinnacle of the temple. Henry Ward Beecher declared, "There are fifty ways of putting out a fire, but shutting your eyes is not one of them."

Independence

Religious maturity is marked by independence of judgment and action. Dependable and unbiased thinking as an outstanding competency of the adult mind can occur only where the myths and illusions of childhood have been discarded. The mature personality has been psychologically weaned, has been buttressed and fortified within, has developed internal resources against the isolations and sorrows which are the inescapable experiences of genuine selfhood, and has learned to think without confusion and assume responsibility for action.

Jesus was religiously self-reliant. He taught the people those principles which he had tested in his own experience and found valuable. He was emancipated from the trammels of tradition and the rigidity of external authority. It is significant that Jesus did not impose upon his followers a complexity of rules for the detailed guidance of daily life, but taught and illustrated principles such as good will, justice, honor, and humility, and relied on men of maturity of judgment to apply them to the special circumstances of each succeeding age. He expected not servile subjection to the letter of a code, but intelligent and courageous devotion to the spirit of his message.

It is admittedly more difficult to apply general principles to concrete instances than it is to obey rules which are relevant. A closed system of regulations may be necessary for children and undeveloped adults. The child or immature man is incapable of controlling his life by social principles and must be governed by simple rules. He whose religious conduct is determined by specific precepts, in a given situation may be guided by a tradition of the Church or a precedent established by the fathers or a current approved custom. The preconditions of the life founded on principles are intelligence, originality, and courage. Some persons ask, What did Jesus do? or, What would he do? Others ask, What was the major objective of Jesus? and, How can we best contribute to its attainment?

St. Paul stood on his own intellectual feet. As a missionary he cultivated virgin ethical soil. In applying the moral principles of the Old Testament prophets and Jesus to the concrete contingencies which arose in the developing life of the churches he had organized, he had no precedents to guide him. One recalls the deplorable conditions which marred the church in Corinth. This church was divided by factions, embittered by the litigation of its members, stained by gross immorality, disturbed by women who overstepped the bounds of social convention, agitated by the problem of personal liberty, harassed by disorderly conduct at the Lord's table, weakened by the misuse of spiritual gifts, and confused by pandemonium in the public meetings. St. Paul might have referred these distressing circumstances to the pillars of the church in Jerusalem for appropriate action, but he was religiously mature enough to attack and dispose of them in his own effectual way. No doubt he made them objects of prayer and then with a mind religiously sensitized exercised his own judgment. He was willing to assume the necessary perils of independent thought, of being personally responsible for any error into which he might fall.

William entered college in the same city in which he had been graduated from high school and in which he and his mother lived. From infancy his life in its various relations had been dominated by his mother. She proceeded to order the details of his college program. William fell in love with Mary, who attended the same college. At first his mother was jealous, but in time Mary won her reluctant approval. The mother told William that if he insisted on associating with a young woman she preferred Mary to anyone else. Mary spent the summer vacations at her home, which was in a city a hundred miles distant from the seat of the college.   Whenever William proposed to visit Mary at her home, his mother purchased the railway ticket, and if possible placed him in the custody of friends of the family who were making the same journey.   After graduation from college he did actually leave his mother and enroll in a theological seminary situated in another city.   Mary and William were now engaged to be married.   The wedding was to occur when he was the pastor of a congregation after his graduation from the seminary.   He preached a succession of trial sermons in various churches, but never received a call. He was in a predicament, for his mother could not preach his sermons for him.   He had become so dependent on her that without her aid he was helpless.   And Mary after a five-year engagement returned the ring.   Such are the experiences of many who have permitted possessive mothers to crush their initiative and to destroy their potential ability to think and act for themselves.

The immature adult is irresolute, timid, unstable, and dependent.   A married woman thirty years old and herself a mother admits that she has never made an important independent decision.   She still relies on her mother for guidance. "Mother knows best," is her explanation and defense.   It is normal for a little girl to bring her problems to her mother for solution, but the same behavior in an adult is a melancholy symptom of mental inferiority.   A pastor reports that fully 90 per cent of the crippled minds that appeal to him for aid request him to make important decisions for them.   The same debilitating attitude can be detected in the desire of religious people to be little children again, to lean upon another for support when aggressive and independent action should be taken, and to let the heavenly Father dispose of all difficulties without effort or thought on their part.   Young, studying 3,000 hymns of Protestant denominations, discovered that the predominant motif of more than one half was the longing to return to infantile security and to reap a heavenly reward.   In his opinion many hymns sung with fervor and conviction, are likely

to intensify retrogression and dependence.[4] No doubt hymns
of this kind, sung when songs of challenge should be selected,
sound a retreat from the conflict of life and express a desire,
perhaps unconscious, to shift all responsibility to God.

Not that the attitude of dependence has no proper function in
religion. In fact, the analysis of mature religion discloses the
value of a sense of dependence on a Determiner of human destiny. So long as reliance on God gives us poise and courage,
fortifies the will to do or endure, or sends us forth, after a
time of refreshing retirement, with fresh zeal and confidence,
religion supports or constructs a victorious personality. In
cases of difficult or delicate personality adjustment passive religion may well serve for a season as a haven of security and
rest. On the other hand, when dependence in religion evokes
or encourages self-pity, pretense, inertia, and inapplicability of
thought, the personality is weakened and unable to cope with
life situations. The quality of dependence is known by its
fruits. Religious reliance which is negative, morbidly self-
regarding, and evasive of reality is one kind of tree, and the assurance that "underneath are the everlasting arms" [5] which
helps us successfully contend with a world of frustrations, dep-
rivations, and inhibitions is quite another. Knowledge of
the existence and outcomes of both types of religious dependence should lead to the uprooting of the one whenever it manifests itself and to the unceasing cultivation of the other. There
is a form of dependence which, so far from fettering one's
mind, sets it free and gives it an opportunity to realize its potentialities.

Self-reliant thought and behavior do not create competencies
where hitherto none have existed, but they do rally and make
effective the abilities one does possess. On the other hand, an
endowment of magnificent gifts may remain undeveloped or
deteriorate under the power of a pernicious attachment to infantile illusions and practices. Furthermore, since aptitudes
differ in kind and degree, not all who have achieved a like

[4] Young, Kimball, "The Psychology of Hymns," *Journal of Abnormal
and Social Psychology,* Vol. XX, pp. 391 ff.
   [5] Deuteronomy 33 : 27.

stage of mental independence are equally competent. Religious maturity stimulates the personality to respond realistically and intelligently to situations to the measure of its ability.

The independence of maturity does not imply that the individual is to proceed without taking cognizance of the contributions which others have made to the solution of personality problems. Such a personal regime would constitute a sin of presumption. To ignore those who have opened gates of beauty and wisdom is to be guilty of the heinous offenses of captiousness and superiority. The wise man, just because he has forsaken infantile associations, is free to benefit by the maturity of others. Although he does include within his purview the experiences of others, he exercises discrimination, arrives at conclusions by his own thought processes, accepts full responsibility for the courses of action adopted, and is willing to take the consequences of his independence.

Emotional Stability

The emotionally mature personality has achieved a considerable degree of poise, serenity, and stability. Such conjunctive emotional values as confidence, courage, good will, and social sympathy impart to the self coherence and unity. Maturity expresses itself in a certain imperturbability, in a constancy of devotion to an ideal in the face of disapproval or opposition, in attention to one's own behavior and that of others with enough detachment to make fairly accurate observations, and in action so planned as to create desired outcomes. Of course no personality is absolutely balanced. Emotional maturity is relative. In even the well-balanced individual emotional experiences occur which are not entirely conjunctive, but such events are subordinated or at the worst incidental to the prevailing mode of the personality. An emotionally mature Christian may, in the phraseology of St. Paul, be pressed hard by grim circumstance yet not be in hopeless straits, perplexed but not in despair, pursued but not captured, struck down but not destroyed.

The emotionally immature adult is preoccupied with self, indulges in orgies of abnormal introspection, and stages tantrums when crossed. He demands an excess of personal attention without giving anything in return, is hypersensitive, easily flattered, and just as easily offended. He laughs when another is the object of a joke, but takes umbrage when he himself is the target of the shaft of fun. Disjunctive emotional responses, such as self-pity, suspicion, jealousy, malice, resentment, exasperation, and depression, torment the emotionally infantile adult. One may be intellectually and volitionally grown up, but an infant in emotional experience. A dictator of a nation may be an independent and fertile thinker, and an executive of amazing ability, but in his lust for personal power, self-aggrandizement, and the plaudits of the multitudes a mere child. He may be intellectual enough to defend his decisions and the causes he espouses with ingenious arguments that are convincing but be consumed by lust for personal power.

The vain and inept emotional form of adult infantilism often originates in babyhood, is the product of defective early training, and expresses itself progressively throughout the stages of the victim's life. As an infant overwhelmed with debilitating tenderness he learned to cry for what he wanted, whether it was attention or food, until he obtained it. Later as a spoiled child he indulged in tantrums whenever he was thwarted, screaming, biting, and kicking until his anguished elders complied with his unreasonable requests. As an adolescent in school, whenever he felt neglected, he pouted and sulked until he received the coveted recognition. As a husband he now demands the constant admiration of his wife, and her prompt attention to every detail that can minister to his comfort and vanity. God, if he is supposed to exist, is a super-parent, whose chief duty it is to protect his child from all harm, to comfort him when he has alienated all normal human relationships by his selfishness, to do for him things he ought to do himself, and at last to reward him for his religious beliefs with admission to an everlasting heaven with more or less material delights. The emotionally infantile adult is likely to have been a pampered child.

Mr. Stockbridge, dining with a friend in a restaurant, overheard a young girl admonish her mother. "Be your age, Mother," she exhorted. Something had gone wrong with the table service, and the overfed, plump mother was ready to burst into tears. She staged a tantrum. The flapper daughter calmly remarked to the embarrassed young man who was her escort, "Don't mind Mother. She was raised a pet, and I don't think she will ever grow up." Mr. Stockbridge remarked to his friend, "That girl has put her finger precisely upon the weakest spot in our civilization." [6]

The world is full of Peter Pans, people who have refused or been unable to outgrow childish emotional inferiority. People who are childishly morbid and unreasonable in their demands are embarrassingly present in every community and in the vast majority of churches. In their social relations they are cold and irritable, feel that they are unappreciated if not actually persecuted, attach too much importance to praise or censure, and participate in co-operative enterprises only when they are accorded positions of honor. Small wonder that church workers are distraught by such "difficult" parishioners! These emotionally arrested adults do not play with dolls or tops, nor roll hoops in the streets, but their social responses are those of little children. It is no easy task to lead such persons into a reintegration of freedom from the myths, unrealities, and emotional immaturities of childhood.

So long as the undeveloped adult secures what he wants he gets along after a fashion. When life begins to impose its discipline upon him, when those with whom he must associate are unimpressed or antagonized by his tantrums, when circumstances withhold the pleasant and present him with the disagreeable, when it is useless to attempt to escape the irksome by ignoring it, when the attention he rages for is not accorded him, he may commit suicide. Death by his own hand is a form of exhibitionism by means of which he proposes to secure the notice which during adult life was refused. Suicide is his final gesture of immaturity, his last temperamental effort to hold the center of the stage.

[6] Stockbridge, Frank Parker, "Your Emotional Age," *Red Book Magazine,* July, 1928.

Socialization

Individualism is an outstanding trait of early childhood. The young child is self-centered, although since he lacks the ability to anticipate imaginally the social consequences of his deeds he cannot be called culpably selfish. Co-operation with others is not an instinctive inclination but a capability which is acquired during the course of time in group situations which make social demands on the growing personality. The play of the young child is solitary. If a dozen infants with simple toys are placed upon the floor of the same room, each will be preoccupied with his own playthings except when he is trying to appropriate the possessions of another child. At a later period boys and girls revel in games in which the individual is in competition with his playmates. In the adolescent stage the individual who has cultivated a sense of social responsibility is willing to submerge himself in the interests of the group as such. The youth who is capable of voluntary and cheerful self-sacrifice for the advancement of the social unit with which he is identified has achieved an important increment of maturity. The inferior adult has never progressed beyond the solitariness of the play world of babyhood or the rivalry which characterizes the games of unsocialized children. In the game of adult life he is likely to withdraw into himself or to pursue his own advantages at any cost to others.

Rugged individualism, the application of the doctrine of personal liberty which takes scant account of the imperiled rights of others, is a typical symptom of adult infantilism. Persons who decline to sacrifice a portion of their individual freedom for the welfare of the group are too immature to participate constructively in our complex modern social order. Furthermore, individualism that discharges itself in rivalry and contention creates a mental attitude which renders an appreciation of higher values practically impossible. Reproving the factious spirit which had produced dissension in the church in Corinth, St. Paul writes, "I fed you with milk, not with meat; for ye were not yet able to bear it . . . for whereas there is among you jealousy and strife." [7] The Corinthians were

[7] 1 Corinthians 3: 2, 3.

prolonging their babyhood by fostering partisanship rooted in the three or four factions which threatened to disrupt the church. St. Paul implies that mutuality, unity of aim, and group solidarity are aspects of maturity which is a precondition of the comprehension of a further revelation of Christian truth. As it was, strife and recriminations had so retarded the religious development of the brethren that they deserved the significant appellation "babes." They did not merit the designation "men." The relation between the socialization of personality and religious progress is one that St. Paul and other religious leaders have grasped.

Social maturity involves not only good will and sympathetic imagination, but also a recognizable degree of detachment from self. It is relatively free from debilitating preoccupation with one's own feelings, preferences, and grievances. Its approach to the exigencies of life is comparatively objective. At Lystra St. Paul was pelted with stones and dragged outside the city. A few followers gathered about the presumably dead leader and began to bewail his untimely and violent demise. To their surprise St. Paul proceeded to show signs of life and soon staggered to his feet. Did he begin to bemoan his lot, to propose flight, or to plot revenge? Nothing was apparently farther from his mind than such individualistic considerations. The cause he served was uppermost in his intentions. He went back to Lystra at once, devoted a short period of time to the strengthening of the church, and then, convinced that he had fulfilled his mission in that city, took his departure.

Those who assert that Christianity entails no social obligations do not understand either the genius of our religion or the nature of soundly integrated personality. It would be absurd to maintain that although society contributes to the organization and content of personality, the individual, in turn, does not achieve fulfillment in active, hearty, and intelligent social participation. The individual and the social order interact. Whether the individual is conscious of it or not, he leaves his impress on the social institutions in which he is enmeshed. Personality, as we know it, cannot emerge apart from its cultural environment, and society cannot maintain itself apart from the individuals who constitute it. The relation which binds them is one of interdependence.

A form of religion exists which while not actively antisocial may well be called nonsocial. It is a system of religious mysticism characterized by a separation of its votary from mundane affairs. It is a form of quietism. Its adherents do not set their wills against eradicable social evils, but propose patiently to endure them until God in his own good time and manner shall come to the rescue. At best this is a policy of passive waiting, and a dependence on God to effect changes in society by a purely divine interposition if and when he sees fit. For example, a pastor in Germany was asked by an American tourist if in his opinion it is possible for the nations to establish and maintain an effective organization for the keeping of the peace of the world. The pastor replied that men are powerless to form such a league, and that if peace is ever to reign among the nations God himself will have to intervene in international relations and grant it. Carried to its logical conclusion, the principle which underlies such statements would forbid the purging of the cinemas of their indecencies and unrealities, the abolition of sweatshops, and the redemption of politics from corruption.

Such a form of quietism is hardly in accord with the message of the succession of the Old Testament prophets and the social teaching of Jesus. We are not to retreat to the wilderness like anchorites, or remain sequestered within a privileged group like the Pharisees of old, or dream away our responsibilities like the romanticists, but, like Jesus, cultivate ethical love and give justice an opportunity to prevail.

Loyalty to the God of Jesus does not render men indifferent to collective wrong, socially entrenched crime, and international iniquity, but makes them his fellow workers in the deliverance of the world from its major evils. They are not mere spectators of the world's parade of industrial and economic tragedies. So far from being inactive beholders of the social pageant, the true followers of Jesus are participants in it, and each according to the measure of his ability determines the character and trend of civilization. They achieve a balance of what might be termed other-worldliness and this-worldliness. In fact, they recognize no such distinction, but regard both as two unified constituents of the Christian religion. They believe that the kingdom of heaven as the rule of God should be established and expanded in themselves as individuals as well as in the institutional life of mankind. No dualism in actual experience is possible in the ongoing experience of the Christian. The one area of Christianity is internal, the other external, but they are inseparable and indivisible in the functioning of the religiously integrated personality.[8]

How Does Personality Mature?

Christian character expands itself in the modes of maturity to which reference has been made—acceptance of reality, constructive independence of thought and action, emotional stability, and the socialization of the personality. The Christian religion, so far from being an escape from the facts of experience or a substitute for the efforts we should put forth, delivers us from pretended attitudes, wish thinking, and imaginary accomplishments, and nerves us for the battle of life. The practice of its principles emancipates us from slavish subjection to the opinions and judgments of others and places at our disposal the intellectual resources of our own personalities. It engenders and directs conjunctive emotions and attitudes, such as love, sympathy, and disinterestedness, and thereby tends to give the self unity and coherence. It stresses the social implications of maturity and teaches us not to presume to exploit God for selfish ends, but to co-operate with him in his redemptive work. Any form of religion which avoids reality, fetters the intelligence, fosters the disjunctive emotions, and encourages the antisocial inclinations, contributes to adult infantilism and delinquency.

How does one develop religious maturity in its several aspects? Ideally the foundations for it are laid during child-

[8] See Quadrennial Report of Federal Council of the Churches of Christ in America, 1932, pp. 57 ff. The Roman Catholic Church has organized a league for social justice which embodies objectives enunciated in the encyclical letter of Pope Pius XI published in *The Examiner*, Vol. 82, numbers 26-31, 1931.

hood in the Christian family. Christian nurture in the home
and church should set conditions and suggest profitable areas
for inquiry and judicious experimentation rather than super-
impose upon the child ideas, customs, and behavior patterns
which have no affiliations with his growing needs and interests.
The child should be reared in an atmosphere of affection and
increasing obligations. He should not be pampered with ex-
cessive attention nor crushed by domination nor embittered
by parental neglect, but be thrown upon his own resources,
gradually emancipated from family dependency, taught by actual life situations to confront reality with courage, and become
socially sensitized through experience in the group. Dr. Hale
recalls that he was at the breakfast table of a distinguished educator on the morning of a commencement day. A visit of a
woman called the host from the table. When he had returned
he explained, "Another of those mothers who are crying their
eyes out because they must bring their boys to us." Dr. Hale
ventured to ask what he had told her. "I said, 'Madam, God
Almighty has educated your son thus far by your agency; now
he purposes to educate him without it.' " [9]

The mere impartation of religious beliefs, principles, and
precepts through formal instruction is not sufficiently motivating to produce the characteristics of maturity. The control by the parent-teacher of the situations which influence the
behavior of the child is the most effective known means. Christian education which is psychologically based incites children
and others to desired behavior through the organization of the
necessary conditions of religious living. Interpretation follows
rather than precedes overt experience. Maturity of personality
is achieved in hearty participation in the program of the Christian group.

Is the case of the immature adult hopeless? Can he be reclaimed? By what process or discipline or change, if any, can
he resolutely face life as it actually is, exercise initiative and
freedom of right decision, achieve emotional stability and so-
cialize his attitudes? The redemption of the infantile adult, it

[9] Hale, Edward Everett, "Formative Influences," *The Forum*, Vol. X,
p. 64.

should be admitted, involves a personality transformation which amounts to a constructive revolution. It entails a recentering of personality, the adoption of a new point of reference; in fact, nothing short of the experience of regeneration.

In many instances a crisis occurs in the height of which the infantile personality feels that it is doomed to collapse. The crisis may be brought about by frantic endeavors to extend in new directions the avoidance of life's realities, the condition of dependence, the disjunctive emotions of envy, jealousy, and vindictiveness, and the expression of antisocial attitudes. The egocentric individual may overreach himself, but instead of ceasing to function as a human being he may to his surprise experience relief. If positive religious forces have made an impression despite his infantilism, a wisdom wrought in the subconscious realm may emerge into awareness. The revelation of the nature of his mode of living makes the egocentric goals he has been pursuing so repugnant that he renounces them. When he thinks that the foundations of his life are blasted and that he will be plunged into gloom and depression he is upborne by potentialities become actualities. Religious resources are now utilized. In the school of Christian experience the newborn individual step by step is emancipated from childishness and develops self-confidence, emotional balance, and loses himself in the building of the Kingdom, but only to find himself enriched beyond measure.

St. Paul urges men to "attain unto the unity of the faith, and of the knowledge of the Son of God, unto a full-grown man, unto the measure of the stature of the fullness of Christ: that we may be no longer children, tossed to and fro and carried about with every wind of doctrine, by the sleight of men, in craftiness, after the wiles of error; but speaking truth in love, may grow up in all things into him, who is the head, even Christ." [10]

[10] Ephesians 4: 13-15.

BIBLIOGRAPHY

ADLER, ALFRED, *The Neurotic Constitution.* New York: Moffat, Yard & Co., 1917.

ADLER, ALFRED, *The Practice and Theory of Individual Psychology.* New York: Harcourt, Brace & Co., 1924.

ADLER, ALFRED, *Understanding Human Nature.* New York: Greenberg, Inc., 1927.

ALLIER, RAOUL, *The Mind of the Savage.* London: G. Bell & Sons, 1929.

ALLPORT, FLOYD HENRY, *Social Psychology.* New York: Houghton Mifflin Company, 1924.

AMES, EDWARD SCRIBNER, *The Psychology of Religious Experience.* Boston: Houghton Mifflin Company, 1910.

AMES, EDWARD SCRIBNER, *Religion.* New York: Henry Holt & Co., 1929.

ANGELL, JAMES ROWLAND, *Introduction to Psychology.* New York: Henry Holt & Co., 1918.

ANGELL, JAMES ROWLAND, *Psychology.* New York: Henry Holt & Co., 1904.

ANGUS, SAMUEL, *The Religious Quest of the Graeco-Roman World.* New York: Charles Scribner's Sons, 1929.

ARNOLD, EDWARD VERNON, *Roman Stoicism.* Cambridge, Eng.: The University Press, 1911.

ATHEARN, WALTER S., *The Malden Survey.* New York: George H. Doran Company, 1920.

ATHEARN, WALTER S., EVENDEN, E. S., HANSON, W. L., CHALMERS, WILLIAM E., *The Religious Education of Protestants in an American Commonwealth,* Vol. 1 in The Indiana Survey of Religious Education, 3 volumes. New York: George H. Doran Company, 1923.

BAGBY, ENGLISH, *The Psychology of Personality.* New York: Henry Holt & Co., 1928.

BERNARD, LUTHER LEE, *Instinct, a Study of Social Psychology.* New York: Henry Holt & Co., 1924.

BETTS, GEORGE HERBERT, *The Beliefs of 700 Ministers and Their Meaning for Religious Education.* New York: The Abingdon Press, 1929.

357

BRENT, CHARLES HENRY, *Adventures in Prayer.* New York: Harper & Brothers, 1932.

BRENT, CHARLES HENRY, *With God in Prayer.* Philadelphia: George W. Jacobs & Co., 1907.

BRUCE, W. S., *The Psychology of Christian Life and Behaviour.* Edinburgh: T. and T. Clark, 1923.

BUCKHAM, JOHN WRIGHT, *Mysticism and Modern Life.* New York: The Abingdon Press, 1915.

BUNDY, WALTER E., *The Religion of Jesus.* Indianapolis: Bobbs-Merrill Company, 1928.

BURNHAM, WILLIAM H., *The Wholesome Personality.* New York: D. Appleton & Co., 1932.

BYINGTON, EDWIN H., *The Quest for Experience in Worship.* New York: Doubleday, Doran & Company, 1929.

CALVIN, JOHN, *Institutes of Christian Religion,* Book IV, translated by John Allen. Philadelphia: Presbyterian Board of Publication, 1844.

CLARK, ELMER T., *The Psychology of Religious Awakening.* New York: The Macmillan Company, 1929.

COE, GEORGE ALBERT, *The Psychology of Religion.* Chicago: University of Chicago Press, 1916.

COE, GEORGE ALBERT, *The Religion of a Mature Mind.* New York: Fleming H. Revell Company, 1902.

COE, GEORGE ALBERT, *A Social Theory of Religious Education.* New York: Charles Scribner's Sons, 1917.

COE, GEORGE ALBERT, *The Spiritual Life; Studies in the Science of Religion.* New York: Fleming H. Revell Company. 1900.

CONKLIN, EDMUND S., *The Psychology of Religious Adjustment.* New York: The Macmillan Company, 1929.

CURNOCK, NEHEMIAH (Editor), *The Journal of John Wesley,* Vol. 1. London: Robert Culley, 1909.

CUTTEN, GEORGE BARTON, *The Psychological Phenomena of Christianity.* New York: Charles Scribner's Sons, 1908.

DARWIN, CHARLES R., *Variation of Animals and Plants under Domestication.* London: Murray, 1868.

DAVENPORT, FREDERICK MORGAN, *Primitive Traits in Religious Revivals.* New York: The Macmillan Company, 1905.

DAWSON, MILES MENANDER, *The Ethical Religion of Zoroaster.* New York: The Macmillan Company, 1931.

DE SCHWEINITZ, KARL, *The Art of Helping People Out of Trouble*. Boston: Houghton Mifflin Company, 1924.

DEARMER, PERCY (Editor), *The Art of Public Worship*, Bohlen Lectures. London: A. R. Mowbray & Co., Ltd., 1919.

DEISSMANN, GUSTAV ADOLF, *Paul*, translated by William E. Wilson. New York: George H. Doran Company, 1926.

DEISSMANN, GUSTAV ADOLF, *The Religion of Jesus and the Faith of Paul*, translated by William E. Wilson. New York: George H. Doran Company, 1923.

DEWEY, JOHN, *A Common Faith*. New Haven: Yale University Press, 1934.

DEWEY, JOHN, *How We Think*. Boston: Heath & Co., 1910. New Edition, 1933.

DEWEY, JOHN, *Human Nature and Conduct*. New York: Henry Holt & Co., 1922.

DOUGLASS, H. PAUL, *How to Study the City Church*. New York: Doubleday, Doran & Co., 1928.

DOYLE, ARTHUR CONAN, *The Vital Message*. New York: George H. Doran Company, 1919.

DRAKE, DURANT, *Problems of Religion*. Boston: Houghton Mifflin Company, 1916.

DRESSER, HORATIO W., *Outlines of the Psychology of Religion*. New York: Thomas Y. Crowell Company, 1929.

DURKHEIM, EMILE, *The Elementary Forms of the Religious Life*, translated by Joseph Ward Swain. New York: The Macmillan Company, 1912.

EDDINGTON, ARTHUR STANLEY, *The Domain of Physical Science*. New York: The Macmillan Company, 1929.

ELLIOTT, HARRISON SACKET, *Bearing of Psychology upon Religion*. New York: Association Press, 1927.

Encyclopaedia of Psychic Science. London: Arthurs Press, Ltd., 1933.

EVERETT, CHARLES CARROLL, *The Psychological Elements of Religious Faith*. New York: The Macmillan Company, 1902.

FARMER, HERBERT H., *Experience of God*. Garden City, N. Y.: Doubleday, Doran & Co., 1929.

FLETCHER, M. SCOTT, *The Psychology of the New Testament*. New York: Hodder & Stoughton, Ltd., 1912.

FLOWER, JOHN CYRIL, *Approach to the Psychology of Religion*. London: Kegan Paul, Trench, Trübner & Co., 1927.

FORTESCUE, ADRIAN, *The Mass.* New York: Longmans, Green & Co., 1914.

FOSDICK, HARRY EMERSON, *The Meaning of Prayer.* New York: Association Press, 1916.

FRAZER, JAMES GEORGE, *The Golden Bough.* New York: The Macmillan Company, 1927.

FREUD, SIGMUND, *The Ego and the Id.* London: The Hogarth Press, 1927.

FREUD, SIGMUND, *A General Introduction to Psychoanalysis.* New York: Boni & Liveright, 1920.

FREUD, SIGMUND, *Psychopathology of Daily Life.* New York: The Macmillan Company, 1914.

GALLOWAY, GEORGE, *The Philosophy of Religion.* New York: Charles Scribner's Sons, 1914.

GALLOWAY, GEORGE, *The Principles of Religious Development.* New York: The Macmillan Company, 1909.

GLOVER, TERROT REAVELEY, *The Conflict of Religions in the Early Roman Empire.* London: Methuen & Co., 1909.

GRANGER, FRANK, *The Soul of a Christian.* London: Methuen & Co., 1900.

HADFIELD, J. A., *Psychology and Morals.* New York: Robert M. McBride & Co., 1925.

HALLIDAY, WILLIAM FEARON, *Psychology and Religious Experience.* London: Hodder & Stoughton, 1929.

HART, BERNARD, *The Psychology of Insanity.* Cambridge, Eng.: The University Press, revised edition, 1935.

HART, HORNELL, and HART, ELLA B., *Visions and Apparitions Collectively and Reciprocally Perceived,* Proceedings of the Society of Psychical Research, Vol. XLI, May, 1933.

HARTSHORNE, HUGH, *The Book of Worship of the Church School.* New York: Charles Scribner's Sons, 1915.

HEGEL, GEORG WILHELM FRIEDRICH, *Lectures on the Philosophy of Religion,* Vol. 1, translated by E. B. Speirs. London: Kegan Paul, Trench, Trübner & Co., 1895.

HEILER, FRIEDRICH, *Prayer; A Study in the History and Psychology of Religion.* London: Oxford University Press, 1932.

HEILER, FRIEDRICH, *The Spirit of Worship,* translated by W. Montgomery. New York: George H. Doran Company, 1926.

HERMAN, E., *The Meaning and Value of Mysticism.* London: J. Clarke & Co., 1915.

HERTZLER, JOYCE O., *The History of Utopian Thought.* New York: The Macmillan Company, 1923.

HICKMAN, FRANK S., *Introduction to the Psychology of Religion.* New York: The Abingdon Press, 1926.

HICKS, ROBERT DREW, *Stoic and Epicurean.* New York: Charles Scribner's Sons, 1910.

HOCKING, WILLIAM ERNEST, *Human Nature and Its Remaking.* New Haven: Yale University Press, 1929.

HOCKING, WILLIAM ERNEST, *The Meaning of God in Human Experience.* New Haven: Yale University Press, 1912.

HODGE, ALEXANDER, *Prayer and Its Psychology.* New York: The Macmillan Company, 1931.

HÖFFDING, HARALD, *The Philosophy of Religion.* New York: The Macmillan Company, 1914.

HOLLINGWORTH, HARRY L., *Psychology, Its Facts and Principles.* New York: D. Appleton & Co., 1928.

HOLMAN, CHARLES THOMAS, *The Cure of Souls.* Chicago: University of Chicago Press, 1932.

HOLT, EDWIN B., *The Freudian Wish and Its Place in Ethics.* New York: Henry Holt & Co., 1915.

HOPKINS, E. WASHBURN, *The Origin and Evolution of Religion.* New Haven: Yale University Press, 1923.

HORTON, WALTER MARSHALL, *A Psychological Approach to Theology.* New York: Harper & Brothers, 1931.

HORTON, WALTER MARSHALL, *Theism and the Modern Mood.* New York: Harper & Brothers, 1930.

HOWLEY, JOHN F. W., *Psychology and Mystical Experience.* St. Louis: B. Herder, 1920.

HUDSON, CYRIL E., *Recent Psychology and the Christian Religion.* New York: George H. Doran Company, 1923.

HUME, ROBERT ERNEST, *The World's Living Religions.* New York: Charles Scribner's Sons, 1924.

HYSLOP, JAMES H., *Contact with the Other World.* New York: The Century Company, 1920.

INGE, WILLIAM RALPH, *Christian Mysticism.* New York: Charles Scribner's Sons, 1899.

INGE, WILLIAM RALPH, *Faith and Its Psychology.* New York: Charles Scribner's Sons, 1910.

JAMES, WILLIAM, "The Moral Equivalent for War," in *Memoirs and Studies*. New York: Longmans, Green & Co., 1912.

JAMES, WILLIAM, *The Principles of Psychology*. New York: Henry Holt & Co., 1890.

JAMES, WILLIAM, *The Varieties of Religious Experience*. New York: Longmans, Green & Co., 1911.

JAMES, WILLIAM, *The Will to Believe and Other Essays in Popular Philosophy*. New York: Longmans, Green & Co., 1897.

JANET, PIERRE M. F., *Principles of Psychotherapy*. New York: The Macmillan Company, 1924.

JONES, E. STANLEY, *The Christ of the Indian Road*. New York: The Abingdon Press, Eighth Edition, 1925.

JONES, RUFUS M., *New Studies in Mystical Religions*, the Ely Lectures delivered at Union Theological Seminary, New York, 1927. New York: The Macmillan Company, 1927.

JONES, RUFUS M., *Some Exponents of Mystical Religion*. New York: The Abingdon Press, 1930.

JONES, RUFUS M., *Spiritual Energies in Daily Life*. New York: The Macmillan Company, 1922.

JONES, RUFUS M., *Studies in Mystical Religion*. New York: The Macmillan Company, 1909.

JOSEY, CHARLES CONANT, *Psychology of Religion*. New York: The Macmillan Company, 1927.

JUNG, CARL G., *Modern Man in Search of a Soul*. New York: Harcourt, Brace & Co., 1933.

JUNG, CARL G., *Psychological Types*. New York: Harcourt, Brace & Co., 1926.

JUNG, CARL G., *Psychology of the Unconscious*. New York: Moffat, Yard & Co., 1916.

KANT, IMMANUEL, *Kritik der praktischen Vernunft*. Riga: Johann F. Hartknoch, 1788.

KING, IRVING, *The Development of Religion*. New York: The Macmillan Company, 1910.

KOFFKA, KURT, *The Growth of the Mind*. New York: Harcourt, Brace & Co., 1924.

KÖHLER, WOLFGANG, *Gestalt Psychology*. New York: H. Liveright, 1929.

KÖHLER, WOLFGANG, *The Mentality of Apes*. New York: Harcourt, Brace & Co., 1925.

LAIRD, JOHN, *The Idea of Value*. Cambridge, Eng.: The University Press, 1929.

LANG, ANDREW, *Magic and Religion*. New York: Longmans, Green & Co., 1901.

LANG, LEWIS WYATT, *A Study of Conversion*. London: George Allen & Unwin, Ltd., 1931.

LAWRENCE, BROTHER, *The Practice of the Presence of God*. Philadelphia: American Baptist Publication Society, 1908.

LEUBA, JAMES H., *The Belief in God and Immortality*. Chicago: University of Chicago Press, 1921.

LEUBA, JAMES H., *A Psychological Study of Religion*. New York: The Macmillan Company, 1912.

LEUBA, JAMES H., *The Psychology of Religious Mysticism*. London: Kegan Paul, Trench, Trübner & Co., 1925.

LEVY-BRUHL, LUCIEN, *How Natives Think*. London: George Allen & Unwin, Ltd., 1928.

LIPPMANN, WALTER, *A Preface to Morals*. New York: The Macmillan Company, 1929.

LODGE, OLIVER JOSEPH, *Raymond*. New York: George H. Doran Company, 1916.

MACKIE, ALEXANDER, *The Gift of Tongues*. New York: George H. Doran Company, 1921.

MALINOWSKI, BRONISLAW, *Argonauts of the Western Pacific*. London: George Routledge & Sons, 1922.

MARETT, ROBERT RANULPH, *The Threshold of Religion*. London: Methuen & Co., 1909.

MATTHEWS, W. R., *The Psychological Approach to Religion*. New York: Longmans, Green & Co., 1925.

McCOMAS, HENRY CLAY, *Ghosts I Have Talked With*. Baltimore: Williams & Wilkins Co., 1935.

McCOMAS, HENRY CLAY, *Psychology of Religious Sects*. New York: Fleming H. Revell Company, 1912.

McDOUGALL, WILLIAM, *An Introduction to Social Psychology*. London: Methuen & Co., 1908.

McDOUGALL, WILLIAM, *Outline of Abnormal Psychology*. New York: Charles Scribner's Sons, 1926.

McDOUGALL, WILLIAM, *Outline of Psychology*. New York: Charles Scribner's Sons, 1923.

McKENZIE, JOHN G., *Souls in the Making*. New York: The Macmillan Company, 1929.

McTaggart, John Ellis, *The Nature of Existence,* Vol. 1. London: Cambridge University Press, 1921.

McTaggart, John Ellis, *Some Dogmas of Religion.* New York: Longmans, Green & Co., 1906.

Menzies, Allan, *History of Religion.* New York: Charles Scribner's Sons, 1906.

Morgan, C. Lloyd, *Emergent Evolution.* London: Williams & Norgate, Ltd. Lectures delivered in 1922.

Morgan, John J. B., *The Psychology of Abnormal People.* New York: Longmans, Green & Co., 1928.

Myers, Frederick William Henry, *Human Personality and Its Survival of Bodily Death.* New York: Longmans, Green & Co., 1903.

Myers, Frederick William Henry, *Science and a Future Life.* New York: The Macmillan Company, 1901.

Myerson, Abraham, *The Psychology of Mental Disorders.* New York: The Macmillan Company, 1928.

Niebuhr, H. Richard, *The Social Sources of Denomination-alism.* New York: Henry Holt & Co., 1929.

Nygren, Anders, *Agape and Eros, a Study of the Christian Idea of Love,* translated by A. G. Herbert. London: Society for Promoting Christian Knowledge, 1932.

Oliver, John Rathbone, *Pastoral Psychiatry and Mental Health.* New York: Charles Scribner's Sons, 1932.

Otto, Rudolph, *The Idea of the Holy.* London: Oxford University Press, 1923.

Paton, Lewis Bayles, *Spiritism and the Cult of the Dead in Antiquity.* New York: The Macmillan Company, 1921.

Perry, William, *The Scottish Liturgy.* London: A. R. Mowbray & Co., Ltd., 1922.

Pfister, Oskar, *The Psychoanalytic Method.* London: Kegan Paul, Trench, Trübner & Co., 1917.

Pillsbury, W. B., *The History of Psychology.* New York: W. W. Norton & Co., 1929.

Pitts, John, *Psychology and Religion.* New York: Fleming H. Revell Company, 1930.

Pratt, James Bissett, *The Pilgrimage of Buddhism and a Buddhist Pilgrimage.* New York: The Macmillan Company, 1928.

Pratt, James Bissett, *The Psychology of Religious Belief.* New York: The Macmillan Company, 1907.

PRATT, JAMES BISSETT, *The Religious Consciousness.* New York: The Macmillan Company, 1930.

PRINCE, MORTON, *The Dissociation of a Personality.* New York: Longmans, Green & Co., 1906.

PYM, T. W., *More Psychology and the Christian Life.* New York: George H. Doran Company, 1925.

PYM, T. W., *Psychology and the Christian Life.* London: Student Christian Movement, 1921.

RAVEN, CHARLES EARLE, *A Wanderer's Way.* New York: Henry Holt & Co., 1929.

REICHELT, KARL LUDVIG, *Truth and Tradition in Chinese Buddhism.* Shanghai: Commercial Press, 1927.

RHINE, J. B., *Extra-Sensory Perception.* Boston: Boston Society for Psychic Research, 1934.

RICHET, CHARLES, *Thirty Years of Psychical Research,* translated by Stanley De Brath. New York: The Macmillan Company, 1923.

ROBACK, A. A., *The Psychology of Character.* New York: Harcourt, Brace & Co., 1927.

ROSENOFF, AARON J. (Editor), *Manual of Psychiatry.* New York: John Wiley & Sons, Inc., 1927.

RUSSELL, BERTRAND, *The Scientific Outlook.* New York: W. W. Norton & Co., 1931.

SANCTIS, SANTE DE, *Religious Conversion,* translated by Helen Augur. New York: Harcourt, Brace & Co., 1927.

SCHAFF, PHILIP, *The Creeds of Christendom,* Vol. III. New York: Harper & Brothers, 1877.

SCHLEIERMACHER, FRIEDRICH, *On Religion,* translated by John Oman. London: Kegan Paul, Trench, Trübner & Co., 1893.

SCLATER, J. R. P., *The Public Worship of God.* New York: George H. Doran Company, 1927.

SCOTT, ERNEST F., *The Spirit in the New Testament.* New York: George H. Doran Company, 1923.

SELBIE, W. B., *The Psychology of Religion.* Oxford: Clarendon Press, 1924.

SHAVER, ERWIN L., *The Project Principle in Religious Education.* Chicago: University of Chicago Press, 1924.

SHELDON, WILLIAM H., *Psychology and the Promethean Will.* New York: Harper & Bros., 1936.

SNOWDEN, JAMES H., *The Psychology of Religion, and Its Application in Preaching and Teaching.* New York: Fleming H. Revell Company, 1916.

SPERRY, WILLARD, *Reality in Worship.* New York: The Macmillan Company, 1925.

STALKER, JAMES, *Christian Psychology.* New York: Hodder & Stoughton, Ltd., 1914.

STARBUCK, EDWIN DILLER, *The Psychology of Religion.* New York: Charles Scribner's Sons, 1899.

STOLZ, KARL R., *Pastoral Psychology.* Nashville: Cokesbury Press, 1932.

STOLZ, KARL R., *The Psychology of Prayer.* New York: The Abingdon Press, 1924.

STRATTON, GEORGE MALCOLM, *Anger, Its Religious and Moral Significance.* New York: The Macmillan Company, 1923.

STRATTON, GEORGE MALCOLM, *Psychology of the Religious Life.* London: George Allen & Unwin, Ltd., 1911.

STRICKLAND, FRANCIS L., *Psychology of Religious Experience.* New York: The Abingdon Press, 1924.

TERMAN, L. M., *The Measurement of Intelligence.* New York: Houghton Mifflin Company, 1916.

THOM, DOUGLAS A., *Mental Health of the Child.* Cambridge: Harvard University Press, 1928.

THOULESS, ROBERT H., *An Introduction to the Psychology of Religion.* Cambridge, Eng.: The University Press, 1923.

THURSTONE, L. L., AND CHAVE, ERNEST J., *Measurement of Attitude.* Chicago: University of Chicago Press, 1929.

TITCHENER, EDWARD BRADFORD, *Experimental Psychology.* New York: The Macmillan Company, 1901.

TITCHENER, EDWARD BRADFORD, *An Outline of Psychology.* New York: The Macmillan Company, 1896.

TITCHENER, EDWARD BRADFORD, *A Primer of Psychology.* New York: The Macmillan Company, 1898.

TITCHENER, EDWARD BRADFORD, *A Textbook of Psychology.* New York: The Macmillan Company, 1909.

TROUT, DAVID M., *Religious Behavior.* New York: The Macmillan Company, 1931.

TYLOR, EDWARD BURNETT, *Primitive Culture.* New York: Henry Holt & Co., 1874.

UNDERHILL, EVELYN, *The Essentials of Mysticism.* New York: E. P. Dutton & Co., 1920.

UNDERHILL, EVELYN, *The Life of the Spirit and the Life of Today*. London: Methuen & Co., 1922.

UNDERHILL, EVELYN, *The Mystic Way—A Psychological Study in Christian Origins*. New York: E. P. Dutton & Co., 1913.

UNDERHILL, EVELYN, *The Mystics of the Church*. London: James Clark & Co., 1926.

UNDERHILL, EVELYN, *Practical Mysticism*. New York: E. P. Dutton & Co., 1915.

UNDERHILL, EVELYN, *Worship*. New York: Harper & Brothers, 1937.

UNDERWOOD, ALFRED CLAIR, *Conversion: Christian and Non-Christian*. New York: The Macmillan Company, 1925.

UREN, A. RUDOLPH, *Recent Religious Psychology*. Edinburgh: T. and T. Clark, 1928.

VOGT, VON OGDEN, *Modern Worship*. New Haven: Yale University Press, 1927.

WARNER, HORACE EMORY, *The Psychology of the Christian Life*. New York: Fleming H. Revell Company, 1910.

WATERHOUSE, E. S., *Psychology and Religion; a Series of Broadcast Talks*. New York: R. R. Smith, Inc., 1931.

WATERHOUSE, E. S., *The Psychology of the Christian Life*. London: Kelly Publishing Company, 1913.

WATSON, GOODWIN, *Experiments and Measurements in Religious Education*. New York: Association Press, 1927.

WATSON, JOHN B., *Behaviorism*. New York: W. W. Norton & Co., 1925.

WATSON, JOHN B., *Psychology from the Standpoint of a Behaviorist*. Philadelphia: J. B. Lippincott Company, 1919.

WEATHERHEAD, LESLIE D., *Psychology and Life*. New York: The Abingdon Press, 1935.

WHITE, WILLIAM A., *Outlines of Psychiatry*. Washington, D. C.: Nervous and Mental Disease Publishing Company, 1919.

WIEMAN, HENRY NELSON, *Methods of Private Religious Living*. New York: The Macmillan Company, 1928.

WIEMAN, HENRY NELSON, *Religious Experience and Scientific Method*. New York: The Macmillan Company, 1926.

WIEMAN, HENRY NELSON, AND WIEMAN, REGINA WESTCOTT, *Normative Psychology of Religion*. New York: Thomas Y. Crowell Company, 1935.

WOLFE, WALTER BERAN, *Nervous Breakdown*. New York: Farrar & Rinehart, 1934.

WOODBURNE, ANGUS STEWART, *The Religious Attitude*. New York: The Macmillan Company, 1927.

WOODWORTH, ROBERT S., *Dynamic Psychology*. New York: Columbia University Press, 1918.

WOODWORTH, ROBERT S., *Psychology*. New York: Henry Holt & Co. Revised edition, 1929.

WRIGHT, HENRY WILKES, *Religious Response*. New York: Harper & Brothers, 1929.

INDEX

Abraham
pioneer of religious faith, 60

Adam
sin of, 194 ff.

Adler, Alfred
doctrine of will to power, 164 ff.
masculine protest, 165
religious implication of Adlerian concepts, 165 ff.
classification of emotions, 247

Adrenal glands
function of, 179

Adult Infantilism
origin and development of, 349
suicide final gesture of, 350
evasion of reality, 342

Ahriman
malevolent god of Persians, 111

Ahura Mazda
benevolent god of Persians, 111

Alexander of Hales
commentaries of on Aristotle, 114

Allier, Raoul
on the primitive mind, 46 ff.

Allport, F. H.
classification of emotions, 246

Ames, Edward Scribner
contribution to sociological approach to religion, 130 ff.

Amos
teaching of monotheism, 64
prophet of social justice, 80

Anaxagoras
idealistic philosophy of, 66

Angell, James R.
advocate of functionalism, 152 ff.

Anger
nature of, 227
transformation of, 227 ff.

Angus, Samuel
on Stoicism, 77 ff.

Apollo
inspirer of prophecy, 59

Arabs
scientific studies of, 108

Ares
Greek god of war, 59

Aristotle
scientific contributions of, 112

Aristotle—(Continued)
thinking as self-communing, 241

Arnold, E. Vernon
on Roman Stoicism, 79

Art
as normative, 18

Artemis
Greek goddess, 59

Asceticism
expressed in monasticism, 91 ff.

Astronomy
Babylonian contributions to, 108 ff.

Athearn, Walter S.
study of church buildings, 143 ff.
survey of religious education in Indiana, 144

Athena
Greek goddess, 59

Aton
sun god of the Egyptians, 60

Augustine, St.
conversion of, 214 ff.
the creation theory of, 117
Confessions of, 138

Automatic Writing
examples of, 311
dissociation of consciousness in, 312

Awe
nature of, 226

Bacon, Roger
scientific contributions of, 115 ff.

Baptism
magical use of, 46

Benedict, St.
order of, 90

Bernard, L. L.
on habit and instinct, 44

Betts, George H.
study of religious beliefs of ministers, 137 ff.

Bible, The
as an outgrowth of religion, 38 ff.
uniqueness of, 39
psychological exegesis of, 141

Böhler, Peter
influence of on John Wesley, 212 ff.

Buddhism,
as a variety of humanism, 84
motivation of by theistic beliefs, 85

369

Stechert 5-20-41